Communications in Computer and Information Science 1154

More information about this series at http://www.springer.com/series/7899

Fabián R. Narváez · Diego F. Vallejo ·
Paulina A. Morillo · Julio R. Proaño (Eds.)

Smart Technologies, Systems and Applications

First International Conference, SmartTech-IC 2019
Quito, Ecuador, December 2–4, 2019
Proceedings

Springer

Editors
Fabián R. Narváez ⓘ
Universidad Politécnica Salesiana
Quito, Ecuador

Diego F. Vallejo ⓘ
Universidad Politécnica Salesiana
Quito, Ecuador

Paulina A. Morillo ⓘ
Universidad Politécnica Salesiana
Quito, Ecuador

Julio R. Proaño ⓘ
Universidad Politécnica Salesiana
Quito, Ecuador

ISSN 1865-0929   ISSN 1865-0937   (electronic)
Communications in Computer and Information Science
ISBN 978-3-030-46784-5   ISBN 978-3-030-46785-2   (eBook)
https://doi.org/10.1007/978-3-030-46785-2

This Springer imprint is published by the registered company Springer Nature Switzerland AG
The registered company address is: Gewerbestrasse 11, 6330 Cham, Switzerland

Preface

This volume contains the papers presented at the First International Conference on Smart Technologies, Systems and Applications (SmartTech-IC 2019) held during December 2–4, 2019, in Quito, Ecuador. The SmartTech-IC conference aims to attract researchers, scientists, and technologists from some of the top companies, universities, research groups, and government agencies from Latin America and around of the world to communicate their research results, inventions, and innovative applications in the area of smart science as well as to showcase the most recent smart technological trends. SmartTech-IC 2019 was organized by the Universidad Politécnica Salesiana, a private institution of higher education with social purposes, and co-financed by the Ecuadorian State for nonprofit purposes. The SmartTech-IC conference was conceived as an academic platform to promote the creation of technical and scientific collaboration networks. The goal of the conference was addressed with relevant topics related to smart technologies, smart systems, smart trends, and applications in different domains in the field of computer science and information systems that represent innovation in current society.

We would like to express our gratitude to all the authors who submitted papers to SmartTech-IC 2019, and our congratulations to those whose papers were accepted. There were 90 submissions in total and each submission was reviewed by three qualified reviewers chosen from our Program Committee (PC) based on their qualifications and experience. Only papers with an average score of ≥ 2.0 were considered for final inclusion, and almost all accepted papers had positive reviews or at least one review with a score of 3 (accept) or higher. Finally, the PC decided to accept 30 full papers.

We would also like to thank the PC members, who agreed to review the manuscripts in a timely manner and provided valuable feedback to the authors.

December 2019

Fabián R. Narváez
Diego F. Vallejo
Paulina A. Morillo
Julio R. Proaño

Organization

Honorary Committee

Javier Herrán Gómez   Universidad Politécnica Salesiana, Ecuador
José Juncosa Blasco   Universidad Politécnica Salesiana, Ecuador
Juan Pablo Salgado   Universidad Politécnica Salesiana, Ecuador
Tatiana Mosquera   Universidad Politécnica Salesiana, Ecuador

Organizing Committee

Fabián R. Narváez   Universidad Politécnica Salesiana, Ecuador
Julio R. Proaño   Universidad Politécnica Salesiana, Ecuador
Paulina A. Morillo   Universidad Politécnica Salesiana, Ecuador
Diego F. Vallejo   Universidad Politécnica Salesiana, Ecuador

Program Committee

Oscar Acosta Tamayo	Université de Rennes 1, France
Patricia Acosta Vargas	Universidad de Las Américas, Ecuador
Alexander Aguila	Universidad Politécnica Salesiana, Ecuador
Hernán Aguirre	Shinshu University, Japan
Pablo Alvarez	Université de Rennes 1, France
Germán Arévalo	Universidad Politécnica Salesiana, Ecuador
Enrique Arias	Universidad de Castilla-La Mancha, Spain
María G. Baldeón	University of South of Florida, USA
César A. Beltrán	Pontificia Universidad Católica del Perú, Peru
Julian Betancur	Safran Group, France
Jack Bravo Torres	Universidad Politécnica Salesiana, Ecuador
Juan C. Caicedo	Broad Institute of MIT and Harvard University, USA
Jorge Camargo	Universidad Antonio Nariño, Colombia
Blanca Caminero	Universidad de Castilla-La Mancha, Spain
Lenin V. Camposano	Universidad Politécnica Nacional, Ecuador
Cármen Carrión	Universidad de Castilla-La Mancha, Spain
Diego Carrión	Universidad Politécnica Salesiana, Ecuador
Carlos Cevallos	Universidad Politécnica Nacional, Ecuador
Christian Cifuentes	Universidad de Zaragoza, Spain
Estefania Coronado	Fundazione Bruno Kessler (FBK), Italy
Germán Corredor	Case Western Reserve University, USA
Erick Cuenca	Université Catholique de Louvain, Belgium
Angel Cruz-Roa	Universidad de Los Llanos, Colombia
Juan DÁmanto	Universidad Nacional UNICEN, Argentina
Gloria M. Díaz	Instituto Tecnológico Metropolitano, Colombia

Diego Vallejo	Universidad Politécnica Salesiana, Ecuador
Pedro Yébenes	Universidad de Castilla-La Mancha, Spain
María A. Zuluaga	University College London, UK

Local Organizing Committee

Tatiana Mosquera	Universidad Politécnica Salesiana, Ecuador
Janneth Pallascos	Universidad Politécnica Salesiana, Ecuador
Jessica Chávez	Universidad Politécnica Salesiana, Ecuador
Maria Belén Sánchez	Universidad Politécnica Salesiana, Ecuador
Mónica Ruiz	Universidad Politécnica Salesiana, Ecuador
Julissa Freire	Universidad Politécnica Salesiana, Ecuador
Christian Guachilema	Universidad Politécnica Salesiana, Ecuador
Byron Fernando Velasco	Universidad Politécnica Salesiana, Ecuador

Sponsoring Institutions

http://www.ups.edu.ec

https://www.springer.com/series/7899

Contents

Smart Technologies

Spectral Power Map Generation Based on Spectrum Scanning
in the ISM Band for Interference Effects   3
  Benjamin Huertas-Herrera, David Góez Sánchez, and Erick ReyesVera

Implementation of a Real-Time Monitoring and Analysis System
for Luminous Flux Test in Integrating Sphere   16
  Ronny De La Bastida, Ricardo Araguillin, Nelson Sotomayor,
  and Carolin Chasi

Soil and Environmental Monitoring on a Vineyard in the Guadalupe Valley
as a Tool for Processes of Precision Viticulture Based on ZigBee
Technology to Improve the E-Agriculture.   29
  J. A. López-Leyva, A. Talamantes-Álvarez, E. Sanabia-Vincent,
  L. Aguilera-Silva, G. Gastelum-Rodríguez, and O. Meza-Arballo

The Network Virtualization to Support the Scalability of the Internet
of Things.   40
  Carlos J. Gonzalez, Olivier Flauzac, and Florent Nolot

Broadcast and Analysis of Traffic Warning Messages
in a VANET Network   52
  Luis Naula and Andrés Segovia

Signal Detection Methods in Cognitive Radio Networks:
A Performance Comparison   63
  Pablo Palacios Játiva, Milton Román-Cañizares, Carlos Saavedra,
  and José Julio Freire

Scalable Electrical Distribution Networks Planning for Medium and Low
Voltage Considering Capacity on Transformers and Voltage Drop.   75
  Milton Ruiz, Esteban Inga, and Silvio Simani

Performance Analysis of a Direct-Expansion Solar-Assisted Heat Pump
Using a Photovoltaic/Thermal System for Water Heating   89
  William Quitiaquez, Isaac Simbaña, C. A. Isaza-Roldán,
  César Nieto-Londoño, Patricio Quitiaquez, and Luis Toapanta-Ramos

Smart Systems

Enabling the Latent Semantic Analysis of Large-Scale Information
Retrieval Datasets by Means of Out-of-Core Heterogeneous Systems.   105
   Gabriel A. León-Paredes, Liliana I. Barbosa-Santillán,
   and Antonio Pareja-Lora

Increasing K-Means Clustering Algorithm Effectivity for Using in Source
Code Plagiarism Detection.   120
   Patrik Hrkút, Michal Ďuračík, Miroslava Mikušová,
   Mauro Callejas-Cuervo, and Joanna Zukowska

Using Machine Learning Techniques for Discovering Latent Topics
in Twitter Colombian News   132
   Vladimir Vargas-Calderón, Marlon Steibeck Dominguez,
   N. Parra-A., Herbert Vinck-Posada, and Jorge E. Camargo

Latent Semantic Index: A Microservices Architecture   142
   Julio Proaño, Andres Reinoso, and Jonnathan Juma

Factors that Affect i-Vectors Based Language Identification Systems.   154
   David Romero, Christian Salamea, Fernando Chica, and Erick Narvaez

Incorporation of Language Discriminative Information into Recurrent
Neural Networks Models to LID Tasks   165
   Christian Salamea, Ricardo Cordoba, Luis D'Haro, and David Romero

A Content-Based Multi Label Classification Model to Suggest Tags
for Posts in Stack Overflow   176
   Fredy A. Moreno and Jorge E. Camargo

Benchmarking of Classification Algorithms for Psychological Diagnosis   188
   Jhony Llano, Vanessa Ramirez, and Paulina Morillo

Proposal for an Integral System for Massive Open Online
Courses (ISMOOC).   202
   Lourdes Atiaja Atiaja and Andrés García Martínez

Security Mechanisms in NoSQL DBMS's: A Technical Review   215
   Irving L. Solsol, Héctor F. Vargas, and Gloria M. Díaz

Corrective Feedback Through Mobile Apps for English Learning:
A Review   229
   Adriana Guanuche, Osana Eiriz, and Roberto Espí

Classification and Visualization of Web Attacks Using HTTP Headers
and Machine Learning Techniques   243
   Nicolás Ricardo Enciso and Jorge E. Camargo

Smart Trends and Applications

Fusion of 3D Radiomic Features from Multiparametric Magnetic
Resonance Images for Breast Cancer Risk Classification   259
   Diana M. Marín-Castrillón, Jaider Stiven Rincón,
   Andrés E. Castro-Ospina, Liliana Hernández, and Gloria M. Díaz

Evaluation of Learning Approaches Based on Convolutional Neural
Networks for Mammogram Classification.   273
   Roberto Arias, Fabián Narváez, and Hugo Franco

Technological Platform for the Control of the Medication Supply
to People with Diabetes   288
   Mauro Callejas-Cuervo, Juan Pablo Contreras Barrera,
   and David Leonardo Cárdenas Rengifo

Emotion Recognition from Time-Frequency Analysis in EEG Signals
Using a Deep Learning Strategy   297
   Ruben D. Fonnegra, Pablo Campáz-Usuga, Kevin Osorno-Castillo,
   and Gloria M. Díaz

Automatic Exercise Recognition Based on Kinect Sensor
for Telerehabilitation   312
   Fernando Velasco and Fabián Narváez

Hand Angle Estimation Based on sEMG and Inertial Sensor Fusion   325
   Alfredo Lobaina Delgado, César Quinayás, Andrés Ruiz,
   Adson F. da Rocha, and Alberto López Delis

Estimation of Spatio-temporal Parameters of Gait Using an Inertial
Sensor Network   337
   Marcelo Bosmediano and Fabián Narváez

A Genetic Algorithm for BAP + QCAP with Imprecision in the Arrival
of Vessels   351
   Flabio Gutierrez, Edwar Lujan, Jose Rodríguez-Melquiades,
   and Miguel Jimenez-Carrion

Data Analysis of Particle Physics Experiments Based on Machine Learning
and the Mitchell's Criteria   364
   Huber Nieto-Chaupis

Quantum Mechanics Formalism for Modeling the Flux of BitCoins.   375
   Huber Nieto-Chaupis

Author Index   389

Smart Technologies

Spectral Power Map Generation Based on Spectrum Scanning in the ISM Band for Interference Effects

Benjamin Huertas-Herrera$^{(\boxtimes)}$ 🆔, David Góez Sánchez🆔, and Erick ReyesVera🆔

Department of Electronic and Telecommunications Engineering,
Instituto Tecnologico Metopolitano, Medellin, Colombia
benjaminhuertas240124@correo.itm.edu.co

Abstract. The use of the non-licensed frequency bands has increased considerably in the last years. The ISM band is widely used for short-range wireless communications systems and low energy consumption. Many technologies operating in the same band generally interfere with each other. This leads to a negative performance of the systems. Literature reports several researches that focus on techniques of medium access, coexistence and interference mechanism among others to attempt improving the deficient performance of the technologies that share the same frequency band. We propose the generation of a spectral power map in order to estimate the location of signal sources that cause interference effects in our systems. We implement GNU Radio, a reconfigurable radio (USRP) and a directional Yagui-uda antenna for capturing and processing signals in the ISM band. The Yagui-uda antenna presents an approximate directivity and bandwidth of 5 dB and 146 MHz respectively. Besides, the rate error of the antenna is 2.75%. This paper shows that, by integrating software-defined radio, signals processing and antennas with high directivity, it is possible to identify the sources of RF signals in a band of interest and in which objects the signals are reflected. Therefore, corrective actions can be taken in order to modify the position of the receivers and if possible the position of surrounding objects to change the incident power in the receiving antenna. As a result, the effects of interference between technologies can be mitigated, increasing the coexistence between them, especially in the ISM bands.

Keywords: Software-Defined Radio (SDR) · Spectrum sensing · Coexistence ISM bands · Spectral power sensing · Directive patch antenna

1 Introduction

In recent decades, electromagnetic occupancy has presented a rapid growth due to the high development of systems of wireless communication and the strong interest to connect anything trough of Internet of Things (IOT) [1–3]. Numerous technologies compete for getting an access to the electromagnetic spectrum, especially in the ISM band since it is widely used for wireless personal and local area networks [4]. Actually,

© Springer Nature Switzerland AG 2020
F. R. Narváez et al. (Eds.): SmartTech-IC 2019, CCIS 1154, pp. 3–15, 2020.
https://doi.org/10.1007/978-3-030-46785-2_1

many of the most employed technologies, such as WIFI, Bluetooth and ZigBee operate simultaneously at 2.4 GHz [5]. As consequence, an overloading and inaccessibility to the electromagnetic spectrum is produced. Likewise, interference effects appear by the presence of different signals that operate in the same frequency range and the surrounding environment, which produces a negative impact in the performance of the wireless communication systems [6].

Recently, many alternatives have been investigated regarding to decrease the interference between technologies, that operate in the ISM bands [7, 8]. Two different coexistent mechanisms based on traffic scheduling were proposed in order to look for solutions to the mutual interference problematic, the first one was applied to the WLAN stations and the second one to the Bluetooth (BT) devices. The results showed that the mechanisms employed were able to mitigate interference between collocated and no collocated BT and 802.11 devices. Furthermore, these mechanisms had a minor impact on the IEEE 802.11 standard and the BT specification [7]. In [9], a study about the performance of Bluetooth technology when there is WLAN interference based on probability of packet collision in frequency and time overlap was developed. It was showed that the packet loss may be significant (up to 27% for data traffic and 25% for voice applications) and may cause extreme performance degradation. In [10], the authors proposed a non-light-of-sight test setup in order to establish a standard practice for wireless coexistence of wireless systems. They showed that in higher wireless channel occupancy environment 802.15.4 coexists better with 802.11n than with 802.11 g. Otherwise, in [8], a similar investigation was performed. They demonstrated through testbed involving physical layer and network/transport layer that WLAN and 802.15.4 may coexist when they operate in close adjacency.

Based on above, the efficient use of the electromagnetic spectrum plays an important role in wireless communications. Thus, cognitive radio has become an interesting alternative to enhance the overwhelm use of the electromagnetic spectrum [4]. Federal communication commission defines cognitive radio as "A radio that can change its transmitter parameters based on interaction with the environment in which it operates". Several researches have shown that the use of cognitive radio to sense the spectrum is a reliable way to detect and use white spaces when there is not presence of primary users [4, 11, 12]. Numerous software defined radio platforms have been used for spectrum sensing [13]. One of the most used platforms is the Universal Software Radio Peripheral (USRP).

We propose the design of a method able to generate a spectral power map using spectrum scanning, considering the frequencies and spectral power of the signals scanned in the 2.4 GHz ISM band. To carry out this task a directive microstrip Yagi antenna in combination with an USRP were implemented to capture the signals into the range from 2.3238 GHz to 2.4698 GHz. Next, the GNU Radio software was used in order to process and build up the spectral power map based on the level of the collected signals. To test the capability of the proposed method to detect interference signals, two different experiments were achieved. Based on the obtained results, we can evidence that the proposed technique could be employed to identify interference signals, which can affect the operation of some wireless communication systems. Thus, this simple method has potential to sense the spectrum occupancy, the presence of other sources and could be used to optimize the use of microwave bands. Likewise, the recorded information will be used to detect the presence of objects close to the antenna that induce interference signals.

The next sections of this paper are organized as follows. Section 2 contains the methods and processes developed along the project. Section 3 presents the results and their analysis. Section 4 contains the conclusion.

2 Methods and Processes

As previously mentioned, we generate a spectral power map using spectrum scanning. In order to accomplish our objective, it is necessary the implementation of scanning systems in signal processing. In this context, it is required a hardware for RF data acquisition, a processing signal software and a directional antenna to capture the signals. Figure 1 shows a block diagram of the proposed architecture. Below we present in more detail each one of the components of the proposed spectrum scanning.

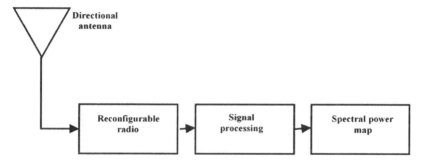

Fig. 1. Flow diagram for the generation of a spectral power map

2.1 Antenna Design and Characterization

Antennas are essential part of any wireless communication system and their electrical characteristic (resonant frequency, bandwidth, impedance, radiation pattern among others) depends on many factors such as materials, size, geometry, etc. [14–16]. Thus, it is one of the most important components to capture the power associated to different signals at specific band. In this section, we present the design and characterization of the proposed microstrip Yagui antenna, since we need to capture smaller signals.

Full wave structure simulation of the antenna is done using CST Microwave Studio [17]. The proposed structure consists of a microstrip Yagui-Uda antenna with a reflector and an array of seven directors, which operate at 2.4 GHz aiming for capturing signals in the ISM band. We select this kind of antenna since different works have demonstrated that the directivity can be improved with the inclusion of director elements [18, 19]. The input impedance of the antenna depends on the h_a (distance between the dipole and the reflector) and the width of the feed-line. In this case, the width of the feed line was calculated using the analytical model of impedance line in order to have a coupled line [14]. Based on this model, we obtain a feed line with a width of 3 mm. On the other hand, the distance h_a was tuned to obtain an input impedance of 50 Ω. Figure 2 shows a 2D schematic of the proposed antenna. The front side is illustrated in Fig. 2a. On the front side, the patch is formed by a single dipole that radiate the energy. The backside of the board the reflector and the directors' array were included. Figure 2b shows that the width of the directors decreases from W_{d1} to W_{d7} since we noticed that if the directors had the same width, they started to interact stronger with the electric field. As a result, new resonance frequency bands appeared, which is not desirable in spectra monitoring. The separation among the directors is periodic with a value of 1 mm. The short separation among the directors allows to generate induced current. In addition, the overall area of the proposed sensor is 4514 mm^2 (61 $\times$ 74 mm) which makes it to look as a compact and portable antenna. Moreover, the small size allows to manipulate and rotate the antenna easily.

The values of the proposed antenna are as follows: $W = 61$ mm, $h = 74$ mm, $W_{d1} = 37$ mm, $W_{d2} = 33$ mm, $W_{d3} = 29$ mm, $W_{d4} = 25$ mm, $W_{d5} = 21$ mm, $W_{d6} = 17$ mm, $W_{d7} = 13$ mm, $W_d = 28$ mm, $W_r = 49$, $h_d = 20$ mm, $h_r = 6$ mm, $h_a = 10$ mm.

To manufacture the proposed antenna, a CNC machine for printed circuit boards (LPKF ProtoMat D104, LPKF Laser & Electronics AG, Hanover, Germany) was used. The antenna is built on commercial dielectric substrate FR4, which has a relative permittivity (ε_r) of 4.4, loss tangent (tan δ) of 0.019, a thickness of 1.6 mm and a copper layer of 35 μm. Likewise, a 50-Ω SMA male connector was soldered in the input of the antenna for testing purposes.

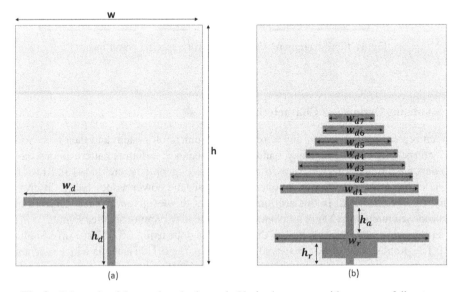

(a)   (b)

Fig. 2. Schematic of the employed microstrip Yagi-uda antenna with an array of directors.

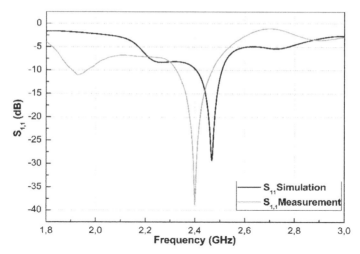

Fig. 3. $S_{1,1}$ Parameter for the simulated and fabricated antenna

A FSH8 vector network analyzer (VNA, Rhode & Schwartz, Munich, Germany) is used in order to validate the performance of the proposed antenna. During the test, the response of the S_{11} parameter is measured with the VNA from 1.8 GHz 3.0 GHz in order to identify the resonant frequency of the Yagui-Uda antenna. Figure 3 shows a comparison between the theoretical and experimental results. From this figure, the theoretical results obtained with CST STUDIO shows that the proposed antenna can operate at 2.468 GHz and it does not present another resonance in the analysis window. However, the experimental result shows that the fabricated antenna operates at 2.4 GHz, i.e., we obtain an error rate of only 2.57% between the resonant frequency simulated and measured. The small differences between them can be due to small fabrication tolerances in the engraved process with the CNC machine. In addition, the bandwidth of the proposed antenna was of 146 MHz, which is desirable for the proposed application in order to not detect too many bands.

In this case, the directivity and the gain of the antenna are others important parameters since they determine the angle of analysis and the operating distance of the antenna respectively. Figure 4 shows the radiation pattern of the antenna. As it is evident, the proposed antenna reached a maximum directivity of 4.97 dB and gain of 4.90 dB. Based on the directivity, the half power beam width was measured and gave a value of 70.5°.

2.2 Universal Software Radio Peripheral (Usrp)

The flexibility of this device allows capturing signals in many frequency bands. Usually, USRP has the capability to operate in a wide frequency range from 50 MHz to 6 GHz. The Fig. 5 shows the configuration and architecture of the USRP device. The USRP fulfills the function of capturing the wireless signal using a variable RF module. Once signal is acquired, this is passed through the amplification and filtering stage (analog signal). In this stage, the displacement from high to low frequency is performed. As a result, the signal is delivered in baseband. Then, it is digitized using the ADC at a

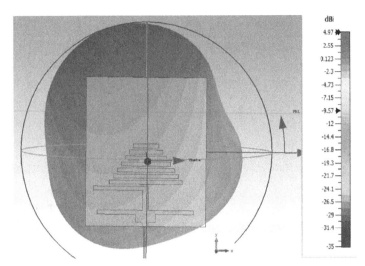

Fig. 4. Radiation pattern of the proposed antenna.

sampling frequency that can be modified based on the type of information received and bandwidth. At the end of this process, the signal is delivered to the signal processing in the complex form (I/Q) where different techniques and algorithms for signal processing can be used. In our case, the signal in the I/Q channels is received and processed to build the spectral power map from the FFT.

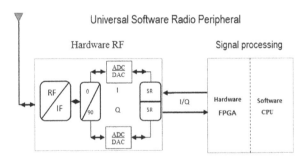

Fig. 5. Configuration and architecture of the USRP device

2.3 Signal Processing Using Software Defined Radio

In general, the radio built from software (SDR) consists of two stages. The first consists of reconfigurable hardware, on which it is possible to modify parameters such as sample rate and RF frequency of radio working in a wide frequency range. At the software level, the system integrates a series of libraries and computer tools that allow to manage the RF hardware, analyze the captured and digitized signal in a complex way, i.e. an I/Q signal. In this way, the design of the algorithm for spectral power map construction consisted of obtaining the RF signal from the reconfigurable radio at a sampling rate of 2 MHz per I/Q channel. Then, Fourier's 1024-point discrete transformation was obtained. Third, the transformed signal was scaled to the frequency domain on a color scale, where a range between −100 dBm and 0 dBm was assigned to construct the color map. Finally, GNU Radio was used (see Fig. 6), which is an "OPEN SOURCE" signal processing tool that allows to integrate algorithms and techniques associated with digital communications with reconfigurable RF hardware [20].

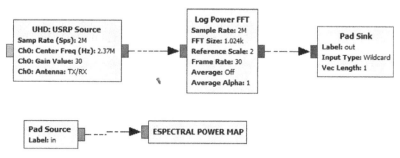

Fig. 6. Generation of the spectral power map using GNU Radio.

3   Experiment and Results

In this section we present the experimental results of the spectral power map using software defined radio (SDR).

3.1   Experimental Setup

The experimental setup consists of two phases. The first phase was developed in a controlled environment in order to validate the correct operation of the antennas and the software developed. Moreover, it was analyzed the variations in the measured spectral power when the receiving antenna changes its capture direction and there is an obstacle close to the communication system. Figure 7 shows the first phase of the experimental setup. To carry out this experiment, the proposed microstrip Yagi antenna was used as receiver (Rx), while a monopole (Tx) with a gain of 2 dB was implemented to transmit our own signal at 2.37 GHz with a maximum deviation in frequency of 250 kHz and a bandwidth of 500 kHz. Both antennas (transmitter and receiver) are placed at a height of 1.20 m with respect the ground in order to avoid interference effect due to ground reflections. Likewise, the microstrip Yagi antenna was mounted on a rotating platform and with a horizontal polarization in order to evaluate the collected signals at different reception directions.

Using the experimental setup illustrated in Fig. 7, we begin the capture of the signal without any obstacle when the receiving antenna was oriented at three different angles on the yaw axis 0°, 90° and 270°. Next, we place an object with a height of 1.60 m and a width of 0.65 m in six different positions close to the transmitter and receptor.

The intention of this prove was to examine how the presence of an object can induce interference signals due to the reflected waves (see the different position of the object in Fig. 7). The antenna capture directions with respect to the obstacle are summarized in Table 1.

The second phase of this experiment was addressed in the ISM band; we capture a signal coming from a router on a second floor, which operate at 2.431 GHz. We set the microstrip Yagi antenna on the first floor and change the inclination angle of it on the pitch axis First, the microstrip Yagi antenna was directly pointed to the router with an inclination angle of 0° and rotate the antenna on the yaw axis at 0°, 90° and 270°. The same experiment was carried out when the inclination angle on the pitch axis changes from 0° to 45°, while simultaneously the yaw axis is oriented at 0°, 90° and 270°.

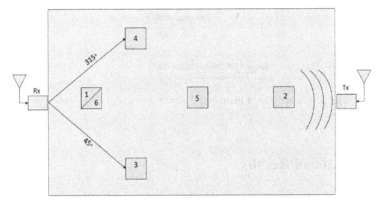

Fig. 7. Experimental setup with an object as an obstacle.

3.2 Spectral Power Map

In this section, we discuss the obtained results for the first phase (controlled environment) and the second phase (when the experiment was carried out to detect signals in the ISM band). The construction of the spectral power map starts from the spectrum sensing using USRP and processing the signals to obtain the frequencies from the FFT.

The implementation of this algorithm consists mainly of 6 steps. The first instance fulfills the function to initialize the SDR system. Secondly, the system scans RF signals. Thirdly, based on the sample rate the system acquires the RF signal. Then, GNU Radio employs the FFT with 1024 points. After that, the spectral power map is built by assigning a color to each spectral power sensed at the particular frequency value. Finally, the system asks for a new scan RF signal.

Figure 8 presents spectral power map obtained in the first phase of the experiment, which is conformed for only three pixels (each pixel is a capture with a particular direction on the yaw axis). The capture of these maps correspond to the impressions obtained when the receiver antenna was pointed at 0°, 90° and 270° on the yaw axis. From these results, it is evident that if the Yagui antenna is oriented at 0°, the spectral power sensed is approximately of −30 dB and it has a bandwidth of 500 kHz. Moreover, when the antenna is pointed at 90°, the sensed spectral power is equal to −62 dB, while the bandwidth is approximately 430 kHz. Finally, if the antenna is oriented at 270°, the system reports a sensed spectral power of −70 dB and a bandwidth of 390 kHz. Then, it can be observed that the spectral power reaches a higher value when the antenna points directly to the transmitter since as it was previously demonstrated in Sect. 2.1, the microstrip Yagui antenna presents a higher directivity at this direction. In addition, it is very remarkable that the bandwidth is wider at 0° because the antenna is able to capture all the frequencies that are sent from the transmitter antenna. It is hoped, that at the 90° and 270° directions the results may be almost equal. However, at the 90° direction there was a wall in the vicinity, which generated some reflections and changes in comparison to the 270° direction. Consequently, there is an appreciable change in the spectral power and visualized bandwidth between 90° and 270°. The visualized bandwidth at 90° and 270° decrease due to the loss of frequencies with low spectral power that the antenna is not able to capture.

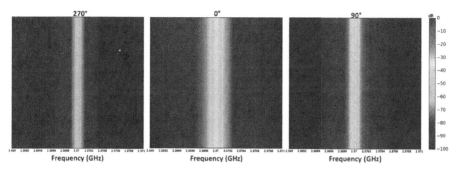

Fig. 8. Spectral power map conformed by three pixels. (a) 270°, (b) 0°, (c) 90°. The central frequency was set at 2.37 GHz and the analysis windows was from 2.369 GHz to 2.371 GHz.

Table 1 presents the values of the experiment with an object as an obstacle in different positions between the transmitter and receptor (Fig. 7). Results show that the obstacle does generate interferences and reflected waves. Drawing a comparison between the position 1 and 2, it can be seen that the spectral power in the receptor is higher when the object is set in position 2. This is because the lobe of the transmitted signal is narrower in position 2 than position 1. Furthermore, as position 1 is farther than position 2, the transmitted signal arrives and interacts with the obstacle in position 1 with lower spectral power.

Figure 9 shows the spectral power measured in the receptor when the antenna points directly to the transmitter with an angle of 0° and with the obstacle in position 1 and 2. The image clearly shows the great difference in spectral power for the obstacle in position 1 and 2. It also shows how the visualized bandwidth decreases greatly because of the distance between position 2 and the transmitter.

Table 1. Experimental measurement with an obstacle

Position	Frequency (GHz)	Antenna capture angle (yaw axis)	Spectral power (dB)
1	2.37	0°	−57
2	2.37	0°	−46
3	2.37	45°	−65
4	2.37	315°	−66
5	2.37	0°	−48
6	2.37	180°	−70

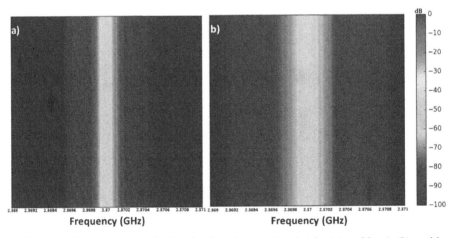

Fig. 9. Spectral power measured when the obstacle was placed at the (a) position 1; (b) position 2. The antenna capture angle on the yaw axis was equal for both position at 0°. Furthermore, the central frequency was set at 2.37 GHz and the analysis windows was from 2.369 GHz to 2.371 GHz.

Figure 10 shows the result of the experiment in the ISM band. The spectral power map displays the spectral power sensed for each inclination angle on the pitch axis, while the antenna was rotated on the yaw axis. As expected, the spectral power sensed with an inclination angle of 45° and rotating position 0° is higher than the other cases. This is because the antenna has a better line of sight at 45° than 0°. Furthermore, due to the directivity and radiation pattern of the antenna, there is a greater scope of the transmitted signal. The results for the rotating position at 90° and 270° exposes the great differences with the rotating position at 0°. It is very evident that the spectral power is lower when the antenna does not point to the direction of the transmitter. The lateral lobes of the antenna receive a low spectral power of the transmitted signal when the rotating position is fixed at 90° or 270°.

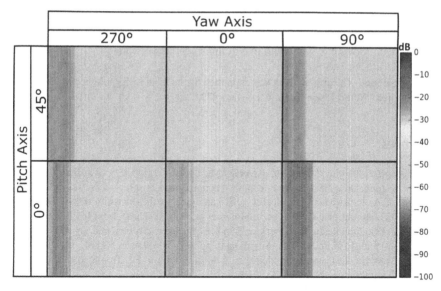

Fig. 10. Spectral power map ISM band.

The spectral power map also shows that the spectral power is higher for the three rotating positions at 45° inclination angle than the rotating positions at 0° inclination angle. As mentioned above, this is due to the capability of the antenna to capture signals pointing with a not good line of sight. Results prove that changing the position of the transmitter, receptor or obstacle the visualized bandwidth changes in function to the spectral power sensed. Therefore, it can be assumed, that if the system or environment configuration is modified, the interference effects caused by undesirable signals can be mitigated.

4   Conclusions

In this paper, the problematic of interference between technologies was addressed. We developed a technique able to generate a spectral power map in order to identify signal sources. Firstly, we worked in a controlled environment for validating the functioning of the software. Then, we used an object as an obstacle to analyze the interference and reflected waves caused by the object. Finally, we captured a signal coming from a router and built up a complete spectral power map conformed by different capturing directions and two inclination angles.

The use of a directional antenna allows to obtain quality results for the spectral map due to its directivity. In that way, the map can be built by capturing in different directions.

The spectral power map provides relevant details such as spectral power, bandwidth and visual representation of signals. Therefore, we conclude that the spectral power map is a very good alternative to attempt decreasing interferences between technologies. The identification of signal sources permits to employ new solutions. For instance, a positioning change of the technology might decrease considerably the interferences caused by others technologies.

In our further work, we propose to improve the directional antenna in order to have more directivity and a more directional radiation pattern. Also, in order to reduce the computational processing, we would like to improve the software.

Acknowledgments. The present work was supported by the Insituto Tecnológico Metropolitano under the project "Young researcher and innovator ITM".

References

1. Reyes-Vera, E., Senior, D.E., Luna-Rivera, J.M., López-Giraldo, F.E.: Advances in electromagnetic applications and communications. TecnoLógicas **21**(43), 9–13 (2018)
2. Medina, C.A., Perez, M.R., Trujillo, L.C.: IoT paradigm into the smart city vision: a survey. In: 2017 IEEE International Conference on Internet of Things (iThings) and IEEE Green Computing and Communications (GreenCom) and IEEE Cyber, Physical and Social Computing (CPSCom) and IEEE Smart Data (SmartData), pp. 695–704, January 2018
3. Botero Valencia, J., Castaño Londoño, L., Marquez Viloria, D.: Trends in the Internet of Things. TecnoLógicas **22**(44), I–II (2019)
4. Perez, M., Jaramillo, D., Pinzon, D., Herrera, F.: Spectrum forecasting model for IoT services. In: 2018 IEEE-APS Topical Conference on Antennas and Propagation in Wireless Communications (APWC), pp. 877–881 (2018)
5. Wetzker, U., Splitt, I., Zimmerling, M., Boano, C.A., Romer, K.: Troubleshooting wireless coexistence problems in the industrial Internet of Things. In: Proceedings - 19th IEEE International Conference on Computational Science and Engnieering. 14th IEEE Conference on Embedded and Ubiquitous Computing. 15th International Symposium on Distributed Computing and Applications for Business Engineering, October 2017, pp. 98–109 (2017)
6. Mahajan, A., Gupta, S.: Interference evaluation of different wireless systems operating in 2.4 GHz ISM band, pp. 3–6 (2013)
7. Chiasserini, C.F., Rao, R.R.: Coexistence mechanisms for interference mitigation between IEEE 802.11 WLANs and Bluetooth. In: Proceedings of the Twenty-First Annual Joint Conference IEEE Computer Communication Society, vol. 2, no. 5, pp. 590–598 (2003)
8. Angrisani, L., Bertocco, M., Fortin, D., Sona, A.: Experimental study of coexistence issues between. IEEE Trans. Instrum. Meas. **57**(8), 1514–1523 (2008)
9. Golmie, N., Mouveaux, F.: Interference in the 2.4 GHz ISM band: impact on the Bluetooth access control performance. ICC 2001. In: IEEE International Conference Communication Conference Record. (Cat. No.01CH37240), pp. 2540–2545 (2002)
10. Lasorte, N.J., Rajab, S.A., Refai, H.H.: Experimental assessment of wireless coexistence for 802.15.4 in the presence of 802.11 g/n. In: IEEE International Symposium on Electromagnetic Compatibility, pp. 473–479 (2012)
11. Dobre, E.I., Martian, A., Vladeanu, C.: USRP-based experimental platform for energy detection in cognitive radio systems. In: IEEE International Conference Communication, vol. 2016, pp. 185–188, August 2016
12. Cosmina-valentina, N., Mar, A., Marghescu, I.: Spectrum sensing based on energy detection algorithms using GNU radio and USRP for cognitive radio. In: 2018 International Conference Communications, pp. 381–384 (2018)
13. Roncancio, G., Espinosa, M., Pérez, M.R., Trujillo, L.C.: Spectral sensing method in the radio cognitive context for IoT applications. In: Proceedings - 2017 IEEE International Conference Internet Things, IEEE Green Computer Communications IEEE Cyber, Physics. Society Computer IEEE Smart Data, iThings-GreenCom-CPSCom-SmartData 2017, pp. 756–761, January 2018

14. Constantine, B.: Antenna Theory: Analysis and Design, 2nd edn. Wiley, Hoboken (1982)
15. Catano-Ochoa, D., Senior, D.E., Lopez, F., Reyes-Vera, E.: Performance analysis of a microstrip patch antenna loaded with an array of metamaterial resonators. In: 2016 IEEE International Symposium on Antennas and Propagation (APSURSI), pp. 281–282 (2016)
16. Reyes-Vera, E., Arias-Correa, M., Giraldo-Muno, A., Catano-Ochoa, D., Santa-Marin, J.: Development of an improved response ultra-wideband antenna based on conductive adhesive of carbon composite. Prog. Electromagn. Res. C **79**, 199–208 (2017)
17. Simulator, M.S.E.: Computer simulation Tool. Dassault Systems, Vélizy-Villacoublay (2017)
18. Floc, J.H., Ahmad, A.E.S.: Dual-band printed dipole antenna with parasitic element for compensation of frequency space attenuation. Int. J. Electromagn. Appl. **2**(5), 120–128 (2012)
19. Barros, I., Gonçalves, S., Fernandes, M., De Andrade, H.D.: Quasi-Yagi microstrip antenna device design for directive wideband ISM application, pp. 3042–3046, May 2017
20. Song, W.: Configure cognitive radio using GNU radio and USRP. In: Proceedings of the 2009 3rd IEEE International Symposium Microwave, Antenna, Propagation. EMC Technology Wireless Communication MAPE 2009, pp. 1123–1126 (2009)

Implementation of a Real-Time Monitoring and Analysis System for Luminous Flux Test in Integrating Sphere

Ronny De La Bastida[1,2] (ID), Ricardo Araguillin[3,4](✉) (ID), Nelson Sotomayor[2], and Carolin Chasi[3] (ID)

[1] Departamento de Física, Escuela Politécnica Nacional, Quito, Ecuador
[2] Departamento de Automatización y Control Industrial, Escuela Politécnica Nacional, Quito, Ecuador
[3] Instituto de Investigación Geológico Energético IIGE, Quito, Ecuador
[4] GLOmAe, Departamento de Física, Facultad de Ingeniería, Universidad de Buenos Aires, Buenos Aires, Argentina

Abstract. One of the methods to determine luminous efficacy is using an integrating sphere following Illuminating Engineering Society (IES) standards. For obtaining reliable results is necessary to monitor and analyze luminous flux stability using specialized measurement devices reporting the test uncertainty. Although, in most of commercial instruments there is not flexibility to program the needed of the costumer and those which have this flexibility are more expensive even when the quality is similar, adding the fact of many research laboratories have their measurement devices but without an option to develop or integrate in a unique central system. For this reason, in this paper is presented a low cost implementation of a real time monitoring and analysis for luminous flux test at Lighting Laboratory of Instituto de Investigación Geológico Energético (IIGE) of Ecuador, taking measurement devices without protocols information (close systems) and using a method of reverse engineering on it to integrate in a central system controlling by LabVIEW. The Automatic Central System (ACS) is validated using standard lamps and comparing with the manual system using manufacture software showing that ACS could monitor and analyze the data in real time, in contrast with manual system, showing normalized errors less than 1% and an increasing productivity of 50% due to the automatic generation of documentation following IES and ISO/IEC 17025 standards.

Keywords: Luminous flux stability · Integrating sphere · Virtual instrumentation · LabVIEW · Color correlated temperature · Reverse engineering

1 Introduction

One of the most study physical phenomena is light for its impact in daily life, being the road lighting a fundamental area for mobility, ornamentation and public safety [1]. Two important optical properties of light source related to luminous efficiency and emission spectral due to the electronic process inside the lamp are total luminous flux and color

© Springer Nature Switzerland AG 2020
F. R. Narváez et al. (Eds.): SmartTech-IC 2019, CCIS 1154, pp. 16–28, 2020.
https://doi.org/10.1007/978-3-030-46785-2_2

correlated temperature (CCT). The total luminous flux is defined as the power light emitted by a light source taking in count the eye photopic vision [2], it could be express in (1) where k_m, $V(\lambda)$ and $\phi_{e,\lambda}(\lambda)$ are a constant of maximum photopic luminous efficacy of radiations, the spectral luminous efficiency in photopic vision and spectral concentration of radiant flux measured in watts per nanometer.

$$\phi = k_m \int_{380}^{780} V(\lambda)\phi_{e,\lambda}(\lambda)d\lambda \tag{1}$$

On the other hand, the CCT is defined as the nearest black body temperature to reproduce spectral radiance from the light source [3]. Some studies have been done for calculating it, the Robertson's method has been used as a reference method in computational determination of CCT that require greater accurate [4] permitting to calculate, using a linear Eq. (2), an unknown iso-temperature line between two known in the Plank locus uniform chromaticity scale [5]. T_j, d_j and T_c are reciprocal color temperature of a black body radiator, the distance between two iso-temperature lines and correlated color temperature respectively.

$$CCT = T_c = \left[\frac{1}{T_j} + \frac{d_j}{d_j - d_{j+1}} \left(\frac{1}{T_{j+1}} - \frac{1}{T_j} \right) \right]^{-1} \tag{2}$$

In order to measure total luminous flux and CCT, it is used an Integrating Sphere (IS) as a standard method provided by IES, which is an empty spherical cavity with a perfectly diffusing and nonselective reflectance surface, where a test lamp placed in the center is considered as punctual source. With those assumptions, the luminance is proportional to the total luminous flux from the light source and it could be express in (3), where ϕ_T, k, E are the total luminous flux express in lumen, the proportional constant and the luminance express in candela per unit area [6].

$$\phi_T = kE \tag{3}$$

The presence of a source having finite dimension, cavities for the measurement devices, a necessary baffle and other characteristics introduce error in measurements [7]. For accurate measurement, self-absorption is taken as correction method using an auxiliary lamp as seen in Fig. 1.

Luminous flux variation is one problem to avoid during the analysis, for this reason, IES standard advice to analyze the luminous flux during its establishment. In this period is important to calculate the percentage of stability using (4), where S, n, ϕ_{max} and ϕ_{min} are the percentage, the number of continuous measurements, maximum and minimum values of total luminous flux. To avoid thermal effects, all measurements are taking under values of continuous operation time (t) before the analysis of lamp, environmental temperature (Te), period of time between two measures (Δt) and maximum percentage of stability to declare the luminous flux settled down, the parameters are shown in Table 1 [8–11].

$$S = \frac{\phi_{max} - \phi_{min}}{\frac{\sum_{i=1}^{n} \phi_i}{n}} \tag{4}$$

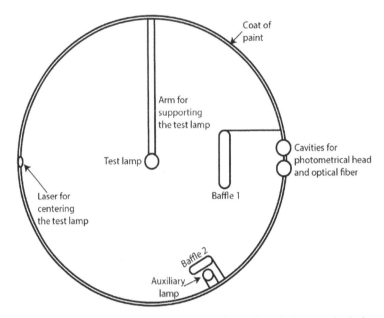

Fig. 1. Scheme of integrating sphere using radiometric and photometric devices.

Table 1. Parameters used for analysis of luminous flux stability depending lamp technology.

Lamp technology	t (min)	Te (°C)	N	Δt	S (%)
Incandescent (INC)	1–3	25 ± 10	5	15 s	0.25
Fluorescent (FL)	30–45	25 ± 5	6	1 min	1
Compact Fluorescent Lamp (CFL)	30–45	25 ± 5	6	1 min	1
High Pressure Sodium (HPS)	15–30	25 ± 5	4	1 min	2.5
High Pressure Mercury (HPM)	15–30	25 ± 5	4	1 min	1
Metal Halide (MH)	15–30	25 ± 5	4	1 min	2
Solid State Lamp (SSL)	30–120	25 ± 1	3	15 min	0.25

A measure of electrical, optical and radiometric parameters allows to evaluate the energy efficiency of a light source technology. According to requires methods for measuring, analysis data and the calculus of uncertainty of the International Organization for Standardization (ISO) and International Electrotechnical Commission (IEC), it is necessary to supply reliable results endorsements. In an economic context, the needed of reliable results implies a strong inversion in measure devices and infrastructure to satisfy with every standard. Adding to it, in our present the automation of process allows to increase the efficiency of production with automatic analysis using computational process in real time, giving some benefits such us less workload to the operator, less fails due to human errors and others, but it involves to have equipment which have technical requirements to connect in a computational automatic system control. This is a problem in countries that depend on the technology of others and even more in countries that have a high quality of measure devices but don't have the inversion necessary to get devices with automation features.

In Ecuador public lighting and other related services represents around 17.31% of the cost of invoiced energy [12]. Due to this fact, Ecuador launched a National Plan of Energy Efficiency for two reasons (1) to improve the efficiency in the consumption of electrical energy in the public lighting and (2) to improve the load factor of the national electrical system where one of the most important strategies were replacing old light technologies for new efficiency light technologies such as compact fluorescents lamps and LED lamps in residential and public sectors [13–15]. In order to improve the efficiency of this sector the Instituto Nacional de Eficiencia Energética y Energías Renovables, that is now part of the Instituto de Investigación Geológico Energético (IIGE), created in 2015, the first Lighting Laboratory of Ecuador to test lamps and luminaries which are commercialized in the country. IIGE's Lighting Laboratory has photometric and electrical devices to analyze the energy efficiency following the criteria of ISO/IEC 17025 and IES methodologies. Initially the devices were not in a central system to acquire data, it means, every device communicated with their own software, where all of them didn't have technical documentation to integrate in a unique software. Adding to it, the design of all devices made impossible the diffusion of technical documentation of protocol communication by manufactures. Another fact is that all the analysis during the test is not made in real time, increasing the period of time service and possible human errors for all the variables imply in data analysis.

Due to the high cost to change all the measure device to create an automatic system, this work present the implementation of an automatic and central system (ACS) developed in LabVIEW using a method of reverse engineering to find the protocols communication from all device to integrate in ACS to analyze luminous flux stability in real time, generate all the documentation following IES and ISO/IEC 17025 standards, improve the efficiency of the system, give less workload to the operator and reduce test time.

2   Implementation of Automatic Central System

The ACS needs control devices, measurement equipment and software elements to evaluate energy efficiency according to ISO/IEC 17025 standard, calibrate equipment using standard light sources, measure different light sources due to the method is a relative method, calculate the combined uncertainty using a mathematical model published by Velazquez et al. [16] and generate all documentation about the test.

2.1   Automatic Central System Hardware

The ACS system is composed by a multiphotometer corrected with the $V(\lambda)$ function to measure total luminous flux, spectroradiometer to measure the spectral power distribution, two temperature sensor was placed in the system: a thermohygrometer MSR-255 to sense the environmental temperature and a wireless temperature sensor developed with an ESP8266 microcontroller and integrated circuit LM35 to obtain the temperature of photometrical head, a summary of all devices with their quantities is shown in Table 2.

Table 2. Measurement quantities and units for system devices.

Device	Quantity	Symbol	Unit
Multiphotometer PR-200D	Total luminous flux	ϕ	lumen (lm)
Spectroradiometer Haas 2000	Color correlated temperature	CCT	Kelvin (K)
Power analyzer Yokogawa WT310	Voltage	V	Volt (V)
	Current	I	Ampere (A)
	Real power	P	Watt (W)
	Power factor	PF	–
Thermo-hygrometer MSR-255	Temperature	T	Celsius (°C)
Wireless temperature sensor	Temperature	T	Celsius (°C)

The main problem to integrate most of all measurements was their unknown communication protocols. Due to this, a methodology of reverse engineering was applied to decodify communication protocols [17], this method follows four stages to decodify protocol communication through OSI layers as shown in Fig. 2.

Initially, a hardware analysis was applied to find primordial characteristic of communication protocol in the physic layer. Once recognized physical characteristic, different values of a quantity was monitored to identify data traffic and collect it for the next stage, that consists in analyze the data and divide it in two groups. The first one a constant data cluster where all information doesn't change even when the value is modified. This cluster carrying the information to establish a successful communication with the equipment such as headers, recognized information, modes of operations as others. The second one dynamic data cluster, which generally carry the information of value of quantity. Finally, an analysis to link data changed with an algorithm to establish communication and codify to display information to the use.

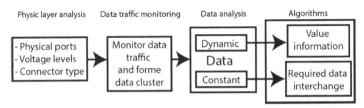

Fig. 2. Applied method of Reverse engineering methodology to decodify communication protocols from measurement devices.

All measurement devices interchange data with a workstation, the devices use a serial RS-232 protocol except the spectra radiometer that uses a USB protocol and the wireless temperature sensor that uses a Wi-Fi protocol. In order to communicate wireless temperature sensor and control ignition of lamp, communication and control devices was developed with an ESP8266 microcontroller that has two main functions: to transmit data from temperature sensor to the workstation and to activate relays located in a control panel to ignite the lamp placed inside the integrating sphere, all of this using Wi-Fi protocol. Adding to it, the workstation is linked to a server where a data base, developed in MySQL, saves all the results data of luminous flux test, the integrated system is observed in Fig. 3.

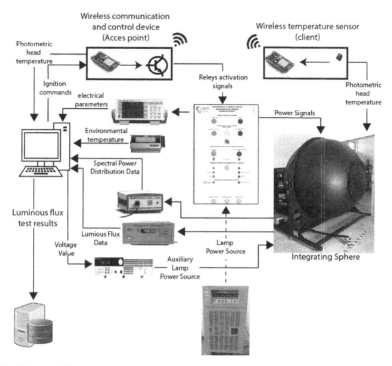

Fig. 3. Scheme of integrated system used to analyze luminous flux with an integrating sphere

Device Calibration. For optimal performance of the spectroradiometer and the wireless temperature sensor, a calibration method is developed before a test. The calibration of the spectroradiometer helps to reduce the noise that occurs for the optical attenuator, placed before its optical fiber that does not allow saturating the CCD sensor when testing a high intensity discharge lamp. To calibrate it is necessary to test a standard lamp with a known Spectral Power Distribution (SPD) and compare it with the SPD taken by the spectroradiometer as shown in (5), the M (λ) function is used to correct the data at each wavelength multiplied by reading of the spectroradiometer.

$$M(\lambda) = \frac{SPD_{standard}}{SPD_{real}} \tag{5}$$

Meanwhile, for wireless temperature sensor calibration used a comparison with the value of temperature of a heating control. The data obtained was used to interpolate in a linear function, whose slope corresponds to gain to convert the counts of ADC to temperature in Celsius. Both correct function for spectroradiometer and gain for wireless sensor temperature are place in a text file to use during the test and refresh every time when a new calibration is made.

Data Collecting. To generate reports according to ISO 17025 standard is necessary to take information about test lamp, measurement devices and temperature values before the test begin [18]. The information about the test lamp like technology, nominal power and nominal voltage are provided manually by an operator at first instance. As quality assurance measures, the operator indicates what devices are calibrated, the ACS compute the voltage percentage difference between power analyzer and power source without load and automatically the application communicates with MSR-255 to determine if the environmental temperature is inside the range shown in Table 1, if all is correct ACS allow perform the test. All this data is given by an operator manually and the application classifies and saves in text files to generate all the documentation and register the test in the data base.

Analysis of Variables. ACS uses a parallel programming taking advantage of Lab-VIEW's characteristics to assign one process to different cores and the actual technology of the workstation which permits to work with more than one task at same time, as result the time for one iteration is reduced. The test for reference lamp and test lamp use this method of programming, having three different process to get better results

The first process gets the data of luminous flux, electrical parameters and temperature in the environment and photometric head. The ACS is designed to show temporal evolution of those variables, with a sampling time defined in the setting of the system, in a graph where the operator has the option to display more than one with an adjustable scale that allows to compare the behavior of different quantities. In this process, PR-200D, WT310, MSR-255 and wireless communication and control device use a RS-232 protocol communication to interchange data and activate relays to control ignition at the begin of each test lamp. The second process is measured the SPD from the light source and show in another graph, creating a cluster with all SPD taken during the test to export at the end of it, the sampling time is the same in the first process. All data interchange uses an USB protocol making more stable the communication and faster than using RS-232 protocol. The third process analyzes the luminous flux stability with data taken in the first process and using parameters described in Table 1. In this process, the sampling time is different, due to analysis of data between two readings, compared to the sample time to monitor variables. When the lamp stabilizes, the system analyzes among all the percentages calculated to determine the lowest value to declare the stabilization time in the report. The analysis is restarted every time the lamp changes from a non-stable to a stable state. All data measured in the three processes is exported in excel files as primary register and it will be used to calculate the uncertainty of the test and complete the information to generate the reports.

Generation of Documentation. In order to generate the two principal reports, the uncertainty is calculated with uncertainty estimation model published by Velazquez et al. [14], importing all data measured during the test. Ones it is calculated, the system imports data of data collecting stage. To create the report with a custom format, Lab-VIEW used Microsoft Office tools to export data into a copy of a template for generating both reports. The virtual system generates four files about the test: two reports, one about uncertainty calculation and data used for it, and other with all data measured from the test lamp. Ones all documents were generated, LabVIEW establishes a communication with a data base for saving all important data such as name of documentation, time stabilization, combined uncertainty of test and others to permit an automatic register giving less workload to the operator and to avoid mistakes that could happen by register manually the results.

3   Experimental Results

To determine the success of the reverse engineering method, incandescent and HID lamps were tested, to compare the results between software developed in LabVIEW and original software. The results, show in Fig. 4, correspond to the difference calculated for the luminous flux, voltage, current and active power, are zero showing the efficacy of reverse engineering method applied. Nevertheless, luminous efficacy and power factor have an small error due to those values are computed and the amount of significant numbers differs between both applications.

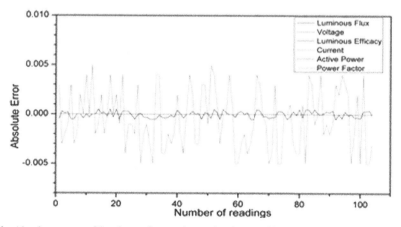

Fig. 4. Absolute error of luminous flux, voltage, luminous efficacy, current, active power and power factor company software and LabVIEW application after using reverse engineering

In the same way, Fig. 5 shows a comparison of the spectral peaks between the manufacture software and the ACS measured from a CFL lamp. It shows a displacement of one nanometer in wavelength between two data processing and an error in spectral power distribution magnitude due to the difference of the calibration method for both applications, considering that the reverse engineering was used to decode protocol communication and not data processing methods. However, the error in the SPD values is 0.84% being 1% using the criteria of the ISO/IEC 17025 standard to analyze the standardized error required by the Ecuadorian Accreditation System (SAE).

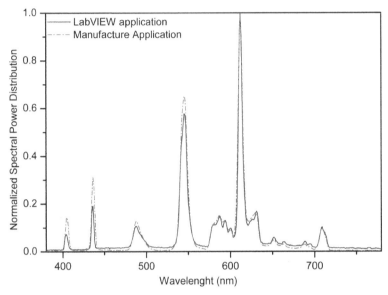

Fig. 5. Normalized spectral power distribution measured from a CFL lamp using LabVIEW application and manufacture application.

Testing standard incandescent and HID lamps permitted to analyze the efficacy of the automatic system. In Fig. 6 is shown the luminous flux stabilization of both lamps, where the data inside blue box was taken to be analyzed. Both lamps have a damped behavior but in Fig. 7(a) exists some undesirable peaks produced by instrumental error that could give errors calculating combined uncertainty. However, later it shall be evidenced that combined uncertainty will not be affected due to the quantity of error in comparison with all data measured during the test taking into consideration that the sampling time was

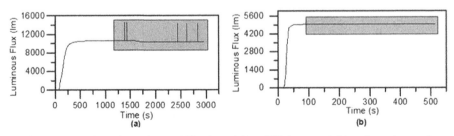

Fig. 6. Behavior of luminous flux stabilization of (a) a HID lamp and (b) an incandescent lamp measured with ACS (Color figure online)

un second per reading. The data outside blue box are measurements during the time of continuous operation that IES standard recommends and data inside blue box is analyzed taking into consideration the parameters of Table 1.

Within the analysis of luminous flux stabilization is important to determine the minimum percentage to declare it according to the procedures of the laboratory, where all the percentages inside blue box of Fig. 7, were taking into consideration to found the minimum values. The reason to analyze just one part of percentage calculated is to ensure the quantity of data to calculated combined uncertainty with a confidence level of 95%. As seen in Table 1 and Fig. 7, both lamps are under the maximum percentage to consider them stabilized.

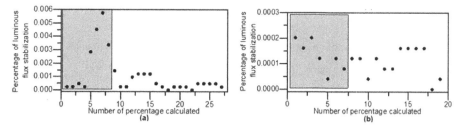

Fig. 7. Behavior of luminous flux stabilization of (a) a HID lamp and (b) an incandescent lamp measured with automatic system (Color figure online)

Due to the technology of the lamp, an identical behavior is not possible, but it is possible to compare the manual and the automatic system using the uncertainty of the test and the normalized error that allows to see how repeatable the results of the automatic method are respecting to the manual system. In Table 3 is shown the values calculated by automatic and manual system for both lamps, where both normalized errors are under a value of one that is the maximum value allowed by SAE. Analyzing in every lamp their uncertainty, they have an error of 0.5% taking as reference the value of manual system.

Table 3. Quantities of uncertainty model estimation and normalized error according to ISO/IEC 17025 standard

Lamp	Quantity	Automatic system	Manual system
Standard incandescent	Average of luminous flux (lm)	4965.87	4963.00
	Combined uncertainty	0.0199	0.0200
	Normalized error	0.02044	NA
HID	Average of luminous flux (lm)	10350	10370
	Combined uncertainty	0.07479	0.07478
	Normalized error	0.01825	NA

Even when the peaks produced by instrumental errors included to analyze and calculate combined uncertainty, the errors aren't greater than one percent. It is because in the analysis there is more than two thousand samples for each variable and calculating their average, it means that the few points out of the trend have a low weighting in the calculation of the averages of their variables and therefore a low contribution to the calculation of combined uncertainty.

The test using either, manual or automatic system, could be classified into five stages: verification of devices, continuous operation of test lamp according IES standards, acquisition and data analysis, compute test uncertainty and register of test information, and generation of reports. The Table 4 shows duration of both stages for each system in a HID test, where the reduction of time is 40 min or 30% of the time using the manual system.

Table 4. Time of operation for each stage during the test lamp in minutes

Quantity	Automatic system	Manual system
Verification of devices	30	20
Continuous operation time according IES standard	40	40
Data acquisition and analysis	21	25
Calculation of combined uncertainty and register information	2	20
Generation of reports	2	30
Total time	95	135

In terms of productivity and taking in consideration that the maximum numbers of test per day is four, it could be increase to six tests per day. However, another consideration is that all this time was taken following the method implemented by the laboratory, having the possibility to reduce it if the continuous operation time of the lamp is reduced to a few minutes, due to the system could analyze the luminous flux from the beginning of the test to the lamp is off. In this way, it could be increased the productivity at least of seven tests per day.

As seen in Table 4, the calculation of combined uncertainty of test, the registration of information about the test and the generation of reports reduced the time in 92%, giving less workload to the operator and minimizing the errors of data analysis. However, the errors of system could not reduce to zero because the operator filled the information about the lamp and information about calibration, being this part where the errors could be introduced.

4   Conclusion

The implementation of a real-time monitoring and analysis system for luminous flux tests in integrating sphere has been proposed in this research. In order to measure photometric, radiometric and electrical parameters, the ACS integrated measurement devices with unknown protocol communication using a reverse engineering methodology to decodify their protocols to communicate all of them into one system. As seen in results using reverse engineering permits integrated all the devices with low cost, high and reliable results. The system was controlled for an application developed on LabVIEW following IES standard to analyze the stability of luminous flux and ISO/IEC 17025 standard, where one of the main characteristics of the system is to control three kind of process using parallel programming to assign a specific task within the test. All the data monitored and analyzed is used to create documentation automatically with the help of Microsoft tools implemented by LabVIEW. It permits to reduce the time of the process giving less workload to the operator, minimizing human errors and increasing the productivity in the laboratory with reliable results validated using the criteria for accreditation in ISO/IEC standard.

All the results had low errors comparing with the manual system, having a more robust system against instrumental errors and giving more details about the temporal evolution of the variables. Proponing for future works to implement current model as deep learning or neural networks to analysis luminous flux stability to reduce the time of analysis and even to implement models to predict the time where the lamp shall be stabilized, improving the current methods to analyze the luminous flux, which would be a great contribution to IES standards methods and it would have an impact on all laboratories of photometry.

Acknowledgment. The corresponding author acknowledges financial support from SENESCYT scholarship.

References

1. Fotios, S., Gibbons, R.: Road lighting research for drivers and pedestrians: the basis of luminance and illuminance recommendations. Light. Res. Technol. **50**(1), 154–186 (2018)
2. Choudhury, A.K.R.: Principles of Colour and Appearance Measurement, 1st edn. Woodhead Publishing, Cambridge (2014)
3. DiLaura David, L., Houser Kevin, W., Mistrick Richard, G., Steffy Gary, R.: Lighting Handbook. Reference and Application, In: 10th edn. Iluminating Engineering Society of North America, New York (2011)
4. Li, C., et al.: Accurate method for computing correlated color temperature. Opt. Express **24**, 14066–14078 (2016)
5. Robertson, A.R.: Computation of Correlated Color Temperature and Distribution Temperature. Journal of the Optical Society of America **58**(11), 1528–1535 (1968)
6. Ohkubo, K.: Integrating sphere theory for measuring optical radiation. J. Light Visual Environ. **34**(6), 111–122 (2010)
7. Lin, F., Li, T., Yin, D., Lai, L., Xia, M.: Research on effects of baffle position in an integrating sphere on the luminous flux measurement. In: 8th International Symposium on Advanced Optical Manufacturing and Testing Technologies: Optical Test, Measurement Technology, and Equipment. SPIE, China (2016)
8. Illuminating Engineering Society of North America: IESNA Approved Method for Electrical and Photometric Measurements of General Service Incandescent Filament Lamps. IESNA, New York (2009)

9. Illuminating Engineering Society of North America: IES Approved Method for Electrical and Photometric Measurement of Single-Ended Compact Fluorescent Lamps. IESNA, New York (2011)

10. Illuminating Engineering Society of North America: IES Approved Method for the Electrical and Photometric measurement of High Intensity Discharge Lamps. IESNA, New York (2013)

11. Iluminating Engineering Society of North America: Approved Method: Electrical and Photometric Measurements of Solid- State Lighting Products. IESNA, New York (2008)

12. Agencia de Regulación y Control de Electricidad (ARCONEL). https://www.regulacionelectrica.gob.ec/boletines-estadisticos. Accecsed 02 June 2019

13. Chavez-Rodriguez, M.F., et al.: Fuel saving strategies in the Andes: long-term impacts for Peru, Colombia and Ecuador. Energy Rev. **20**, 35–48 (2018)

14. Ponce-Jara, M.A., Castro, M., Palaez Samaniego, M.R., Espinoza-Abad, J.L., Ruiz, E.: Electricity sector in Ecuador: an overview of the 2007-20017 decade. Energy Pol. **113**, 513–522 (2018)

15. Espinoza, V.S., Guayanlema, V., Martínez-Gómez, J.: Energy efficiency plan benefits in ecuador long-range energy alternative planning model. Int. J. Energy Econ. Pol. **8**(4), 42–54 (2018)

16. Velásquez, C., Espín, F.: Cálculo de la incertidumbre combinada en un goniofotómetro de espejo rotante tipo C y una esfera de Ulbricht, I + T+C Investigación. Tecnología y Ciencia **9**, 29–35 (2015)

17. de la Bastida, R., Araguillin, R., Sotomayor, N.: Reingeniería como metodología para el desarrollo de instrumentación virtual y aplicaciones integrales. Proc. XXVII Jornadas en Ingeniería Eléctrica y Electrónica 61–69 (2017)

18. Servicio Ecuatoriano de Normalización. Requisitos generales para la competencia de los -laboratorios de ensayo y calibración. NTE INEN-ISO/IEC 17025, pp. 17–18 (2018)

Soil and Environmental Monitoring on a Vineyard in the Guadalupe Valley as a Tool for Processes of Precision Viticulture Based on ZigBee Technology to Improve the E-Agriculture

J. A. López-Leyva$^{(\boxtimes)}$ ⓘ, A. Talamantes-Álvarez ⓘ, E. Sanabia-Vincent,
L. Aguilera-Silva, G. Gastelum-Rodríguez, and O. Meza-Arballo ⓘ

CETyS Universidad, Centro de Innovación y Diseño, 22860 Ensenada, BC, Mexico
{josue.lopez,oscar.meza}@cetys.mx,
{ariana.talamantes,eduardo.sanabia,luis.aguilera,
guillermo.gastelum}@cetys.edu.mx

Abstract. This paper presents the design and field tests of a system to remotely monitor environmental variables in a vineyard in the Guadalupe Valley, Mexico. In particular, the environmental variables are temperature, humidity, and luminosity, some of them monitored in the subsoil. These variables affect the quality of the grapes, and these quality parameters are also different according to each grape variety according to the different stages of the crop. The presented prototype is based on the ZigBee technology and is part of the E-Agriculture process, particularly related to Precision Agriculture concept. In addition, measurements were made with the early-adopters in order to determine the performance of the prototype and consider the feedback to improve the overall performance. Finally, the prototype shows an adequate performance with respect to the measurements of the environmental variables, the reliability of the interconnection, the storage and presentation of the data. Also, there are some findings that could improve the performance and installation of the prototype to enhance the E-Agriculture process and the widespread use in the Guadalupe Valley through a sectorization process according to the grape variety crops.

Keywords: Monitoring · Precision viticulture · Prototype

1 Introduction

Nowadays, guarantee the availability and quality of diverse natural resources are crucial for social development for any country. In this case, agriculture is one of the many important activities for reaching this development. In fact, technology and engineering have been very involved in agriculture processes and activities with the objective of increasing the quality of products, among other objectives [1–3]. In particular, Precision Agriculture (PA) (in our case, precision viticulture) is a technological concept that involves

© Springer Nature Switzerland AG 2020
F. R. Narváez et al. (Eds.): SmartTech-IC 2019, CCIS 1154, pp. 29–39, 2020.
https://doi.org/10.1007/978-3-030-46785-2_3

integrated information and production systems in whole farms in order to enhance the efficiency, profitability, and productivity; all the mentioned based on sustainability [4–7]. In addition, the PA concept also describes continuous smart decision-making based on data set related to the soil and crops. In this case, Site-Specific Crop Management (SSCM) term is used. Thus, the smart decisions making process is performed based on particular features regarding the environmental, soil and crops, to optimize the quality and production efficiency, and minimize the environmental impact and risks. In particular, the SCCM term can management's crops and soils, either based on an uniform or site-specific features. In order to clarify, SCCM term applied for uniform crop and soil involves a bulk or composite soil and crop sampling, considering that all measurements will be the same along the time and the crop terrain [8–10]. However, when the SCCM is applied to site-specific crop and soil, the technical and methodological requirements are so different, for example, fine grid sampling and sensing are crucial issues to increase the resolution for in-situ measurements [11]. Considering the aforementioned, the PA technique involves a complete crop, soil and climate monitoring as a basic activity. Next, an attribute mapping is performed in order to describe the overall terrain (although there exist basic and high-end suitable options to attribute mapping). Considering the intensive data sets, post-processing is needed to analyze and support smart decisions, and next make specific actions regarding the variables monitored and processes related. Thus, PA term also involves the product and process innovations, i.e. PA projects change the crop production from Open-loop to Closed-loop [12, 13]. On the other hand, PA applied to vineyards allows monitored many environmental and soil features along the different stages of the grapes crop (which implies monitor at different elevations), in order to improve the quality and increase competitiveness. For example, grapes varieties such as Cabernet Sauvignon, Pinot Noir, Chardonnay, Sauvignon Blanc, among others, require particular environmental conditions respect to temperature, intensity luminosity, humidity on specific period time to ensure a quality level required by the final customers [14, 15]. Although exist some technical options to PA application in vineyards, the business model is still the principal issue [16, 17].

Also, how to adopt technology in agriculture is still an open problem in Latin America, furthermore it is more difficult if this decision is regulated by the cost of implementation. Thus, in the research field of real-time monitoring, the first layer is devoted to the construction of low-cost reliable hardware. Hence, a friendly and cheap prototype for PA projects in vineyards is an important tool to increase the quality and competitiveness based on Closed-loop crop production. Also, considering the Information and Communication Technology in agriculture (ICT, or called E-agriculture), the connectivity and application of the prototype mentioned allowing strengthening the E-agriculture in the Guadalupe Valley. In this paper, a novel friendly and cheap technological development to monitor some in-situ environmental and soil variables in a Vineyard located in the Guadalupe Valley is presented as part of a potential whole PA and E-agriculture project. The paper is organized as follows: Sect. 2 describes the technical background of the prototype. Section 3 shows the in-situ measurements and the analysis of the performance of the prototype. Finally, Sect. 4 presents the conclusion, challenges, and future work.

2   Theoretical and General Background

2.1   E-Agriculture Framework

In general, the E-Agriculture concept is based on different advantages and function-alities of different areas related to business, communication, automation, resilience, sustainability, social and policy aspect, among others. In this paper, aspects of the E-Agriculture such as the acquisition of real-time information, data storage and analytics are considered, which are part of the PA concept mentioned [18–20]. In order to clarify, E-Agriculture considers four categories (see Fig. 1) to reach optimal performance, i.e. systems, tools, informatics and data mining. In particular, regarding systems, it is based on the Global Positioning System (GPS) and geographic information system (GIS) in order to acquire and handling geographical data based on a very precise geo-referenced based on the GPS performance [21, 22]. Also, data mining allows analyzing a lot of information related to agricultural-related activities in order to extract significant data in an effort to obtain important knowledge and trends to promote smart decisions. In addi-tion, the custom design and easy implementation of a wide variety of tools with specific objectives is a high demand by E-Agriculture customers. Tools based on data feed of location-specific weather and related crop-specific commercial impacts are highly used as decision support tools, but still, there are many factors that affect the uptake process and use of such support tools by farmers and consultants [23, 24]. On the other hand, the informatics category considers remote sensing and digital imaging. In fact, the new techniques related to designing and using sensors, platforms and correctly acquiring and managing remotely sensed data are more important issues regarding this category. Considering the aforementioned, the technical contribution of the prototype proposed is acquiring environmental data from remote locations and the transmission of them to a central unit., i.e. it is related to the remote sensing aspect of the E-Agriculture concept.

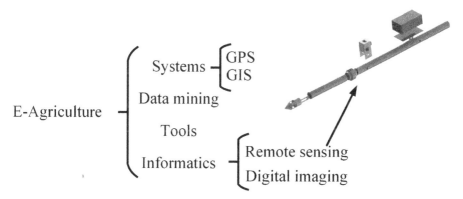

Fig. 1. The general framework of E-Agriculture.

2.2 Design and General Implementation of the Prototype

In general, the prototype was designed and manufactured using the integrated technology concept, i.e. Commercial-Off-The-Shelf (COTS) devices were used in order to create the prototype, making possible the product innovation based on a priori market analysis. Figure 2 shows the overall electronic diagram of the prototype, where the following sensors were used: (1) advanced digital light sensor (TSL2561) which support separately measurements of infrared, full-spectrum and human-visible light, (2) digital environmental humidity and temperature sensor (SHT85) with high-accuracy and long-term stable and, (3) soil moisture sensor (SEN-13322) and soil temperature sensor (DS18B20). Thus, the sensors mentioned were controlled using a microcontroller with nano-watt technology (PIC18F4550). Regarding the transmitter-receiver signal, two XBee Pro modules were used at 2.4 GHz, the output power of 60 mW and the technical standard, 802.15.4, which is the base of the Low-Rate Wireless Personal Area Networks (LR-WPANs) and ZigBee. In particular, ZigBee technology allows transmission distances from 10 to 1,500 m, depending on power output and environmental characteristics (mainly, Line-Of-Sight, LOS) [25–27]. Thus, considering the aforementioned, many scenarios for applications in vineyards are suitable, for example, (1) long-distance, low data rate & low consumption power applications for uniform monitoring vineyards, and (2) short-distance & high data rate applications for site-specific crops and soils. In our case, the second scenario was chosen. For the initial version of the prototype, a conventional battery (+9 V) was used, but a rechargeable battery also can be adapted using a photovoltaic panel.

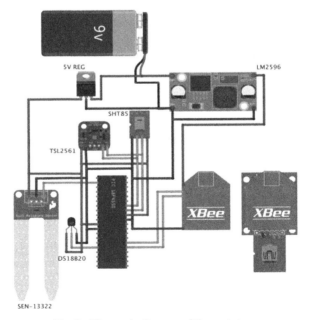

Fig. 2. Electronic diagram of the prototype.

Next, Fig. 3 shows the complete diagram of the prototype that consists of six parts designed take into account the requirements established by the early adopter. Basically, the prototype consists of a conventional PVC (Polyvinyl Chloride) pipe as principal support, and other structures manufactured using additive manufacturing techniques where the sensors and other devices will be located. In the principal support different sensors (i.e. temperature, humidity, and luminosity sensors) are implemented at different heights (i.e. $\approx+30$, $\approx+60$ and $\approx+90$ cm) according to the growth stages and varieties of the grapes crop. Also, the prototype has a temperature/humidity sensor in order to monitor the subsoil (≈-30 cm). Although stainless steel material presents a better performance in extreme environmental conditions, this increases the cost of the prototype and reduces accessibility for small farmer producers. It is important to mention the capability to variate the heights of the sensors or adding more similar sensors at different heights in order to perform wide monitoring of the crop. Thus, the information related to different heights is transmitted in a simultaneously way, being this feature an important innovation because it is not presented in the actual technological options in the market.

In addition, the prototype has a power & controlling subsystem (wireless commu-nication + DC source) in order to send the information monitored in a wireless way to the central control unit, which can be a computer in a build near or a specific location within the vineyard.

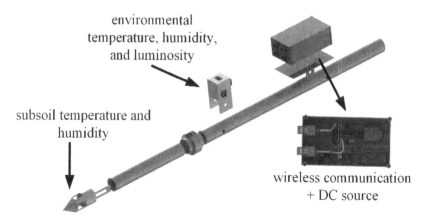

Fig. 3. The complete diagram of the prototype

After the design and manufacturing processes, the prototype was tested in real con-ditions (Beta testing). Thus, Fig. 4 shows the real implementation of the prototype in a vineyard located in the Guadalupe Valley, Baja California, where the diverse heights to monitoring are shown according to the stage of the grape crop. It is important to mention that, according to each grape variety and terrain conditions, the testing conditions can be modified, so the height has to be adapted to the conditions mentioned [28–30].

Fig. 4. Prototype implemented in the vineyard.

3   Measurements and Analysis

This section shows some results about the monitored environment variables using the prototype. It is important to clarify that the results that will be showed are presented in a representative way because the objective of the in-situ testing is to determine the overall performance of the prototype in order to enhance the prototype and the agricultural informatics as a future task. Thus, Fig. 5 shows the luminous intensity measurements in a specific groove of the vine-yard. In order to clarify, the period of measurements is a parameter that is available to modify according to the requirements of the early adopters. In order to clarify, the early adopters are the first real enterprises or individual that use the prototype in order, and the purpose of that is to improve the overall performance of the prototype based on their technical feedback. Thus, the period of measurements was 10 s approximately. However, for real applications in vineyards (or others crops) and due to the semi-stationary dynamic of the monitored variables, the period of measurements should be 30 min, approximately.

Now, the measurements performed by the prototype will be shown and analyzed. The initial measurements show a saturation of the sensor at ≈65,000 lumens. After, the luminous intensity was monitored correctly without intensity saturation, reaching a mean intensity value of ≈25,000 lumens with reduced variations (from ≈18,000 lumens to ≈30,500 lumens). In this case, the sensor used presented an extreme sensitivity, which promotes two possible scenarios to improve the measurements: (a) the sensor has to be replaced by others with less sensitivity, or (b) an attenuation system is required in order to decrement the luminosity monitored; obviously, the attenuation system imposes add a calibration process.

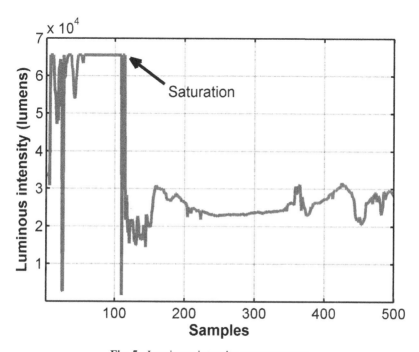

Fig. 5. Luminous intensity measurements.

Figure 6 shows the environmental and subsoil humidity measurements (at ≈+30 cm). In particular, an extreme intentional modification was made in order to change drastically the humidity of the subsoil to determine the sensing velocity of the prototype. Thus, the subsoil humidity level changed from ≈30% to ≈82% with adequate response time, i.e. 20 measurement samples were required to visualize the drastic humidity change, which means 200 s to detect the change. While the environment humidity remains with small and continuous slow variations, presenting minimum and maximum values, ≈45% and ≈74%, respectively. Considering the performance of the measurements shown in Fig. 6, the prototype is capable to monitor these variables in the vineyard in a proper way.

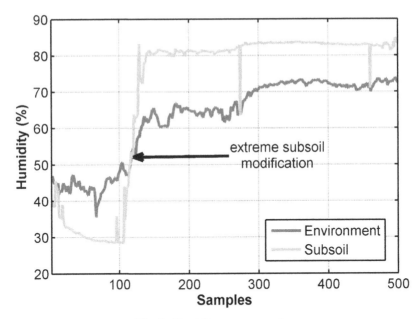

Fig. 6. Humidity measurements.

Figure 7 shows the environmental and subsoil (at ≈-30 cm) temperature measurements. As can be seen, the subsoil temperature is always higher than the ambient temperature (temperature difference of $\approx4°$ approximately), and also, it is also more stable. For example, the maximum subsoil temperature variation is $\approx0.75°$, while the maximum environment temperature variation is $\approx1.6°$. Regarding the minimum temperature values variations, the environment and subsoil variations are very close, $\approx0.04°$. In addition, a sudden intentional change in the temperature was performed (see the sample 200) in order to observe the performance of the prototype. In order to clarify, the difference between the temperature measurements of subsoil and the environment is very important because it affects the level of subsoil moisture. In addition, this difference must be constantly calibrated due to variations of the sensors.

It is very important to clarify that, the measurements presented correspond to only one point in the vineyards, which is assigned to a particular Grape Variety (GV). However, to achieve a more detailed analysis of information it is necessary to replicate the prototype proposed and installs it in various vineyards with different grape varieties. In fact, for the reasons mentioned above, we believe that the complete scenario for the potential application of the prototype, which is shown in Fig. 8, is highly important to visualize in order to promote future improvements. In addition, the installation of prototypes is not a trivial task because require a specific and well design protocol. In fact, according to our experience, the advice of a person skilled in agricultural engineering is extremely important to ensure that the measurements are representative of each grape variety according to the different types of soils.

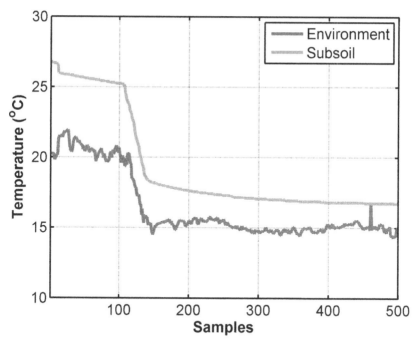

Fig. 7. Temperature measurements.

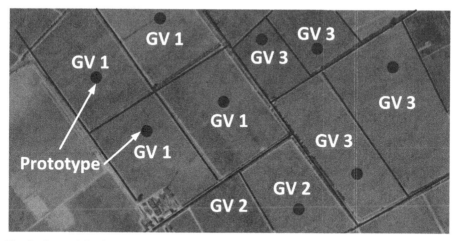

Fig. 8. General distribution proposed of various prototypes (red spots) in different vineyards that correspond to different grape varieties. (Color figure online)

4 Conclusions

Precision Viticulture is a technological process and tool that, working efficiently with other processes can increase the quality product and services, and thus, also the competitiveness of the agro-industry sector. This paper presented the general design and performance of a prototype to monitor environmental variables that affect the production of wine in the Guadalupe Valley, Mexico. Based on the initial requirements of the project, the prototype was designed in such a way that it was accessible and friendly to users and the environment. In addition, the prototype was based on ZigBee technology with the aim of proposing a wireless sensor network in the short or medium term, although our article only showed a prototype connected to a communication server, which will then have to be reconfigured to accept multiple bidirectional communication channels of various prototypes. In particular, some technical parameters (e.g. throughput, delay, load, distances links, power consumption, among others) impose important challenges to the development of the Precision Viticulture, not only related to technical performance but with accessibility for any type of user on the viticulture sector [31–33].

Finally, the proposed prototype and its scaling to large crops will improve the remote acquisition of data in order to be subsequently analyzed and implement smart decisions and processes. Thus, considering the E-agriculture framework, there is an important potential of sharing information into the community to enhance the current viticulture processes, that, by the way, they are still very traditional. Also, considering the opinion of the early adopters, the prototype must ensure connectivity and energy supply for various terrestrial topologies. Although the performance of the prototype proposed has been adequate based on the presented results, it is important to clarify that the evaluation of the prototype needs more development respect to repeatability and accuracy.

References

1. Walls, H., Baker, P., Chirwa, E., Hawkins, B.: Food security, food safety & healthy nutrition: are they compatible?. Global Food Security (2019). (In Press)
2. Barrett, C.B., Palm, C.: Meeting the global food security challenge: obstacles and opportunities ahead. Global Food Secur. **11**, 1–4 (2016)
3. Kasturi, P.: Technology and food security. Humanomics **25**(2), 163–168 (2009)
4. Bongiovanni, R., Lowenberg-Deboer, J.: Precision agriculture and sustainability. Precision Agric. **5**(4), 359–387 (2004)
5. McBratney, A., Whelan, B., Ancev, T., Bouma, J.: Future directions of precision agriculture. Precision Agric. **6**(1), 7–23 (2005)
6. Santesteban, L.G.: Precision viticulture and advanced analytics. Short Rev. Food Chem. **279**, 58–62 (2019)
7. Newson, D.N., Ratcliff, A.R., Freckleton, J.C.: Practical applications of precision viticulture in Australia. Acta Hort. **978**, 37–46 (2013)
8. Zhu, Q., Lin, H.S., Doolittle, J.A.: Functional soil mapping for site-specific soil moisture and crop yield management. Geoderma **200–201**, 45–54 (2013)
9. Gili, A., Álvarez, C., Bagnato, R., Noellemeyer, E.: Comparison of three methods for delineating management zones for site-specific crop management. Comput. Electron. Agric. **139**, 213–223 (2017)

10. Braga, R.P., Jones, J.W.: Using optimization to estimate soil inputs of crop models for use in site-specific management. Trans. ASAE **47**(5), 1821–1831 (2004)
11. Schramm, H.: On Farm Tools for Site Specific Crop Management. SAE Technical Paper Series (1995)
12. Zhang, Q.: Precision Agriculture Technology for Crop Farming. CRC Press, Boca Raton (2015)
13. Pedersen, S.M., Lind, K.M.: Progress in Precision Agriculture. Springer, Cham (2017). https://doi.org/10.1007/978-3-319-68715-5
14. Cao, F., Wu, D., He, Y.: Soluble solids content and pH prediction and varieties discrimination of grapes based on visible–near infrared spectroscopy. Comput. Electron. Agric. **71**, S15–S18 (2010)
15. D'Agata, I.: Native Wine Grapes of Italy. University of California Press, Berkeley (2019)
16. Pedersen, S.M., Lind, K.M. (eds.): Precision Agriculture: Technology and Economic Perspectives. PPA. Springer, Cham (2017). https://doi.org/10.1007/978-3-319-68715-5
17. Adamchuk, V.I., Morgan, M.T., Lowenberg-Deboer, J.M.: A model for agro-economic analysis of soil ph mapping. Precision Agric. **5**(2), 111–129 (2004)
18. Li, Daoliang, Zhao, Chunjiang (eds.): CCTA 2008. IAICT, vol. 293. Springer, Boston, MA (2009). https://doi.org/10.1007/978-1-4419-0209-2
19. Kondawar, D.G.: Information and communication technology in agriculture. J. Commer. Manag. Thought **9**(4), 509 (2018)
20. Demiryürek, K.: Information systems and communication networks for agriculture and rural people. Agric. Econ. **56**(5), 209–214 (2010)
21. Zhang, N., Taylor, R.K.: Applications of a Field Level Geographic Information System (FIS) in Precision Agriculture. Appl. Eng. Agric. **17**(6), 885–892 (2001)
22. Rahmadian, R., Widyartono, M.: Machine vision and global positioning system for autonomous robotic navigation in agriculture: a review. J. Inf. Eng. Educ. Technol. **1**(1), 46–54 (2017)
23. Fernandez, G.: Applications of statistical data mining methods. In: Conference on Applied Statistics in Agriculture, pp. 1–16 (2004)
24. Georg, R.: Computational Intelligence in Intelligent Data Analysis. Springer, Berlin (2013). https://doi.org/10.1007/978-3-642-32378-2
25. Mašík, I.: Reliability of ZigBee transmission in agriculture production. Res. Agric. Eng. **59**(4), 153–159 (2013)
26. Lin, Y.G.: An intelligent monitoring system for agriculture based on ZigBee wireless sensor networks. Adv. Mater. Res. **383–390**, 4358–4364 (2011)
27. Bakó, K.I.: ZigBee technology in precision agriculture. Acta Agraria Debreceniensis **47**, 15–17 (2012)
28. Planinić, M.: Influence of temperature and drying time on extraction yield of phenolic compounds from grape pomace variety 'Portogizac'. Chem. Biochem. Eng. Q. **29**(3), 343–350 (2015)
29. Lante, A.L.: Characterization of esterase activity in the Bianchetta trevigiana grape variety under reducing conditions. Int. J. Wine Res. **2012**(4), 45 (2012)
30. Pradel, E., Pieri, P.: Influence of a grass layer on vineyard soil temperature. Aust. J. Grape Wine Res. **6**(1), 59–67 (2000)
31. Smit, J.L., Sithole, G., Strever, A.E.: Vine signal extraction – an application of remote sensing in precision viticulture. S. Afr. J. Enol. Vitic. **31**(2), 65–74 (2016)
32. Morais, R., Fernandes, M.A., Matos, S.G., Serôdio, C., Ferreira, P.J.S.G., Reis, M.J.C.S.: A ZigBee multi-powered wireless acquisition device for remote sensing applications in precision viticulture. Comput. Electron. Agric. **62**(2), 94–106 (2008)
33. Matese, A., Di Gennaro, S.F.: Technology in precision viticulture: a state of the art review. Int. J. Wine Res. **7**, 69–81 (2015)

The Network Virtualization to Support the Scalability of the Internet of Things

Carlos J. Gonzalez[1,2]([⊠]), Olivier Flauzac[1,2], and Florent Nolot[1,2]

[1] Autonomous University of Chiriqui, David, Panama
carlos.gonzalez5@unachi.ac.pa
[2] University of Reims Champagne Ardenne, Reims, France
{Olivier.flauzac,florent.nolot}@univ-reims.fr

Abstract. The network's functions virtualization emerges as one of the most promising technologies for the management of the new generation of internet. In recent years, computer and communication systems evolved enormously at influencing the development of network infrastructures in terms of scale, programmability and dynamic management. On one hand, the number of connected devices grows exponentially with the development of the Internet of Things (IoT) and multiple online applications. On the other hand, the diversity of proprietary protocols and programs does not allow the evolution of new network architectures with dynamic requirements. The scientific community has focused efforts on optimizing the administration of networks with the implementation and redesign of configurations techniques to improve the performance. The integration of a new emerging technology such as the Software Defined Networking (SDN) allows a flexible, dynamic and adaptable management by optimizing network resources in the proposed framework. In an IoT environment, we develop a testbed platform, which allows us to evaluate the orchestration of an implemented distributed SDN controllers in order to achieve scalability and flexibility management. Based on the simulation results, the developed SDCIOT architecture shows some performance metrics and the effectiveness management of large scale-networks. The SDCIOT framework includes a fault tolerance system with distributed SDN controllers. This study presents the development of an IoT framework to manage scale and distributed system using the network's functions virtualization. Finally, some of the most important future research directions are highlighted and the development of new IoT applications.

Keywords: Software Defined Networking · Openflow · Cluster · SDCIOT · ONOS

1 Introduction

In the last years, with the proliferation of connected devices to Internet, a new networking paradigm has evolved, the Internet of Things (IoT). Due to the evolutionary nature, the security risks and the difficulties to manage the large-scale

© Springer Nature Switzerland AG 2020
F. R. Narváez et al. (Eds.): SmartTech-IC 2019, CCIS 1154, pp. 40–51, 2020.
https://doi.org/10.1007/978-3-030-46785-2_4

networks increase [1]. As one of the most important emerging technologies, the IoT currently concerns a large part of the industrial and academic communities. The computer systems included in this new digital communication paradigm allow us to program objects that are related to many aspects of our daily life. In addition, the IoT can be used to monitor and control autonomously various areas such as smart cities, environment, education, health, transportation, and so on. With the large number of interconnected devices, a high volume of data is generated, establishing an IoT ecosystem with new requirements for scalable networks, security and privacy. The projections of communication systems until 2020 will be around 26 billion of connected devices [2]. Regarding to the degree of complexity and the heterogeneity of systems, the new network architectures require an adaptable development to the fourth industrial generation with pervasive connectivity between machines and objects. A promising solution is provided by another emerging technology called the Software Defined Networks [3].

The control function is decoupled from the data transfer plan function by providing a scalable, programmable and dynamic network architecture. In the control function, the intelligence of network is centralized in one SDN controllers or may be distributed in multiple nodes SDN controllers. Traditional network equipment is proprietary, making it difficult to program, to innovate and to deploy scalability that emerging networks such as the IoT can. One of the most promising alternatives that can overcome these barriers is the SDN. With its open source environment, it is possible to program network functions and to customize administration and security applications.

This article presents the development of a virtualized SDN platform in order to support the scalability of integrated devices with IoT capability. The testbed platform includes open source implementation tools integrating a virtualized environment.

1.1   The Internet of Things

The development of a wide variety of integrated devices with internet requirements generates a large volume of data which requires a network architecture for collection, processing and storage of information [4]. Currently, there are several models of IoT architecture. Moreover, the academic and industrial sectors propose various solutions according to the needs and products developed. The models vary according to the number of communication layers and the protocols used. Therefore, there is no consensus for a single type of IoT architecture. The standardization of a universal model evolves with the contributions of different developers [4].

This emerging technology provides a wide range of opportunities to create value-added in industrial and academic sectors. In one of the published projections, Cisco forecasts about 3.6 devices connected per person and approximately 396 exabytes of data traffic per month and approximately 4.8 zettabytes per year by 2022 [5].

Due to the evolutive nature of the IoT technology, it is important to mention some features of the architecture. However, after a study of the main characteristics of those architectures, the functionalities have been simplified to understand the processing of the data. From this perspective, a three-layer architecture can be defined into the perception layer, the network layer and the application layer.

– Application layer: allows the development of applications to interact with users, used industrial sectors, such as home automation, smart cities, logistics, environment, public safety and healthcare. In addition, the functions of control decision and security are integrated.
– Network layer: its main function is to establish a link between the perception layer and the application layer. The transfer of data is done through different technologies and protocols that guarantee the flow of information.
– Perception layer: includes the physical objects known as sensors and actuators. The main objective of these devices is to recompile data and identify other objects using Radio Frequency Identification RFID and wireless networks.

The heterogeneity of multi-networks creates a complex administration to address scalability and security in IoT environments. The scientific community is focusing its efforts on an emerging technology under the SDN concept, being one of the most promising technologies for this kind of networks.

1.2   The Software Defined Networking

The complexity in the administration of traditional networks is due to the coupled control plane and data plane. Each network interconnection device is managed individually, which prevents the evolution and innovation in the implementation of data flow policies and rules. The majority of systems are closed and proprietary impeding the access to the deployment of new communication protocols or security policies, with an extensive and complex process to be developed.

With a dynamic management, the SDN architecture simplifies the network management by separating control functions from data plane. Instead of individually configuring each network interconnection device, a node called SDN controller manages the control plane in a centralized way. The packet transfer is organized by routing tables at the data plane level. The controller given the overall vision of the network performs all routing decisions. The SDN architecture composed of three layers: application layer, control layer and infrastructure layer.

– The application layer allows network administrators to configure, manage, automate and optimize network resources through an application programming interface.
– The control layer uses an algorithm based on data management for specific protocols. Network policies can be distributed among multiple SDN controllers.
– In the infrastructure layer, it is included all the network interconnection devices where traffic is forwarded or processed with forwarding decisions received from the controller.

The communication protocol most commonly used to access the data plane is OpenFlow (OF) and it is standardized by the Open Networking Foundation [6]. Currently, a large part of network hardware manufacturers supports the SDN. The exchanged messages between the controller and the OF switches are secured with TLS encryption. Each OF switch contains flow tables with a set of entries representing the data packet routing rules. In this way, the SDN controller collects information from the network devices and establishes the necessary configurations.

2   Related Works

The scalability of the NFV resources has been studied and there exists some scaling techniques to integrate new emerging technologies. The study in [7] highlights the Virtual Objects (VO) as a key component to provide energy efficient management, heterogeneity and scalability for the IoT. The authors propose a Smart Devices as a Service (SDaaS) including the VO of each physical device. The proposed virtual architecture includes a Platforms-a-Services (PaaS) model, Network Function virtualization (NFV) and Fog Computing techniques. PaaS cloud solution is placed close to the edge of the network enabling direct communication with the end virtual devices. In this way, the testbed platform provides network performance result and an overview of the VO functionalities. However, the proposed solution has no information about the integration of the cloud services with NFV to make forwarding decisions.

The research in [8], presents a scalable architecture based on NFV. In this perspective, this work addresses the benefits and challenges to support the expected increasing IoT technology. Obviously, the increasing mobility and ubiquitous computing emerge as one of the most important challenges to be integrated with NFV. Network connectivity at the southbound interface is provided by IoT gateways and the IP protocol communicates the collect information to the northbound interface. All network functions and IoT application are centralized in a Data Center. As part of future work, the authors plan the integration of an implementation platform in order to evaluate the proposed approach.

In [9], the SDIoT architecture extends high scalability, management, and security of IoT. Essentially, this architecture consists of three layers: physical layer, middleware/control layer, and data service layer. The physical layer includes the end-point devices. The middleware/control layer consists in a block of software defined applications: Software Defined Security (SDSec), Software Defined Storage (SDStore), Internet of Things Controller (IoT-C), and Software Defined Controller (SDN-C). The collected data is processed from an IoT gateway. The SDSec process the authentication of connected devices. In case of success authentication, the data is tagged including a positive flag (P), otherwise a flag is tagged a (N). Then, the IoT-C compute the datapath to the destination devices. The SDN-C processes the forwarding rules to be added into the network switches. For scalability, the SDIoT architecture involves many software defined applications which avoid the evolution of the IoT environment.

Erran *et al.* in [10], proposed a framework called CellSDN. It is focused on simplifying cellular networks management. Based on SDN applications, they specify the attributed policies and forwarding rules of each end user devices allowing fine-grained control over the LTE network. The local control agent added to the switches is key to handle deep packet inspection. The verification process can monitor traffic flow applications such as video, peer-to-peer, web and VoIP. With an efficiency performance of these local agents should increase the scalability, reducing the excessive load on multiple controllers. It is provided fast reaction time to overcome critical events. An extension of this work was presented in [11]. The proposed SoftCell architecture is based in four main components: the controller, the access switches, the core switches, and middle-boxes. The middle-boxes defines the security rules or transcoder applications for multimedia transfer received by the controller and processed at the switch-level. The traffic flows received from the end users is fine-grained verified at the access switch level in order to locate it on the base station. Each access switch includes a local agent which specifies a classification of packets received from end users. The flows are processed locally minimizing the overload between controllers. Core switches act as a gateway connected to the Internet. The network traffic is forwarded from the gateway through the middle-boxes switches. In this architecture, the LTE networks do not need specialized network elements including the Serving Gateways (S-GWs) or the Packet data network Gateways (P-GWs).

A similar research is pursued in [12], wherein the authors present a monitoring framework with NFV/SDN functions virtualization integrating the SONATA project to support 5G applications and services. The scalability is based on a distributed cascade monitoring system. A push gateway collects information of the LXC container in order to send the information to the monitoring server. Each container defines a point of presence (PoP) that communicate with its respective websocket server. The framework is an initiative to monitor 5G services.

Tennison [13] is a distributed framework on the context of different security scenarios to evaluate the SDN controllers performance in case of attack. It allows monitoring the request and processing the incoming flow from the nodes. The experimentation framework includes 350 nodes and 19 switches using mininet. The distributed controllers uses cbench to test the scalability performance handling large amount of traffic. This test performs only the scalability of nodes and it does not necessarily determine the conductivity of IoT devices.

The proposed solutions have been developed to overcome the IoT scalability. However, these framework lacks of an experimental evaluation platform.

3   SDN Scalability Solution

Due to the large number of IoT devices connected, the new network infrastructures need scalability support. From a centralized point, with SDN it is possible to create an automation system with protocols that allow a macro management of data flows [14]. It is also possible to predefine the communication and security policies for the connected devices, and even to define these policies before the connectivity request, which basically allows a dynamic administration without taking into account the new connected devices. SDN allows including an inherent scalability due to its centralized conception for the administration of applications and protocols, allowing rapidly response to expand scalable networks.

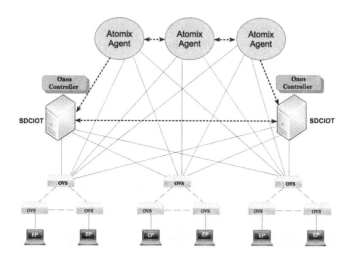

Fig. 1. Scalable cluster architecture with ONOS.

With the abstraction of network equipment such as switches, routers and intermediary devices induces a significant cost reduction [3]. These equipments in traditional networks use programmed proprietary systems with specific rules and complex protocols to establish the communications. Therefore, configuring appropriate policies to meet specific IoT application requirements is a challenge that can be solved by applying software-defined networks technologies.

We introduce the concept of Software Defined Clustered IoT (SDCIOT) assuming that each controller contains hundreds or thousands of embedded devices. Normally, a large-scale network cannot achieve an organization structure efficiently. For this reason, we propose SDN cluster assuming that each controller manages its own domain. Each SDCIOT is in charge of managing the operation end-points devices (Fig. 1). With this clustering architecture, the data of the network environment is processed at the controller level, and will be routed to the neighbor controller. Moreover, having a global view of entire domain the controller node can monitor, inject, and defines reactive flow rules. By using Atomix cluster of Open Network Operating System (ONOS), the controller node discovers its peers neighbor using dynamic discovery mechanisms. The Atomix ONOS cluster is a fault tolerate system in case of a clustered node fails. Each controller has full access control to the switches and policies rules. Based on this clustering architecture, it is possible to set configuration management, process the data collected and aggregate the information in the domain or send the information to the other controller.

ONOS is an open source SDN controller available to build testbed platform of the next-generation of SDN and NFV technologies. The ONOS controller integrates network and functions' applications in a virtualized environment. The core of ONOS uses a modular architecture, which combine the different component the controller. This modularity separates the northbound/southbound from the eastbound/westbound data flows allowing the customization of the entire network. To develop scale networks, the ONOS controller permits the distribution of physical or virtual system devices. In a clustered environment, ONOS allows to add new switches, components and services without interrupting the operation of the system. The Atomix framework, a fault tolerant system with distributed controllers, provides the high availability of ONOS controller.

Atomix contains a set of features such as the shared raft cluster and the multi-primary protocol to provide distributed systems including cluster communication, management and failure detection with a distributed coordination. Each node has a local configuration including the IP address, member id and group information. It allows the Atomix Agent to discover the others nodes into the cluster.

The agent Atomix has an unique memberId and a TCP address to identify the others clustered nodes. Once the cluster member information is provided, it is necessary to set up the instances including the discovery process. The bootstrap procedure uses an id and the IP address of each Atomix agent joining the cluster. In general, all members of the cluster participates in the election to define state on the Atomix environment. When an Atomix candidate starts the election process, it counts the votes from the peers. Depending on the votes, the raft protocol selects the leader, which receives the requests from the clients and the followers replicate the leader information. If a cluster member cannot reach, the Atomix agent can replace it by promoting another replica preventing the loss of high-availability.

The distribution of cluster member is done by using the replication protocols Primary-backup and Gossip. In order to facilitate the replication process, the clusters must be organized in a set of partition groups. The partition groups may be configured with the Atomix instances to include, and the replication protocols share cluster information. The members of the cluster can be organized into a set of partition groups in which each member resides in accordance to its configuration.

The deployment of a Cluster-based High Availability model is based in ONOS project [15]. The fact of a better network performance, fault tolerance and scalable network management introduce new challenges to deploy SDN controllers. Because each clustered SDN controller has a partial view of its domain and exchanges full information, it causes an overload of the system. By using multiple controller, if one controller fails, another one can take the control over the entire network. The proposed cluster model provides high level of scalability, large flows management and easy management deployment.

4   Implementations

In this section, we describe the framework for IoT scalability and applications used, specifically designed to be integrated with SDN technologies. Our IoT environment provides, virtualization of IoT embed devices, Openvswitch and SDN controllers.

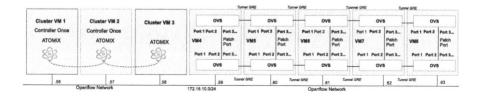

Fig. 2. SDN clustered tesbed platform.

After analyzing the currently existing platforms and tools, it does not exist one to be adapted to a realistic scenario of SDN-IoT experimentation. For this reason, we build a tested platform that was designed in a virtualized environment, which allows inserting data flow between end-devices, monitor the requests, and verify the policies rules for each device connected to the cluster. The integration process between simulations tools are performed by algorithm, which automated the task of the network deployment. The developed platform consists of an external network for the remote management, and an internal network to establish OpenFlow communication. The platform includes 8 Linux servers, 3 servers for the cluster setup and 5 servers for virtualization of IoT embed-devices (Fig. 2).

The infrastructure management is performed in a cloud-computing environment, based on VMware vSphere. With this software, it is possible to manage, install and configure multiple virtual machines simultaneously on a single physical node. The emulation of the architecture of an IoT-capable device is done with the open source qemu tools. Qemu emulator allows to adapt the system requirements such as the type of processor, network interfaces, hard disk, RAM memory among others. There are other kinds of OS to simulate devices with limited resources such as Contiki, RIoT, LiteOS. The TinyOS contains several functions designed to allow scalability and integrity in an IoT tested architecture.

The SDN test platform consists of open source tools such as the ONOS and OpenvSwitch (OVS). ONOS project is supported Windows and Linux distribution, also some important network developers' devices. OpenFlow protocol is set up to create a communication channel between the controller and the OVS switches. OpenFlow, organizing the data in flow tables, manages the control management application and the data transfer decisions. ONOS controller has an integrated plug-in which allows the automation process of switching in IPv4 and IPv6. However, the routing process for optimal scalability requires many successive operations to add flows into the Openflow switches. To enable the

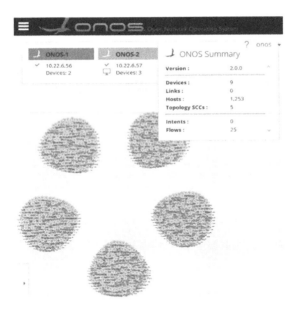

Fig. 3. ONOS controller test environment.

automation process of SDN scalable networks with Openflow, it is necessary an extensive knowledge of flow table segmentation including the instructions of routing, as well as Shell scripting or python. We developed a shell script that reads the input nodes and creates automatically flows rules establishing an Openflow communication path between end devices and the end devices to the SDN controller. Besides this, based on the IPv4 address, the script creates new forwarding rules from one subnet to another.

The experimental scenario allows the verification of good performance of the cluster solution in scalable networks including 1,235 nodes (Fig. 3). The nodes are distributed into two clustered nodes, *Onos-1* and *Onos-2*. The experimental case of use is able via the OpenFlow protocol 1.3. Regarding the Openflow operations process, the security policies implementation does not provide the appropriate tools at the application layer. Openflow only allows the management of data transfer decision and the communication flow tables. Hence, once the flow rules are installed, only the switches perform the switching and routing transfer decisions.

ONOS cluster adopted a distributed election of the master controller using Raft protocol. Once the elected leader is connected in the cluster, the members share a global network view. The time election depends on the repetition, for every discovery process started immediately after that the cluster members are initialized. The first member initialized have a high probability to reach the master election. Each clustered client node receives an entry from the leader to join the cluster. The leader receives requests response from the others cluster client and share the network inventory. The clustering process indicate that the leader election procedure and the exchange of information highly depends on the starting time of each member of the cluster and the election timeout.

In this study we evaluate the hardware resources performance only in the clustered nodes. Figure 4, shows the CPU usage of the controller ONOS 1. Once the Atomix agents join the controller, the CPU usage increases significantly. Compare to the Fig. 5, the average of CPU usage is lower than the controller ONOS 2. This is due to the election of roles between the cluster members. The controller ONOS 1 has a network load more important with a master role within the cluster. In this experiment, for a cluster with approximately 1,000 embed devices, the percentage of CPU usage of the controller is 90% at the starting point. When the cluster is formed, the CPU performance is stabilized but always with a high usability. The experiments' results demonstrate the effectiveness of the proposed cluster architecture including Atomix agent and ONOS Controllers. However, by increasing the number of nodes within the cluster, we can measure the scalability of our tested platform.

A transcendental experiment with our SDN architectures is the cluster organization. The clustered SDN controllers allow to limit the number of devices connected in a domain, the amount of data and device to manage. The cluster information exchanged between controllers is done through the atomix tools provided by interconnection ONOS controllers. Within the developed testbed platform, we are able to perform simulations with more than 1,000 devices performing an IoT environment.

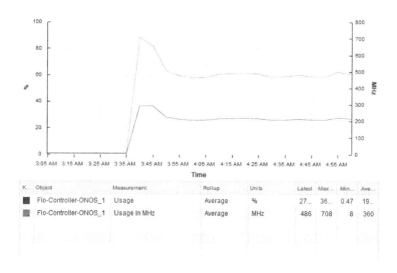

Fig. 4. CPU usage of clustered ONOS controller 1.

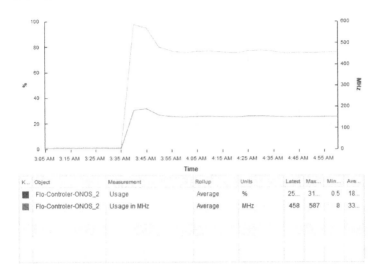

Fig. 5. CPU usage of clustered ONOS controller 2.

5   Conclusion and Future Works

In this article, we present the main contributions of network virtualization for IoT. The number of devices with heterogeneous connectivity increases daily raising the experimental scenarios to create network architectures oriented towards the new generation of Internet. With the performed tests, we observe a high degree of scalability, dependability, and high fault of tolerance of SDN. The distributed architecture devices allow the control, the configuration and the management of complex networks in an efficient manner. The developed framework support many controllers instances with a multi-level monitoring system including a large size of nodes connected into an intra-cluster environment. The cluster evaluation of ONOS shows an effective adaptability to integrate testing tools and embedded operating system for the IoT.

Based on the results obtained from our SDN-based distributed architecture implementation and evaluation, we consider new research topics to study. The developed platform handles communications between clustered nodes, but future work needs an intra-cluster management protocol over SDN controller. With this approach, a better datapath of flows may be provided for objects/devices connected on the cluster. In addition, we plan to include more scalability simulations with other SDN controllers and analyze the better performance including the time joining and leaving the clustered nodes. Another future work for scalable deployment is to include a combination of IPv4 and IPv6 protocols providing a performance of the emerging network virtualization concept.

Acknowledgment. This work has been supported by the SENACYT Panama under the program SNI Sistema Nacional de Investigación.

References

1. Al-Garadi, M.A., Mohamed, A., Al-Ali, A.K., Du, X., Guizani, M.: A survey of machine and deep learning methods for internet of things (IoT) security. CoRR, vol. abs/1807.11023 (2018)
2. i3forum: Internet of things whitepaper, April 2017
3. Bizanis, N., Kuipers, F.A.: SDN and virtualization solutions for the internet of things: a survey. IEEE Access **4**, 5591–5606 (2016)
4. Alam, I., et al.: IoT virtualization: a survey of software definition & function virtualization techniques for internet of things. CoRR, vol. abs/1902.10910 (2019)
5. Barnett, T., Jain, S., Andra, U., Khurana, T.: Cisco visual networking index (VNI) complete forecast update, 2017–2022 (2018)
6. Open Networking Foundation: Software-Defined Networking: The New Norm for Networks. White Paper, April 2012. https://www.opennetworking.org/images/stories/downloads/sdn-resources/white-papers/wp-sdn-newnorm.pdf
7. Atzori, L., et al.: SDN&NFV contribution to IoT objects virtualization. Comput. Networks **149**, 200–212 (2019)
8. Miladinovic, I., Schefer-Wenzl, S.: A highly scalable IoT architecture through network function virtualization. OJIOT **3**, 127–135 (2017)
9. Jararweh, Y., Ayyoub, M.A., Darabseh, A., Benkhelifa, E., Vouk, M.A., Rindos, A.: SDIoT: a software defined based internet of things framework. J. Ambient Intell. Hum. Comput. **6**(4), 453–461 (2015)
10. Li, L.E., Mao, Z.M., Rexford, J.: Toward software-defined cellular networks. In: 2012 European Workshop on Software Defined Networking, pp. 7–12, October 2012
11. Jin, X., Li, L.E., Vanbever, L., Rexford, J.: Softcell: scalable and flexible cellular core network architecture. In: Proceedings of the Ninth ACM Conference on Emerging Networking Experiments and Technologies, CoNEXT 2013, New York, NY, USA, pp. 163–174. ACM (2013)
12. Panagiotis, T., et al.: Scalable monitoring for multiple virtualized infrastructures for 5G services. In: The Seventeenth International Conference on Networks, pp. 7–12, June 2018
13. Fawcett, L., Scott-Hayward, S., Broadbent, M., Wright, A., Race, N.: Tennison: a distributed SDN framework for scalable network security. IEEE J. Sel. Areas Commun. **36**, 2805–2818 (2018)
14. Salman, O., Elhajj, I., Chehab, A., Kayssi, A.: IoT survey: an SDN and fog computing perspective. Comput. Networks **143**, 221–246 (2018)
15. ONOS Project, 10 March 2019

Broadcast and Analysis of Traffic Warning Messages in a VANET Network

Luis Naula[✉] and Andrés Segovia[✉]

Departamento de Ingeniería Eléctrica,
Electrónica y Telecomunicaciones Universidad de Cuenca,
Av 12 de Abril, CP. 010203 Cuenca, Ecuador
{fernando.naula,andres.segoviav}@ucuenca.edu.ec

Abstract. Within the current cities the number of vehicles has shown a increase, giving rise in increase traffic, caused that the number of traffic accidents also increase. This is where the role of VANET networks can intervene with the goal of reducing and trying to avoid this type of accidents. A VANET network provides connection between a vehicle-to-vehicle (V2V), vehicle-to-infrastructure (V2I) or a hybrid combination between these two, allowing a wide variety of safety, traffic management and assistance applications with safety precautions for drivers. With the increase of VANETS and its large number of applications, in this work is proposed to send warning messages to vehicles that are near intersections or circulate on a road using a Raspberry Pi development platform, websockets that is based on Node.js together with the Socket.io library in order to avoid collisions between vehicles, reduce traffic and warn drivers about the traffic signs that are to come.

Keywords: VANETS · Traffic signal · Warning · Messages · Socket.io

1 Introduction

VANETs (Vehicular Ad-Hoc Network) are networks in which vehicles are the nodes that participate in the communication process. VANETs are created when vehicles get connected with each other without using any infrastructure. Communication in this network is divided into two, which can be V2V (vehicle to vehicle), that generates the existence of exclusive communication between vehicles, and V2I (vehicle to infrastructure), in which vehicles are allowed to communicate with elements from traffic signs or a base station. One of the most outstanding applications in VANETs implies sending and receiving warning messages and the major challenges focus on the transmission of them. On the other hand, many facts such as de the re-transmission, broadband usage, duplication of messages are additional aspects to consider. In this sense, this paper presents the development of message transmission in a VANETs network using the Raspberry development platforms with the Raspbian and Node.js operating system through websockets and their available libraries. This article is organized into

© Springer Nature Switzerland AG 2020
F. R. Narváez et al. (Eds.): SmartTech-IC 2019, CCIS 1154, pp. 52–62, 2020.
https://doi.org/10.1007/978-3-030-46785-2_5

sections described below. Section 2 describes the main work related to the established proposal. Section 3 describes the message dissemination system created. The results from both, implementation and simulation are developed in Sect. 4. Conclusions of the article and results are presented in Sect. 5.

2   Related Work

Within of development of intelligent cities, several projects have been developed using VANETs network [4]. A brief description of the main proposals available in the literature is featured below. In [9] Inter-vehicular communication describes an architecture for traffic signal control. The aim of the system is reducing the waiting time at some intersections as well as in transit signal. It uses a clustering algorithm based in the direction followed by vehicles that arrive to the intersections and at the same time in an opportunistic diffusion techniques and cluster combination. It recollects data on vehicles arriving at the intersections and send the information to the traffic signal controls. In addition, GPS and digital maps are used to calculate correctly the direction that the vehicle follows. As regards the detection of road accidents in [6], the e-NOTIFY is proposed allowing the sending of messages to an emergency centre using vehicular networks additional to V2V and V2I communication. e-NOTIFY pretends to improve care for post-accidents patients by increasing the possibility of recovery and survival. The vehicles that will be part of this network, will have to incorporate an On-Board Unit (OBU), the same one that will detect the moment when there has been a serious accident for the occupants an recollect information from the vehicle sensors. In [8], it is proposed the dissemination of warning massages to vehicle using intelligent traffic lights (ITL), which will provide drivers the information about current traffic conditions and notify the vehicles the best routes and they will be able to avoid traffic congestion. In addition, ITL will send warning messages to vehicles in case of accidents to avoid collisions. In this process, some routing protocols have been included obtaining the best expected result with AODV, that provides a good performance and the minimal delay.

Continuing with the intelligent traffic lights, in [5] introduces an innovative perspective using virtual traffic lights to control the intersections. Behind the proposal, the protocol for the creation of virtual traffic lights is distributed in a synchronized and organized way between vehicles, but without using Andy centralized control infrastructure, but with the existence of a DIVERT simulator where they can simulate several situations and test the protocol used. In [7], there is an analysis of dissemination of warning messages strategies and communication metrics, using a VEINs vehicle network simulator. For the experiment development, is considered de evaluation of three fundamental aspects y the communication: (a) The distance between Tx and Rx, (b) The number of jumps that a message takes to get from Tx to Rx, and (c) Probabilistic retransmission. The results obtained from the variation of the numbers of cars, were that the lost of packets and duplicated packets have increased, so it means the waste of broadband because of the duplicated packets and a poor quality of service because of the lost packets. In order to solve this problem, the proposed solution implies the use of low-value TTL packets at the time of keep increasing the number of vehicles as the communication performance falls for TTL of higher packets. This trend was also observed in low power transmissions, and in this area of re transmissions and hops, in [12] presents a proposal based on the probabilities calculation to decide the number of units on board that can relay messages, analyzing several dissemination schemes of warning messages [3], including probabilistic re transmission. One of the VANET consideration, and in any communication system, is the type of routing protocol as this is developed according topologies an position, such protocols are used in security apps, based on transmissions. In this context, at [13], the proposal focuses on sending warning messages when a setback occurs on the road. Then, a node which knows the situation, notifies its neighbors about the problem [3], so the message must be relayed to other neighbors. One of the important facts perform this operation is the high reliability of the messages, due to the redundancy of packets [17], but it also represents an important waste of broadband because of the duplicated packets.

In relation to the package redundancy, in [14], are presented some schemes that help with the redundant retransmissions reduction, and avoiding collisions. This document presents five model solutions: (a) Probability scheme, (b) Scheme based on counter, (c) Scheme based on distance, (d) Scheme based on location, and (e) Scheme based on cluster. The results obtained show that the location scheme is the best option to eliminate redundant retransmissions, without affecting the users accessibility. Based on the probability scheme, [15] proposes an analytical model able to calculate the survival packets delivery. This model was validated with a single hop and the results matched the data obtained analytically. In [11] the transmission of Layer 2 (L2) devices and routing with 3 (L3) devices are evaluated using routing AODV and GPRS protocols for messages forwarding, however, some network simulators were used for its development too, such as OMNet++ in addition to SUMO in the context of VEINs simulations. The results obtained in these tests, showed that the delay in forwarding packets between nodes is directly proportional to the number of hops that the protocol uses to forward packets, so the power of the transmitter must be considered because it is an important effect on the transmission. Power control must also be considered due to its importance for VANET nodes, it must find the optimization between the amount of hops needed for a successful, timely communication, and an interface with fewer nodes. In [16] presents a WAVE protocol performing a synchronization between all WAVE devices. The following section details the proposal designed for the messages broadcast on a VANET network.

3   Message Diffusion Systems on a VANET

This section presents de architecture designed for the warning messages generation by a specific detail of the tools used in the implementation of the app and the experiments carried out to calculate an optimal distance for the sending of packets on a VANET network.

3.1 VANET Network Architecture via Node.js and Raspberry Pi Development Platforms

The objective of this VANET network, is the Exchange of warning messages altogether the users connected to the network. The diagram of Ad Hoc network is presented in Fig. 1.

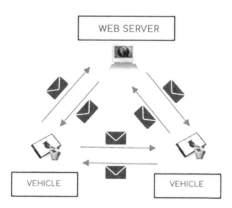

Fig. 1. VANET network architecture to be implemented

To establish an Ad-hoc communication, it is necessary the configuration of the *interfaces* file, located on each Raspberry platform, while on the computer with a graphical interface already implemented, a new network whose IP addresses are included in 10.10.10.xxx and with a mask of 24 are created. To achieve this communication, it must be used *Node.js* which is based on the JavaScript programming language. The messages to be transmitted by the users are prepared by websockets built under *Node.js* and *Socket.io* library. The *browser* is used in the sending of warning messages by clients, in which the IP address of the server must be placed with the port where requests should be Heard, for example *10.10.10.10:8080*. This web page created, allows us the messages Exchange and for this reason, two fields were enabled to be filled by costumers: name and message, followed by a send button, in addition to viewing the number of connected users. Another option that is enabled in the web interface is the load of the location map using *OpenStreetMap*. The best way to load the map and its location is through an iframe, where the code that belongs to the map is obtained from the same OpenStreetMap website. To perform the programming to the server and the client, on the computer was installed *Atom*, a text editor that is coupled to the different programming languages to be used, in this case HTML and JavaScript. It is necessary to create two independent files, *server/main.js* where will be shown the server, and *public/main.js* where the information about clients will be placed [2].

In the server part, we used *express* which is nothing more than an app that will be linked to the websockets server and http server created with socket.io. It also listens to the server via 8080 port. To know the number of users connected to the network, is defined a *clients* variable that is incorporated into two events called *Connection* and *Disconnect* using the *sockets.emit* function, and it will be responsible for broadcasting messages with information on the number of clients connected to the network [1]. We created a new event called *new-message* that will count the information that comes from the client in the fields of the form such as its name and the warning message and in the same event using *io.socket.emit* we issue the message array to all the network clients.

The client part of the *public/main.js* file starts with the creation of the *socket* variable which will be where the connection to the server is by placing the IP address and the port used. As in the server part, a *broadcast* event is created that comes to the user from the server with the information of the number of users connected to the network. This information is in the *data2* variable that is printed on the website created by the use of *div* of HTML. It makes use of the function created *addMessage* in which the information will be extracted from the fields to be filled by the users and it is saved within the variable *message* and via *socket.emit* and the *new-message* sends the entire event to the server and it will do the broadcast (Fig. 2).

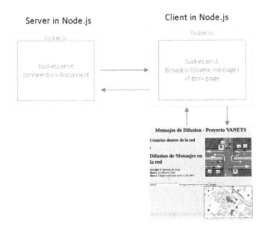

Fig. 2. Functional diagram to the server and clients programming using Node.js

3.2 Prototype Node Implementation

For the development of the node and communication with the other nodes of the network, an Ad Hoc network is implemented that will be formed by two platforms Raspberry Pi+ and a computer with Linux operating system. The feed for the Raspberry is made by a *power bank* of 20000 mAh capacity. It also makes use of a Display with touch technology for the manipulation of the device.

This prototype will be part of the Ad-hoc network located on each vehicle that is part of the VANET network. Once inside the network you can write the warning message on the screen and send the broadcast message. The message sent will be observed on the other devices along with the number of users connected to the network (Fig. 3).

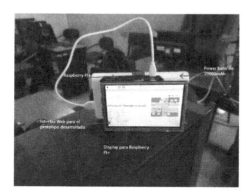

Fig. 3. Prototype node for client part

3.3 NS3 VANETS Networks Simulations

Using the example that comes within NS3 with the name AODV that comes incorporated with the LENA distribution of NS3, besides the LTE technology is loaded in the example mentioned. For the analysis, we place 6 nodes whose *step* separation distance is a variable that will vary by using bash script [10]. The schema to simulate is shown in Fig. 4. With the example used and the changes made in the script, we performed several simulation environments modifying the distance between the nodes, to verify the sending and receiving of the data packets. It starts with a minimum distance between the nodes of 10 m to reach a distance of 200 m between nodes with Steps of 5 m and in addition, a seed of a random value is placed for each simulation.

4   Results

The physical implementation of the scenario for the Ad-hoc network is shown in Fig. 5 where 2 Raspberry Pi is observed and a computer on which the client part and the server are mounted respectively.

Once the server is started, in the implementation of the website the results are those shown in Fig. 6 and 7. Here it is clear that the number of users in the network is 2, user 1 has sent a warning message about an *accident at 1 km* while a user 2 has sent a message about a *vehicle crash* on a certain avenue in the city.

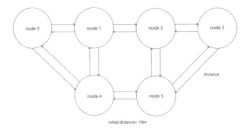

Fig. 4. Nodes scheme to the VANET network messages Exchange simulation

Fig. 5. Physical implementation of scenario for VANET network

Fig. 6. Web interface for a network client

On the right side of website there is an image about a VANET network and the use of platforms to send warning messages. Below the image, we can find the map of the cities from where the warning messages were sent (OpenStreetmap). For this experiment, the warning messages were sent from the same place, so

Fig. 7. Web interface for a network client

the map localization will be the same. At the moment that the map is loaded to the website, the university and its surroundings are chosen as a central point to the map. Another scenario that happens in a real environment is to gradually move away the three nodes that are part of the Ad-hoc network up to a distance in which the warning messages cannot be sent because the node is outside the coverage area of the network. In order to verify and analyze the range of coverage that a VANET network will present, the NS3 simulation environment is used to observe the behavior in the sending of packets and what distance reaches an acceptable coverage without losing the connection to the network. With the script performed we make the necessary variations to select the percentage of packets received (PRR) and the distance to which it was sent to be able to graph packets received vs distance between the nodes of the VANET network. These results are shown in Fig. 8 and 9 where the seed is not used in this case. The behavior of the packets is observed depending on the distance between the nodes.

As seen in the above two figures the loss of packets beyond 100 m distance is total due to the already lost all type of connection within the Ad Hoc network, this is one of the limitations to the implementation of a VANET network in a city. When a random seed is used in Fig. 8 it is observed that the loss of packets resembles a daily situation because there is loss of packets at very few distances and in other situations, the sending of packets is almost constant. Whereas, in Fig. 9 the percentage of packets losses is affected only by the distance factor and it is noted that around 100 m between nodes there is a 100% loss of packets.

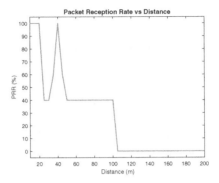

Fig. 8. Percentage of packets received vs distance between nodes, simulation 1

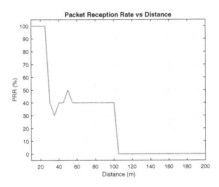

Fig. 9. Percentage of packets received vs distance between nodes, simulation 2 without seed use

5   Conclusions

This paper has developed the design and implementation of broadcast and warning messages within a VANET network using the Raspberry Pi device and a graphical interface for sending and receiving messages based on websockets and the socket.io library. In this sense, a prototype node has been implemented with the goal of issuing warning messages taking into account the separation distance between the nodes. At small distances such as 10 m these warning messages are issued successfully by the prototype. As the distance increases the range of coverage of the network decreases so, as shown in the simulations in different scenarios, there are broadcast messages in distances less than 100 m although with a PRR of 40%. At distances greater than 100 m there is loss of packages completely. The application of the prototype developed in a real environment must be tested although this prototype in terms of cost is economical because a Raspberry, a display with touch technology and a powerbank are electronic devices available in the market. The prototype node inside a vehicle will be placed without major difficulty since it has a small size and the implemented server has no limit of connections so the warning message issuing system is scalable, it has reliability in battery life due to the power bank capacity.

References

1. Socket. IO Broadcasting. https://www.tutorialspoint.com/socket.io/socket.io_broadcasting.htm
2. Usando Websockets con NodeJS y SocketIO. https://carlosazaustre.es/websockets-como-utilizar-socket-io-en-tu-aplicacion-web/
3. Akhil, M., Vasudevan, N., Ramanadhan, U., Devassy, A., Krishnaswamy, D., Ramachandran, A.: Collision avoidance at intersections using vehicle detectors and smartphones. In: 2015 International Conference on Connected Vehicles and Expo (ICCVE), pp. 389–390. IEEE (2015)
4. Ayyappan, B., Kumar, P.M.: Vehicular ad hoc networks (VANET): architectures, methodologies and design issues. In: 2016 Second International Conference on Science Technology Engineering and Management (ICONSTEM), pp. 177–180. IEEE (2016)
5. Fernandes, R.J.: VANET-enabled in-vehicle traffic signs. Ph.D. thesis, Master's thesis, University of Porto (2009)
6. Fogue, M., et al.: Prototyping an automatic notification scheme for traffic accidents in vehicular networks. In: 2011 IFIP Wireless Days (WD), pp. 1–5. IEEE (2011)
7. Gama, O., Nicolau, M.J., Costa, A., Santos, A., Macedo, J., Dias, B.: Evaluation of message dissemination methods in VANETs using a cooperative traffic efficiency application. In: 2017 13th International Wireless Communications and Mobile Computing Conference (IWCMC), pp. 478–483. IEEE (2017)
8. Khekare, G.S., Sakhare, A.V.: A smart city framework for intelligent traffic system using VANET. In: 2013 International Mutli-conference on Automation, Computing, Communication, Control and Compressed Sensing (iMac4s), pp. 302–305. IEEE (2013)
9. Maslekar, N., Boussedjra, M., Mouzna, J., Labiod, H.: VANET based adaptive traffic signal control. In: 2011 IEEE 73rd Vehicular Technology Conference (VTC Spring), pp. 1–5. IEEE (2011)
10. Palaguachi, A., Tenempaguay, E., Estuardo, E.: Diseño de una red de comunicación vehicular inteligente, integrando la tecnología Ad-Hoc con LTE, para la movilidad en la zona urbana de la ciudad de Cuenca. B.S. thesis (2015)
11. Petrov, T., Dado, M., Kortis, P., Kovacikova, T.: Evaluation of packet forwarding approaches for emergency vehicle warning application in VANETs. In: 2018 ELEKTRO, pp. 1–5. IEEE (2018)
12. Sanguesa, J.A., Fogue, M., Garrido, P., Martinez, F.J., Cano, J.C., Calafate, C.T.: A survey and comparative study of broadcast warning messagedissemination schemes for VANETs. Mob. Inf. Syst. **2016** (2016)
13. Singh, S., Agrawal, S.: VANET routing protocols: issues and challenges. In: 2014 Recent Advances in Engineering and Computational Sciences (RAECS), pp. 1–5. IEEE (2014)
14. Tseng, Y.C., Ni, S.Y., Chen, Y.S., Sheu, J.P.: The broadcast storm problem in a mobile ad hoc network. Wirel. Netw. **8**(2–3), 153–167 (2002)

15. Virdaus, I.K., Kang, M., Shin, S., Lee, C.G., Pyim, J.Y.: A counting-based broadcast model of emergency message dissemination in VANETs. In: 2017 Ninth International Conference on Ubiquitous and Future Networks (ICUFN), pp. 927–930. IEEE (2017)
16. Wang, Y., Ding, Z., Li, F., Xia, X., Li, Z.: Design and implementation of a VANET application complying with wave protocol. In: 2017 International Conference on Wireless Communications, Signal Processing and Networking (WiSPNET), pp. 2333–2338. IEEE (2017)
17. Xia, Y., Qin, X., Liu, B., Zhang, P.: A greedy traffic light and queue aware routing protocol for urban VANETs. China Commun. **15**(7), 77–87 (2018)

Signal Detection Methods in Cognitive Radio Networks: A Performance Comparison

Pablo Palacios Játiva[1]([✉]), Milton Román-Cañizares[2]([✉]), Carlos Saavedra[3], and José Julio Freire[2]

[1] Department of Electrical Engineering, Universidad de Chile, Santiago, Chile
`pablo.palacios@ug.uchile.cl`
[2] Department of Telecommunications Engineerings, Universidad de las Américas, Quito, Ecuador
{`milton.roman,jose.freire`}`@udla.edu.ec`
[3] Faculty of Electrical and Computation Engineering, Escuela Superior Politécnica del Litoral (ESPOL), Guayaquil, Ecuador
`casaaved@espol.edu.ec`

Abstract. In this paper, the performance of several detection methods for primary user (PU) signals used to Cognitive Radio Networks (CRNs) are compared. Singular Value Decomposition Scheme (SVD), Eigen-value Decomposition Scheme (EVD), and Cyclo-stationary Detection Scheme (CD) are fairly compared based on Probability of Detection (P_d) as function of Signal-to-Noise ratio (SNR) in a CRN that coexists with a primary network based on Wireless Fidelity (WiFi) and Long Term Evolution (LTE) technologies. Results of the three methods implementation are obtained via numerical simulations. The Maximum Likelihood Estimator (MLE) is used to check the efficiency under established system measurement parameters such as the Standard Deviation (SD) and Standard Error (SE). Based on the results of the evaluation, it is concluded that the SVD scheme outperform the EVD and CD methods, according to the P_d.

Keywords: Cognitive Radio Networks (CRNs) · Cyclo-stationary Detection method (CD) · Eigen-Value Decomposition (EVD) · Probability of detection (P_d) · Singular Value Decomposition (SVD).

1 Introduction

Cognitive Radio (CR) is a paradigm presented as a solution to the inefficiency in the use of the electromagnetic spectrum, which is generally caused by a high demand for wireless technologies, especially WiFi and LTE [1]. A CR system detects spectral holes by assigning them to secondary users (SUs) or unlicensed users, without causing interference to primary users (PUs) or licensed users [2,3].

© Springer Nature Switzerland AG 2020
F. R. Narváez et al. (Eds.): SmartTech-IC 2019, CCIS 1154, pp. 63–74, 2020.
https://doi.org/10.1007/978-3-030-46785-2_6

In general, dynamic access to the spectrum requires four functionalities closely linked to the cognitive cycle [4], as we can see in Fig. 1:

1. Identify the opportunities for spectrum access.
2. Select the frequency bands to be used (spectrum decision).
3. Coordinate access to the spectrum with other secondary users (spectrum sharing).
4. Undock the channels used when required by the PU (spectrum mobility hand-off).

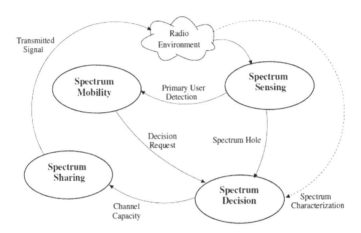

Fig. 1. Cognitive cycle. Adapted to [4].

The main difference between the PUs and the SUs is the authority for use of the spectrum by the PUs, while the SUs is waiting to apply. CR technology has the following characteristics and advantages:

- **Cognitive Capability:** It refers to the ability of the CR user to detect and collect information from their environment, which may be transmission frequency, bandwidth, power or modulation, adjusting them to have the best SU detection [5].
- **Reconfigurability:** It adjusts the technical parameters, based on the information collected in the first phase of the cognitive radio cycle, without having to modify the hardware [6].

In the cognitive cycle the spectrum detection is the most complex stage and can be described as follows:

- **Detection of whites spaces:** this stage detects the whites spaces, and make models to meet the transmission requirements of SUs [7].

– **Signal classification according to the interference analysis:** the signal at this stage is also classified according to its characteristics and its interference level [7].

Spectrum detection has two objectives: to reduce harmful interference between PUs communication while using the channel and at the same time improve the effective use of the spectrum while it is not being used by PUs. Based on these parameters, fast and effective signal detection is a priority for CRNs. To comply with this principle, several detection schemes have been proposed, including Energy Detection Schemes (ED) [8], Waveform Detection (WD), Matched filtering detection (MFD), Radio identification Detection (RID), CDM [9], SVD [10], EVD [11], among others.

For the EVD [12], the threshold value that determines the signal presence is obtained from the Random Matrix Theory (RMT). In contrast with EVD, SVD scheme can be applied to any matrix dimension [13]. In the case of CD, this scheme has greater resistance to noise uncertainty than the ED schemes. If the signal transmitted by a PU has a cyclo-stationarity component, it can be detected by periodicity of this cyclo-stationary parameter. The cyclo-stationary signal can be detected even when the SNR is poor. Nevertheless, CD scheme is more difficult than the ED methods because requires prior information about the transmitted signal [14].

The main contribution of this research is to compare the performance of the SVD, EVD, and CD schemes applied separately to a CRN, that coexist with a primary network based on Long Term Evolution (LTE) and Wireless Fidelity (WiFi) technologies, implemented in Network Simulator 3 (NS-3) modules [15]. The efficiency of the three methods in a state-of-the-art functional mobile network is validated in terms of probability of detection (P_d) as function of signal-to-noise ratio (SNR) through numerical simulations. Finally, the performance is verified, using the Maximum Likelihood Estimator (MLE) with its respective error and deviation.

The rest of this article is organized as follows: in Sect. 2, the detection methods and algorithms used in the work are explained. In Sect. 3, the design of the experiment and the parameters of the simulation are presented. Section 4 describes the results of the simulation, its interpretation and the analysis using the statistical estimator, presented in a CDF and numerical values. Finally, in Sect. 5 the results of the paper are described.

2   Spectrum Detection Techniques Evaluated

In this work we evaluate the performance of spectrum sensing techniques, specifically implemented in a secondary network based on the CR interweave paradigm, that coexist with a primary network based on LTE and WiFi technologies, which are state-of-the-art technologies in heterogeneous networks [16].

Algorithm 1. Eigen-value Detector Algorithm

Require: k, L, N.
Ensure: $PU_{detection\ bit}$.
 1: **while** the users are transmitting **do**
 2:     Setup $k = 2$, $L = 18$ and $N = 18000$
 3:     Obtain $CovMat = CreateMatrixCovariance(L)$
 4:     Obtain $Max = Maximum(CovMat)$ and $Min = Minimum(CovMat)$
 5:     Obtain $Threshold = CalculateThreshold()$
 6:     **if** $(Max/Min < Threshold)$ **then**
 7:         **return** $PU_{detection\ bit}=1$
 8:     **else**
 9:         **return** $PU_{detection\ bit}=0$
10:     **end if**
11: **end while**

2.1 Eigen-values Signal Detector

The detection problem can be established as a hypothesis test: noise only and signal with Additive White Gaussian Noise (AWGN) component [17]. The hypothesis test is given by

$$x(t) = \begin{cases} n(t) & H_0 \\ h(t) * s(t) + n(t) & H_1, \end{cases} \tag{1}$$

where $x(t)$ is the signal received by the SU, $s(t)$ is the signal transmitted by the PU, $n(t)$ is the AWGN and $h(t)$ is the channel gain.

Considering the N, L and k values, such that $k < L < N - k$ must be fulfilled, we define N as the number of samples to be taken by the receiver, L is the number of consecutive values co-variance matrix of the received signal can take, and k is the number of singular values [13]. For this work, $N = 18000$, $L = 18$, and $k = 2$. Then, the matrix of co-variances is as follows

$$R(N) = \frac{1}{N} \sum_{n=L}^{L-1+N} \hat{x}(n)x^\dagger(n), \tag{2}$$

where $R(N)$ is the sample co-variance matrix of the received discrete signal $\hat{x}(n)$ received by the SU, and $x^\dagger(n)$ is the Hermitian of $\hat{x}(n)$.

By setting a very large N value, and based on properties assumptions of the transmitted signals and the noise [17], is possible to verify that

$$R(N) \approx R = E(\hat{x}(n)x^\dagger(n)), \tag{3}$$

where $E(.)$ is the expected value.

The approach of this method is summarized in Algorithm 1.

2.2 Singular Value Decomposition Detector

To obtain the singular value decomposition detector, we need factorize the co-variance matrix R, i.e. apply the SVD scheme to obtain the singular values, base on [13]. The expression is given by

Algorithm 2. SVD Detector Algorithm

Require: k, L, N.

Ensure: $PU_{detection\ bit}$.

1: **while** the users are transmitting **do**
2:     Setup $k = 2$, $L = 18$ and $N = 18000$
3:     Obtain $CovMat = CreateMatrixCovariance(L)$
4:     Factorize(CovMat)
5:     Obtain $Max = Maximum(CovMat)$ and $Min = Minimum(CovMat)$
6:     Obtain $Threshold = CalculateThreshold()$
7:     **if** $(Max/Min < Threshold)$ **then**
8:         **return** $PU_{detection\ bit}=1$
9:     **else**
10:        **return** $PU_{detection\ bit}=0$
11:    **end if**
12: **end while**

$$R = U\Sigma V^t, \tag{4}$$

where $R_{(m \times n)}$ is the co-variance matrix, $U_{(N-L+1) \times (N-L+1)}$ is the singular vector matrix of columns, $\Sigma_{(m \times n)}$ is the diagonal matrix of singular values, and $V^t_{(N-L+1) \times (N-L+1)}$ is the singular vector matrix of rows.

The maximum and minimum eigenvalues (λ_{max} and λ_{min}) of the covariance matrix R are obtained [13]. After that, we calculate the threshold detection value and compare it with the eigenvalues, according to [13]

$$\gamma = \frac{(\sqrt{N} + \sqrt{L})^2}{(\sqrt{N} - \sqrt{L})^2} * (1 + (\frac{(\sqrt{N} + \sqrt{L})^{-\frac{2}{3}}}{N * L^{\frac{1}{6}}}) * F_1^{-1}(1 - P_{fa})), \tag{5}$$

this expression is an asymptotic formula of signal detection threshold based on the probability of false alarm P_{fa} proposed in [18]. It is our consideration that the P_{fa} required must be equal or less than 0.1 ($P_{fa} <= 0.1$). F_1^{-1} is the inverse cumulative distribution function (CDF) of the Tracy-Widom distribution of first order, which is the normalized probability distribution for the eigenvalues described in [18].

The decision about the signal presence is defined as the ratio of the maximum and minimum singular values of the received signal matrix, then, this value is compare with the threshold. Therefore, if $\frac{\lambda_{max}}{\lambda_{min}} < \gamma$, the signal is present, otherwise the signal is absent. The approach of this method is summarized in Algorithm 2.

2.3 Cyclo-stationary Detector

In wireless networks, the PU signal contains sine and cosine carriers, propagation and synchronization sequences, which provide information about the

---

Algorithm 3. Cyclostationary Detector Algorithm

Require: $x(t)$, α, N.
Ensure: *PU detection bit.*
 1: **while** the users are transmitting **do**
 2:    Setup $N = 18000$
 3:    Obtain $CAF = Cyclic\ Autocorrelation\ Function(x(t), \alpha)$
 4:    Obtain $S_r = SpectralCorrelationFunction(CAF)SU$
 5:    Obtain $S_n = SpectralCorrelationFunction(CAF)noise$
 6:    **if** $(S_r = S_n)$ **then**
 7:       **return** $PU_{detection\ bit} = 0$
 8:    **else**
 9:       **return** $PU_{detection\ bit} = 1$
10:    **end if**
11: **end while**

---

signal nature. A signal with auto-correlation and periodic mean is called a cyclo-stationary process [14]. For any SU signal received $x(t)$, with a period T, the function of the auto-correlation (ACF) $R_{xx}(t, \tau)$ is represented by [19]

$$R_{xx}(t, \tau) = E(x(t) * x^{\dagger}(t + \tau)), \tag{6}$$

Since the signal $x(t)$ is cyclo-stationary, assuming it is periodic in the time t for each lag parameter τ, the ACF has a period that is a function of the cyclic frequency α, is called Cyclic Auto-correlation Function (CAF) and is defined as follows [19]

$$R_{xx}(\tau) = E(x(t) * x^{\dagger}(t - \tau)e^{-j2\pi\alpha(t-\tau/2)}), \tag{7}$$

Therefore, the spectral correlation function (SCF), is present as follow [19]

$$S_x(f) = \int_{-\infty}^{\infty} R_{xx}(\tau)e^{-j2\pi f\tau}\,d\tau, \tag{8}$$

As an OFDM symbol has periodicity incorporated into it, this method was adapted to the proposed cognitive system, based on WiFi and LTE technologies. According to this principle, the SU has to decide if the PU is present or not via a hypothesis test problem, given by [19]

$$\begin{cases} H_o : S_r = S_n \\ H_1 : S_r = S_x + S_n, \end{cases} \tag{9}$$

where S_r is the SCF of the signal received by the SU, S_x is the SCF of the PU signal and S_n is the SCF of the noise. For H_o PU is absent, otherwise PU is present.

The approach of this method is summarized in Algorithm 3.

3   Implementation and Simulation

We implemented CRN and simulated it in a mixed CR network that coexist with a primary network composed to LTE and WiFi technologies in a module developed in Network Simulator 3 (NS-3.23). In the spectrum detection, there is the option of using the EVD [17], SVD [13] or CD [19], separately, to be able to analyze it at work. The spectrum decision is based on coalition game theory [7] and spectrum sharing and mobility is based on the Received Signal Strength Indicator (RSSI), parameter used to carry out the hand-off between WiFi and LTE technologies [20].

The simulation is based on a network topology shown in the Fig. 2. As we can see, the proposed topology is configured so that the position and movement of the PU and SU should be dynamic and randomly during the simulation time.

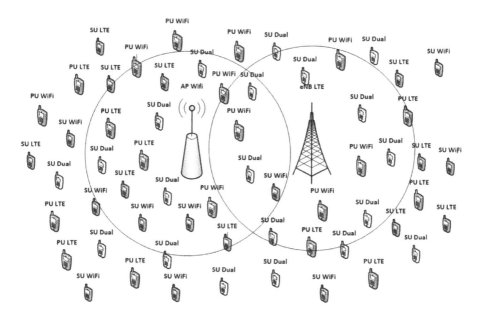

Fig. 2. Proposed network topology for simulation

Several simulation characteristics are explained as follows:

- We assume the slow Rayleigh channel fading for PUs and SUs, with complex coefficient mean square value that tends to a Normal distribution of parameters $N(0, 1)$.
- The path loss exponent (α) is considered to be 2.7, because it is a classic value in communications systems for representing an urban area propagation [17].
- There are several nodes in the proposed network topology, as depicted in Fig. 2.
- The propagation and mobility models used and that are provided by the NS-3 simulator [15]. For the propagation model the range propagation loss was chosen, which only depends on the distance between transmitter and receiver. The mobility model is the random way-point, which is oriented for the movement of mobile users in order to known their location, velocity, and acceleration in terms of the time.

- The range of coverage of the access point (AP) and the range of coverage of the evolved-node B (eNB) are fixed to 100 m and 350 m, respectively. This configuration was done to generate interference between the evaluated technologies in the simulation.

The principals parameters used in the system simulation are shown in Table 1. The same parameters were used for each type of detection method, in order to obtain a fair comparison.

Table 1. System parameters

Parameters	Values
AP range of coverage	100 m
Channel model PU	Slow Rayleigh fading [15]
Channel model SU	Slow Rayleigh fading [15]
CR SU	4
eNB range of coverage	350 m
LTE bandwidth	20 MHz [13]
LTE frequency	729 MHz [13]
Mobility model	Random Waypoint [15]
Noise	AWGN, $\sigma = 1$
Path loss exponent (*alpha*)	2.7 [17]
Propagation model	Range propagation loss [15]
PU	10
Samples	18000
SU, PU distribution	Uniform random distribution [15]
Time of simulation	1200 s
Traffic	TCP
WiFi bandwidth	20 MHz [13]
WiFi frequency	2400 MHz* [13]

*Note: According to the research in [15], NS-3 has not implemented any module for the band of 5.9 MHz, for this reason, it was decided to evaluate the system in 2.4 GHz.

4   Results

P_d as a function of SNR is presented as a Cumulative Distribution Function (CDF) for SVD, EVD and CD, as shown in Fig. 3. The curves of the three methods were obtained through the implementation and simulation of the algorithms in NS-3 separately. The simulation iterations was defined based on the Monte Carlo method, with 21 iterations for each SNR value, this is to have reliable estimates in the distributions of the generated data [21, 22]. Before performing the experiments, we must take into account an important factor for the simulator, that the simulation time is not the same as the real time. An important feature of this simulator is that it contains a built-in pseudo-random number generator (PRNG), which ensures that the iterations of the developed experimentation are independent of each other.

It is possible to observe by the Fig. 3 the linear and increasing behavior of the curves. In addition, is important to note that the SVD method has the best performance in terms of P_d, with respect to the EVD and CD methods, approximately 10% improvement with respect to the EVD scheme and a 2% improvement compared to the CD scheme. This is due to its accuracy and precision in the detection process, through its unique value search algorithm. For low levels of SNR, specifically -20 dB, SVD has a P_d of 20%, while CD has a P_d of 10%. In contrast, for high levels of SNR, specifically 20 dB, SVD has a P_d of 88% approximately, while CD has a P_d of 82% approximately.

To compare the performance of the proposed schemes and according to the data and models obtained from Fig. 3, it is necessary to use a reliable statistical method that allows the Validation of these results. The statistical estimator MLE derived in [23] is used and its methodology applied in a development in R[24]. The MLE estimates the parameters of a given probabilistic model, in this case the models of the detection methods obtained experimentally, allowing a statistical comparison.

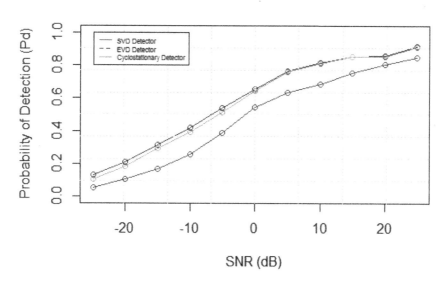

Fig. 3. Probability of detection vs SNR

It should be noted that Standard Error (SE) and Standard Deviation (SD) of the parameters MLE are included in the work, because a data model is incomplete if the error associated with the data is not indicated and the validity range of the presented models could not be estimated. With this statistical estimator, the numerical results obtained are shown in Table 2. It is shown that, the SVD method [13] outperforms the EVD and Cyclo-stationary methods proposed in [17] and [19], respectively. This is due to the fact that it is more likely to detect PUs with the SVD algorithm, as it is their largest estimator compared to the two detection algorithms studied.

Table 2. MLE detection methods

	MLE	SE	SD
SVD	0.587388	0.08495629	0.2817681
EVD	0.476233	0.08872702	0.2942742
CDM	0.574531	0.08807605	0.2921152

5 Conclusions

In this work we compare and analyze the performance of three PU energy detection methods applied to a CRN that coexist in the same communication environment with a primary network based on WiFi and LTE technologies. These methods are evaluated in terms of the P_d as function of SNR. The MLE statistical estimator, its standard deviation and the standard error parameters are used to test the system performance and efficiency of the schemes. Through this analysis, we conclude that the SVD detection method is more efficient than EVD and CDM in terms of P_d.

Acknowledgments. This work was funded by CONICYT PFCHA/Beca de Doctorado Nacional/2019 21190489, SENESCYT "Convocatoria abierta 2014-primera fase, Acta CIBAE-023-2014", and UDLA Telecommunications Engineering Degree.

References

1. Haykin, S.: Cognitive radio: brain-empowered wireless communications. IEEE J. Sel. Areas Commun. **23**(2), 201–220 (2005)
2. Muchandi, N., Khanai, R.: Cognitive radio spectrum sensing: a survey. In: 2016 International Conference on Electrical, Electronics, and Optimization Techniques (ICEEOT), pp. 3233–3237, March 2016
3. Patil, V.M., Patil, S.R.: A survey on spectrum sensing algorithms for cognitive radio. In: 2016 International Conference on Advances in Human Machine Interaction (HMI), pp. 1–5, March 2016
4. Liu, X., Zhang, Y., Li, Y., Zhang, Z., Long, K.: A survey of cognitive radio technologies and their optimization approaches. In: 2013 8th International Conference on Communications and Networking in China (CHINACOM), pp. 973–978, August 2013

5. Alias, D.M., Ragesh, G.K.: Cognitive radio networks: a survey. In: 2016 International Conference on Wireless Communications, Signal Processing and Networking (WiSPNET), pp. 1981–1986, March 2016
6. Sun, H., Nallanathan, A., Wang, C.X., Chen, Y.: Wideband spectrum sensing for cognitive radio networks: a survey. IEEE Wirel. Commun. **20**(2), 74–81 (2013)
7. Palacios, P., Saavedra, C.: Coalition game theory in cognitive mobile radio networks. In: Botto-Tobar, M., Pizarro, G., Zúñiga-Prieto, M., D'Armas, M., Zúñiga Sánchez, M. (eds.) CITT 2018. CCIS, vol. 895, pp. 3–15. Springer, Cham (2019). https://doi.org/10.1007/978-3-030-05532-5_1
8. Verma, R., Mahapatro, A.: Cognitive radio: energy detection using wavelet packet transform for spectrum sensing. In: 2017 Third International Conference on Advances in Electrical, Electronics, Information, Communication and Bio-Informatics (AEEICB), pp. 168–172, February 2017
9. Liu, Z., Ali, R., Khan, I., Khan, I.A., Shah, A.A.: Performance comparison of Energy and cyclostationary spectrum detection in cooperative cognitive radios network. In: 2016 IEEE International Symposium on Circuits and Systems (ISCAS), pp. 1734–1737, May 2016
10. Xu, S., Kwak, K.S., Rao, R.R.: SVD based wideband spectrum sensing and carrier aggregation for LTE-Advanced networks. In: 2014 IEEE 25th Annual International Symposium on Personal, Indoor, and Mobile Radio Communication (PIMRC), pp. 1190–1194, September 2014
11. Jacob, S.M., Nandan, S.: Spectrum sensing technique in cognitive radio based on sample covariance matrix. In: 2015 International Conference on Control, Instrumentation, Communication and Computational Technologies (ICCICCT), pp. 139–144, December 2015
12. Ali, S.S., Liu, C., Jin, M.: Minimum eigenvalue detection for spectrum sensing in cognitive radio. Int. J. Electr. Comput. Eng. **4**(4), 623–630 (2014)
13. Palacios, P., Castro, A., Azurdia-Meza, C., Estevez, C.: SVD detection analysis in cognitive mobile radio networks. In: 2017 Ninth International Conference on Ubiquitous and Future Networks (ICUFN), pp. 222–224, July 2017
14. Yawada, P.S., Wei, A.J.: Cyclostationary detection based on non-cooperative spectrum sensing in cognitive radio network. In: 2016 IEEE International Conference on Cyber Technology in Automation, Control, and Intelligent Systems (CYBER), pp. 184–187, June 2016
15. ns-3 Model Library, Release ns-3.23, August 2015. https://www.nsnam.org/docs/release/3.23/models/ns-3-model-library.pdf
16. Galanopoulos, A., Foukalas, F., Tsiftsis, T.A.: Efficient coexistence of LTE with WiFi in the licensed and unlicensed spectrum aggregation. IEEE Trans. Cogn. Commun. Netw. **2**(2), 129–140 (2016)
17. Omar, M.H., Hassan, S., Nor, S.A.: Eigenvalue-based signal detectors performance comparison. In: The 17th Asia Pacific Conference on Communications, pp. 1–6, October 2011
18. Zeng, Y., Liang, Y.C.: Maximum-minimum eigenvalue detection for cognitive radio. In: 2007 IEEE 18th International Sympsium on Personal, Indoor and Mobile Radio Communications, pp. 1–5, September 2007
19. Thomas, A.A., Sudha, T.: Primary user signal detection in cognitive radio networks using cyclostationary feature analysis. In: 2014 IEEE National Conference on Communication, Signal Processing and Networking (NCCSN), pp. 1–5, October 2014

20. Gerasimenko, M., Himayat, N., Yeh, S.P., Talwar, S., Andreev, S., Koucheryavy, Y.: Characterizing performance of load-aware network selection in multi-radio (WiFi/LTE) heterogeneous networks. In: 2013 IEEE Globecom Workshops (GC Wkshps), pp. 397–402, December 2013
21. Ramírez, I.C., Barrera, C.J., Correa, J.C.: Efecto del tamaño de muestra y el número de réplicas bootstrap. Ingeniería Compet. **15**(1), 93–101 (2013)
22. Alfonso, U.M., Carla, M.V.: Modelado y simulación de eventos discretos. Editorial UNED (2013)
23. Held, L., Sabanés Bové, D.: Applied Statistical Inference, vol. 10. Springer, Heidelberg (2014). https://doi.org/10.1007/978-3-642-37887-4
24. R Core Team: R: a language and environment for statistical computing. R Foundation for Statistical Computing, Vienna (2014). www.R-project.org

Scalable Electrical Distribution Networks Planning for Medium and Low Voltage Considering Capacity on Transformers and Voltage Drop

Milton Ruiz[1]([⊠]) [iD], Esteban Inga[1] [iD], and Silvio Simani[2] [iD]

[1] Universidad Politécnica Salesiana, Quito, Ecuador
{mruizm,einga}@ups.edu.ec
[2] University of Ferrara, Ferrara, Italy
silvio.simani@unife.it

Abstract. This paper shows a heuristic algorithm for design of a scalable and reliable distribution networks using real data. The database uses a geographic information system (GIS), which contains the coordinates of households, buildings, streets, parks, etc. The data is used by the algorithm to determine the optimal path for the primary network of medium voltage (MV), secondary network of low voltage (LV), location of transformers and inspection wells. Medium and low voltage distribution networks are underground; the conductors must be deployed along the streets. This algorithm computes the capacity that each transformer needs and the voltage drop in each branch. Finally, the software CYMDIST are used to analyze the model of the distribution system, in order to validate the results of the power flow analysis, line losses, transformers load capacity and verify that voltage profiles fulfill technical specifications.

Keywords: Dimensioning · Cymdist · Underground electrical distribution grids · Optimization · Planning

1 Introduction

The electrical distribution systems play an essential role since it interconnects the transmission system and the users. Due to the constant increase of electrical energy demand and the high investments costs, research efforts in the area have been directed toward developing methodologies for optimal design, planning and expansion of modern electrical distribution systems. Such methodologies should consider the topology of the network of interest, namely ring, radial or mixed [1,2]. The ring topology is generally used for high and medium voltage networks and significantly improves the reliability of the system, but its cost is higher due to a more complex implementation and additional equipment such as extra breakers and conductors. On the other hand, the radial topology is

© Springer Nature Switzerland AG 2020
F. R. Narváez et al. (Eds.): SmartTech-IC 2019, CCIS 1154, pp. 75–88, 2020.
https://doi.org/10.1007/978-3-030-46785-2_7

typically used in medium and low voltage networks; its cost is lower, but a failure (e.g. of a feeder or a transformer) will cause a power outage of the associated users due to the lack of alternative supply paths. Problems of interest when planning electrical distribution networks are design of substations, path of medium voltage lines, location of transformers and path of low voltage lines to the users (households) [3–5]. Traditional design methodologies may not result in an economically optimal planning; it is necessary to minimize the associated costs, such as investment, energy losses, operation and maintenance of the system, while keeping satisfactory levels of security and reliability. In other words, optimal planning of an electrical distribution network involves minimizing costs and maximizing load of transformers and cost/benefit ratio, while fulfilling security and reliability requirements during the operation and maintenance of the system [6,7]. Information about the electrical distribution network, such as location and ratings of generators, substations, transformers and lines, and the electric energy demand of the users, is key for solving this optimization problem. However, publicly available data from a real network is generally scarce. Therefore, considering the demand increase, when planning distribution networks, typically requires the use of artificial models that emulate the real infrastructure [8,9]. Optimal design of smart distribution networks is a combinatorial problem defined as NP-complete; where the connection between customers and the main network on a georeferenced scenario is build using a heuristic model based on Minimum Spanning Tree (MST) techniques. The project deals with the optimal location of distribution transformers using a modified-prim algorithm based on the minimal cost of low voltage network between transformers and users. Secondly, clustering algorithms are used to break the dataset (number of distribution transformers) up into groups, then k-medoids algorithm determines a defined number of clusters, which can be used as primary feeders. The next stage deals with the built up the medium voltage network based on modified-prim to determine the lowest path between main substation and distribution transformers on a georeferenced path [10–12]. The minimum spanning tree are estimated with Prim algorithm and graph theory. Prim is used to find the subset of branches and all vertices that will constitute the tree. The constraint related to the losses due to distances are taken into account during the process. In each iteration, the algorithm increases the tree size, starting from an initial vertex representing a transformer and successively adding vertices corresponding to the users, such that the distances between the transformer and the users are minimized, initial works in telecommunications are presented in [13]. This process considers variables such as location of the householders' main feeders, location and ratings of transformers and path of medium and low voltage along the streets; it also takes into account constraints such as power flow balance/equality, the location of a substation, the path of lines, bus voltage and ratings and coverage of each transformer. Regarding the latter, any transformer that does not satisfy the requirements are replace [14]. The proposed model in this paper is develop considering a multigraph, that defines a layer for the medium voltage network and another layer for the low voltage network, ensuring the connectivity of users in the deployment depending on demand. To achieve the objectives a deployment is carried out in urban areas using an open street map (OSM) file with the information of longitude and latitude within a model developed in Matlab and simulated in Cymdist. The efficiency of model is estimate for varying densities of the electric load, to assess adaptation capability and resources availability to fulfill the demand of different number of users. The k-means algorithm is used for generating the clusters, and the nodes inside an area are treated as PQ loads. Such network is generated through the Delaunay-Voronoi triangulation, thus resulting in a partially connected mesh. If such mesh network shows a redundancy larger than desired, branches are iteratively suppress starting with the one connecting two nodes with the highest degree [15,16]. Henceforth, this article is organized as follow. Section 2 presents the formulation of the problem. Section 3 presents the results. Section 4 analyzes the results of the model and its simulation. Finally, in Sect. 5 presents the conclusions about this research.

2   Problem Formulation

For design of a reliable distribution network is necessary to consider that only one transformer should cover each user in low voltage. Each transformer should be covered by a substation in medium voltage. Each transformer has a maximum capacity for supply power for a defined number of users. Transformers can only be connected to household main feeders that are within its coverage area of radius. Connections between transformers are done through the medium voltage network, and the ampacity of each conductor in the network depends on its cross section, material properties and distribution voltage [17,18]. The length of the lines of the medium and low voltage distribution networks should be limited, in order fulfill regulations related to maximum voltage drops due to Joule effect losses. Since it is a geo-referenced system, the distance is estimate using the Haversine formula [19]. The cost of the transformers depends of his capacity. In order to determine the location of the transformers, a set of possible sites are generate based on the geographic features of the area where the network will be implemented. The implementation cost of the distribution network only considers the unit cost of the conductor per Km. When the current flows through a conductor, there a voltage drops across it. Therefore, the voltage of a PQ bus is different from the voltage of the PV bus. Equation 1 show the voltage Vi in every bus PQi must be within the specified range [4,20].

$$V_{min} \le V_i \le V_{max} \tag{1}$$

The reactive power losses in the low voltage line of the distribution network are negligible compared with the resistance of the conductor; hence, it is not analyzed in this research [21]. The model can be formulated as follow: Eq. 2 considers minimizing the implementation cost of the network. Equation 3 maximizes the capacity of transformers to be installed, including the cost of the transformers. Equation 4 is the constraint that limits to M the maximum number of users that can be connected to a transformer, while Eq. 5 is the constraint that sets the maximum capacity of the transformer to its last household main feeder. Equation 6 limits the maximum numbers of transformers.

$$min \ \sum_{j=1}^{M} \sum_{i=1}^{N} X_i Y_j \tag{2}$$

$$max \ Cmax_j \tag{3}$$

Subject to:

$$X_i * Y_j = 1 \qquad \forall X_i / \{X_i \in only \ Y_j\} \tag{4}$$

$$\sum_{i=1}^{N} X_i * P_i \le Cmax_j \qquad \forall X_i / \{X_i \in coverage \ area \ Y_j\} \tag{5}$$

$$Y_j \in 0, 1 \qquad \forall Y_j \tag{6}$$

A real scenario consists of a geographical location of electricity users, which require coverage by a transformer. In order to determine how such coverage will be supplied, the Steiner Tree combinatorial optimization heuristics is used to find the shortest path between users and transformers, and generate the minimum spanning tree (MST) [22]. The sets are established by groups of users of the electric service prior to routing, and clustering algorithms such as k-means and Delaunay-Voronoi triangulation are used to determine subsets of interconnected users such that the total length of branches. The optimal location of transformers is a Set-Cover problem, which is a combinatorial NP-complete problem whose solution requires the use of heuristics [23]. Algorithm 1 comprises the execution of the following steps: Step 1: Acquire data from Open Street Map, including the geo-referenced coordinates of the households and streets. Step 2: Build sets of users, intersections and transformers. Step 3: Calculate the size of each group. Step 4: Build sets clusters. Step 5: Generate the allocation of random loads.

Algorithm 1. Reconstruction and clustering

1: Step 1: Acquire data from OSM
2: $\quad\quad\quad x^u, y^u, m_{con}, x^{in}, y^{in}$
3: Step 2: Build sets
4: $\quad\quad\quad \Omega_u = [x^u, y^u], \ \Omega_{in} = [x^{in}, y^{in}], \ \Omega_s = [x^{in}, y^{in}]$
5: $\quad\quad\quad Se = [x^{se}, y^{se}]$
6: Step 3: Calculate the size of group
7: $\quad\quad\quad clust = round(N/2^{nc})$
8: Step 4: Build cluster
9: $\quad\quad\quad [idx, m^{xy} \ = \ kmedoids(clust, \Omega_u)]$
10: $\quad\quad\quad tri \ = \ dalaunay(m^{xy}(:, 1), m^{xy}(:, Z))$
11: $\quad\quad\quad voronoy(m^{xy}(:, 1), m^{xy}(:, Z), tri);$
12: Step 5: Allocation of random loads
13: $\quad\quad\quad m^U_{idx} = [(1:N), idx]$
14: $\quad\quad\quad for \ C_1 = 1 : N$
15: $\quad\quad\quad\quad m^U_{idx}(C_1, 3) = random(idx(C_1))$
16: $\quad\quad\quad endfor$

Algorithm 2 generates a minimum spanning tree that covers all users, before solving the SetCover problem. The step 2, greedy algorithm selects the number of transformers required to cover all users. The households are grouped based on ratings and maximum allowed distances (to limit voltage drops). This corresponds to a Setcover problem, which is estimate using a Greedy algorithm [24] that selects a suboptimal solution at each step in the search for the optimal solution that supplies electric coverage to all residential users.

Algorithm 2. Placement of transformation centers

1: Step 1: PRIM modified
2: $\quad\quad\quad$ Define: C_{max}, D_{ct}
3: $\quad\quad\quad X = [x^u, x^s, x^{se}, mean(x^u)]$
4: $\quad\quad\quad Y = [y^u, y^s, y^{se}, mean(y^u)]$
5: $\quad\quad\quad for \ C_2 = 1 : M$
6: $\quad\quad\quad\quad x_a = X_N + C_2$
7: $\quad\quad\quad\quad y_a = Y_N + C_2$
8: $\quad\quad\quad\quad gp = primmodified(\Omega_u, x_a, y_a, D^{min}_{ct}, C^{max}_t)$
9: $\quad\quad\quad\quad u^{mn}_p(C_2, gp) = 1$
10: $\quad\quad\quad endfor$
11: Step 2: Greedy algorithm
12: $\quad\quad\quad greedy(u^{mn}_p)$
13: $\quad\quad\quad$ Return: $solC, solL$

Algorithm 3: size of the transformer capacity in function of the number of users that transformer provide service to. It is subject to the distance constraint and one transformer provides service to one user.

Algorithm 3. Sizing

1: Step 1: Define: C_{max}, D_{ct}
2: Step 2: Redundance Error:
3:       $for\ C_3 = 2 : N$
4:          $aux = find(solC(C_{3,:} == 1)$
5:          $if\ length(aux) > 1$
6:             $for\ C_4 = 2 : length(aux)$
7:                $solC(i, aux(m)) = 0$
8:             $endfor$
9:          $endif$
10:       $endfor$
11: Step 3: Power demand
12:       $for\ C_5 = 1 : M_{C_T}$
13:          $ind = find(solC(C_{5,:} == 1)$
14:          $S_{pt} = 0$
15:          $for\ C_6 : length(ind)$
16:             $S_{pt} = S_{pt} + m^u_{idx}(ind(C_6, 3))$
17:             $P_T(C_5) = S_{pt}$
18:          $endfor$
19:       $endfor$

The algorithm 4 compute the drop voltage in all circuits using the connection path between elements, subject to the distance constraints.

Algorithm 4. Drop voltage in circuits

1: Step 1: Define: T_j^{xy}
2: Step 2: Calculate
3:       $d_{ui}^{sj}; \forall\ U\ |\ U \in cobert(T_j)$
4: Step 3: Assignments
5:       Define conductor: ρ_c, S_c
6:       Define network parameters: Φ_c, v_L
7: Step 2: Calculate
8:       $d_{U_i S_j} = haversine(U_i\ ,\ T_j)$
9:       $for\ C_6 = 1 : length(P_{T_j})$
10:          Section resistance: $R_c(C_6) = d_{U_i S_j} * \rho_c / S_c$
11:          Current by line: $I = P_T(C_6)/(v_L)$
12:          $\Delta V = R_C(C_6) * I(C_6))$
13:       $endfor$

---

3   Results

This algorithm is applied on the Borgo Punta neighborhood in the city of Ferrara, Italy. Figure 1 shows Delaunay-Voronoi tessellation. User's loads are divided in five zones that defines different profiles. The model includes power levels that vary regionally: orange region is zone 1 with 4 kW users, blue region is zone 2 with 5 kW users, red region is zone 3 with 6 kW users, green region is zone 4 with 7 kW users and purple region is zone 5 with 8 kW users. The coordinates are 11.6352 W 44.8391 S and 11.6504 E 44.8485 N. The area of interest has a base of 1.182 miles and a height of 0.829 miles, for a surface of 0.98 square miles, with approximately 600 buildings and 20 streets.

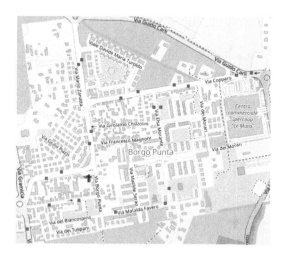

Fig. 1. Scenario for deployment of underground electrical distribution networks (Color figure online)

Using an OSM file, that contains the coordinates of households and streets, which were acquired from Open Street Map. Each household has four coordinates in the geo-referenced space, corresponding to latitude and longitude. The algorithm is use to distribute users among transformers and inspection wells. The distances are calculated using Haversine formula. The Prim algorithm is used to generate the minimum spanning tree (MST) of an underground medium voltage radial network that should run along the streets, ensuring a minimum total length of branches. This algorithm considers the active nodes, and identifies the shortest path between a user and the closest transformer, while honoring voltage and power ratings of the transformers. In addition, it is required that the voltage drop in the lines, is below 3%. Figure 2 shows the results obtained after implementing the optimization algorithm in Matlab. The optimal trajectory of the radial distribution feeder is close to 1 mile long. The green rectangles represent the transformers; the white rectangles represent the candidate inspection wells that could be build; the triangles represent the loads of the users, each color indicating the nominal installed It can be see that five load profiles are build and the substation is represented by a black square.

Figure 3 shows the ratings of transformers used are between 15 KVA and 125 KVA and average load capacity of 85%.

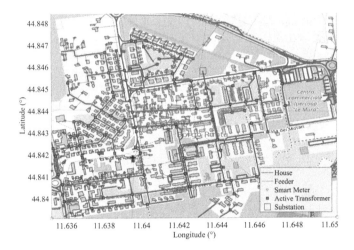

Fig. 2. Results of optimization. Source: Author (Color figure online)

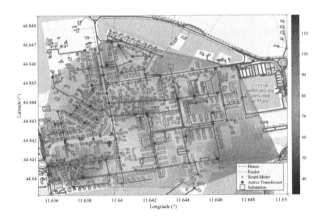

Fig. 3. Voltage drop per user. Source: Author

4   Analysis of Results

The AC models are realistic representations of the power flow in electric lines. Due to their nonlinearity, solving the power flow problem is a task of high computational cost. In this work, a standard AC model of power flow is used, which decomposes the network to improve performance when solving large-scale power flow problems. In other words, a power system is divided in parts in which the problem is estimated independently to reduce the time of execution. In particular, the power flow model implemented in CYMDIST uses the algorithm of Unbalanced Voltage Drops with a 3% tolerance to solve the AC power flow problem. Figure 4 shows the unifilar circuit of distribution power system and the power flow using Cymdist software.

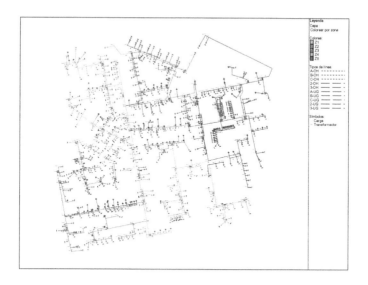

Fig. 4. CYME unifilar. Source: Author

Information about the most representative feeders in each zone is described. The length of the medium voltage main feeder of zone 1 is 1.23 Km; the low voltage secondary feeder has a length of 147 m and supplies 21 users, with a maximum voltage drop of 4.81 V in phase A. The length of the medium voltage main feeder of zone 2 is 1.53 Km; the low voltage secondary feeder has a length of 152 m and supplies 20 users, with a maximum voltage drop of 9.3 V in phase A. The length of the medium voltage main feeder of zone 3 is 0.72 Km; the low voltage secondary feeder has a length of 178 m and supplies 16 users, with a maximum voltage drop of 7.9 V in phase A. The length of the medium voltage main feeder of zone 4 is 1.22 Km; the low voltage secondary feeder has a length of 72 m and supplies 13 users, with a maximum voltage drop of 9.7 V in phase A. The length of the medium voltage main feeder of zone 5 is 0.52 Km; the low voltage secondary feeder has a length of 80 m and supplies 15 users, with a maximum voltage drop of 6.8 V in phase A. Figure 5 shows the phase voltage profiles in the five zones under consideration.

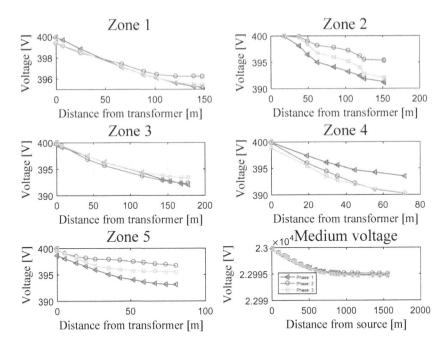

Fig. 5. Voltage profiles maximum lengths: (a) Zone 1: 21 users with 148 m, (b) Zone 2: 20 users with 154 m, (c) Zone 3: 26 users with 186 m, (d) Zone 4: 13 users with 76 m, (e) Zone 5: 15 users with 80 m. Source: Author

In the final analysis, none of the feeders should exceed the maximum length Lmax from the low voltage side of the transformer to the user meter. The medium voltage network should be deployed in order to connect all transformers that are required to provide coverage to 100% of the users. The proposed model uses N transformers to provide coverage to M users with loads ranging from 4 KW to 8 KW. It is important to remark that the power transmitted by the low voltage network is the sum of the power consumed from the transformers by the intermediate users. The installed load is 3810 KVA, distributed in 1272, 1268 and 1270 for phases A, B and C, respectively. The nominal medium voltage is 23000 VLL and 13279 VLN, and nominal currents are 97.6 A, 94.8 A and 94.5 A for phases A, B and C, respectively. Based on the results obtained with the power flow analysis in the distribution network, it can be concluded that there is a load balance between the phases.

The Table 1 presents a summary of the power flow analysis, including the power source, the load installed in each zone, the conductor ampacity, and the losses in lines, conductors and transformers.

Table 1. Summary of the power flow in the power distribution grid - Source: Authors

Total summary	Active Power [kW]	Reactive Power [kVAR]	FP [%]
Sources (Balance power)	3804,47	206,03	99,85
Total production	3804,47	206,03	99,85
Load Zone 1	629,98	87,65	99,05
Load Zone 2	634,97	14,57	99,97
Load Zone 3	930,95	14,42	99,99
Load Zone 4	447,99	−0,04	100
Load Zone 5	1092,93	81,4	99,72
Total loads	3736,82	198	99,86
Cable capacitance	0	158,08	0
Line capacitance	0	0	0
Total shunt capacitance	0	158.08	0
Losses in lines	30,93	24,69	78,16
Losses in cables	1,7	1,33	78,77
Losses in transformers	35,02	140,09	24,25
Total losses	67,65	166,1	37,72

5   Conclusions and Future Works

The proposed heuristic algorithm solves the np-complete problem of setcover, obtaining quasi-optimal results of the routing of electrical lines in medium and low voltage found the interconnections between users and active transformers. The algorithm found in a close to optimal manner the location of transformers and inspection wells deployed to supply electric power to a particular number of users involving geo-referenced zones with specific populations.

The problem of dimensioning the electrical distribution grid are solve by selecting a minimum number of spots for transformer locations from those candidate sites initially defined, considering constraints related to the rating of each transformer and the maximum grid radius of coverage. This optimization reduces the cost of infrastructure and implementation of the electrical distribution grid.

The simulation of the distribution grids with software Cymdist has been use to verify that all users are cover, while attaining power losses of about 1.8% of the total power flow, acceptable voltage profiles and maximum voltage drops of 3%.

This research is the first step for design resilient and reliable distribution networks with the inclusion of renewable energies.

Nomenclature

The Table 2 presents a summary of the power flow analysis, including the power source, the load installed in each zone, the conductor ampacity, and the losses in lines, conductors and transformers.

Table 2. Used variables

SETS	
Ω_u	Set of users in georeferenced area
Ω_{in}	Set of intersections in georeferenced area
Ω_s	Set of candidate sites for the location of transformation centers
Ω_Z	Set of active transformation centers

VARIABLES	
X^u, Y^u	Longitude and latitude of the i-th user
X^{in}, Y^{in}	Longitude and latitude of the i-th intersection
m_{con}	Connectivity matrix for the extraction of coordinates of intersections
S_e	Location of the electrical distribution substation
idx	Indices assigned to each user based on their cluster
m^{xy}	Location of medians obtained when applying K-medoids
m^u_{idx}	User matrix and assigned cluster index
tri	Matrix with the set of triangles formed in the triangulation delaunay
d_{eT}	Distances between transformers
gp	Graph obtained by applying the Prim algorithm
m_p^{MN}	Preliminary matrix of candidate sites and users
$solC$	Distribution Transformers and users with coverage
$solL$	Labels of the coverage matrix
T_i^{xy}	Coordinates of the i-th active transformer
$d_{u_i Z_j}$	Distance from user i to the transformer j
R_c	Electric resistance of the conductor
ΔV_u	Voltage loss per user
P_Z	Powers of transformers
C_1, C_2, C_3, C_4, C_5	Counters
S_{pt}	Adder
aux	Auxiliary variables

PARAMETERS	
N	Number of users
M	Number of candidate sites
N^{in}	Number of intersections
x^{se}, y^{se}	Longitude and latitude of the distribution substation
n_c	Number of regions for clustering
$clust$	Number of users belonging to the same cluster
C_{max}	Transformers maximum rating
D_{ct}	Minimum distance between transformers
M_{Tac}	Number of active transformers
ρ	Electrical resistivity of the employed conductor
S_c	Cross section of the employed driver
V_L	Line voltage in secondary circuit
Φ	Power factor

Conflict of Interest. The authors declare that there are no conflicts of interest regarding the publication of this paper.

References

1. Aghaei, J., Muttaqi, K.M., Azizivahed, A., Gitizadeh, M.: Distribution expansion planning considering reliability and security of energy using modified PSO (Particle Swarm Optimization) algorithm. Energy **65**, 398–411 (2014). https://doi.org/10.1016/j.energy.2013.10.082

2. Rad, H.K., Moravej, Z.: An approach for simultaneous distribution, sub-transmission, and transmission networks expansion planning. Int. J. Electr. Power Energy Syst. **91**, 166–182 (2017). https://doi.org/10.1016/j.ijepes.2017.03.010

3. Injeti, S.K., Prema Kumar, N.: A novel approach to identify optimal access point and capacity of multiple DGs in a small, medium and large scale radial distribution systems. Int. J. Electr. Power Energy Syst. **45**(1), 142–151 (2013). https://doi.org/10.1016/j.ijepes.2012.08.043

4. Gouin, V., Alvarez-Hérault, M.C., Raison, B.: Innovative planning method for the construction of electrical distribution network master plans. Sustain. Energy Grids Netw. **10**, 84–91 (2017). https://doi.org/10.1016/j.segan.2017.03.004

5. Zubo, R.H., Mokryani, G., Rajamani, H.S., Aghaei, J., Niknam, T., Pillai, P.: Operation and planning of distribution networks with integration of renewable distributed generators considering uncertainties: a review, May 2017. https://doi.org/10.1016/j.rser.2016.10.036. https://www.sciencedirect.com/science/article/pii/S1364032116306840

6. Mendoza, J.E., López, M.E., Peña, H.E., Labra, D.A.: Low voltage distribution optimization: site, quantity and size of distribution transformers. Electr. Power Syst. Res. **91**, 52–60 (2012). https://doi.org/10.1016/j.epsr.2012.05.004

7. Santos, M.M., Abaide, A.R., Sperandio, M.: Distribution networks expansion planning under the perspective of the locational transmission network use of system tariffs. Electr. Power Syst. Res. **128**, 123–133 (2015). https://doi.org/10.1016/j.epsr.2015.07.008

8. Abeysinghe, S., Wu, J., Sooriyabandara, M., Abeysekera, M., Xu, T., Wang, C.: Topological properties of medium voltage electricity distribution networks. Appl. Energy **210**, 1101–1112 (2018). https://doi.org/10.1016/j.apenergy.2017.06.113

9. Noussan, M.: Performance based approach for electricity generation in smart grids. Appl. Energy **220**, 231–241 (2018). https://doi.org/10.1016/j.apenergy.2018.03.092

10. Esmaili, M., Firozjaee, E.C., Shayanfar, H.A.: Optimal placement of distributed generations considering voltage stability and power losses with observing voltage-related constraints. Appl. Energy **113**, 1252–1260 (2014). https://doi.org/10.1016/j.apenergy.2013.09.004

11. Zubo, R.H.A., Mokryani, G., Abd-alhameed, R.: Optimal operation of distribution networks with high penetration of wind and solar power within a joint active and reactive distribution market environment. Appl. Energy **220**, 713–722 (2018). https://doi.org/10.1016/j.apenergy.2018.02.016

12. Mohandas, N., Balamurugan, R., Lakshminarasimman, L.: Optimal location and sizing of real power DG units to improve the voltage stability in the distribution system using ABC algorithm united with chaos. Int. J. Electr. Power Energy Syst. **66**, 41–52 (2015). https://doi.org/10.1016/j.ijepes.2014.10.033

13. Inga, J., Inga, E., Hincapié, R., Cristina, G.: Optimal planning for deployment of FiWi networks based on hybrid heuristic process. IEEE Lat. Am. Trans. (Revista IEEE America Latina) **15**(9), 1684–1690 (2017). https://doi.org/10.1109/TLA.2017.8015053

14. Masoum, M.A.S., Moses, P.S., Hajforoosh, S.: Distribution transformer stress in smart grid with coordinated charging of plug-in electric vehicles. In: 2012 IEEE PES Innovative Smart Grid Technologies (ISGT), pp. 1–8 (2011). https://doi.org/10.1109/ISGT.2012.6175685. https://ieeexplore.ieee.org/document/6175685/

15. Nagarajan, A., Ayyanar, R.: Application of minimum spanning tree algorithm for network reduction of distribution systems. In: 2014 North American Power Symposium (NAPS), pp. 1–5 (2014). https://doi.org/10.1109/NAPS.2014.6965353

16. Das, S., Das, D., Patra, A.: Reconfiguration of distribution networks with optimal placement of distributed generations in the presence of remote voltage controlled bus. Renew. Sustain. Energy Rev. **73**, 772–781 (2017). https://doi.org/10.1016/j.rser.2017.01.055

17. Phetlamphanh, V., Premrudeepreechacharn, S., Ngamsanroaj, K.: Technical losses reduction of electrical distribution system in Vientiane capital. In: 2012 International Conference on Renewable Energy Research and Applications, ICRERA 2012 - (Mv) (2012). https://doi.org/10.1109/ICRERA.2012.6477309

18. Tang, Y., Ayyanar, R.: Modeling and validation of a distribution system with high PV penetration using zone division method. In: IEEE PES T&D Conference and Exposition 2014, pp. 1–5 (2014). https://doi.org/10.1109/TDC.2014.6863357

19. Chouhan, S., Mohammadi, F.D., Feliachi, A., Solanki, J.M., Choudhry, M.A.: Hybrid MAS fault location, isolation, and restoration for smart distribution system with microgrids. In: IEEE Power and Energy Society General Meeting 2016, pp. 1–5, November 2016. https://doi.org/10.1109/PESGM.2016.7741213

20. Singh, B., Mishra, D.K.: DA survey on enhancement of power system performances by optimally placed DG in distribution networks. Energy Rep. **4**, 129–158 (2018). https://doi.org/10.1016/j.egyr.2018.01.004

21. de Oliveira, E.J., Rosseti, G.J., de Oliveira, L.W., Gomes, F.V., Peres, W.: New algorithm for reconfiguration and operating procedures in electric distribution systems. Int. J. Electr. Power Energy Syst. **57**, 129–134 (2014). https://doi.org/10.1016/j.ijepes.2013.11.038. http://linkinghub.elsevier.com/retrieve/pii/S0142061513004961

22. Li, H., Mao, W., Zhang, A., Li, C.: An improved distribution network reconfiguration method based on minimum spanning tree algorithm and heuristic rules. Int. J. Electr. Power Energy Syst. **82**, 466–473 (2016). https://doi.org/10.1016/j.ijepes.2016.04.017

23. Bretas, A., Cabral, R., Leborgne, R., Ferreira, G., Morales, J.: Multi-objective MILP model for distribution systems reliability optimization: a lightning protection system design approach. Int. J. Electr. Power Energy Syst. **98**. https://doi.org/10.1016/j.ijepes.2017.12.006

24. Sun, Y., Zhang, Y., Fang, B., Zhang, H.: Succinct and practical greedy embedding for geometric routing. Comput. Commun. **114**, 51–61 (2017). https://doi.org/10.1016/j.comcom.2017.10.014

Performance Analysis of a Direct-Expansion Solar-Assisted Heat Pump Using a Photovoltaic/Thermal System for Water Heating

William Quitiaquez[1]($\boxtimes$), Isaac Simbaña[1], C. A. Isaza-Roldán[2], César Nieto-Londoño[2], Patricio Quitiaquez[1], and Luis Toapanta-Ramos[1]

[1] Universidad Politécnica Salesiana, Quito 170607, Ecuador
wquitiaquez@ups.edu.ec
[2] Universidad Pontificia Bolivariana de Medellín, Medellín 050031, Colombia

Abstract. This work presents the performance of a direct-expansion solar-assisted heat pump (DX-SAHP) to supply 60 L per day of domestic hot water. The operating values in tests, such as refrigerant pressure and temperature, were taken in a built prototype every five minutes. The weather data measurements were obtained with a WS-1201 meteorological weather station and a CMP3 pyranometer. Boiling took place in a bare flat-plate solar collector using ambient temperature and the solar radiation intensity, with an emissivity value of 0.10. The system used a photovoltaic panel to turn on a variable speed compressor with 95 W of maximum power at 3600 rpm using R134a as working fluid. The measured condensation average temperature was 41.2 °C, meanwhile boiling temperature was 5.5 °C, gaining 252.8 W in the collector/evaporator and allowing releasing 335.8 W in the condenser while water reached a maximum temperature of 39.7 °C. In Test 1, when solar radiation had an average daily value of 607.5 W/m^2 with an average ambient temperature of 25.5 °C, water raised its temperature from 17.5 to 39.3 °C in 35 min. The maximum coefficient of performance (*COP*) of the system was 5.75 under rainy conditions in Test 2. Results showed that while the solar radiation intensity or ambient temperature were increased, the water heating time decreased. The environmental study also showed that by the implementation of the DX-SAHP, it could stop emitting 1065.6 kg of CO_2 per year due to the system using renewable energy for its working.

Keywords: Solar energy · R134a · Experimental analysis · Solar-assisted heat pump

1 Introduction

Climatic change and air pollution are the most significant environmental impacts generated by burning fossil fuels at industries, vehicles and domestic applications [1]. Due to the industrial growth, the greenhouse gas emissions have increased, where carbon dioxide (CO_2) is the main pollutant [2]. The worldwide energy consumption increases

© Springer Nature Switzerland AG 2020
F. R. Narváez et al. (Eds.): SmartTech-IC 2019, CCIS 1154, pp. 89–102, 2020.
https://doi.org/10.1007/978-3-030-46785-2_8

every year; primary energy consumption has grown an average of 2.2% in 2017, up 1.2% more than last year and the fastest since 2013, close to the 10-year average of 1.7% per year [3]. Nowadays continuous effort worldwide are focus to develop substitutes to traditional energy consumption appliances for new ones that use alternative energy sources (i.e. solar, wind and geothermal), with the aim of reducing CO_2 emissions associated with fuel fossil burning [4].

Current technology should adopt a sustainability perspective due to the global energy consumption increases every year, emitting more greenhouse gas emissions. Solar energy is a renewable energy source able to satisfy the energy demand. Domestic energy consumption covers about one-third of the global consumption, therefore, by implementing a solar-assisted system, it is going to conduce to a pollution reduction [5]. Domestic heating water devices are among the sources of pollution, regardless of the type of energy source that they use. A conventional electric water heater requires 5.5 kW to work for 20 min per day generating 226.6 kg of CO_2 each year [6]. The implementation of a direct-expansion solar-assisted heat pump (DX-SAHP) represents a reduction of 1065.6 kg of CO_2 emissions contributing to stop damaging the ozone layer [7]. Comparing a resistance water heater and a solar-assisted heat pump, the last one can save about 40 to 60% of energy consumption [8].

Yousefi and Moradali [9] investigated the thermodynamic performance of a DX-SAHP water heater. This system can heat water from 20 to 45 °C at an ambient temperature of 10 °C. The DX-SAHP system reached a *COP* of 8.25 with 900 W/m^2 of average solar radiation intensity. The rotational speed of the compressor has a significant influence in the performance by the system depending of the required parameters. Increasing the speed from 1100 to 1700 rpm, the *COP* decrease from 11 to 7, respectively, with an average solar radiation of 950 W/m^2.

Zhang et al. [10] developed a study about the effects of refrigerant charge and structural parameters on the performance of a DX-SAHP system. This investigation allowed affirming that the refrigerant is mainly in the heat exchangers; more of the 50% of the refrigerant is in the condenser, while the remaining 20–30% is in the collector. The refrigerant charge in the compressor was between 1.2 and 1.8 kg and with these values, the *COP* ranges between 36.7 and 42.3%, respectively. It is important to mention that the *COP* of the system depends of collector area; therefore, the *COP* decreases its value when collector area is increased.

Malali et al. [11] predicted the thermal performance of DX-SAHP systems for water heating applications by applying an approximate method. These types of solar pumps are more efficient than a conventional water heater having a significant energy conservation potential. CO_2 emissions reduce from 31 to 70% compared against a conventional electric water heater, giving COP values between 3.6 and 5.6. Despite that these values depends of the location; they will be better than the conventional systems.

Paradeshi et al. [12] performed parametric studies of a simple DX-SAHP operating in a hot and humid environment by using R22. The heating capacity is within the range of 2.09 to 3.57 kW with a 2 m^2 solar collector. This heat pump evidently depends of weather conditions, but there are other influencing factors, such as the materials and its geometric design. The system attains *COP* values between 2.09 to 2.72 depending on the season of the year and a larger collector's area could influence on the *COP*.

Zhu et al. [13] analyzed the characteristics of three types of solar collectors for a direct-expansion solar-assisted heat pump. They studied a bare plate collector, a glass plate collector and a double glass plate collector with a useful area of 1.82 m². The authors noted that the *COP* of the double glass plate collector is higher than just using the bare plate collector, the *COP* values are 3.47 to 3.26, respectively, because there is a higher energy absorption due to the glass. In other hand, they mentioned that the system performance was affected by solar radiation, although if the solar collector's area is larger, the system will earn more energy increasing *COP* value.

A mathematical model to evaluate the performance of a DX-SAHP is presented by De Leon-Ruiz and Carvajal-Mariscal [14]. This model compared with experimental tests presented a relative error of 20% validating it by using a statistical analysis to demonstrate that the relation between experimental and analytic results were within a 95%. The built model had 8 bare flat-plate solar collectors able to heat 300 L of water to a temperature about 51 °C in four hours using R134a as working fluid. The experimental tests took place for all the year, changing the refrigerant in different seasons to obtained similar results. R22 were used to get 150 L of heat water at 50 °C in two hours.

Therefore, this work presents the evaluation of a solar-assisted heat pump that uses the vapor-compression refrigeration cycle to harness the solar energy to generate domestic hot water. The obtained results are evaluated under three different weather conditions (i.e. clear, rainy and cloudy) at an altitude of 2850 m above sea level. Refrigerant properties are evaluated using Engineering Equation Solver software. The main objective is to study experimentally the performance of the DX-SAHP system. Parameters such as mass flow rate, water temperature, the *COP* variation, solar radiation and gained heat in the condenser are presented. The system studied in this work, differs from others found in the literature, due to use of a variable speed compressor powered by photovoltaic panels to supply the required electric energy and an environmentally friendly refrigerant. The inclusion of such a device like that, allows evaluating the effect of the compressor speed variation on the performance DX-SAHP operation.

This paper has the following structure. Section 2 presents the system description of the developed DX-SAHP. Section 3 details the used materials and methods about the theoretical background to present the energy balance of the components. Section 4 discusses the obtained experimental results. Finally, Sect. 5 shows conclusions about the obtained results.

2 System Description

A heat pump is a device that transfers heat from a low temperature source to a higher one by compressing a refrigerant. It keeps a heated space at a high temperature absorbing heat from a low temperature source. The developed system in this investigation is a direct-expansion solar-assisted heat pump that works with both, photovoltaic and thermal solar energy by using photovoltaic panels and a collector (Fig. 1).

Fine et al. [15] determined that the implementation of this kind of systems for domestic hot water production could reduce electric energy consumption 12% in comparison with conventional water heaters (i.e. an electric shower or burning fossil fuel heater). The refrigerant evaporates directly when the solar radiation is absorbed by the collector, allowing the working fluid to receive solar thermal energy and releasing it at the condenser [16]. Table 1 describes the characteristics of each component of this prototype. Manometers and thermocouples are installed at the inlet and outlet of each component to measure the refrigerant pressure and temperature.

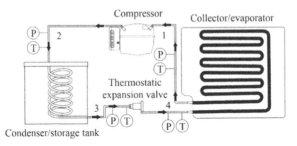

Fig. 1. DX-SAHP scheme (P is a manometer and T is a thermocouple).

Table 1. Components description.

System	Element	Description
Compressor	Only piston	Variable speed
	Rotational speed (max)	3500 [rpm]
	Volumetric displacement	2×10^{-6} [m^3]
	Refrigerant R134a (charge)	0.1 [kg]
Condenser	Water mass inside tank	5 [kg]
	Tank area	0.1261 [m^2]
	Outside pipe area	0.0394 [m^2]
Collector/Evaporator	Inside pipe area	0.0300 [m^2]
	Pipe thickness	7.62×10^{-4} [m]
	Thermal conductivity (Al)	237 [W/m·K]
	Plate area	1 [m^2]
	Plate thickness	0.0015 [m]
	Outside pipe diameter	0.01 [m]
	Distance between pipe	0.026 [m]

A heat pump works under a vapor-compression refrigeration cycle; therefore, this system is going to be studied with a thermodynamic analysis. The resulting superheated steam (state 1) is compressed until the condensation pressure (state 2) remaining in the superheat zone. After the heat is exchanged between the refrigerant and water, the refrigerant leaves the condenser (state 3). In an ideal process, there would be saturated liquid; however, the real process requires a subcooling step to increase the range of heat transfer in the condenser. The throttling process in the expansion valve (state 4) brings saturated liquid-steam mix of refrigerant to the collector/evaporator where it is evaporated. Finally, the refrigerant flows to evaporate while it absorbs solar thermal energy through the collector and the cycle starts again [11]. Figure 2 presents the *T-s* and *P-h* diagrams of the vapor-compression refrigeration cycle.

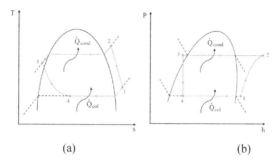

(a)   (b)

Fig. 2. Refrigeration cycle diagrams (a) *T-s*, (b) P-h.

Figure 3 describes the design of the heat pump, its sizing and correct operation in a vapor-compression refrigeration cycle by applying the mathematical modeling concerning to solar-assisted heat pumps and energy balances.

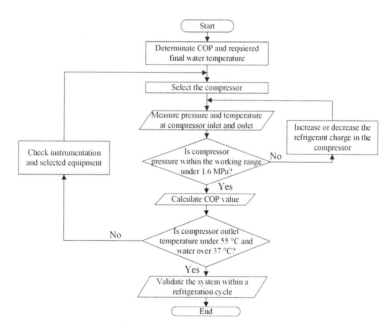

Fig. 3. Flow diagram of DX-SAHP.

3 Materials and Methods

The vapor-compression refrigeration cycle is used for the analytic study of this proto-type. To determine the *COP* of the system, it was necessary to apply global energy, mass and momentum balances over the system components by applying thermodynamic laws for each element. Enthalpies calculated with the measured refrigerant pressure and temperature by the installed instrumentation in the experimental system. The experimental tests let to measure parameters, such as ambient temperature, wind speed, operational pressures and temperatures, solar radiation. To select the days without carrying out a thermodynamic analysis, the solar radiation was considered due to it is the influential parameter on the performance of the system. The selected days had the highest solar radiation under different weather conditions.

3.1 Collector/Evaporator

Kong et al. [17] presented the mathematic analysis of a DX-SAHP that uses a bare flat-plate solar collector without insulation. The useful gained heat by the collector/evaporator ($\dot{Q}_{col}$) expressed as:

$$\dot{Q}_{col} = \dot{m} \left(h_{col,o} - h_{col,i} \right), \tag{1}$$

where $h_{col,o}$ and $h_{col,i}$ are the enthalpies of the refrigerant at the collector outlet and inlet, respectively, and $\dot{m}$ is the mass flow rate.

3.2 Compressor

In the energy balance reported by Moreno-Rodriguez et al. [18], the electric power consumption of compressor ($\dot{W}_{comp}$) can be evaluated by:

$$\dot{W}_{comp} = \dot{m} \left(h_{comp,o} - h_{comp,i} \right), \tag{2}$$

where $h_{comp,o}$ and $h_{comp,i}$ are the enthalpies of the refrigerant at the compressor outlet and inlet, respectively. Mass flow rate could calculate with the equation reported by Deng and Yu [19]:

$$\dot{m}_r = \frac{s_{rot} \, \eta_V \, V_d}{60 \, v_{suc}}, \tag{3}$$

where N is the rotatory compressor speed, V_d is the volumetric displacement, v_{suc} is the refrigerant specific volume at compressor inlet. According to Kong et al. [17] the volumetric efficiency (η_V) was:

$$\eta_V = 0,959 - 0,00642 \, \frac{P_o}{P_i}, \tag{4}$$

where P_i and P_o are the compressor pressures at inlet and outlet, respectively.

3.3 Condenser

The condenser is made of a copper coil pipe, submerged in the storage water tank. The energy balance in the condenser allowed knowing the heat gained ($\dot{Q}_{con}$), as follows [20]:

$$\dot{Q}_{con} = \dot{Q}_{col} + \dot{W}_{comp}, \tag{5}$$

3.4 Expansion Valve

In a thermostatic expansion valve, the throttling process is considered approximately isenthalpic, therefore, the energy balance is expressed as [21]:

$$h_{val,i} = h_{val,o}, \tag{6}$$

where $h_{val,o}$ and $h_{val,i}$ are the enthalpies of the refrigerant at the expansion valve outlet and inlet, respectively.

3.5 System Performance

The coefficient of performance could reach different values, depending the ambient air temperature, solar radiation, as well as the discharge temperature [11]. The *COP* is calculated by using the equation reported by Kokila and Rajakumar [22]:

$$COP = \frac{\dot{Q}_{con}}{\dot{W}_{comp}} = \frac{h_{con,o} - h_{con,i}}{h_{comp,o} - h_{comp,i}}, \tag{7}$$

4 Results

An analysis of a DX-SAHP was carried out testing it for almost 10 months under different weather conditions, from March to December to determine its *COP*, evaluating the heat transfer in the collector/evaporator and condenser. The system was studied within a vapor-compression refrigeration cycle, superheating the refrigerant at the compressor inlet and subcooling it at the condenser outlet. Results for water and average ambient temperature, average solar radiation, average wind speed and *COP* as shown in Table 2.

An aluminum bare flat plate with piping of 0.01 m of external diameter performs as collector/evaporator. Power is supplied by a variable speed compressor of 95 W that uses R134a as fluid work with a displacement of 2×10^{-6} m^3. A photovoltaic system is used to provide the required energy by the compressor. A potentiometer allowed controlling the increase or reduction of the rotatory speed. The condenser is a copper coil pipe, submerged in a water storage tank of five liters. The experimental analysis took place for almost one year, beginning every day at 10:00 to take data information even 5 min. Table 3 presents the representative values for average ambient temperature and solar radiation under different weather conditions. It also shows the measured parameters, compressor rotatory speed, maximum and minimum radiation, and water temperature.

Table 2. Experimental data.

Date [mm/dd/yy]	T_a [°C]	I [W/m^2]	w_s [m/s]	$T_{w,i}$ [°C]	$T_{w,o}$ [°C]
03/21/2018	25.5	607.5	0.2	17.5	39.3
04/05/2018	24.1	840.5	0.5	17.1	40.1
04/21/2018	24.3	796.0	0.1	17.0	39.0
05/10/2018	19.0	729.7	0.8	17.7	38.6
05/20/2018	24.1	584.3	0.2	17.3	37.9
06/05/2018	18.7	212.5	0.4	18.0	39.4
06/17/2018	19.3	177.3	0.8	17.5	40.9
07/04/2018	18.3	100.0	1.7	17.5	35.8
07/28/2018	20.4	594.5	0.1	17.6	37.3
08/15/2018	24.5	752.3	0.2	17.8	41.7
09/01/2018	24.6	771.2	0.8	17.5	39.1
09/15/2018	25.0	611.6	1.0	18.0	38.6
10/19/2018	22.4	539.8	0.6	17.5	39.4
11/14/2018	24.9	707.1	0.3	17.4	41.6
12/01/2018	25.1	772.7	0.2	17.5	42.8
12/21/2018	25.0	611.6	0.5	18.0	38.6

Table 3. Representative values for average ambient temperature and solar radiation.

	Test 1	Test 2	Test 3	Test 4	Test 5
Date	March-21	May-20	July-28	Sep-15	Dec-21
Weather condition	Clear	Rainy	Cloudy	Cloudy	Clear
Ambient temperature [°C]	25.5	19	20.4	21.2	25.0
Min. radiation [W/m^2]	407.9	429.6	406.3	392.3	401.1
Max. radiation [W/m^2]	841.9	850.0	797.4	809.1	758.0
Average radiation [W/m^2]	607.5	584.3	594.5	603.1	611.6
Max. water temp. [°C]	39.3	37.9	37.3	38.7	38.6

Temperature measurements is corroborated by using a Fluke Ti400 infrared camera and these images are checked in SmartView 3.7 software (Fig. 4), the estimated uncertainty has been provided for measurements of ±2%. Thus, it is possible to analyze the influence and effect of the refrigerant in each component of the DX-SAHP.

Several studies about DX-SAHP systems were considered to develop the present research [17, 21]. Results presented by Kong et al. [17] are similar to obtained results shown in Fig. 7, Fig. 8 and Fig. 9a where water temperature showed a gradual increasing

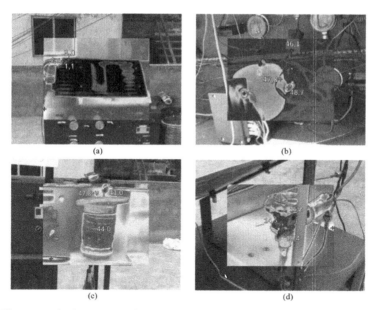

Fig. 4. Thermography images (a) collector/evaporator, (b) compressor, (c) condenser, (d) expansion valve.

and *COP* decreased gradually. Wang et al. [23] conducted a review of solar-assisted heat pumps noting the *COP* variation in function of the time and the compressor speed, as shown in Fig. 8 and Fig. 9b. Zhou et al. [24] carried out an experimental investigation of a direct-expansion heat pump presenting the variation of each operating parameter as function of time. Similar results about the gained heat over the collector/evaporator and condenser were obtained as shown in Fig. 5. Sun et al. [8] compared the performance of a solar-assisted heat pump and an air heat pump. They proved that *COP* reduces its value while the water temperature is increasing, similar to the Fig. 9a.

Sunrise is at 6:00 am and sunset at 6:00 pm approximately, reaching an average solar radiation value of 600 W/m^2 at noon due to the country location (i.e. longitude 78°31′29″ O, latitude 0°13′47″ S). Several experimental tests occurred throughout each day and the following results were of the most significant (e.g., between 11:50 to 12:25). Solar radiation heated the collector surface; a great percent is absorbed and transported to the working fluid to raise its temperature allowing the refrigerant boiling. Figure 5a shows that the maximum gained heat in the collector/evaporator was 314.24 W in a clear day (Test 1) and a minimum gained heat of 201.74 W. For this reason, different water temperatures were obtained, showing a difference no higher than 2 °C as shown in Fig. 7. The refrigerant flows from the collector/evaporator to the compressor, then to the condenser where the refrigerant released the gained heat to the water in the storage tank (Fig. 5b). The maximum gained heat in the condenser was 314.24 W under a clear day, water reached 39.3 °C and the *COP* attained a value of 3.89. Comparing the obtained results between clear and cloudy conditions, the average gained heat was an 11.53% lower, produced by the effect of weather conditions variation.

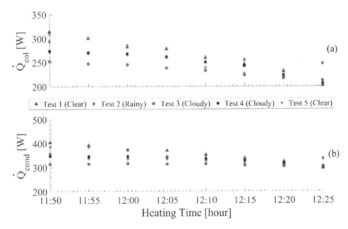

Fig. 5. Gained heat by the (a) collector/evaporator, (b) condenser/storage tank.

The compressor required an amount of energy depending of the system operation conditions at determinate instant. Considering the weather conditions for a clear day, the obtained results in the experimental test indicated that by increasing the $\dot{W}_{comp}$, $\dot{m}$ had a gradual increase trend. When $\dot{W}_{comp}$ increased from 76 to 93.7 W in Test 5, the $\dot{m}$ increased from 0.0085 to 0.0104 kg/s (as can be seen in Fig. 6) and the *COP* decreased from 5.08 to 3.25 in 35 min (Fig. 8).

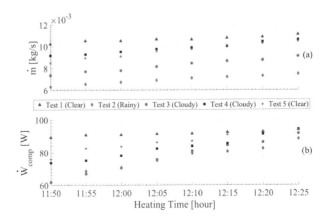

Fig. 6. Variation of the (a) mass flow rate, (b) compressor power.

The water temperature had a constant increase as shown in Fig. 7. This prototype can heat water until 39.3 °C in 35 min; during the tests, average water initial temperature was 17.6 °C. The increase in water temperature was a function of weather conditions; on a clear day (Test 1), there was an increase of 21.8 °C in water temperature, meanwhile during a cloudy day, the value is about 19.7 °C.

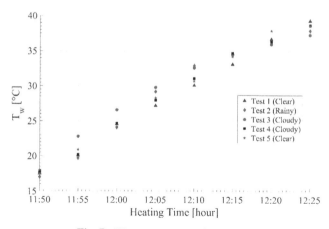

Fig. 7. Water temperature increasing.

The coefficient of performance relates the amount of released heat to the storage tank with the supplied energy in the form of work at the compressor. Due to the variable operation of the compressor, the *COP* of the system depend on the available solar radiation intensity. In other hand, an increase of the water tank temperature produces a decrease of the *COP* (Fig. 8). In Test 2, under rainy conditions, at 11:50, the *COP* value was 5.75 and water temperature was 17 °C, while at 12.25, the *COP* and water temperature values were 3.8 and 37.9 °C, respectively. Thus, it was notable the influence of water temperature in the *COP* of the system.

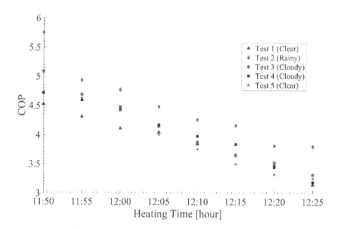

Fig. 8. Variation of COP with heating time

Figure 9a shows that the *COP* decrease with the passage of time, however when the water increases its temperature, the *COP* of the system also reduce. The rotational speed influence in the system performance inasmuch as increasing the compressor speed, the *COP* value decrease. Figure 9b presents the effect of the compressor speed variation on the system. By increasing the compressor speed from 1200 to 3500 rpm in a clear day, it results in a reduction of the *COP* of the system, from 4.52 to 3.15, meanwhile the water temperature reached 39.3 °C. Comparing the experimental results of the *COP* at different water temperatures in a clear and a rainy day, an increasing of 15.56% was reported on this last one.

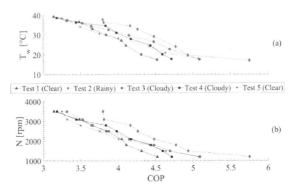

Fig. 9. COP in function of (a) water final temperature, (b) compressor speed.

Solar radiation influences the system performance directly due to when radiation intensity is higher, the *COP* also increased (as can be seen in Fig. 10a). In an experimental test, the solar radiation intensity fluctuated between 400 and 800 W/m^2 and the *COP* increased from 3.2 to 5.7. The behavior was similar with the water temperature because under these conditions, it increased from 17 to 38 °C (as can be seen in Fig. 10b).

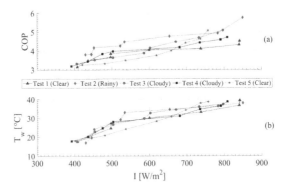

Fig. 10. Solar radiation against (a) COP, (b) final water temperature.

Therefore, the *COP* reduce in a 51.4% when the minimum and maximum water temperatures were 17 and 37.9 °C, respectively. Considering a clear day, water temperature raised from 17.5 to 39.3 °C and the *COP* decreased from 4.52 to 3.15. Results showed that when the solar radiation intensity or ambient temperature increase, the heating time decreased and the *COP* and water temperature increase.

5 Conclusions

A direct-expansion solar-assisted heat pump used to supply domestic hot water under different weather conditions was studied. A thermodynamic analysis was performed, and the following conclusions were obtained.

The thermal performance of the DX-SAHP system is affected directly by the weather conditions. The ideal conditions were in a clear day, with an average radiation of 607.5 W/m^2 and ambient temperature of 25.5 °C, where water raised up to 37 or 40 °C, depending the weather conditions. For non-favorable weather conditions (i.e. cloudy and rainy days), the final water temperature was 5.36% lower (i.e. 37.7 °C with 96.16% of the mentioned radiation).

Experimental tests were performed with a high solar radiation intensity due to the country location (i.e. longitude 78°31′29″ O, latitude 0°13′47″ S). It should be mentioned that the boiling flow took place in an aluminum bare flat-plate collector with an emissivity value of 0.10, being a parameter, which affects directly the system. This was shown in the system operation; when solar radiation increased, the *COP* of the system also increased. By increasing the compressor rotational speed, the *COP* decreased; at 1200 rpm on a clear day, the maximum *COP* was of 4.52, and when the compressor was working at 3500 rpm, the *COP* reduced its value by 30.31%.

References

1. Akhmat, G., Zaman, K., Shukui, T., Sajjad, F.: Does energy consumption contribute to climate change? Evidence from major regions of the world. Renew. Sustain. Energy Rev. **36**, 123–134 (2014)
2. Mondani, F., Aleagha, S., Khoramivafa, M., Ghobadi, R.: Evaluation of greenhouse gases emission based on energy consumption in wheat Agroecosystems. Energy Rep. **3**, 37–45 (2017)
3. BP, Statistical Review of World Energy. https://www.bp.com/en/global/corporate/energy-economics/statistical-review-of-world-energy.html. Accessed 30 June 2018
4. Lim, J., Chinnici, A., Dally, B., Nathan, G.: Assessment of the potential benefits and constraints of a hybrid solar receiver and combustor operated in the MILD combustion regime. Energy **116**, 735–745 (2016)
5. Kong, X., Jiang, K., Dong, S., Li, Y., Li, J.: Control strategy and experimental analysis of a direct-expansion solar-assisted heat pump water heater with R134a. Energy **145**, 17–24 (2018)
6. Parra, R.: Factor de emisión de CO2 debido a la generación de electricidad en el Ecuador durante el periodo 2001–2014. Av. Cien. Ing. **7**, 80–85 (2015)
7. Comisión Interdepartamental de Cambio Climático, Guía Práctica para el Cálculo de Emisiones de Gases de Efecto Invernadero. Oficina Catalana del Canvi Climatic, Catalunya (2011)
8. Sun, X., Dai, Y., Novakovic, V., Wu, J., Wang, R.: Performance comparison of direct expansion solar-assisted heat pump and conventional air source heat pump for domestic hot water. Energy Procedia **70**, 394–401 (2015)
9. Yousefi, M., Moradali, M.: Thermodynamic analysis of a direct expansion solar assisted heat pump water heater. J. Energy South. Afr. **26**, 110–117 (2015)

10. Zhang, D., Wu, Q.B., Li, J.P., Kong, X.Q.: Effects of refrigerant charge and structural parameters on the performance of a direct-expansion solar-assisted heat pump system. Appl. Therm. Eng. **73**, 522–528 (2014)
11. Malali, P., Chaturvedi, S., Abdel-Salam, T.: An approximate method for prediction of thermal performance of direct expansion-solar assisted heat pump (DX-SAHP) systems for water heating applications. Energy Conv. Manag. **127**, 416–423 (2016)
12. Paradeshi, L., Srinivas, M., Jayaraj, S.: Parametric studies of a simple direct expansion solar assisted heat pump operating in a hot and humid environment. Energy Procedia **90**, 635–644 (2016)
13. Zhu, M., Xie, H., Zhang, B., Guan, X.: The characteristics of the evaporator/evaporator for direct expansion solar assisted heat pump system. J. Power Energy Eng. **1**, 73–76 (2013)
14. De León-Ruiz, J., Carvajal-Mariscal, I.: Mathematical thermal modelling of a direct-expansion solar-assisted heat pump using multi-objective optimization based on the energy demand. Energies **11**, 2–27 (2018)
15. Fine, J.P., Friedman, J., Dworkin, S.B.: Detailed modeling of a novel photovoltaic thermal cascade heat pump. Renew. Energy **101**, 500–513 (2016)
16. Kamel, R.S., Fung, A.S.: Solar systems and their integration with heat pumps: a review. Energy Build. **87**, 1–41 (2014)
17. Kong, X.Q., Li, Y., Lin, L., Yang, Y.G.: Modeling evaluation of a direct-expansion solar assisted heat pump water heater using R410A. Int. J. Refrig **76**, 136–146 (2017)
18. Moreno-Rodríguez, A., García-Herando, N., González-Gil, A., Izquierdo, M.: Experimental validation of a theoretical model for a direct-expansion solar-assisted heat pump applied to heating. Energy **60**, 243–253 (2013)
19. Deng, W., Jianlin, Y.: Simulation analysis on dynamic performance of a combined solar/air dual source heat pump water heater. Energy Conv. Manag. **120**, 378–387 (2016)
20. Huang, W., Ji, J., Xu, N., Li, G.: Frosting characteristics and heating performance of a direct-expansion solar-assisted heat pump for space heating under frosting conditions. Appl. Energy **171**, 656–666 (2016)
21. Chen, J., Yu, L.: Theoretical analysis on a new direct expansion solar assisted ejector-compression heat pump cycle for water heater. Sol. Energy **142**, 299–307 (2017)
22. Kokila, R., Rajakumar, S.: Thermal performance analysis and optimization of solar assisted heat pump water heater. Appl. Mech. Mater. **592**, 2416–2421 (2014)
23. Wang, Z., Guo, P., Zhang, H., Yang, W., Mei, S.: Comprehensive review on the development of SAHP for domestic hot water. Renew. Sustain. Energy Rev. **72**, 871–881 (2017)
24. Zhou, J., et al.: Experimental investigation of a solar driven direct-expansion heat pump system employing the novel PV/micro-channels-evaporator modules. Appl. Energy **178**, 484–495 (2016)

Smart Systems

Enabling the Latent Semantic Analysis of Large-Scale Information Retrieval Datasets by Means of Out-of-Core Heterogeneous Systems

Gabriel A. León-Paredes[1]([📧]) [iD], Liliana I. Barbosa-Santillán[2] [iD],
and Antonio Pareja-Lora[3] [iD]

[1] Universidad Politécnica Salesiana, Cuenca 010102, Ecuador
`gleon@ups.edu.ec`
[2] Universidad de Guadalajara, 45100 Zapopan, Jalisco, Mexico
`ibarbosa@cucea.udg.mx`
[3] Universidad Complutense de Madrid, 28040 Madrid, Spain
`aplora@ucm.es`

Abstract. Latent Semantic Analysis (LSA) has already been widely and successfully applied in many applications for Natural Language Processing (NLP), usually working with fairly small or average sized datasets and no actual time constraints. Even so, LSA is a high time and space consuming task, which complicates its integration in real-time NLP applications (as, for example, information retrieval or question answering) on large-scale datasets. For this reason, an implementation of LSA that can both allow and accelerate as much as possible its execution on large-scale datasets would be most useful in these data-intensive, real-time NLP scenarios. However, to the best of our knowledge, such an implementation of LSA has not been achieved so far.

Towards this end, a new, out-of-core, scalable, heterogeneous LSA (hLSA) system has been built and run on the clinical decision support large-scale dataset from the Text REtrieval Conference (TREC) 2015 competition. Results show that the out-of-core hLSA system can process this large-scale dataset (that is, 631,302 documents) with a full-ranked term-document matrix of 566 GB fairly fast and, besides, with a better precision (at least for one of the topics) than the TREC 2015 competing systems.

Keywords: GPU · Multi-CPU · Heterogeneous system · Information retrieval · Distributed system · Latent Semantic Analysis · Parallel computing · Question answering

1   Introduction

Latent Semantic Analysis (LSA) is a mathematical method widely and successfully applied so far in many applications for Natural Language Processing

© Springer Nature Switzerland AG 2020
F. R. Narváez et al. (Eds.): SmartTech-IC 2019, CCIS 1154, pp. 105–119, 2020.
https://doi.org/10.1007/978-3-030-46785-2_9

(NLP) [1,4,11,13]. Firstly, LSA creates a semantic vector space based on a term-document matrix constructed from a training corpus. Then, secondly, it applies the Singular Value Decomposition (SVD) algorithm on this matrix to reflect the major associative patterns in the data. And, thirdly, it reduces its complexity and/or dimensionality by truncating it to the first k values.

One of the fields of NLP where LSA has already been used is information retrieval [1–3,5,6,8]. However, LSA is a high time and space consuming task. Thus, applying LSA to retrieve information from a large-scale dataset is still an open issue, since (1) the amount of memory required to create, reduce and use the different matrices associated with the standard (*i.e.*, sequential) LSA algorithm is larger than the largest main memory available nowadays; and (2) the amount of time required for this process to run in these circumstances does not allow relevant information retrieval systems, such as Question/Answer (Q&A) systems, to respond in real time.

Even so, some steps have already been taken towards solving this problem. For example, [7] presents a Heterogeneous Latent Semantic Analysis (hLSA[1]) system that is eight times faster than the standard LSA version, when run on a dataset of 5,000 documents. Nonetheless, this hLSA system had quite a reduced scalability and could not be used to process a dataset of some hundred thousand documents (as it is usually required in real-world scenarios). Therefore, thus far, the problem of retrieving information from large-scale datasets in a reasonable time using LSA has remained unsolved.

Accordingly, the goal of this work has been to solve such a hard problem by means of an hLSA system. In other words, this work shows that an hLSA system can process a large-scale dataset and retrieve some information from it fairly fast (thanks to its multi-CPU and GPU architectures). Towards this end, a new, out-of-core, more scalable hLSA system has been built and run on the large-scale dataset from the Text REtrieval Conference, 2015 (TREC 2015) for clinical decision support.

The results obtained with this new out-of-core hLSA system show that it can process this large-scale dataset (containing 631,302 documents) in a reasonable time. In particular, (a) the LSA reduced semantic vector space can be created in approx. 2 h; and (2) the out-of-core hLSA system can retrieve the most similar documents for some test queries in 4 min (averagely) when using some lower k values. In addition, even though this has not been the main aim of this research, the answers of the out-of-core hLSA system have been fairly adequate. Indeed, it has been found out that (i) for at least one topic, this out-of-core hLSA system is more precise than the most precise TREC 2015 competing systems; and (ii) for eight topics, this LSA implementation provides better or similar precision values than the median precision values of the TREC 2015 competition.

The rest of the paper has been organized as follows. Section 2 introduces some related works. In Sect. 3, the new out-of-core hLSA system built to solve this problem is presented. Section 4 describes the experiments carried out with

---

[1] An hLSA system integrates multi-CPU and GPU architectures in order to accelerate the execution of the LSA algorithm.

this out-of-core hLSA system on information retrieval with large-scale datasets, and discusses the results of these experiments. Finally, Sect. 5 summarizes the conclusions drawn from this work.

2   Related Works

This section presents some previous works that have tried to solve the scalability challenge of the LSA algorithm. To start with, [12] presents a technique, called *index interpolation*, that efficiently calculates the term cooccurrence matrix for large document collections (*i.e.*, the first phase of the standard LSA algorithm). The associated symmetric eigenvector problem is then solved by distributing its computation among any number of computational units without increasing the overall number of multiplications[2]. One of the experiments carried out with this system, with a term-document matrix of around 6.1 GB (only non-zero values), 300,000 terms and 300 eigenvectors, could be executed (i) in 42.5 h on 16 CPUs; and (ii) in 493 h on one CPU. Yet, no matter how good these results are, this work did not aim at a complete execution of the LSA algorithm on large-scale datasets. Besides, the documents in the dataset consisted basically of lists of terms (they were no real documents).

Besides, and rather independently, a distributed algorithm for incremental SVD updates [9] was developed to efficiently compute the SVD in a distributed architecture so as to support the execution of LSA on large datasets with a more realistic content. This algorithm was then run on a large corpus that contains 3.2 million documents and 100,000 terms, which could be represented as a sparse term-document matrix of 0.5 GB (only non-zero entries). It took 8.5 h to complete this experiment using a single commodity laptop with a one-pass online algorithm. Using six nodes, the execution time dropped to 2 h 23 min. Nevertheless, these performance results comprise only the SVD updates. In effect, no results of this experiment were reported on a full execution of the LSA algorithm or on the whole information retrieval task. In fact, the goal of this work was, basically, to propose a quicker and more scalable algorithm to obtain a SVD for a pretty large term-document matrix.

Therefore, even though these previous works provide quite interesting and promising results on processing large-scale datasets using LSA, they are only partial as for the whole set of tasks of LSA computation and/or information retrieval. And yet, to the best of our knowledge, no more ambitious works have ever been carried out so far. Table 1 shows some comparisons referring to the scalability and phases of the LSA algorithm covered by these two previous proposals, as well as our proposed out-of-core hLSA system. Further and more detailed comparisons (such as execution times, memory space consumed, etc.) cannot be performed, since (1) these data are not provided by the researchers who carried out the corresponding works; (2) their experiments cannot be replicated so that these parameters can be obtained; (3) their datasets are not

---

[2] This computation is performed (sequentially) in the third phase of the standard LSA algorithm.

publicly available and, hence, the out-of-core hLSA system cannot be executed on them for a suitable comparison; (4) the contents of their datasets have a lower complexity; and/or (5) their systems cannot be run on the datasets used in the experiments described in this paper (either because their source code is not open or because it would require a big amount of reprogramming).

Table 1. Scalability and coverage comparisons with previous approaches, systems and/or results as for the LSA algorithm executions

	[12] Vigna (2008)	[9] Řehůřek (2011)	out-of-core hLSA system
Phase (0) Document reading and parsing	No	Yes	Yes
Phase (a) List of token calculation (Yes/No)	No	No	Yes
Phase (b) Semantic vector space creation (Yes/No)	Yes	Yes	Yes
Phase (c) Semantic vector space normalization (Yes/No)	No	No	Yes
Phase (d) Semantic vector space reduction (SVD) (Yes/No)	Yes	Yes	Yes
Phase (e) Document/information retrieval (Yes/No)	No	No	Yes
Executes the whole LSA algorithm (Yes/No)	No	No	Yes
Scalability for large-scale datasets	Yes	Yes	Yes
Type of algorithm	Distributed	Distributed	Batch-Based GPU/Multi-CPU

3   The Out-of-Core Heterogeneous Latent Semantic Analysis (hLSA) System

A new, out-of-core, more scalable hLSA system had to be built in order to show that, indeed, the LSA algorithm can process a large-scale dataset and retrieve some information fairly fast from it. However, developing this system has entailed facing previously some other challenges. First, in order to train the model, the system has to (a) obtain the list of tokens (terms) from the large-scale dataset, (b) create a semantic vector space using a term-document matrix, (c) normalize the semantic vector space (e.g., using the weighting scheme: Term Frequency - Inverse Document Frequency) and (d) reduce the semantic vector space using the SVD algorithm. Second, in order to test the model, the system needs to (e) retrieve the most similar documents from the reduced semantic vector space.

Hence, each of these five challenges mentioned above ((a) to (e)) have been faced in a dedicated phase of the out-of-core hLSA system architecture as described below.

Phase (a): Obtaining the List of Tokens from the Large-Scale Dataset
For the purpose of generating the term-document matrix, the out-of-core hLSA system needs to obtain a list of unique terms gathered from the large-scale dataset. In the original LSA algorithm, the list of terms that indexes the rows of the term-document matrix is calculated dynamically, together with the matrix itself. However, this is not feasible and/or efficient when LSA is applied on large-scale datasets. Indeed, this list of terms or tokens has to be previously obtained by the out-of-core hLSA system due to two main reasons, namely (i) memory limitations; and (ii) new restrictions imposed by the parallelization and distribution of the LSA algorithm.

Therefore, the documents of the dataset have to be grouped and processed in small subsets (each subset at a time and, in general, in different cores of the architecture). As a result, new restrictions emerge for the parallelization and distribution of the LSA algorithm, concerning the calculation of the term-frequency matrix. Indeed, processing the dataset documents in this distributed way complicates and/or makes it fairly inefficient to calculate the term-document matrix in just one go, since it would require to keep it somehow in main memory as well. In effect, firstly, all the cores would have to access and update it anytime, which would both (i) overload the communication and the main memory subsystems of the architecture, and (ii) result in a poor performance. Secondly, specifying the calculation of the term-frequency matrix in terms of a straightforward divide-and-conquer scheme (the obvious approach for the parallelization and distribution of this algorithm) implies a quite inefficient specification of its merging procedure (as for time and memory space), which makes inefficient as well a whole straightforward divide-and-conquer solution specification. Then again, implementing this inefficient specification would result in a poor performance of the system.

Thus, the calculation of the term-document matrix was divided into two different phases. In the first one (that is, in (a)), the list of [relevant] tokens (or, equivalently, of document terms) is determined; and, in the second one (i.e., (b)), these tokens are used to calculate the term-frequency matrix and index its rows.

Phase (b): Creating a Semantic Vector Space Using a Term-Document Matrix
In this stage, the out-of-core hLSA system creates a semantic vector space. To begin with, it divides dynamically the document set into multiple subsets of a similar size, as in phase (a). Then, each subset is processed by the multi-CPU architecture, where each core is responsible for running concurrently an instance of the *Bag_of_words* model [14].

When the *Bag_of_words* model has been completely run in each core, the out-of-core hLSA system takes the list of term-frequency pairs and saves it in a term-document sparse matrix in CSR/CSC format, where only the non-zero values are taken into account to save some memory space. For optimization purposes, the out-of-core hLSA system uses a Hierarchical Data Format[3] (HDF) to save and manage the sparse matrix.

Phase (c): Normalizing the Semantic Vector Space
The out-of-core hLSA system converts the raw frequency counts of the term-document sparse matrix into TF-IDF (Term Frequency - Inverse Document Frequency) values. The TF-IDF scheme takes the number of occurrences ($A_{t,d}$) of each term (t) in the list of the T terms [previously obtained] within each document (d) of the large-scale dataset, and normalizes it with respect to (i) the total number of occurrences of the T terms in the same document; (ii) the total number of documents (D) in the dataset; and, (iii) the total number of occurrences of the term t across the whole document dataset.

Thus, TF-IDF calculates the weight ($W_{t,d}$) of each and every term in the corpus (the document dataset) using the following formula:

$$W_{t,d} = \frac{A_{t,d}}{\sum_{i=1}^{T} A_{i,d}} \times log(\frac{D}{\sum_{j=1}^{D} A_{t,j}}) \tag{1}$$

In this phase, the out-of-core hLSA system takes advantage of the GPU capabilities in order to enable and speed up this processing of the large-scale sparse matrix. Firstly, the hierarchical data associated to the matrix are obtained, and then provided as input to a GPU kernel function. Towards this end, the GPU executions include CUDA kernels and CUDA functions using a floating-point representation for numbers. Each CUDA core is in charge of normalizing the raw frequencies of all the terms in a document. Finally, the normalized/weighted sparse matrix is saved using the Hierarchical Data Format again.

Phase (d): Reducing the Semantic Vector Space Using the SVD Algorithm
Then, the out-of-core hLSA system has to calculate the SVD (Singular Value Decomposition) of $P_{t \times d}$, the TF-IDF matrix obtained in the previous phase, as with the original LSA algorithm. SVD is applied on LSA to obtain a rank reduced approximation of the large-scale matrix obtained in phase (c). In our case, this is achieved by obtaining the following factorization of $P_{t \times d}$:

$$P_{t \times d} = U_{t \times t} \cdot S_{t \times d} \cdot V^{T}{}_{d \times d} \tag{2}$$

where $U_{t \times t}$ and $V^{T}{}_{d \times d}$ are orthogonal matrices whose columns contain, respectively, the left-singular and the right-singular vectors of $P_{t \times d}$; and $S_{t \times d}$ is a diagonal matrix that lists its singular values in descending order. Subsequently, in order to reduce the semantic vector space, the out-of-core hLSA system truncates the three resultant SVD matrices into their first k dimensions, which helps saving both memory space and processing time.

---

[3] HDF is a data model, library, and file format for storing and managing data. It was designed for flexible and efficient input/output access to big and/or complex data. For further info., see https://support.hdfgroup.org/HDF5/.

Thus, as previously mentioned, in this phase, the out-of-core hLSA system has to truncate the SVD for the large-scale dataset. The input for this phase is the term-document sparse matrix that has been created in phase (b) and normalized by the TF-IDF weighted scheme in phase (c). This matrix summarizes and generates the semantic vector space that represents the large-scale document dataset and, as described above, it is saved in CSR/CSC format.

Nevertheless, calculating the SVD associated to large-scale matrices has a very high computational cost and requires some preprocessing to be conveniently accomplished. Therefore, firstly, the out-of-core hLSA system divides the term-document sparse matrix, $P_{t \times d}$, by column-partitioning it into X sub-matrices, where X equals the total number of documents (D) divided by the k factor (that is, $X = D$ **div** k). Secondly, each sub-matrix is transformed into a full-ranked matrix of size $t \times k$. Accordingly,

$$P^{t \times d} = \sum_{i=1}^{X} P_i^{t \times k} \tag{3}$$

Thirdly, the system calculates the SVD of each $P_i^{t \times k}$ sub-matrix. Also in this case, the out-of-core hLSA system benefits from the GPU architecture capabilities to enable and accelerate these calculations. Towards this end, the out-of-core hLSA system decomposes each sub-matrix and retains in GPU memory only the $U_i^{t \times k}$ matrix and the $S_i^{k \times k}$ diagonal matrix, whereas the $(V_i^{k \times d})^T$ matrix is discarded to save memory space for other computations in this phase.

Finally, the out-of-core hLSA system has to merge into a single decomposition all the resulting SVD sub-matrices. In order to do this merging, the out-of-core hLSA system implements the optimized merge algorithm that is described in [9] in thx e GPU architecture.

Phase (e): Retrieving the Most Similar Documents from the Reduced Semantic Vector Space

In this phase, the out-of-core hLSA system takes a user query as input and retrieves the most similar documents in the large-scale dataset using the cosine similarity measure. Towards this end, the out-of-core hLSA system sends the user query to the *tokenizer* algorithm in the multi-CPU architecture, and obtains the unique terms of the user query that are included in the list of tokens of the large-scale dataset documents as shown in Fig. 1.

When the multi-CPU architecture has completed the execution of the *tokenizer* algorithm, the out-of-core hLSA system outputs a vector query, $\boldsymbol{Q}_t$. Accordingly, the out-of-core hLSA system benefits one more time of the GPU architecture capabilities to project the query vector onto the reduced semantic vector space, by applying the following transformation scheme:

$$q_k = \boldsymbol{Q}_t \cdot U_{t \times k} \cdot S_{k \times k}^{-1} \tag{4}$$

In order to retrieve the most similar documents, the out-of-core hLSA system has to find the similarity between the $\boldsymbol{q}_k$ vector and each of the documents in the large-scale dataset. Therefore, the out-of-core hLSA system needs the V^T

matrix, where each column represents a document from the large-scale dataset in the reduced semantic vector space. However, the V^T matrix was discarded in the previous stage. Thus, the V^T matrix has to be recalculated using the formula

$$V_{k \times d}^T = S_{k \times k}^{-1} \cdot U_{t \times k}^T \cdot P_{t \times d} \tag{5}$$

But then again, as the out-of-core hLSA system has to process large-scale datasets, it cannot keep the original P matrix in memory either, due to lack of space. Therefore, the out-of-core hLSA system relies one more time on the GPU architecture capabilities to recover the P matrix and to compute the V^T matrix using batch-processing. Each batch takes N columns from the P matrix and computes the V^T matrix. With the V^T matrix in the GPU memory, the out-of-core hLSA system can find the similarity between the q_k vector and each d_i vector, where d_i corresponds to a column-vector of the V^T matrix.

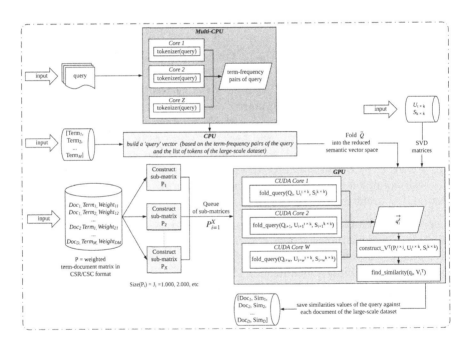

Fig. 1. The architecture implemented in the out-of-core hLSA system to retrieve the most similar documents from the reduced semantic vector space, using the cosine similarity measure.

4   Experiments and Results

This section presents the results of the experiments carried out in order to evaluate the performance of the out-of-core hLSA system presented in the previous section. Thus, the experiments have been executed on a Linux Open-SUSE 13.2

(3.16.6-2 kernel) system with Core i7-4710HQ Intel processors at 2.50 GHz with 16 GB DDR3L of main memory and 4 cores and an NVIDIA GeForce GTX 970M. The GPU has 10 streaming multiprocessors (SMs) with 128 CUDA cores for each SM, that is, 1280 CUDA cores in total. The GPU global memory space amounts to 3064 Mbytes in total and the GPU clock speed has been 2.5 GHz.

The experiments conducted with the out-of-core hLSA system have taken as input one of the large-scale datasets from the Text REtrieval Conferences (TREC). The TREC 2015 collection contains 733,138 articles compiled on January 21, 2014, and it is divided into four bundles, which can be downloaded from http://trec-cds.appspot.com/2015.html.

Also, four term-document matrices have been created, each one corresponding to one of the four values for the minimum number of word occurrences ($f_m = 5, 15, 25, 50$). Moreover, eight different values (k = 75, 175, 275, 300, 375, 500, 750, 1,000) have been defined for the parameter k, which refers to the number of dimensions into which the SVD of the term-document matrix is truncated. These values have been empirically and incrementally determined, while looking for the one(s) that provided a better global document retrieval precision. The out-of-core hLSA system has been executed thirty-two times and each time it has read and processed the documents from the large-scale dataset in batches of 20,000 documents. Table 2 shows some relevant statistics for the four term-document matrices created by the out-of-core hLSA system in this way.

Table 2. Some relevant statistics for the 4 term-document matrices created by the out-of-core hLSA system.

Term-document matrix number	Min. required frequency of terms (f_m)	Total number of tokens	Non-zero values	Size of non-zero values (Gb)	Size of sparse term-document matrix (Gb)
1	5	112,039	49,813,914	0.40	566
2	15	28,563	47,601,540	0.38	144
3	25	16,974	45,987,551	0.37	86
4	50	9,063	43,101,901	0.34	46

4.1 Results Regarding the Execution Time

Three different results regarding the out-of-core hLSA system execution times are presented and discussed here, namely the execution times for the part of the experiments relating (i) the creation of the term-document matrices; (ii) the calculation of their respective (truncated) SVDs; and (iii) the information (or document) retrieval task itself.

Thus, to begin with, Table 3 shows the respective execution times for each of the phases implemented in the out-of-core hLSA system to create the four term-document matrices (that is, phases (a) to (c) –see Sect. 3– plus a previous phase to read and parse the documents, henceforth referred to as phase (0)).

Table 3. Results – Execution times of the whole term-document matrix creation task in the out-of-core hLSA system (using a multi-CPU architecture with 4 processors).

Term-document matrix number	Phase (0) Document reading & parsing (hours)	Phase (a) List of token creation (secs.)	Phase (b) Term-document matrix construction (mins.)	Phase (c) Normalization with TF-IDF scheme (mins.)	Total execution time (hours)
1	1.10	3.26	1.94	1.12	1.15
2	1.10	1.37	1.82	1.02	1.15
3	1.10	0.96	1.77	0.99	1.15
4	1.10	0.57	1.65	0.92	1.15

As it can be observed in Table 3, firstly, the computational cost of the system training task is dominated by the document reading procedure. Averagely, the out-of-core hLSA system reads a batch of 20,000 documents in 1.82 min, parses these 20,000 documents in 15.57 s, and creates the term-document sub-matrix for this batch in 3.70 s.

Secondly, phase (0) (that is, the read and parse phase) deals with the same input data for the creation of the four term-document matrix. This is why the execution times of this phase are the same for the four matrices.

Thirdly, the out-of-core hLSA system shows different execution times for the rest of phases (or, equivalently, the columns in Table 3) because of the minimum frequency (f_m) required to include terms in the token list. Obviously, as expected, the higher f_m is, the less number of tokens to be included in the token list and, hence, the less time elapsed (i) to build this list (phase (a)); (ii) to create the term-document matrices (phase (b)); and (iii) to apply the TF-IDF scheme to them (phase (c)).

Fourthly, the out-of-core hLSA system keeps the documents read in the CPU memory to re-process them again together with the list of tokens, in order to create the term-document matrix (phase (b)). Due to this, the execution times for the four matrices in this phase show only slight differences.

Fifthly, in phase (c), the TF-IDF weighting scheme is applied by the out-of-core hLSA system to the non-zero values of the four term-document matrix in order to create the respective semantic vector spaces. This phase is completely run in approximately one second.

Finally, in spite of the few time spent by the system to run phases (a) to (c), this time is almost negligible when compared to the total execution time. Indeed, the total execution time needed to create the term-document matrix is around 1.15 h, whereas the highest time to compute any of these three phases is lower than 2 min.

Then, concerning the execution times of phase (d), that is, the calculation of the (truncated) SVDs for the four term-document matrices, they are summarized in Table 4. For this phase, eight k values have been defined for the truncation of these four matrices ($k = 75, 175, 275, 300, 375, 500, 750, 1,000$). These values

Table 4. Results – Execution times for the computation of the four term-document matrix truncated SVDs ($k = 75, 1000$) in the out-of-core hLSA system (with a GPU architecture and a multi-CPU architecture with four processors).

Term-document matrix number	Number of sub-matrices	Number of rows per sub-matrix	Sub-matrix Size (MB)	Truncated SVD total execution time (hours)
Number of columns in each sub-matrix = $k = 75$				
1	8418	112039	67	1.44
2	8418	28563	17	0.68
3	8418	16974	10	0.61
4	8418	9063	5	0.56
Number of columns in each sub-matrix = $k = 1000$				
1	632	112039	896	1.83
2	632	28563	229	0.61
3	632	16974	136	0.47
4	632	9063	73	0.38

have been empirically and incrementally determined, while looking for the one(s) that provided a better global document retrieval precision.

Thus, the SVD phase was run on each term-document matrix with each k truncation value, which makes a total of 32 executions in order to create the reduced semantic vector spaces. However, Table 4 includes only the execution times referring to the lowest and highest k truncation values for the four term-document matrices. These execution times are the most representative of the system performance.

As it can be observed in this table, quite surprisingly, the out-of-core hLSA system has an overall better performance (in terms of a lower total execution time) for higher values of k when running on the same input matrix, due to the use of the GPU architecture. This entails that using low values of k when truncating the matrices might not only reduce the precision of the system, but also its speed.

Lastly, regarding the execution times for the document retrieval task itself (phase (e)), they are also summarized in Table 5. In this case, the out-of-core hLSA system was run for 30 querying documents in order to retrieve the most similar documents using as input each of the 32 reduced semantic vector spaces. Thus, the out-of-core system was executed 960 times in total to complete this series of experiments. Table 5 includes only the execution times referring to the lowest and highest k truncation values for the four term-document matrices (*i.e.*, $k = 75$ and $k = 1,000$).

As it can be observed in this table, the execution time of the phase (e) of the out-of-core hLSA system depends much more than the previous phases on the size of the input matrix. Indeed, for a given truncation value (k), the lowest execution time corresponds to the smallest input matrix (that is, matrix 4, the one with a highest term minimum frequency, $f_m = 50$, and thus, with the lowest dimension as for terms). Analogously, for a given input matrix, the lowest

Table 5. Results – Execution times for the task of document retrieval in the out-of-core hLSA system, using the 4 term-document matrices truncated to $k = 75, 1000$ columns (with a GPU architecture and a multi-CPU architecture with four processors).

Term-document matrix number	Total execution time for all topics (hours)	Average execution time per topic (mins.)
Number of columns in each sub-matrix = $k = 75$		
1	2.94	5.88
2	1.90	3.80
3	1.77	3.54
4	1.60	3.21
Number of columns in each sub-matrix = $k = 1000$		
1	5.84	11.69
2	2.64	5.28
3	2.23	4.45
4	1.94	3.88

execution time corresponds to the smallest truncation value ($k = 75$), that is, to the truncated matrix with less columns.

4.2 Results Regarding the Precision of the System

In order to evaluate the precision of the out-of-core hLSA system when retrieving documents from the large-scale dataset for a given query, the standard TREC evaluation procedures for retrieval tasks [10] have been followed. Towards this end, each of the nine-hundred-sixty executions discussed above has been scored according to four measures, $i.e.$, its precision at 10 ($P@10$), its R-precision (R-$prec$), its inferred normalized discounted cumulative gain ($infNDCG$) and its inferred average precision ($infAP$). Then, these scores have been compared to the median precision values of the one-hundred-three submissions that competed within Task A of TREC 2015.

As shown in Fig. 2, the precision values obtained after retrieving the 30 querying documents with the out-of-core hLSA system are not better than the average TREC 2015 results. Nevertheless, it should be noted that the primary metric for comparing the retrieval submissions in the TREC 2015 Clinical Decision Support track was, in fact, the $infNDCG$ measure, according to which the out-of-core hLSA system retrieves some relevant document in 96.7% of cases.

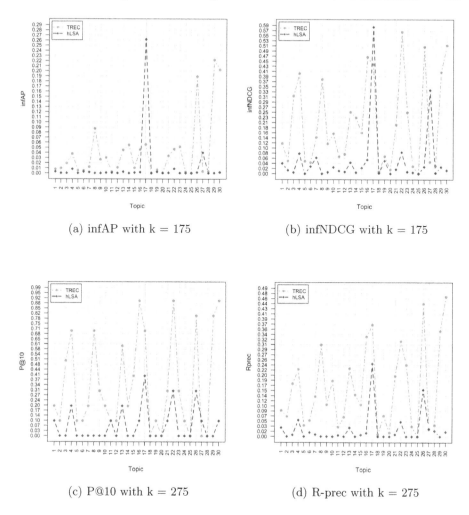

(a) infAP with k = 175

(b) infNDCG with k = 175

(c) P@10 with k = 275

(d) R-prec with k = 275

Fig. 2. Results – Best values for the 4 precision measures obtained with the out-of-core hLSA system (for term-document matrix #2, the 8 truncation values of k), compared with the analogous median precision values of the 103 submissions for Task A of the TREC 2015 Clinical Decision Support Track.

5   Conclusions

This paper proposes a new out-of-core heterogeneous latent semantic analysis system able to process large-scale datasets for information retrieval.

The results show that the integration of batch processing and the use of multi-CPU and GPU architectures reduces the execution time of the system and improves its capability of processing and retrieving documents from a large-scale dataset, even though it may be too large to fit altogether in the main CPU memory. In effect, in this work, a system has been implemented according to the design described in Sect. 3. This system includes four processors in a multi-CPU architecture as well as one-thousand-two-hundred-eighty CUDA cores in a GPU architecture, and has been tested by running it in several experiments on a well-know TREC 2015 large-scale dataset (containing more than 600,000 valid documents). The results obtained have also shown that (i) creating the semantic vector space takes 1.15 h; (ii) reducing it takes the out-of-core hLSA system just 0.82 h (averagely); and (iii) retrieving the most similar documents for a query (document) takes the out-of-core hLSA system only 4 min (averagely) when using lower k (truncation) values – which is the actual relevant time as for its use in real-time scenarios.

However, the performance as for precision of the out-of-core hLSA system in all these experiments on the TREC 2015 dataset are quite low when compared to the official results of the TREC conference. Nevertheless, the goal of this work has not been to improve the precision of the latent semantic analysis algorithm in information retrieval, but rather to allow a full execution of this algorithm to retrieve documents from a large-scale dataset in a reasonable time. In any case, it has been found out that, (i) for at least one topic (out of the 30 TREC 2015 pre-defined topics or document queries), the out-of-core hLSA system has a better precision than the best precision values of the TREC 2015 results; (ii) for eight topics, the out-of-core hLSA has a better or similar precision than the median precision values of the TREC 2015 results; and, finally, (iii) the precision results of the out-of-core hLSA system are better than the worst precision values of the TREC results.

Acknowledgements. This work has been supported by the Universidad Politécnica Salesiana (UPS) through its research group of Cloud Computing, Smart Cities & High Performance Computing (GIHP4C). It has also been supported by the Sciences Research Council (CONACyT) through the research project no. 262756, as well as (partially) by the projects RedR+Human (Dynamically Reconfigurable Educational Repositories in the Humanities, ref. TIN2014-52010-R) and CetrO+Spec (Creation, Exploration and Transformation of Educational Object Repositories in Specialized Domains, ref. TIN2017-88092-R), both financed by the Spanish Ministry of Economy and Competitiveness.

References

1. Bouadjenek, M.R., Hacid, H., Bouzeghoub, M.: Social networks and information retrieval, how are they converging? A survey, a taxonomy and an analysis of social information retrieval approaches and platforms. Inf. Syst. **56**(C), 1–18 (2016)
2. Deerwester, S., et al.: Indexing by latent semantic analysis. J. Am. Soc. Inf. Sci. **41**(6), 391–407 (1990)
3. Dumais, S.T., Furnas, G.W., Landauer, T.K., Deerwester, S., Harshman, R.: Using latent semantic analysis to improve access to textual information. In: the SIGCHI Conference, pp. 281–285. ACM Press, New York (1988)
4. Ignatow, G., Evangelopoulos, N., Zougris, K.: Sentiment analysis of polarizing topics in social media: news site readers' comments on the Trayvon Martin Controversy. In: Communication and Information Technologies Annual, pp. 259–284. Emerald Group Publishing Limited, February 2016

5. Landauer, T.K.: Automatic essay assessment. Assess. Educ.: Princ. Policy Pract. **10**(3), 295–308 (2003)
6. Landauer, T.K., Dumais, S.T.: A solution to Plato's problem: the latent semantic analysis theory of acquisition, induction, and representation of knowledge. Psychol. Rev. **104**(2), 211–240 (1997)
7. León-Paredes, G.A., Barbosa-Santillán, L.I., Sánchez-Escobar, J.J.: A heterogeneous system based on latent semantic analysis using GPU and multi-CPU. Sci. Program. **2017**, 19 (2017)
8. León-Paredes, G.A., Barbosa-Santillán, L.I., Sánchez-Escobar, J.J., Pareja-Lora, A.: Ship-SIBISCaS: a first step towards the identification of potential maritime law infringements by means of LSA-based image. Sci. Program. **2019** 14p. (2019)
9. Řehůřek, R.: Subspace tracking for latent semantic analysis. In: Clough, P., et al. (eds.) ECIR 2011. LNCS, vol. 6611, pp. 289–300. Springer, Heidelberg (2011). https://doi.org/10.1007/978-3-642-20161-5_29
10. Roberts, K., Simpson, M.S., Voorhees, E., Hersh, W.R.: Overview of the TREC 2015 clinical decision support track. In: The Twenty-Fourth Text Retrieval Conference TREC, pp. 1–12 (2015)
11. Stathopoulos, S., Kalamboukis, T.: Applying latent semantic analysis to large-scale medical image databases. Comput. Med. Imaging Graph. **39**, 27–34 (2015)
12. Vigna, S.: Distributed, large-scale latent semantic analysis by index interpolation. In: Proceedings of the 3rd International Conference on Scalable Information Systems. ICST (Institute for Computer Sciences, Social-Informatics and Telecommunications Engineering) (2008)
13. Zhang, W., Kong, S., Zhu, Y., Wang, X.: Sentiment classification and computing for online reviews by a hybrid SVM and LSA based approach. Cluster Comput. **22**, 1–14 (2018)
14. Zhang, Y., Jin, R., Zhou, Z.H.: Understanding bag-of-words model: a statistical framework. Int. J. Mach. Learn. Cybern. **1**(1–4), 43–52 (2010)

Increasing K-Means Clustering Algorithm Effectivity for Using in Source Code Plagiarism Detection

Patrik Hrkút[1]([⊠]) [iD], Michal Ďuračík[1], Miroslava Mikušová[2] [iD],
Mauro Callejas-Cuervo[3] [iD], and Joanna Zukowska[4] [iD]

[1] Department of Software Technologies, Faculty of Management Science and Informatics,
University of Žilina, Univerzitná 1, 010 26 Zilina, Slovakia
{patrik.hrkut,michal.duracik}@fri.uniza.sk

[2] Department of Road and Urban Transport, Faculty of Operation and Economics of Transport,
University of Žilina, Univerzitná 1, 010 26 Zilina, Slovakia
mikusova@fpedas.uniza.sk

[3] Centro de Investigación y Extensión de la Facultad de Ingeniería, Universidad Pedagógica y
Tecnológica de Colombia, UPTC, Tunja, Boyacá, Colombia
maurocallejas@gmail.com

[4] Faculty of Civil and Environmental Engineering, Gdansk University of Technology,
11/12 Gabriela Narutowicza Street, 80-233 Gdansk, Poland
joanna.zukowska@pg.edu.pl

Abstract. The problem of plagiarism is becoming increasingly more significant with the growth of Internet technologies and the availability of information resources. Many tools have been successfully developed to detect plagiarisms in textual documents, but the situation is more complicated in the field of plagiarism of source codes, where the problem is equally serious. At present, there are no complex tools available to detect plagiarism in a large number of software projects, such as student projects, which are created hundreds per year at each faculty of informatics. Our project aim is to create such a system for finding plagiarism in a large dataset of source codes. The whole system consists of several parts. A classification of source code is an essential part of the whole system because it makes it much more efficient to manipulate source code and divide data into individual clusters so that searching in large volumes of source code is as efficient as possible. The paper discusses how to optimize the implementation of clustering, so the whole system would deliver results in a reasonable time because allocating the different parts of the source code into suitable clusters will allow faster and more memory-efficient search for similar parts of the code.

Keywords: Source code classification · Plagiarism · Effective K-Means implementation

1 Introduction

Nowadays the plagiarism (a term usually used in an academic field) is increasingly occurring in everyday life. With the expansion of information technology, it is becoming

F. R. Narváez et al. (Eds.): SmartTech-IC 2019, CCIS 1154, pp. 120–131, 2020.
https://doi.org/10.1007/978-3-030-46785-2_10

easier to access various sources and create plagiarism. On the other hand, this boom also encourages the development of tools that can detect such forms of plagiarism.

The greatest emphasis is currently being put on the development of methods and tools for detecting plagiarism in textual documents. This approach is understandable as hundreds of thousands of academic papers are created annually worldwide. Finding plagiarism in the source code is an interesting area that brings new challenges. Several tools allow to search for plagiarism in the source code, but no one of them searches for source code plagiarism to the extent that happens in textual documents.

1.1 Motivation

The problem of plagiarism and other ways of cheating has recently been a much-debated topic [1]. There were cases where academic degrees were awarded for final theses that contained a high proportion of matches with other theses or literature. The Antiplagiarism System (APS) attempts to identify identical parts of documents. In Slovakia, the ANTIPLAG system is used for this purpose.

The problem of plagiarism is not present in the academic environment only. Increasing plagiarism can be found in various fields like academia [2], journalism [3] or patents [4] in the commercial sphere.

On the other hand, there are studies [5, 6] that show a gradual reduction in the level of plagiarism in the academic environment in recent years. These studies demonstrate the importance of APS existence. Both studies reported a decrease in the level of plagiarism after the integration of APS into the final thesis defence process.

Our contribution does not cover the whole process of development an anti-plagiarism system. Individual problems were addressed in a series of our articles [16–22]. We want to focus on a small part and that is the solution of optimal implementation of clustering algorithm for our purposes. We chose the K-Means method because it was verified and used for a long time. Clustering is not a fundamental problem that we had to solve when creating the system. It only helped us divide the data into groups in order to save a lot of unnecessary operations in finding matches in the source code. The aim of this paper is to point out several optimization techniques, which help us to quickly split data into clusters.

2 Plagiarism in the Source Code

In general, the perception of plagiarism in the source code is not very different from plagiarism in textual documents. The reasons for plagiarism are the same in both cases. We live in a time of easy access to various information on the Internet.

From our point of view, the problem of plagiarism discovery in the source code is that there is not currently available a complex system or service that would allow plagiarism to be detected on a global scale. As a result, there are no global statistics available to describe the level of plagiarism in this area.

The most widely used plagiarism detection systems are the *Measure of Software Similarity system* (MOSS) from Stanford University and the *JPlag system* from Germany.

Both systems were created more than ten years ago and are still being developed. Besides, we can find other systems such as Plague, YAP and others.

These systems can search for plagiarisms within a relatively small sample of data. If we want to use such systems in the teaching process, we encounter a serious problem. The learning process is characterized by the fact that every year a lot of new data is being generated, which needs to be checked on year-to-year basis, and therefore it is necessary to introduce some incremental analysis of this data, as is performed by successful textual APS.

2.1 Shortcomings of Current Methods

Commonly used methods for detecting plagiarism in source code have been developed along with methods for textual documents since the last century. In the case of textual documents, development is progressing with more advanced methods that rely on deep machine learning to detect plagiarism [9] and large systems integrate these methods.

We have revealed these main shortcomings of currently available systems:

- obsolescence,
- systems are closed (no open source),
- the complicated process of plagiarism evaluation,
- the inability to using on a large-scale basis.

In our opinion, all these shortcomings result from the fact, that they were designed to detect plagiarism within a small group of source code files.

2.2 Proposal of a New Method

In this chapter, we will describe a method that allows searching for plagiarism in a large number of source codes and we show its components. The proposed method is shown in Fig. 1.

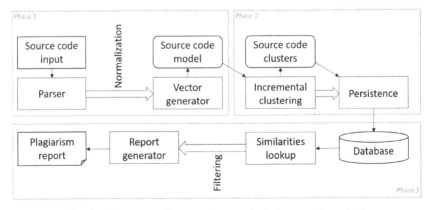

Fig. 1. Component diagram of a new plagiarism search method.

The main advantage of the proposed method is its modularity because it is divided into 3 phases each consisting of two algorithms. The phases represent:

1. Processing and representation of source code.
2. Clustering and persistence of data.
3. Searching for similarities and creating a report.

In the first phase, there are algorithms for processing the source code. These algorithms are divided into two groups. The first one contains algorithms that process the source code and creates a model in the form of a syntax tree. These algorithms will always be specific to each programming language we want to process.

The second phase groups algorithms that transform the syntax tree into a structure suitable for further processing. We chose *characteristic vectors* as a suitable form for the source code representation. Among the processing and vectorization, we can include algorithms that will normalize the syntax tree, what allows to detect plagiarism even in the case of commonly used APS tricks [7, 8].

In the second phase, the clustering of similar vectors is performed. For clustering of similar vectors, we use the K-Means algorithm, which is slightly modified for our purposes. The result of this phase is data ready to be stored in a database in an efficiently searchable form. The aim of clustering is, in addition to pre-preparing data for searching, a certain logical distribution of data into related groups. Such a distribution allows the better scalability of the whole method.

The last phase deals with obtaining individual matches from the database and their evaluation. At this stage, before the report is generated, an *insignificant matches filter* can be used to make reports easier to read.

The phases are almost independent of each other. The only element on which they depend is the format of the data transferred between phases. A processed source code model, represented by characteristic vectors, is transmitted between the first and second phase and a database of vectors is an interface between phase 2 and 3. Such data separation brings us further chances for scaling the whole method.

A detailed description of the individual phases can be found in our previous papers [16–22]. In this paper, we will focus on aspects of an effective clustering implementation and optimization of its performance. The reader can find more information about how clustering was designed in [22].

3 Suggested Optimization Methods for an Implementation of K-Means Algorithm

Clustering is typically used to cluster different data samples into groups or in data mining field. In our case, we want to use clustering as a vector pre-sorting tool, which then allows us to simplify the search for similar vectors. By default, using clustering methods in the data mining field, the input data set is divided into two groups – the training and control set. The training set is used to create clusters and the data from the control set verifies the accuracy of this classification. Our goal was to design a clustering method that would allow new data to be added gradually and to maintain the clusters in an optimal configuration.

3.1 The Efficiency of Computational Complexity of the K-Means Algorithm

The basic K-Means algorithm in its specification only describes the principal ideas, but not the ways of effective implementation. If we want to use this algorithm in our method, we need to design and implement several improvements. To improve the algorithm efficiency, we need to identify which parts of it are significant for us. In most cases, the improvement of the initial phase of the algorithm – finding the initial centres [10, 11] – is the good starting point for such attempts. The starting distribution is important for two reasons – a better start-up distribution speeds up the algorithm and can eliminate the problem of suboptimal solutions where the algorithm drops to a local minimum [12].

Despite the importance of this initial distribution, we decided not to focus on optimizing the initial cluster distribution in our approach. This does not make sense to our algorithm because it is done only at the beginning and the centres are being recalculated during the algorithm run. This calculation is based on the previous state and there is no need to reinitialize the clusters again. The K-Means algorithm is relatively simple, so there are only a few aspects that can be improved. Our analysis showed that the most ineffective part is the assignment of vectors to clusters because this kind of operations has the complexity of $O(n*k)$ where n is the number of vectors and k is the number of clusters. For each vector cluster combination, their distance must be calculated, and the calculation of the Euclidean distance for vectors of length 162 also takes some time.

In this section, we will focus on optimizing the second part of the K-Means algorithm because this part runs very often. We suggest the improvement of the algorithm in several points:

- Adding parallelization,
- improving the logical structure of the algorithm,
- improving implementation techniques,
- pre-processing of input data.

The following chapters we will detail the mentioned points. At the end, we will evaluate the suggested techniques and compare the speed of the algorithm before and after the application of these techniques.

3.2 Parallelization of the Algorithm

One of the basic techniques of algorithm acceleration is their parallelization. In the literature, we can find several methods that attempt to parallelize the K-Means algorithm [13, 14]. In our work, we decided to explore and implement some basic parallelization methods.

In general, a parallelization of algorithms is not a trivial task [15]. The main goal is to use most of the available computing power of the CPU. In the basic implementation of the algorithm, we observed 25% CPU usage during the run (Example 1 in Fig. 2) because the test was run on a processor that had 2 hyperthreaded cores.

Given the large dimension of the input data and the frequency of the distance calculation operations, we decided first to parallelize the Euclidean distance calculation. We divided the input vectors into several groups and calculated the distances of these parts in parallel. Finally, we combined the partial results. This principle is generally known as *MapReduce*. We used the same approach by new cluster centres calculating, where we calculated the individual elements of the resulting centre in parallel. As can be seen in Example 2 of Fig. 2, this method has already been able to utilize almost all available CPU computing resources. On the other hand, this approach (as will be shown in the results) brings considerable overhead costs. Managing threads (through which parallelization has been implemented), synchronization, and other aspects of this approach do not allow full utilization of the parallelization capabilities and the amount of computing power is consumed by the operating system. Some approaches can partially reduce this overhead by using the *thread workers* pool that eliminates some resource management overhead. Although this approach utilized the available computing resources to the maximum, the benefit we gained was less than the added overhead of the operating system.

Fig. 2. Utilization of CPU during parallelization methods.

Based on these results, we built our final parallelization proposal at a higher level of the algorithm. We will parallelize the operation of assigning vectors to clusters as the first step. The single assignments are independent of each other, so we can perform this operation in parallel. At the beginning, we divide a set of vectors that we can assign to n groups (n equals to the number of available CPU cores) and then we perform the vector assignment in parallel. When implementing, we need to be aware of how the assignment operation is implemented, as it may require some degree of synchronization. In the second step, we divide the clusters into n groups, and then we calculate the centres for the individual clusters in parallel as well. As in the previous case, the clusters are independent of each other, so such an approach should not cause any synchronization problem.

As can be seen in Example 3 of Fig. 2, this approach does not reach 100% utilization of available computing resources. This problem is caused by uneven cluster size, so some cluster groups are calculated faster than others. The solution could be to smarter inclusion of clusters into groups or to use an approach where the calculation of each cluster would represent a separate task, and these tasks would be planned based on the current availability of computing resources. On the other hand, our results show that performance improvements using this approach are minimal, but implementation complexity increases significantly.

3.3 Heuristics for Vector Clustering

In this chapter, we detail how we can speed up the phase of assigning vectors to clusters. Based on the analysis of runtime calculations, we found that up to 68% of the time spent by clustering vectors takes distance calculations. Another interesting result was that, except for a negligible number of initial steps, 99% of the vectors remain in the same cluster (they don't change their cluster). Despite this fact, the algorithm must calculate the distance to all other centres, what costs a lot of computing time.

To solve this problem, we proposed a modification that will eliminate unnecessary distance calculation operations.

```
1: function K_Means(V : vector list, k : int, C : list of clusters): list of clusters
2:     repeat
3:         change ← 0
4:         m ← {}
5:         for all cluster c in C do
6:             m(c) ← Sort(Distance(c, Cⱼ)), ∀ j∈{1..k} ∧ Cⱼ != c)
7:         end for
8:         for all vector v in V do
9:             c ← LastCluster(v)
10:            dToLast ← Distance(v, c)
11:            c ← Min(Distance(v, b), dToLast), ∀ b∈m(c)∧Distance(v, m(c))<2*dToLast
12:            Assign(v,c)
13:        end for
14:        for all cluster c in C do
15:            change ← change + Recalculate(c)
16:        end for
17:    while change > 0
18:    return C
19: end function
```

Algorithm 1. Algorithm for reducing of the number of vector distance calculations.

At the beginning of each step, the modified algorithm calculates a matrix of distances between clusters and assigns to each cluster a list of pairs – distance and the other cluster, sorted by distance in ascending order. Thanks to this, we can know for each cluster how far the other clusters are. We will use this list in the assigning vectors procedure. For each vector, we first calculate the distance to the original cluster (denoted as `dToLast` in the algorithm), then sequentially iterate through the list of the nearest clusters of the cluster where the vector was originally, until the distance between clusters is greater than `2*dToLast`. During this iteration, we check the distance of the vector to other clusters, and if necessary, we update the lowest distance found.

We can compute how many distance calculation operations are saved this way. Let k denote the number of clusters and n the number of vectors. In the basic implementation of the algorithm, exactly $n * k$ calculations of the distances between the vectors and the clusters are needed. In our proposed implementation, only $\frac{k*k-1}{2}$ calculations are required to compute the matrix of the distance between clusters. Another n calculations are needed to calculate the distances to the centres of the original clusters (this can be reduced by remembering the original distance and using it if the centre of the cluster has not changed). The last part to be counted in is the average number of clusters (denoted by x), which must be examined near the original cluster. Based on our measurements for the tested dataset, this value was equal to 3.2. The total number of distance calculation operations is therefore $\frac{k*k-1}{2} + (x + 1) * n$. Obviously, this number is less than the original $n * k$.

3.4   Implementation Efficiency

In addition to previously mentioned optimization at a higher level, we also examined the optimization of specific implementation details of the algorithm depending on the programming language and physical hardware. Our algorithm was implemented in.net framework in C# programming language. This language is a high-level programming language and does not allow directly affect the operations that the hardware physically perform. Also, we cannot directly set the compiler to use, for example, vector instructions.

The initial algorithm implementation used various LINQ[1] extensions for convenience. As an example, we can use the `zip`[2] method to calculate the Euclidean distance. When we replaced this method with a loop, it slightly accelerated the algorithm. We used a similar approach to calculate centres, and the replacement of the expression for a simple loop slightly accelerated the algorithm as well. However, these changes brought an acceleration in a few percent only.

The analysis showed yet another way to speed up the algorithm for calculating centres. The original centre calculation algorithm (Algorithm 2) calculated each component of the vector separately. This may not seem like a problem at first glance, but when we realize how single vectors are stored in memory, such an approach means that the algorithm must load a large amount of data from the operating memory into the processor when calculating each component.

```
1: mean ← [sizeof(vector)]
2: for i in 1..sizeof(vector) do
3:     mean(i) ← average(v(i))∀ v ∈ V
4: end for
```

Algorithm 2. The algorithm for calculation of new cluster centres.

Besides that, the current processors use cache massively and include various techniques to prepare data they might need in the future (*CPU prefetch*). Since the vectors are stored in random locations in the memory, the CPU cannot predict which data will need, and thus processing each additional vector means waiting for the value to be read from the RAM. To improve this behaviour, we modified the algorithm to calculate the average of all vector components at once. Although this approach has the same number of operations as the previous one, the results show that it is about an order of magnitude faster.

```
1: mean ← [sizeof(vector)]
2: for all vector v in V do
3:     for i in 1..sizeof(vector) do
4:         mean(i) ← mean(i) + v(i)
5:     end for
6: end for
7: mean(i) ← mean(i) / count(V) ∀ i ∈ {1..sizeof(vector)]}
```

Algorithm 3. The more efficient algorithm for calculating cluster centres.

If we analyse why this version of the algorithm is more efficient, we will find that this version uses the CPU cache and the mentioned prefetch more effectively. Accessing

---

[1] https://docs.microsoft.com/en-us/dotnet/csharp/programming-guide/concepts/linq.

[2] https://docs.microsoft.com/en-us/dotnet/api/system.linq.enumerable.zip.

the CPU cache is much faster than accessing data in the RAM. Another reason is that the CPU is loading data from the memory into its cache memory in blocks, so when we try to access a component of the vector, there is a good chance that the component will already be in the cache. Also, such a sequential approach (step by step through all vector components) also facilitates the prediction of CPU prefetch, which prepares the data that will be needed in the future.

As we have seen, the proper implementation of algorithms and utilization of CPU caches can often help to speed up algorithms without modifying their operations.

3.5 Data Size Reduction

So far, we have described optimization methods which focused on improving algorithms or their implementation. None of these methods has any effect on the algorithm output. In this chapter, we will describe a slightly different approach to effectivity raising.

In the article [22] we discussed the selection of elements suitable for indexing. It has been shown that our vectors contain a lot of dependent components whose removal would make the algorithm more efficient. As this task is more complex, we will not deal directly with it in this section. Instead, we will show that even if we reduce the number of vectors, the main reason of a clustering use will not be affected.

The first option we will look at is the removal of long vectors. Since our algorithm does not limit the maximum length of the generated vectors, it often happens that created vectors cover the entire source code. There is no point in comparing such vectors because they will always be too specific, and it is more efficient to compare smaller parts of source code, and then combine these smaller parts into larger ones. It is important to add that by removing some long vectors we do not lose almost any source code information, since such vectors have always been made up by joining smaller ones, and these smaller vectors sufficiently cover the source code. The principal question is how to determine the maximal vector length. Based on our experiments, we set this value to 250. Smaller vectors still can cover source code well enough at this value.

The second option to make clustering more efficient is to reduce the dimension of the vectors. We considered two approaches to reduce the number of components. In the first approach, we decided to remove any components that have a low entropy, as they will not help us in searching vectors anyway. And in the second approach, we selected components based on their frequency – we omitted components that had zero in most vectors. We decided to use the second approach. Based on the tested dataset, we selected to remove 80 components that occurred in less than 0.1% of the vectors.

In this proposed approach, however, it is important to realize that the removal of the 80 components applies only to the clustering phase. We will work with the original vectors in other algorithms (especially when searching for matches).

As can be seen in Fig. 3, the individual characteristics behave similarly to the method of clustering, where all vectors (without reducing) has been used. The only difference is in absolute values, where the average entropy is lower by 25–30%. The average minimum distance is about 50% lower, which was caused by the removal of the "protruding" components of the vector. Other characteristics have also decreased, but their decline is not so significant.

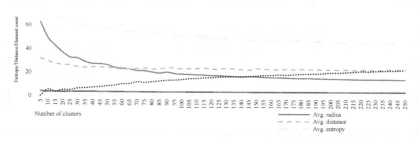

Fig. 3. Selected characteristics of clusters using simplified vectors.

Based on these results, we can say that the created clusters are smaller and more compact. We did not assess the effect of this reduction on plagiarism search efficiency, as it is not critically dependent on the way of clustering. On the other hand, we can say that reducing the amount of data will speed up the clustering process.

3.6   Experimental Evaluation

In this chapter, we evaluate the effect of individual optimization approaches on the resulting speed of the K-Means algorithm. All presented time values are based on an average of 5 measurements using data from the tested dataset. The initialization of clusters was the same for each of the measured cases. We did not measure initialization and initial assignment of vectors to clusters. In measuring, we examined *the average length of one cycle* of the algorithm, that means assigning vectors to clusters and a centre recalculation. We set the number of clusters to 100. Each additional measurement also includes the use of techniques from the previous phase. The configuration of the system on which the measurements were performed was as follows (Table 1):

- Intel Core I5 6200U CPU,
- 16 GB RAM,
- SSD hard disk.

Table 1. Computational speed comparison of K-Means algorithm (in seconds).

	Inserting of vectors	Calculation of centres	Distance calculations	Total
Original version	153.6	1.7	–	155.3
Parallelization added	49.9	1.1	–	51.0
Heuristics for vector assignment	16.3	1.1	–	17.4
Implementation optimization	5.1	0.1	–	5.2

4 Conclusion

Optimization of the algorithm is often very important when creating systems with large data volumes. We can take appropriate steps to speed up the algorithm by tens of percent. Similarly, in this case, the algorithm was accelerated without compromising its original purpose. As the results from the table show, the modifications described in the text have even achieved a triple acceleration compared to the basic implementation without any optimization.

Even the further implementation of the system revealed that the most important component of the system will be a database, initially, some computing power is needed to calculate clusters from the initial data. During the run of the system, the main component will use a database where the vectors for a given cluster configuration are stored and the database will be used for searching source code matches.

Such a design of the system, together with the fact that the need for re-clusterization will decrease as the number of data increases, will allow the system to use computing resources very effectively. As already mentioned, the only necessary running component is a database, and if re-clusterization is necessary, the computing power should be temporarily added.

References

1. Skalka, J.: Prevencia a odhaľovanie plagiátorstva. Zber prác za účelom obmedzenia porušovania autorských práv v kvalifikačných prácach na vysokých školách (2019)
2. Hammond, M.: Cyber-plagiarism: are FE students getting away with words? (2002)
3. Vesely, O.: Results of similarity analysis of online news (2015)
4. Holbrook, T.R., Osborn, L.: Digital patent infringement in an era of 3D printing (2014)
5. Curtis, G.J., Vardanega, L.: Is plagiarism changing over time? A 10-year time-lag study with three points of measurement. High. Educ. Res. Dev. 35(6), 1167–1179 (2016)
6. Kravjar, J.: SK Antilpag is bearing fruit (2015)
7. Tao, G., et al.: Improved plagiarism detection algorithm based on abstract syntax tree. In: IEEE Emerging Intelligent Data and Web Technologies (EIDWT) (2013)
8. Zhao, J., et al.: An AST-based code plagiarism detection algorithm. In: 10th International Conference on IEEE Broadband and Wireless Computing, Communication and Applications (BWCCA) (2015)
9. Rakian, S., Safi, E.F., Rastegari, H.: A Persian fuzzy plagiarism detection approach, pp. 182–190 (2015)
10. Celebi, M.E., Hassan, A.K., Vela, A.: A comparative study of efficient initialization methods for the k-means clustering algorithm. Expert Syst. Appl. 40(1), 200–210 (2013)
11. Pena, J.M., Lozano, J.A., Larranaga, P.: An empirical comparison of four initialization methods for the k-means algorithm. Pattern Recogn. Lett. 20, 1027–1040 (1999)
12. Selim, S.Z., Mohamed, A.I.: K-means-type algorithms: a generalized convergence theorem and characterization of local optimality. IEEE Trans. Pattern Anal. Mach. Intell. 1, 81–87 (1984)
13. Zhao, W., Ma, H., He, Q.: Parallel K-Means clustering based on MapReduce. In: Jaatun, M.G., Zhao, G., Rong, C. (eds.) CloudCom 2009. LNCS, vol. 5931, pp. 674–679. Springer, Heidelberg (2009). https://doi.org/10.1007/978-3-642-10665-1_71

14. Stoffel, K., Belkoniene, A.: Parallel *k/h*-Means clustering for large data sets. In: Amestoy, P., et al. (eds.) Euro-Par 1999. LNCS, vol. 1685, pp. 1451–1454. Springer, Heidelberg (1999). https://doi.org/10.1007/3-540-48311-X_205
15. Wolf, M.E., Lam, M.S.: A loop transformation theory and an algorithm to maximize parallelism. IEEE Trans. Parallel Distrib. Syst. **2**(4), 452–471 (1991)
16. Duracik, M., Krsak, E., Hrkut, P.: Using concepts of text based plagiarism detection in source code plagiarism analysis. In: Plagiarism across Europe and Beyond 2017: Conference Proceedings, pp. 177–186. Mendel University, Brno (2017). ISBN 978-80-7509-493-3
17. Duracik, M., Krsak, E., Hrkut, P.: Current trends in source code analysis, plagiarism detection and issues of analysis big datasets. In: Procedia Engineering, vol. 192, pp. 136–141 (2017). ISSN 1877-7058
18. Ďuračík, M., Kršák, E., Hrkút, P.: Source code representations for plagiarism detection. In: Uden, L., Liberona, D., Ristvej, J. (eds.) LTEC 2018. CCIS, vol. 870, pp. 61–69. Springer, Cham (2018). https://doi.org/10.1007/978-3-319-95522-3_6. ISBN 978-3-319-95521-6
19. Duracik, M., Krsak, E., Hrkut, P.: Issues with the detection of plagiarism in programming courses on a larger scale. In: Proceedings 16th IEEE International Conference on Emerging eLearning Technologies and Applications, ICETA 2018, pp. 141–147. Institute of Electrical and Electronics Engineers, New Jersey (2018). ISBN 978-1-5386-7912-8
20. Duracik, M., Krsak, E., Hrkut, P.: Scalable source code plagiarism detection using source code vectors clustering. In: Proceedings of 2018 IEEE 9th International Conference on Software Engineering and Service, pp. 499–502. Institute of Electrical and Electronics Engineers, Danvers (2018). ISBN 978-1-5386-6564-0
21. Duracik, M.: Semi-automatic identification of non-significant source code parts using clustering. In: Mathematics in Science and Technologies: Proceedings of the MIST Conference 2019, pp. 17–21 (2019). ISBN 9781794002180
22. Duracik, M., Krsak, E., Hrkut, P.: Searching source code fragments using incremental clustering. Concurr. Comput. Pract. Exp. (2019, in press)

Using Machine Learning Techniques for Discovering Latent Topics in Twitter Colombian News

Vladimir Vargas-Calderón[1]($\boxtimes$) iD, Marlon Steibeck Dominguez[2],
N. Parra-A.[1] iD, Herbert Vinck-Posada[1], and Jorge E. Camargo[3]

[1] Grupo de Superconductividad y Nanotecnología, Departamento de Física,
Universidad Nacional de Colombia, 055051 Bogotá, Colombia
{vvargasc,nparraa,hvicnkp}@unal.edu.co
[2] Facultad de Ingeniería, Unipanamericana Fundación Universitaria,
111321 Bogotá, Colombia
madominguez@unipanamericana.edu.co
[3] Departamento de Ingeniería de Sistemas e Industrial,
Universidad Nacional de Colombia, 055051 Bogotá, Colombia
jecamargom@unal.edu.co

Abstract. We propose a method to discover latent topics and visualise large collections of tweets for easy identification and interpretation of topics, and exemplify its use with tweets from a Colombian mass media giant in the period 2014–2019. The latent topic analysis is performed in two ways: with the training of a Latent Dirichlet Allocation model, and with the combination of the FastText unsupervised model to represent tweets as vectors and the implementation of K-means clustering to group tweets into topics. Using a classification task, we found that people respond differently according to the various news topics. The classification tasks consists of the following: given a reply to a news tweet, we train a supervised algorithm to predict the topic of the news tweet solely from the reply. Furthermore, we show how the Colombian peace treaty has had a profound impact on the Colombian society, as it is the topic in which most people engage to show their opinions.

Keywords: Latent topic analysis · Text mining · Information visualisation · Machine learning

1 Introduction

Social interaction on social networks has been a central research topic during the last decade. It has applications in modernisation of government's Twitter-based networking strategies [7,11,20–22], e-commerce [13,15,27] and business performance [5,9]. Of particular interest is the study of how people respond to a stimulus, forming either strong collective responses or weak, isolated responses. For example, [4,18], studied users' influence in microblogging networks, where implementing the InfluenceRank Algorithm for identifying people with high social

© Springer Nature Switzerland AG 2020
F. R. Narváez et al. (Eds.): SmartTech-IC 2019, CCIS 1154, pp. 132–141, 2020.
https://doi.org/10.1007/978-3-030-46785-2_11

media influence can be of great commercial value. An interesting area within the stimulus–response field in social networks is the response of people to the news. In the case of Twitter, it has been identified since its early days as a news-spreading social network [12] where mass media are central actors. Previous work in this area is typically focused on topics such as sports, politics, health, education, travel, business, and so on [1,6,28].

In this work, we inquire on the recognition of the semantic structure of people's response to news tweets by one of the largest Colombian news mass media, Radio Cadena Nacional (RCN), with (7,7 million followers by August 2019). If there is a distinction between how people respond to different kinds of news, then state of the art natural language processing and machine learning techniques should be able to detect this difference. Testing this hypothesis is the objective of this work. Therefore, we propose a two-stage pipeline to investigate the claimed differences. During the first stage, topic analysis is performed over the tweets by RCN, showing the main latent topics that they tweet about. In the second stage, we take the comments by regular users to those tweets and ask ourselves if it is possible to predict which is the topic of the tweet they are responding to. Our research is two-folded. On the one hand, we investigate the characterisation of how people respond to news from different topics. On the other hand, we pay particular attention to one of the most critical social phenomena of the past decade worldwide: the response by Colombian population to the peace treaty between the Colombian government and the Colombian Revolutionary Armed Forces guerrilla (FARC) [25]. These two entities were in a war for over 50 years, a conflict responsible for hundreds of thousands of deaths and millions of people forced from their homes, and being one of the largest human tragedies of modern times [3].

This paper is divided as follows: in Sect. 2 we describe in detail the dataset that we used to carry out our study as well as the workflow of the proposed method. In Sect. 3, we present the results and analysis of the research. Finally, the main conclusions and future work are presented in Sect. 4.

2   Method and Materials

In this section, we describe in detail the two stages of our research: a topic modelling and a topic prediction stage. The work pipeline is shown in Fig. 1.

We collected tweets from the Twitter account @NoticiasRCN from 2014 to the present using the Twitter API. During this period, the mass media giant published 258,848 tweets, having 1,447,440 comments from their public. Then, we proceeded to pre-process our tweet database. We removed punctuation, links, hashtags and mentions from all the tweets. We further lemmatised the text in lowercase.

With the pre-processed data, we trained topic modelling algorithms in order to discover topics in the tweet corpus. Particularly we used the Latent Dirichlet Allocation (LDA) model [8] and a combination of unsupervised FastText model [2,10] and K-Means clustering [14].

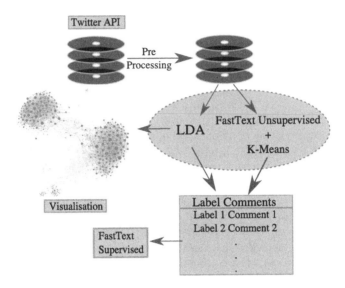

Fig. 1. Overview of the proposed method. We crawl tweets from @NoticiasRCN Twitter account. Then, pre-processing is made over this set of tweets. After that, two different unsupervised topic models are trained, from which visualisations of the tweets only from @NoticiasRCN can be built. We use the discovered latent topics to label comments to @NoticiasRCN tweets. Finally, we train a supervised FastText model to predict the topics of the comments.

LDA assigns K probabilities to a tweet of belonging to K different classes. The classes are learnt in an unsupervised fashion from the co-occurrence of words within the tweets of the corpus. Each of the classes is called a latent topic. Therefore, the K probabilities assigned to a tweet by LDA can be interpreted as a vector of K components, where the k-th one shows the content percentage of the k-th topic in a tweet. The number of latent topics K is a parameter that one provides to the model. In principle, each latent topic corresponds to a topic a human would understand. However, if a low number of latent topics is provided, each latent topic may contain several real topics. On the other hand, if a high number of latent topics is provided, many latent topics may refer to the same real topic. To keep a good correspondence between latent topics and human-understandable topics or real topics, the number of latent topics should be carefully selected. Refs. [19,24] have shown that the best way to pick the number of latent topics is by measuring the C_V coherence, which has shown a large correlation with human judgements of the interpretability of the topics extracted by LDA. For the @NoticiasRCN tweets, the optimum number of latent topics is 12, as it is shown in Fig. 2.

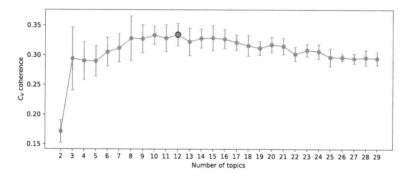

Fig. 2. C_V coherence as a function of number of topics for an LDA model trained with tweets from @NoticiasRCN. For each number of topics, a total of 20 LDA training runs were performed, and bars indicate a standard deviation of the corresponding 20 measured C_V coherences.

The other topic modelling algorithm consisted of training an unsupervised FastText model and performing K-means clustering on the unsupervised learnt vector representations for the tweets in the corpus. FastText is a memory-efficient and fast vector embedding algorithm based on the ideas of Word2Vec [17]. An important remark is that FastText uses sub-word information to enrich word vectors. This is particularly useful in a language such as Spanish, because it is largely inflected. What vector embedding algorithms do is to represent text as vectors of N components. Again, based on the co-occurrence of words or sequences of characters, FastText assigns N-dimensional vectors to each tweet. Here, the components do not have a human interpretation, as they embody abstract semantic features of the tweets. Once the embedded vectors for each tweet are learnt from FastText, the K-means clustering algorithm is used to group vectors in the embedded vector space. This combination of a vector embedding algorithm and a clustering algorithm has been used before with excellent results in unsupervised community detection models [26]. In order to compare both topic modelling algorithms (LDA and FastText + K-means), we used K-means to form 12 clusters, where each one represents a latent topic.

After that, we labelled the comments to the news tweets. Let $t_N^{(i)}$ be a news tweet from @NoticiasRCN indexed by i, which runs from 1 to M, the total number of news tweets. Let $t_C^{(j_i)}$ be a comment made by some Twitter user to the news tweet $t_N^{(i)}$ indexed by j_i, which runs from 1_i to $N_i^{(i)}$, where $N^{(i)}$ is the total number of comments to the i-th news tweet $t_N^{(i)}$. Then, we created a labelled comment dataset for each of the two considered topic modelling algorithms as follows,

$$\left\{ \left(\ell_1, t_C^{(1_1)} \right), \left(\ell_1, t_C^{(2_1)} \right), \dots, \left(\ell_1, t_C^{(N_1^{(1)})} \right), \dots, \left(\ell_M, t_C^{(N_M^{(M)})} \right) \right\}, \quad (1)$$

where ℓ_i is the latent topic (from either LDA or FastText + K-means) assigned to the i-th news tweet $t_N^{(i)}$. Recall that ℓ_i is one of the 12 different latent topics.

From the vector representation of the tweets built with the unsupervised FastText model, we generated visualisations of the tweets in a 2D map. To do this, we applied a state of the art dimensionality reduction model called the Uniform Manifold Approximation and Projection (UMAP) [16]. UMAP learns topological relations between the FastText vectors of N components and finds representative projections of the data onto a two-dimensional vector space.

Finally, a supervised FastText model is trained to learn to predict the labels ℓ_i (provided by the two topic modelling algorithms) from the vector representations of the tweets $t_C^{(j_i)}$, which are efficiently learnt by FastText. A 10-fold cross-validation was performed.

3   Results and Discussion

After performing an LDA analysis on the news tweets, each news tweet was assigned a 12 component probability vector. We built the visualisation of such tweets by selecting the tweets that better represented each latent topic. To do this, we imposed a probability threshold on the LDA probability vectors. Tweets whose maximum LDA probability for some topic is above this threshold are called representative tweets for the corresponding latent topic. For a threshold of 0.8, Fig. 3 shows an annotated visualisation of the most representative tweets. A couple of clusters are not annotated since their topic is not unique or simply not clear.

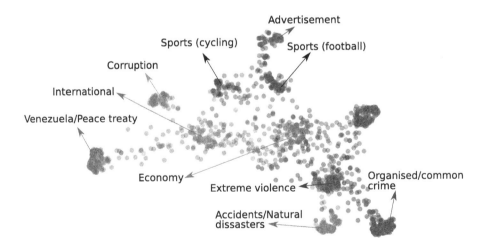

Fig. 3. Visualisation of topics discovered with LDA.

Concerning the FastText and K-means combination, a different selection mechanism for representative tweets was taken into account. K-means groups news tweets geometrically, building 12 vectors called the cluster centroids. We define the most representative tweets of each cluster as the set of tweets grouped in a cluster nearest to its corresponding centroid. Therefore, after defining a maximum distance threshold, we can visualise the clusters and their corresponding representative tweets. Note that this threshold does not have a probabilistic interpretation, and is in general different for different datasets, depending on the mean distance between the data points. In our case, the visualisation is shown in Fig. 4. Topics were easier to identify, and the visualisation shows clear clusters well-separated from the others. In terms of visualisation, the FastText + K-means technique is superior for our case study.

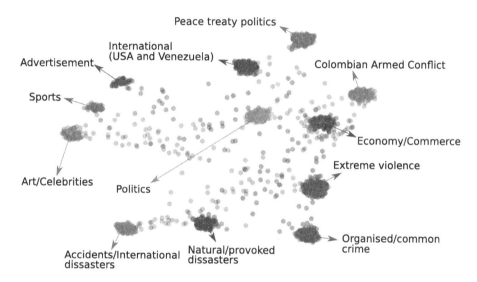

Fig. 4. Visualisation of topics discovered with the combination of unsupervised Fast-Text and K-means clustering.

Now, we focus on the second stage of our research, where we predict the topic of a news tweet from a comment to that tweet. The precision and recall at $k = 1, \ldots, 10$ [23] are shown in Fig. 5. From the results at $k = 1$ it is clear that for both LDA and FastText + K-means, the precision and recall are well-above the expected result of a random classifier. Again, FastText + K-means performs better. Of course, as k gets larger, recall increases and precision decreases.

Remarkably, having a 40% precision and recall at 1 means that there is a difference between how people respond to different topics. This result is quite good considering that topics were discovered with unsupervised learning, and that documents for classification are single tweets. This difference in response can be further examined with a histogram of the impact caused in the public by

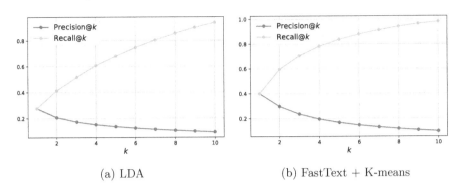

(a) LDA   (b) FastText + K-means

Fig. 5. Precision and Recall at $k = 1, \ldots, 10$ for the LDA and FastText + K-means topic modelling algorithms.

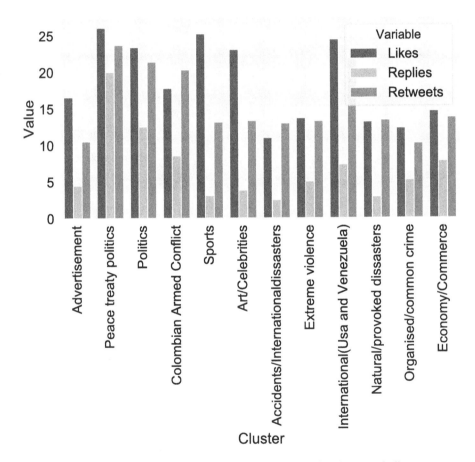

Fig. 6. Bar plot of number of likes, replies and retweets for the set of all news tweets belonging to each latent topic discovered by the FastText + K-means method.

each latent topic. We do so only considering the FastText + K-means method, as it has consistently shown to yield better results. Figure 6 shows that the topic identified as peace treaty politics is by far the more engaging one, having the most number of likes, retweets and replies per news tweet related to that topic. Therefore, our analysis confirms that the peace treaty has been the phenomenon with the largest impact on Colombian society.

4   Conclusions and Future Work

We presented two methods to automatically detect latent topics in news tweets and assess how significant were the differences between the response from the public to tweets from different topics. The first method consisted on discovering latent topics using the widely used LDA model. The second method consisted on generating embedded vectors with FastText and performing K-means clustering on those vectors. We visualised the most representative tweets for each latent topic using both methods and showed that the FastText + K-means method was superior both in the visualisation and in the interpretability of the topics.

Also, using the comments to the news tweets, we trained a supervised Fast-Text method to predict the topic of a news tweet from a comment of that tweet. Again, the better results were obtained with the FastText + K-means method, yielding 40% precision and recall at 1 in a 12-class classification problem. This indicates that the proposed methods are able to identify semantic differences between tweets from different topics.

The examination of the impact of each topic on the news Twitter account followers revealed that the topic identified as peace treaty politics was the most relevant topic, having the most number of likes, retweets and replies per news tweet, compared to the other topics. Furthermore, some applications of the proposed methods include: topic discovery for marketing, automatic classification of new events in real time and monitoring activity in different latent topics.

We intend in the future to perform a sentiment analysis on the followers response in order to measure controversiality of topics as well as study which topics evoke positive/negative sentiment in the public.

References

1. Almutairi, N., Alhabash, S., Hellmueller, L., Willis, E.: The effects of Twitter users' gender and weight on viral behavioral intentions toward obesity-related news. J. Health Commun. **23**(3), 233–243 (2018). https://doi.org/10.1080/10810730.2018. 1423648. pMID: 29388884
2. Bojanowski, P., Grave, E., Joulin, A., Mikolov, T.: Enriching word vectors with subword information. arXiv preprint arXiv:1607.04606 (2016)
3. Cely, D.M.F.: Grupo de memoria histórica,¡ basta ya! colombia: Memorias de guerra y dignidad (bogotá: Imprenta nacional, 2013), 431 pp. 1. Historia y sociedad (26), 274–281 (2014)

4. Chen, W., Cheng, S., He, X., Jiang, F.: Influencerank: an efficient social influence measurement for millions of users in microblog. In: 2012 Second International Conference on Cloud and Green Computing, pp. 563–570 (2012). https://doi.org/10.1109/CGC.2012.31

5. Culnan, M.J., McHugh, P.J., Zubillaga, J.I.: How large US companies can use twitter and other social media to gain business value. MIS Q. Exec. **9**, 243–259 (2010)

6. Garrett, R.K.: Social media's contribution to political misperceptions in US presidential elections. PLOS ONE **14**(3), 1–16 (2019). https://doi.org/10.1371/journal.pone.0213500

7. Golbeck, J., Grimes, J.M., Rogers, A.: Twitter use by the US congress. J. Am. Soc. Inf. Sci. Technol. **61**(8), 1612–1621 (2010). https://doi.org/10.1002/asi.21344

8. Hoffman, M.D., Blei, D.M., Bach, F.: Online learning for latent dirichlet allocation. In: Proceedings of the 23rd International Conference on Neural Information Processing Systems - Volume 1, NIPS 2010, pp. 856–864. Curran Associates Inc., USA (2010)

9. Ioanid, A., Scarlat, C.: Factors influencing social networks use for business: Twitter and Youtube analysis. Procedia Eng. **181**, 977–983 (2017). https://doi.org/10.1016/j.proeng.2017.02.496. 10th International Conference Interdisciplinarity in Engineering, INTER-ENG 2016, 6–7 October 2016, Tirgu Mures, Romania

10. Joulin, A., Grave, E., Bojanowski, P., Mikolov, T.: Bag of tricks for efficient text classification. arXiv preprint arXiv:1607.01759 (2016)

11. Kim, S.K., Park, M.J., Rho, J.J.: Effect of the government's use of social media on the reliability of the government: focus on twitter. Public Manage. Rev. **17**(3), 328–355 (2015). https://doi.org/10.1080/14719037.2013.822530

12. Kwak, H., Lee, C., Park, H., Moon, S.: What is Twitter, a social network or a news media? In: Proceedings of the 19th International Conference on World Wide Web, WWW 2010, pp. 591–600. ACM, New York (2010). https://doi.org/10.1145/1772690.1772751

13. Linda, S.L.A.I.: Social commerce - e-commerce in social media context. World Acad. Sci. Eng. Technol. **72**, 39–44 (2010)

14. Lloyd, S.: Least squares quantization in pcm. IEEE Trans. Inf. Theory **28**(2), 129–137 (1982)

15. Mata, F.J., Quesada, A.: Web 2.0 social networks and e-commerce as marketing tools. J. Theor. Appl. Electron. Commer. Res. **9**, 56–69 (2014)

16. McInnes, L., Healy, J., Melville, J.: UMAP: Uniform Manifold Approximation and Projection for Dimension Reduction. ArXiv e-prints, February 2018

17. Mikolov, T., Sutskever, I., Chen, K., Corrado, G.S., Dean, J.: Distributed representations of words and phrases and their compositionality. In: Advances in Neural Information Processing Systems, pp. 3111–3119 (2013)

18. Nargundkar, A., Rao, Y.S.: InfluenceRank: a machine learning approach to measure influence of twitter users. In: 2016 International Conference on Recent Trends in Information Technology (ICRTIT), pp. 1–6 (2016). https://doi.org/10.1109/ICRTIT.2016.7569535

19. Röder, M., Both, A., Hinneburg, A.: Exploring the space of topic coherence measures. In: Proceedings of the Eighth ACM International Conference on Web Search and Data Mining, WSDM 2015, pp. 399–408. ACM, New York (2015). https://doi.org/10.1145/2684822.2685324

20. de Rosario, A.H., Sáez-Martín, A., del Carmen Caba-Pérez, M.: Using social media to enhance citizen engagement with local government: Twitter or Facebook? New Media Soc. **20**(1), 29–49 (2018). https://doi.org/10.1177/1461444816645652

21. Small, T.A.: e-government in the age of social media: an analysis of the canadian government's use of Twitter. Policy Internet **4**(3–4), 91–111 (2012). https://doi.org/10.1002/poi3.12
22. Sobaci, M.Z., Karkin, N.: The use of twitter by mayors in turkey: tweets for better public services? Gov. Inf. Q. **30**(4), 417–425 (2013). https://doi.org/10.1016/j.giq.2013.05.014
23. Sokolova, M., Lapalme, G.: A systematic analysis of performance measures for classification tasks. Inf. Process. Manage. **45**(4), 427–437 (2009). https://doi.org/10.1016/j.ipm.2009.03.002. http://www.sciencedirect.com/science/article/pii/S0306457309000259
24. Syed, S., Spruit, M.: Full-text or abstract? Examining topic coherence scores using latent dirichlet allocation. In: 2017 IEEE International Conference on Data Science and Advanced Analytics (DSAA), pp. 165–174, October 2017. https://doi.org/10.1109/DSAA.2017.61
25. Tellez, J.F.: Peace agreement design and public support for peace: evidence from colombia. J. Peace Res. **56**, 827–844 (2019). https://doi.org/10.1177/0022343319853603
26. Vargas-Calderón, V., Camargo, J.E.: Characterization of citizens using word2vec and latent topic analysis in a large set of tweets. Cities **92**, 187–196 (2019)
27. Zhao, W.X., Li, S., He, Y., Chang, E.Y., Wen, J., Li, X.: Connecting social media to e-commerce: cold-start product recommendation using microblogging information. IEEE Trans. Knowl. Data Eng. **28**(5), 1147–1159 (2016). https://doi.org/10.1109/TKDE.2015.2508816
28. Zhao, W.X., et al.: Comparing Twitter and traditional media using topic models. In: Clough, P., et al. (eds.) ECIR 2011. LNCS, vol. 6611, pp. 338–349. Springer, Heidelberg (2011). https://doi.org/10.1007/978-3-642-20161-5_34

Latent Semantic Index: A Microservices Architecture

Julio Proaño$^{(\boxtimes)}$, Andres Reinoso, and Jonnathan Juma

Universidad Politécnica Salesiana, Morán Valverde s/n y Rumichaca, Quito, Ecuador
{jproanoo,areinosoo.est,jjuma.est}@ups.edu.ec

Abstract. Nowadays, searching for a topic on the Internet can be a frustrating experience because of all the excessive information. Thus, a strategy for automatically classifying the results can improve user experience and work efficiency. Latent Semantic Indexing (LSI) algorithm is used to classify documents by meaning due to its effectiveness. However, there is a problem with the implementation of this algorithm. LSI is computationally intensive because the cost is directly related to the number of documents. In particular, the Singular Value Decomposition (SVD) that is mainly used in LSI is unscalable in terms of both memory and computation time. One possible solution is to use more powerful computational resources, such as multiple computing nodes. In this paper, a novel distributed architecture for the LSI algorithm is proposed. It is based on the use of microservices in a Google Cloud environment. We evaluated the performances of the proposed Cloud-based LSI, and comparison is made with standalone LSI. The results show the benefits of using distributed systems based on runtime, concurrency, and processing.

Keywords: Latent Semantic Index · Distributed computing · Micro services

1 Introduction

Nowadays, the use of indexes is critical process for gathering relevant information in a search engine. Searching for a topic on an index website such as Scopus, Google Scholar, and so on, may return a considerable amount of results. Thus, researchers have to spend a lot of time determining if the information is useful or not. Latent Semantic Indexing (LSI) [14] can help to reduce the space of coincidences throughout the identification of patterns between terms, concepts and how they are related mathematically. LSI is a methodology for identifying trends in documents base on a list of contained words. For instance, if some words are provided in two or more documents, these words can have a relationship with those documents because they contain these words [14]. So, in other words, all these documents might be related to a particular concept.

LSI uses a Singular Value Decomposition (SVD) algorithm to build a matrix of documents (namely Corpus) with a set of essential concepts that each correspond to a topic in the entire Corpus. All of these concepts have a level of relationship (scores) between them, the documents, and words [12].

© Springer Nature Switzerland AG 2020
F. R. Narváez et al. (Eds.): SmartTech-IC 2019, CCIS 1154, pp. 142–153, 2020.
https://doi.org/10.1007/978-3-030-46785-2_12

The LSI time of processing is directly related to the size of the Corpus [1].

In short, the Corpus is a matrix, where the number of columns is given by the number of documents, and the number of rows is the number of words. Each document corresponds to a column, and each term belongs to a row of the matrix in which all the information of the Corpus ordered, can be processed mathematically by the SVD algorithm [1,12].

The SVD algorithm is based on a matrix factorization technique. Thus, the algorithm can reproduce the original matrix through the combination of its factors (decomposed matrices).

However, data processing is enormous in computational costs, sometimes even impossible to implement in a reasonable time [3]. LSI could be deployed in a computing system such as microservices, where complex applications are decomposed into the smallest distributed microservices. Distributed Computing consists of a set of computers interconnected through a network, and the user sees them as one supercomputer. Some advantages offered by Distributed systems are (a) Investment savings: allows working in together with all the resources, instead of working in a centralized system. (b) Reliability: if a machine fails, the system is still working with the other devices. (c) Scalability: allows increasing resources depending on the demand [3].

So, in this work, we propose the use of LSI search-oriented to a distributed microservices architecture developed entirely in Google Cloud Platform using Redis, Docker, and Kubernetes tools [4,11]. Finally, an evaluation of the proposal is shown.

This article is organized as follows. Section 2 describes some related works. Section 3 describes some background concepts. Section 4 describes the methodology that includes: architecture, software, and hardware, in Sect. 5 the tests of the LSI Server and distributed applications are carried out, finally in Sect. 6 detailed discussion of the results obtained the tests.

2   Related Works

Nowadays, as a result of a search, many users are overloading with a lot of information. In the 90s Deerwester S, Dumais S, Landauer T, Furnas G and Harshman R, published in the Journal of Information Sciences the first article called Indexing by latent semantic analysis. They show that LSI is a search technique that allows the recovery of documents that are similar in terms and content with a search keyword called a query. Next, a lot of studies show the effectiveness of LSI in text mining [5,13,16,17,19]. However, LSI is computationally intensive with large data size. To achieve this problem, several approaches have been perused. A number of researchers focus on decentralized P2P architectures due to its scalability and versatility of searching mechanisms [2,6,7,15,18]. Other researchers focus on distributed architectures such as Hadoop and Apache Spark [8–10]. The authors implement algorithms such K-mean LSI in a distributed architecture and evaluate its performance.

3   Latent Semantic Indexing

3.1   Latent Semantic Indexing

LSI is a methodology for identifying patterns in documents base on a list of contained words. LSI uses Singular Value Decomposition (SVD) algorithm to build a matrix of documents (namely corpus) with a set of important concepts that each correspond to a topic in the entire corpus. For instance, if some words are contained in two or more documents, these words can have a relationship with those documents due to the fact that they contain these words [14]. So, in other words, all these documents might be related to a certain concept.

So, LSI allows quantifying similar scores. These similarities can be used for classifying documents based on a search query, grouping into topics or concepts and finding related documents.

3.2   SVD

SVD factorizes the original matrix into three matrices that each represent concepts in the entire Corpus. In this matrix, documents correspond to columns, terms correspond to rows, and each value in the matrix represents the number of times a given the word occurs in a corresponding document. Singular Value Decomposition is the latent semantic indexing algorithm, a document library can be taken as an example. It can be expressed as a word $m \times n$, a large matrix of document A. Where n indicates the number of documents in the library, m that contains the entire library the number of different words. Each line of matrix A corresponds to a different word, each column of matrix A corresponds to a document, A is expressed as:

$$A = [a_{ij}]$$
$$1 \leq i \leq m \tag{1}$$
$$1 \leq j \leq n$$

SVD allows to identify and order the dimensions along which data point show the greatest variation, consisting of an orthogonal matrix U, a diagonal matrix S and a transpose of the orthogonal matrix V. Where the Transpose of U multiplied by the original U is equal to $I = U^T U$, where the columns of V are orthonormal eigenvectors of AA^T, S is a diagonal matrix containing the square roots of eigenvalues from U or V in descending order.

$$A_{mn} = U_{mm} S_{mn} V_{nn}^T \tag{2}$$

In the next section the proposal architecture is explained in detail (Fig. 1).

4   Microservices LSI Architecture Design

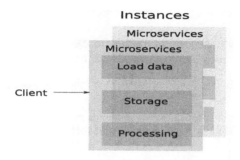

Fig. 1. Proposed architecture

Figure 3 shows the elements of the architecture in the Cluster that works in a distributed way by creating microservices.

The architecture is composed of 3 modules: load, store and processing. The *load module* is in charge of load all the documents that are the Corpus. Users can upload all the files that will be the Corpus. The *storage* is responsible to store the corpus in order to be process. Finally, the last module *processing* contains the SVD algorithm to perform LSI.

The software uses a microservices architecture that means that we will always have the process methods available, if a method fails another instance of it will be available to meet the request, helping the consistency of the processing. The architecture has as input a query (keywords) and number of documents that will be chosen for the Corpus and as output a list of documents with the percentage of relevance with respect to the query.

Two parameters are sent in JSON format, the query (keywords) and the number of documents to be obtained from the Corpus.

This last parameter was implemented exclusively to be able to measure the speed of response of the applications according to the number of elements processed and be able to compare them in the testing phase. The parameters are sent with the address of the services exposed by the server.

The output sends a list of names of the documents according to their relevance in descending order as can be seen an example in Fig. 2. With the use of the keyword process as a query. This word will be used in the testing phase because with the LSI methodology reflects a percentage of more than 33% relevance.

```
[
    {
        "name": "B Learning en la educación superior.txt",
        "relevance": 0.6475716457842186
    },
    {
      "name":"UN REQUISITO IMPRESCINDIBLE.txt",
        "relevance": 0.4578400982625404
    },

    {
        " name ": "chiller de absorción de 1 y 2 etapas.txt",
        " relevance ": 0.2863658409540783
    },
    {
        " name ": "PERFIL DE UNA ÉTICA EN CRISIS.txt",
        " relevance ": 0.2850426844736486
    }
]
```

Fig. 2. Architecture input and output example

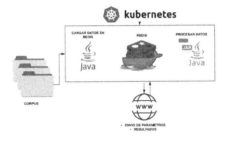

Fig. 3. Microservices implementation

5   Evaluation

The Kubernetes Cluster is composed of 4 nodes, and each node has the hardware characteristics as is detailed in Table 1.

In this section, tests have been carried out to compare the two applications in terms of the response speed of the two servers:

– LSI Virtual Server Application (LSI Server)
– Kubernetes Cluster application (distributed)

The LSI Server application on the virtual server is composed of 2 components hosted on the server:

– Corpus: documents stored

- LSI Methods: allows to perform the LSI document management with the Process module data and Load module data methods that allow showing the results of the application, processing the requests sequentially

On the other hand, the application by microservices was developed in the Kubernetes Cluster. It divides the main methods in Docker containers to save resources and to be able to administer to the containers with Kubernetes. Kubernet allows to increase the efficiency of the algorithm and thus have a faster response. It is composed of the following elements:

- Corpus.- Document store.
- Redis data loading docker as the Load module. It is in charge of a store the data into memory for the Redis
- Data Process Docker. It makes comparisons using SVD from the JAMA library to be able to show the results
- Kubernetes, it is responsible for managing the containers, create Pods if necessary to help the application process maintaining a high availability and load balancing.

Table 1. Hardware details

Parameters	Details
Nodes	4
CPU	Intel Haswell
RAM	3.75 Gb
SSD	5 Gb

The tests that have been performed are concurrency and document processing.

Both applications show the same results as they use the same Corpus documents as input. One of the essential components in terms of data processing is the JAMA library V1.0.3. It is a basic linear algebra package to build and manipulate real and dense matrices. From this library, the Singular Value Decomposition class is used. The SVD algorithm can automate the processes with matrix management [8]. In the case of the application by microservices, it is divided the application into individual services within a container (Docker). Additionally, Redis is used to optimize the query of the documents through the use of a data warehouse. Finally, all these containers will be managed by Kubernetes, improving the behavior of the application in the cluster, shortening the response times to the other application and optimizing the use of the resources of the cluster.

6   Results and Discussion

In this section we test the model presented in Section

6.1   Concurrency

For the concurrency tests, several requests have been made to the two applications, in which forty Corpus Documents and a keyword that represents more than 33% relevance were used to measure the response time of each request.

To measure the behavior of the system based on the results: 50, 100, 200 and 400 requests were made. You can compare the results between each server using the response time according to the number of requests made. These tests are intended to show the advantages of the proposed architecture with the use of microservices in the cluster managed by Kubernetes.

As is shown in Fig. 4 the two servers with 50 request have executed correctly, and there are not timeouts in their response. However, the processing speed of the Kubernetes Cluster is higher than that of the LSI Virtual Server.

The response speed of Kubernetes compared to the LSI server is 7.58 times faster with an average time of 12951 ms and 98142 ms (Table 2). This difference is because Kubernetes increases automatically the number of Pods depending on the workload. As a result, it can process more requests in parallel and avoid losing requests.

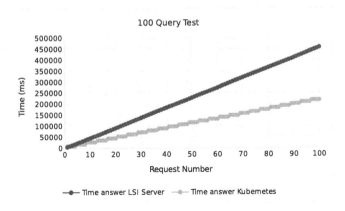

Fig. 4. Results using 50 Requests

On the other hand, in the previous test, when 100 requests have been made, there are no failed request in the two applications as can be seen in Fig. 5. However, with 100 requests, the server average response time drops to 2.02, as is shown in Table 3. Although it is a considerable speed, you can see that the server load increases depending on the number of requests. With 200 requests, the LSI Server application has several dropped requests and an error rate of 46%.

Table 2. Summary of results using 50 Requests

Services	Detail	Total
LSI Server	Number of request	50
	% of Processed requests	100.00%
	% Error	0.00%
	Time averenge requests	98142 ms
Kubernetes	Number of request	50
	% of processed requests	100.00%
	% Error	0.00%
	Time averenge requests	12951 ms

In the Kubernetes cluster, it can be observed that for 200 requests, 100% were fulfilled. Thus, the tests show the high availability of distributed environments to centralized applications. The average time is 1.71 times faster than the LSI Server.

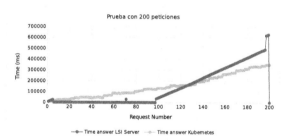

Fig. 5. Results using 100 requests

In Fig. 6, it can be seen how the LSI Server loses most of the requests for 400 requests. In the Kubernetes cluster, the percentage of error for each request is 0%. Therefore, the work that Kubernetes does with the Pods is still useful with an average response in all requests for 349962 ms, which is a time longer than the LSI Server application, but we must take into account that only 28.75% of the requests entered were processed, thus shows the efficiency of the use of the tools used in the application (Tables 4 and 5).

6.2 Load Tests

For the load tests, 25 independent requests were generated for both applications. The metric considered was the average of the response time. That means the time for the applications to return the results of the queries. The purpose of the load tests is to verify the processing that each of them has applications with the increase in the number of documents in the Corpus.

Table 3. Summary of results using 100 requests

Services	Detail	Total
LSI Server	Number of request	100
	% of Processed requests	100.00%
	% Error	0.00%
	Time averenge requests	113940 ms
Kubernetes	Number of request	100
	% of processed requests	100.00%
	% Error	0.00%
	Time averenge requests	230381 ms

Table 4. Results using 200 requests

Services	Detail	Total
LSI Server	Number of request	200
	% of Processed requests	54.00%
	% Error	46.00%
	Time averenge requests	257715 ms
Kubernetes	Number of request	200
	% of processed requests	100.00%
	% Error	0.00%
	Time averenge requests	159470 ms

Table 5. Summary of results using 400 requests

Services	Detail	Total
LSI Server	Number of request	400
	% of Processed requests	71.25%
	% Error	28.75%
	Time averenge requests	276897 ms
Kubernetes	Number of request	400
	% of processed requests	100.00%
	% Error	0.00%
	Time average requests	349962 ms

The tests will start with 25 documents, and 25 more documents will be taken from the Corpus for each test process as can be seen in Fig. 7.

A comparison of the response times between the LSI Server and the Kubernetes Cluster can be observed in Fig. 7. The Kubernetes Cluster has lower response times than the LSI Server application, as can be observed in Table 6.

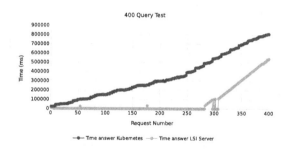

Fig. 6. Results using 400 requests

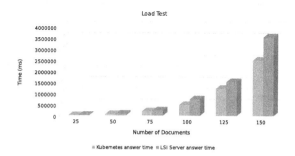

Fig. 7. Results with different documents

The response times of the Kubernetes cluster are lower, however, Kubernetes is still better in each process of the testing stage with 100, 125 and 150 documents processed, Kubernetes is 1.54, 1.24 and 1.42 times faster than the LSI Server application.

Table 6. Results summary

Number of documents	AVG kubernetes	AVG LSI server
25	1699.32	16904.28
50	67119	80852.48
75	197799.32	238926.2
100	484731.16	745101.32
125	1228607.04	1531941.84
150	2520085.76	3566740.68
	% Error	0.00%
	Average requests	349962 ms

7 Conclusions and Future Work

In this work, the efficiency provided by a microservices architecture to process information has been tested. In the case of the LSI Server application shows several problems with response times. On the other hand, Kubernetes and Redis used throughout fulfilled all their characteristics and benefits. Kubernetes allows to manages the resources of the cluster more efficiently with the promising response time.

In the concurrence tests, Kubernetes manages all the request efficiently with a lower percent of error in comparison to the LSI Server application. Finally, the use of the resources of the cluster is minimal since an escalation is made to the other nodes depending on the load sent, thanks to the fact that Kubernetes manages the containers.

Acknowledgments. This work was supported by IDEIAGEOCA Research Group of Universidad Politécnica Salesiana in Quito, Ecuador.

References

1. Baird, H.S.: Fast algorithm for LSI artwork analysis. In: Papers on Twenty-Five Years of Electronic Design Automation, pp. 154–162 (1988)
2. Cohen, E., Fiat, A., Kaplan, H.: Associative search in peer to peer networks: harnessing latent semantics. Comput. Netw. **51**(8), 1861–1881 (2007)
3. Bermúdez, J.G.: Diseño de elementos software con tecnologías basadas en componentes (2015)
4. Geewax, J.: Google Cloud Platform in Action. Manning Publications, Shelter Island (2018)
5. Heyman, G., Vulic, I., Moens, M.F.: C-BiLDA extracting cross-lingual topics from non-parallel texts by distinguishing shared from unshared content. Data Min. Knowl. Disc. **30**(5), 1299–1323 (2016)
6. Liu, F., Ma, F., Li, M., Huang, L.: Distributed information retrieval based on hierarchical semantic overlay network. In: Jin, H., Pan, Y., Xiao, N., Sun, J. (eds.) GCC 2004. LNCS, vol. 3251, pp. 657–664. Springer, Heidelberg (2004). https://doi.org/10.1007/978-3-540-30208-7_88
7. Liu, Y., Jing, W., Liu, Y., Lv, L., Qi, M., Xiang, Y.: A sliding window-based dynamic load balancing for heterogeneous hadoop clusters. Concurr. Comput. Pract. Exp. **29**(3), e3763 (2017)
8. Liu, Y., Li, M., Khan, M., Qi, M.: A mapreduce based distributed lsi for scalable information retrieval. Comput. Inform. **33**(2), 259–280 (2014)
9. Maarala, A.I., Rautiainen, M., Salmi, M., Pirttikangas, S., Riekki, J.: Low latency analytics for streaming traffic data with apache spark. In: IEEE International Conference on Big Data, pp. 2855–2858. IEEE (2015)
10. Mbah, R.B.K., Rege, M., Misra, B.: Using spark and scala for discovering latent trends in job markets. In: 3rd International Conference on Compute and Data Analysis, pp. 55–62 (2019)
11. García, J.N.: Orquestación de contenedores con Kubernetes. B.S. thesis (2018)
12. Peter, R., Shivapratap, G., Divya, G., Soman, K.: Evaluation of SVD and NMF methods for latent semantic analysis. Int. J. Recent Trends Eng. **1**(3), 308 (2009)

13. Soriano, J., Au, T., Banks, D.: Text mining in computational advertising. Stat. Anal. Data Min. **6**(4), 273–285 (2013)
14. Sosa Erazo, M.V., Zambonino Altamirano, M.A.: Estado de arte de" Latent Semantic Index" con una prueba experimental. B.S. thesis (2018)
15. Tang, C., Xu, Z., Dwarkadas, S.: Peer-to-peer information retrieval using self-organizing semantic overlay networks. ACM SIGCOMM Comput. Commun. Rev. **33**(4), 175–186 (2003)
16. Thorleuchter, D., Van den Poel, D.: Weak signal identification with semantic web mining. Expert Syst. Appl. **40**(12), 4978–4985 (2013)
17. Thorleuchter, D., Van den Poel, D.: Semantic compared cross impact analysis. Expert Syst. Appl. **41**(7), 3477–3483 (2014)
18. Zhang, S., Wu, G., Chen, G., Xu, L.: On building and updating distributed LSI for P2P systems. In: Chen, G., Pan, Y., Guo, M., Lu, J. (eds.) ISPA 2005. LNCS, vol. 3759, pp. 9–16. Springer, Heidelberg (2005). https://doi.org/10.1007/11576259_2
19. Zhang, W., Yoshida, T., Tang, X.: A comparative study of TF*IDF, LSI and multi-words for text classification. Expert Syst. Appl. **38**(3), 2758–2765 (2011)

Factors that Affect i-Vectors Based Language Identification Systems

David Romero[1]([⊠]), Christian Salamea[1,2], Fernando Chica[1], and Erick Narvaez[1]

[1] Interaction, Robotics, and Automation Research Group, Universidad Politécnica Salesiana,
Calle Vieja 12-30 y Elia Liut, Cuenca, Ecuador
{dromerom,csalamea,jchicao,enarvaez}@ups.edu.ec
[2] Speech Technology Group, Information and Telecomunication Center,
Universidad Politécnica de Madrid, Ciudad Universitaria Av. Complutense 30,
28040 Madrid, Spain

Abstract. The performance of a language identification (LID) system that uses i-vectors as features depends on several parameters, such as algorithm parameters and data parameters. In this study, an analysis of performance of a language identification system is considered, for which we focused only on data parameters in the "Back End" of the system, analyzing the influence of the amount of data and the speaker variability in the training phases of the UBM and the total variability Matrix T. Also, the Multiclass logistic regression (MLR) classifiers were analyzed, by balancing the classes of the database to train the classifiers on each language. These tests have been carried out in the Kalaka-3 database; we have used the average detection cost function (Cavg) to evaluate the performance. It is shown experimentally that in the training phase of the UBM, speaker variability is more important than a large amount of data. In the training phase of the total variability matrix T a better performance was obtained when a larger number of audios were used. And finally, balancing classes on each language to train the MLR classifiers allowed us to get a better performance only in certain languages. Using all of these proposed variations, we got a Cavg improvement of 37% in a standard language identification system.

Keywords: Data · i-Vector · Language identification

1 Introduction

1.1 Language Identification with i-Vectors

Language identification refers to the process of identifying the language spoken in a speech sample. Many methods have been proposed to perform this task, focusing on phonotactic information to systems based on spectral characteristics referred to as acoustic systems [1], as Gaussian Mixture Models (GMM's) [2], GMM with universal background model (GMM-UBM framework) [3], Joint factor analysis (JFA) [4] and i-Vectors [1, 5]. The i-Vector subspace modeling is one of the methods that has become the state-of-the-art technique in the domain of acoustic systems [6].

© Springer Nature Switzerland AG 2020
F. R. Narváez et al. (Eds.): SmartTech-IC 2019, CCIS 1154, pp. 154–164, 2020.
https://doi.org/10.1007/978-3-030-46785-2_13

This method can be seen as the application of a simplified version of JFA that allows projecting a voice segment that is normally expressed by a supervector in a high-dimensional speaker/language and channel variability space into a low-dimensional variability space, separating the effects of speaker, language and session variability [7]. Unlike the separate speaker and channel-dependent subspaces of JFA, i-Vectors represent the GMM super-vector by a single total-variability space [8]. After the success of i-vectors in speaker recognition, they have been used extensively for language identification tasks [6]. Being this method used in this work to build a standard language identification system.

For a given speech segment, the GMM mean supervector based on a total variability space can be expressed by the following formula:

$$M = m + Tw \tag{1}$$

Where m is the speaker - and channel-independent supervector, T is a low rank rectangular matrix and w is hidden variable that is defined by a Gaussian Distribution and the average of this distribution is an i-Vector [5, 7].

The typical i-Vector extraction process is shown in Fig. 1. Firstly, Mel-Frequency Cepstral Coefficient (MFCC) features [9] are extracted, which are coefficients for speech representation, after that Shifted Delta Cepstral (SDC) features [10], these are parameters that model the cepstral coefficients curve at a certain point in time, so they are able to handle longer context information, these are used to add temporal information or contextual information. Then, the Universal Background Model - Gaussian Mixture Model – (UBM-GMM) and the total variability matrix T are trained using SDC features, the matrix T is a matrix that represent the total variability space used to extract i-vectors [11]. Finally, the i-vectors are obtained for each speech segment according to the formula (1). To make the classification task many types of classifiers are used, such as multiclass logistic regression, neural networks, etc. [12, 13].

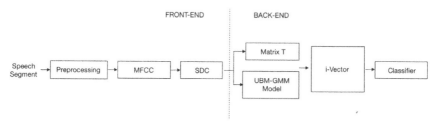

Fig. 1. i-Vector extraction

1.2 Parameters to Analyze in an i-Vector-Based Language Identification System

There are many different parameters involved in the i-Vector extraction process. There are algorithm parameters and data parameters. Algorithm parameters are the variations of the training process, which include training methods, number of interactions, initialization methods, etc. Data parameters are different ways of defining a subset of available training data, these parameters include the amount of data, amount of data per language, variability, data balancing according to each language and so on [14]. The only way of measuring the quality of the language identification system is with the overall/final system performance, finding good results will rely on a trial and error-based endeavor to find the optimal parameters in each phase of the i-vector extraction process. In this research, we will focus only on the "Back end" of the language identification system, which has the training phases of the UBM-GMM, Matrix T, and the logistic regression classifiers. Also, we will focus only on a limited set of data parameters (Amount of data, Data variability and Data balancing) and analyze those to see their effect on the overall/final performance of the language identification system.

After obtaining the MFCC and the SDC features, we train the UBM. A common assumption with the training phase of the UBM is that more data used, the better the system performance. In [14] the authors show for speaker identification that, increasing the inter-speaker variability while maintaining the overall data size constant to train the UBM, gradually improves system performance, also that if the selected data is well-chosen, is not necessary to use all the features of each utterance, being enough just ~1.5 h of data, since this amount of data contains all the inter-speaker variabilities present in all the utterances in the original NIST SRE 04 corpus that was used by the authors. We will analyze this aspect in the training phase of the UBM in the field of language identification using a different database and relate this to system performance.

After getting the UBM, the total variability matrix T has to be trained, usually, this matrix is trained using the same background data used for UBM training [15, 16]. Since total variability matrix T is a low-rank rectangular matrix that includes important inter- and intra-speaker variability [17], we will analyze for language identification whether is better to train the matrix T using a large amount of data or if using a fixed amount of data that contains all the variabilities of the corpus is enough to get a good performance.

Finally, the multiclass logistic regression classifiers were analyzed. The performance will be measured with the average detection cost function (Cavg). This metric uses the error rate of false acceptance and false rejection [18], the function is given by the following Eq. (2):

$$C_{avg} = \frac{1}{N_L} \sum_{LT} C_{miss} P_{trgt} P_{miss}(LT) + \sum_{LN} C_{FA} P_{NONtrgt} P_{FA}(L_T, L_N)$$
$$+ C_{FA} P_{OutSet} P_{FA}(L_T, L_O) \tag{2}$$

N_L is the number of languages to recognize, L_t is the target language, L_N is the non-target language, L_O represents a language that is outside the set of languages.

$$C_{miss} = C_{FA} = 1$$

$$P_{trgt} = 0.5$$

$$P_{OutSet} = 0.0 \text{ for the plenty closed condition}$$

$$P_{OutSet} = 0.0 \text{ for the open - set condition}$$

$$P_{NONtarget} = \frac{1 - P_{target} - P_{out-of-set}}{(N_L - 1)}$$

To get the Cavg we have to take the target language and treat the others as non-target languages, due to taking the other classes as non-target languages there will be an imbalance in the classes, having more files in the class with non-target languages compared to the target language that is being analyzed. We will analyze how this imbalance affects or improves the quality of the predictions, observing which languages improve and which languages are affected in the classification due to this imbalance.

This paper is organized as follows. In Sect. 2 we describe our baseline system and the database used in this research. In Sect. 3 we analyze the effect of the amount of data, data variability and data balancing in language identification. Finally, in Sect. 4 we draw conclusions.

2 Baseline System

2.1 Database

The database used for these experiments is KALAKA-3, this database consists of three subsets: training, development and evaluation. The training database have TV broadcast recordings, including speech in diverse environment conditions and spoken by multiple speakers. The development and evaluation datasets consist of YouTube audio signals in different formats and qualities, all of them stored as single-channel 16 kHz 16-bit PCM encoded WAV files. The training dataset amounts to around 113 h of speech, 80% clean, 20% noisy, with nearly 19 h on average for each one of the 6 target languages (Basque, Catalan, English, Galician, Portuguese, Spanish) [19]. A summary of the dataset is shown in Table 1, and the distribution of files of the training set is shown it Table 2.

Table 1. Kalaka-3 database

Files	Training	Dev	Eval
Files	4656	458	941
Clean files	3060	–	–
Noisy files	1596	–	–
$0 < t < 30$ s	2855	121	267
$30 < t < 120$ s	1801	337	674

2.2 System Overview

The LID system has two phases. The first is called "Front-End", in this phase the preprocessing of the audio signal and the creation of the supervectors are performed. The second phase is called "Back-End", here two processes are carried out, first, the creation

Table 2. Training set distribution

	Clean speech		Noisy speech	
Files	#	T(h)	#	T(h)
Basque	579	14.3	215	3.2
Catalan	440	15.8	209	3.1
English	322	15.5	265	3.7
Galician	675	14.6	300	3.8
Portuguese	558	15.7	295	4.5
Spanish	486	14.2	312	5.3
Total	3060	90.1	1596	23.6

of i-vectors and secondly the classification process with MLR classifiers which determines the language of the audio signals. Since the objective of this research is focused only on the back-end phase of the system, a standard i-vector system is used, that is implemented using "Sidekit" [19].

In the first phase (Front End), for each audio file, 12 Mel cepstral coefficients (MFCCs) are extracted. The silence and noise segments of the acoustic signal are suppressed using a voice activity detector (VAD), the type of VAD used was Signal Noise to Ratio (SNR) with snr of 40. In order to reduce the noise variations in the frequency bands, a Rasta filter and a Cepstral mean and variance normalization (CMVN) are used. A window size of 25 ms and a separation of 10 ms was established for the speech frames, and for each one a feature vector of dimension 56 was extracted from the concatenation of SDC parameters, using a 7-1-3-7 configuration. The second phase (Back End) will be analyzed in the following section, in this phase the UBM and matrix T training are performed to get the i-vectors. Finally, the training phase of the multiclass logistic regression classifiers for each language was performed, taking each language as the target and all other languages are treated as non-target languages in each classifier. The structure of the acoustic system is shown in Fig. 2.

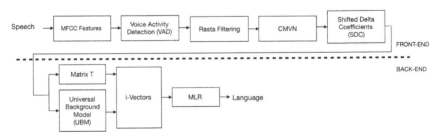

Fig. 2. Acoustic system structure

3   Experimental Approach and Results

3.1   UBM

After extracting the SDC parameters in the "Front end" phase of the system, we train the UBM, as expressed in Sect. 1.2, the authors in [14] show for speaker recognition that increasing the inter-speaker variability in the UBM data while maintaining the overall total data size constant gradually improves system performance, being ~1.5 h the sufficient amount of data to get good performance. We have analyzed this for the language identification field, training an UBM with 512 gaussians, using the expectation maximization algorithm (EM). In Sidekit the training process of the UBM is as follows: initialize one Gaussian distribution given all the training data, iterate n_i iterations of EM with the current size of model (fixed number of distributions), split all distributions in two according to their variance in order to double the number of distributions of the GMM, and finally save the resulting model.

The UBM is trained using, firstly ~1 h of speech per language, then ~2 h per language and finally with ~4 h and ~6 h per language. In each test, half of the data is of clean speech and the other half noisy speech. The amount of audio used for each language is shown in Fig. 3.

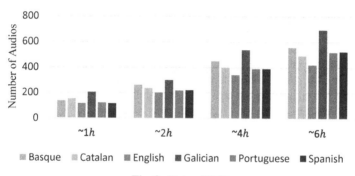

Fig. 3. Data – UBM

The data selected for each test were the shortest audios for each language, to take a greater amount of audios to have a greater variability of speakers, because if larger audios are used, a lot of information of a single speaker will be present in the corpus having less variability in the data. In these tests, the Matrix T has been trained with the same amount of data that was trained the UBM in each test. The multi-class logistic regression classifiers were trained to take each language as the target and all the other languages as non-target languages in each classifier. The results are shown in Fig. 4.

In Fig. 4 it can be seen that the performance with only ~2 h data per language is comparable with using ~4 h and ~6 h of data per language. For language identification it can be concluded that training the UBM with ~2 h of data is enough to get good results, due to this amount of data contains all the variabilities present in all utterances in the corpus, using on average 241 audios per language in the Kalaka-3 database. If the selected dataset is well chosen all the features for each utterance is not necessary for

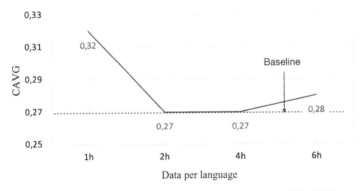

Fig. 4. Cavg – Variation of data in the training phase of the UBM

training the UBM. So, using a large database to train the UBM in language identification may not be necessary for the best performance, as long as the required variability is maintained.

3.2 Matrix T

Since total variability matrix T includes important inter and intra-speaker variability, in this section the performance is analyzed by increasing the variability on each test, incrementing the total amount of data while maintaining the overall total data size constant. The matrix T was trained with 10 interactions with a rank of 400, all the tests use the UBM trained on ~2 h data for each language. The multi-class logistic regression classifiers are trained to take each language as the target and to treat all the other languages as non-target languages.

The number of audios used for each language is shown in Fig. 5. The test performed were:

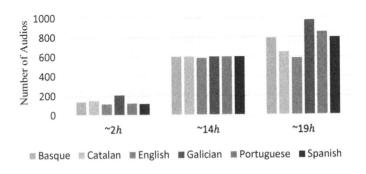

Fig. 5. Data – Matrix T

1. Firstly, training the matrix T with the same amount of data used to train the UBM, using ~2 h of data, on average 241 audios per language, to see if a fixed amount of audio per language that contains all the variabilities is enough or if increasing the number of audios per language help to get a better performance.
2. The second case that was analyzed was by increasing the number of audios per language. In this test, 600 audios (300 clean, 300 noisy) per language are used. In the Kalaka-3 database the lowest number of audios is 587 (322 clean, 265 noisy) corresponding to the English language, for this reason to not create a large imbalance in the number of audios per language we take 600 audios per language except in English that has 587 audios, which is on average ~14 h of speech per language.
3. The third case that was analyzed was by using all the audios of the training set of the database that have 4656 audios (3060 clean, 1596 noisy), on average ~19 h of speech per language.

In Fig. 6 it can be seen that the Cavg decreases as we increase the number of audios to train the matrix T, being the test 3 the one that provides the lowest Cavg value using all the data available in the training set of Kalaka-3. Unlike UBM training where a fixed size of data representing all the variability of the corpus was enough to get a good performance, in this case the system has a better performance by increasing the number of audios. So, with the Kalaka-3 database it can be concluded that a large number of audios to train the matrix T is necessary to get a better performance in the system.

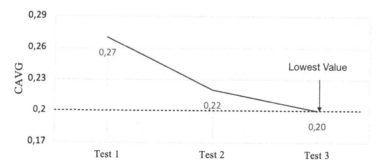

Fig. 6. Cavg – Variation of data in the training phase of the Matrix T.

3.3 Multi-class Logistic Regression Classifier

After analyzing the UBM and the matrix T, the performance was analyzed by balancing the number of audios of each class to train the multi-class logistic regression classifiers, we train 6 MLR classifiers, one classifier for each language. To get the Cavg we have to take each language as the target and treat all the other languages as non-target languages for each classifier. In this case if we take the audios of a language as the target language and all the other audios as non-target languages, we will have an imbalance in the number of audios in each class. The previous tests were performed with this imbalance.

In this section, the performance is analyzed by balancing the classes for each MLR classifier. For each target language we proceeded to take all the audios of that specific language, this being the target class, and then we take a certain amount of audios from the non-target languages, the number of audios per non-target language should be such that when adding all the non-target audios of each language, has to be the same amount of audios as in the target language class.

These tests were performed in the 3 cases that are shown in Fig. 6. The balance of the audios on each class did not provide an improvement in the classification of all languages, causing some classifiers to do not improve or even decrease its performance. The only classifiers that had an improvement were the English and Portuguese classifiers, that for test 3 shows a relative improvement of 6.25% in the accuracy of the English classifier and 2.10% in the Portuguese Classifier with the development set of the database. Due to the improvement in these two classifiers we got an overall improvement in Cavg. These tests are shown in Fig. 7.

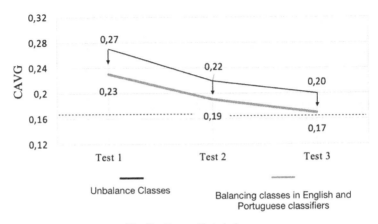

Fig. 7. Cavg – Data balance

In Fig. 7 is shown that after balancing the classes of each language that showed an improvement in its classification (English and Portuguese) the overall performance (Cavg) of the system improves in each test, being the test 3 the test that provides the lowest Cavg value. It can be concluded that balancing the classes to train the MLR classifiers provide an improvement only on certain languages (English and Portuguese) using Kalaka-3.

With all the improvements made to the system on each phase of the "Back End", the Cavg value decreased from 0.27 of the initial system to 0.17 the was the best performance obtained with this standard i-vector system, getting a relative improvement of 37%.

4 Conclusions

In this paper, many tests were performed to determine the data to be selected for an effective i-vector-based language identification system. The test performed showed the importance of data variability in UBM training, showing that a large database to train the UBM in language identification may not be necessary for the best performance, as long as the required variability is maintained, which also shows a benefit in the computation time. Also, that a large number of audios to train the matrix T is necessary to get a better performance, unlike the UBM where a certain amount of data that contains all the variabilities present in all the utterances of the corpus are enough, in this case, we obtained a better performance using all the training set of the database, showing that in this case is better to get a larger number of audios. Also, data balancing showed benefits only on certain languages, although it does not provide an improvement in all languages, there is an improvement in the final performance. Using all of these proposed variations, we got a relative improvement of 37% of Cavg in a standard language identification system.

References

1. Dehak, N., Torres-Carrasquillo, P.A., Reynolds, D., Dehak, R.: Language recognition via i-vectors and dimensionality reduction. In: Proceedings of the Annual Conference of the International Speech Communication Association – INTERSPEECH, pp. 857–860 (2011)
2. Torres-Carrasquillo, P., Reynolds, D., Deller, J.: Language identification using Gaussian mixture model tokenization. In: 2002 IEEE International Conference on Acoustic, Speech, and Signal Processing, vol. 1, pp. 757–760 (2002)
3. Qu, D., Wang, B., Wei, X.: Automatic language identification based on Gaussian mixture model and universal background model. In: Proceedings of SPIE – The International Society for Optical Engineering (2003)
4. Jancik, Z., Plchot, O., Brummer, N., Burget, L., Glembek, O.: Data selection and calibration issues in automatic language recognition - investigation with BUT-AGNITIO NIST LRE 2009 system. In: The Speaker and Language Recognition Workshop, pp. 215–221 (2010)
5. Dehak, N., Kenny, P., Dehak, R., Dumounchel, P., Ouellet, P.: Frond-end factor analysis for speaker verification. IEEE Trans. Audio Speech Lang. Process. **19**(4), 788–798 (2011)
6. Verma, P., Pradip, K.: i-Vector in speech processing applications: a survey. Int. J. Speech Technol. **18**(4), 529–546 (2015)
7. Salamea, C.: Diseño y Evaluación de Técnicas de Reconocimiento de Idioma mediante la Fusión de Información Fonotáctica y Acustica. Tesis Doctoral. Universidad Politécnica de Madrid (2018)
8. Kanagasundaram, A., Vogt, R., Dean, D., Sridha, S., Mason, M.: i-Vector based speaker recognition on short utterances. In: Proceedings of the Annual Conference of the International Speech Communication Association – INTERSPEECH, pp. 2341–2344 (2011)
9. Davis, P., Mermelstein, P.: Comparision of parametric representations for monosyllabic word recognition in continuously spoken sentences. IEEE Trans. Acoust. Speech Signal Process. **28**(4), 357–366 (1980)
10. Longting, X., Kong, A., Haizhou, A., Zhen, Y.: Sparse coding of total variability matrix. In: 2012 International Conference on Signal Processing and Communications, SPCOM 2012, pp. 1–5 (2012)
11. Torres-Carrasquillo, P., Singer, E., Kohler, M., Greene, R., Reynolds, D., Deller, J.: Approaches to language identification using Gaussian mixture models and shifted delta cepstral features. In: International Conference on Spoken Language Processing, ICSLP 2002, pp. 89–92 (2002)
12. Villegas, A.: Optimización de un Sistema de Reconocimiento de Idioma Fusionando Información Fonotáctica y Acústica con Redes Neuronales Profundas. Trabajo Fin de Master. Universidad Politécnica de Madrid (2017)

13. Wang, W., Song, W., Chen, C., Zhang, Z., Xin, Y.: I-vector features and deep neural network modeling for language recognition. In: 2018 International Conference on Identification, Information and Knowledge in the Internet of things, IIKI 2018 (2019). Procedia Comput. Sci. **147**, 36–43
14. Hasan, T., Hansen, J.: A study on universal background model training in speaker verification. IEEE Trans. Audio Speech Lang. Process. **19**(7), 1890–1899 (2011)
15. Ghahabi, O.: Deep learning for i-vector speaker and language recognition. Thesis doctoral. Universidad Politécnica de Catalunya (2018)
16. Chen, M., Yang, Z., Liang, J., Li, Y., Liu, W.: Improving deep neural networks based multi-accent mandarin speech recognition using i-vectors and accent-specific top layer. In: Proceedings of the Annual Conference of the International Speech Communication Association – INTERSPEECH, pp. 3620–3624 (2015)
17. Cumani, S., Laface, P.: Speaker recognition using e-vectors. IEEE Trans. Audio Speech Lang. Process. **26**(4), 736–748 (2018)
18. NIST: The 2015 NIST Language Recognition Evaluation Plan (LRE15). https://www.nist.gov/itl/iad/mig/2015-language-recognition-evaluation. Accessed 21 June 2019
19. Rodriguez, L., Penagarikano, M., Varona, A., Diez, M., Bordel, G.: KALAKA-3: a database for the assessment of spoken language recognition technology on YouTube audios. Lang. Resour. Eval. **50**(2), 221–243 (2016)

Incorporation of Language Discriminative Information into Recurrent Neural Networks Models to LID Tasks

Christian Salamea[1,2(✉)], Ricardo Cordoba[2], Luis D'Haro[2], and David Romero[1]

[1] Interaction, Robotics and Automation Research Group, Universidad Politecnica Salesiana, Calle Vieja 12-30 y Elia Liut, Cuenca, Ecuador
{csalamea,dromerom}@ups.edu.ec
[2] Speech Technology Group, Information and Telecommunications Center, Universidad Politecnica de Madrid, Ciudad Universitaria Av. Complutense, 30, 28040 Madrid, Spain
{cordoba,lfdharo}@die.upm.es

Abstract. Language Identification (LID) is an essential research topic in the Automatic Recognition Speech area. One of the most important characteristics relative to language is context information. In this article, considering a phonotactic approach where the phonetic units called "phone-grams" are used, in order to introduce such context information, a novel technique is proposed. Language discriminative information has been incorporated in the Recurrent Neural Network Language Models generation (RNNLMs) in the weights initialization stage to improve the Language Identification task. This technique has been evaluated using KALAKA-3 database that contains 108 h of audios of six languages to be recognized. The metric used in this work has been the Average Detection Cost metric C_{avg}. In relation to the phonetic units called "phone-grams" used in order to incorporate context information in the features used to train the RNNLM, it has been considered phone-grams of two elements "2phone-grams" and three elements "3phone-grams", obtaining a relative improvement up to 17% and 15,44% respectively compared to the results obtaining using RNNLMs.

Keywords: Language Identification · Automatic Recognition Speech · Recurrent Neural Networks · Language discriminative information

1 Introduction

Automatic spoken language identification (LID) is the process of identifying the actual language of a sample of speech using a known set of trained language models [1]. There are currently two main ways of achieving this goal: the first one uses acoustic features extracted from the speech signal in which the spectral information is used to distinguish among languages, while the second method uses the phonetic sequences obtained using an automatic phonetic recognizer (ASR) as features.

In general, the best results for the LID task are achieved using acoustic-based systems. However, their fusion with phonetic/phonotactic-based systems provides a higher accuracy [2]. This paper focuses on the study of two phonotactic techniques: A ranking

© Springer Nature Switzerland AG 2020
F. R. Narváez et al. (Eds.): SmartTech-IC 2019, CCIS 1154, pp. 165–175, 2020.
https://doi.org/10.1007/978-3-030-46785-2_14

of discriminative information based on text categorization [3] and recurrent neural network based language models generation [4]. Besides, the combination of scores from different levels and sources of information (e.g. acoustic features, higher n-gram orders) provide complementary information, so fusion techniques [5] are also applied to get better performances.

Both referred phonotactic techniques, generate scores which need to be normalized in case that they were getting compared, due to the different number of phone units used by each Automatic Speech Recognition System (ASR) to determinate the corresponding phoneme sequences and the amount of training data, a calibration step is required before the classifier. In this work a novel technique to improve the language recognition task through the incorporation of discriminative information into the weight initialization process of the neural networks is proposed.

This paper is organized as follows. In Sect. 2, the different techniques are described as well as the acoustic system used in the fusion with the phonotactic system. In Sect. 3, the experiments and the final results are presented. Finally, in Sect. 4, the conclusions and future work are presented.

2   System Description

2.1   The Concept of Phone-Gram Units

Frequently, languages models are designed to model phonetic structures at a word level, which is clearly efficient. However, the problem gets worse when the phonetic structures are phonemes as the model needs a state layer which is three times bigger than the layer used with words [6] to obtain similar results. There are two important drawbacks for phonemes. First, there is an important increase of the computational cost, and second, the systems can be easily over-trained [7]. Therefore, the Recurrent Neural Network Language Model proposed by Mikolov adapted to phonemes has been considered as baseline. This model uses the Backpropagation through Time algorithm [8] to recover past information to build the language model and uses a 1-N codification for the phonetic units in order to avoid the input layer duplication [9]. N is the total number of phonemes in the vocabulary. Taking account these drawbacks, using phonetic units bigger than phonemes but smaller than words could be better.

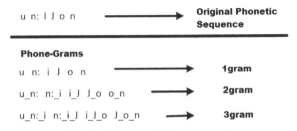

Fig. 1. Concept of "phone-gram"

Phonotactic systems use context information to improve the performance of language identification (LID). In this regard, in this paper the use of phonetic units that implicitly incorporate context information as features is proposed. They have been called phone-gram and they can be defined as the grouping of two or more phonemes in a new unit. An example of these units is presented in Fig. 1.

2.2 Database

As regards the database, KALAKA-3 [10] has been used due to its suitable size when considering the computational cost of the system. It was created for the Albayzin 2012 Language Recognition Evaluation (LRE). It is designed to recognize up to 6 languages in the closed set condition (i.e. Basque, Catalan, English, Galician, Portuguese and Spanish) using noisy and clean files with an average duration of 120 s and includes 108 h in total. The KALAKA-3 database contains training, development, testing, and evaluation examples distributed as shown in Table 1.

Table 1. KALAKA-3 database.

Files	Train	Dev	Test	Eval
N Files	4656	458	459	941
N clean files	3060	–	–	–
N noisy files	1596	–	–	–
Length $<= 30$	2855	121	113	267
Length 120 seg	1801	337	346	674

To compare the systems, C_{avg} metric has been considered, besides that it is one of the most useful metrics in Language Identification tasks. C_{avg} weights the number of false acceptances and false alarms generated by the recognizer [11], representing them as a detection cost function [12]. With this metric, lower values correspond to better systems.

2.3 Phoneme Recognizers in RNNLMs

The work developed in this paper is supported on the PPRLM (Parallel Phone Recognition and Language Modeling) architecture [13] as a reference. It consists of two components: Front-End and Back-End. The main process into the Front-End component is the phoneme recognizer, which obtain the phoneme sequences corresponding to the voice utterances. For this work, the Brno University (BUT) phoneme recognizer [14] which uses monophone three state HMMs has been used. There are three sets of HMMs (for Hungarian, Russian and Czech) with 61, 46 and 52 different phonemes respectively. In the Back-End component, the phoneme sequences obtained in the Front-End component are converted in "phone-grams" sequences that has been used to train the language models for each language in a supervised way using RNNs. The system is shown in the Fig. 2.

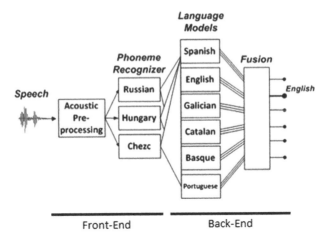

Fig. 2. Architecture of the system

2.4 RNNLM-P Applied to Language Identification

A Recurrent Neural Network is formed by three layers, one entry layer, one state layer and one output layer including an inner connection between the state layer and the entry layer. The number of entries in the entry layer is the number of n-grams of the vocabulary.

To obtain the language model, the next procedure is followed: From the "phone-gram" sequence, one by one, every "phone-gram" is introduced into the RNN using the 1-V codification. This way, each of the phone-grams are related with, one of the entries of the RNN and one weight, this last is random in principle, but after of some iterations characterize to every activated entry. Joint, the generated weight set in *(t)* and the corresponding stored in *(t − 1)* are projected in the state layer where through a sigmoid function the output signals are obtained, with a higher weight in the n-gram most likely in *(t + 1)*. To normalize these outputs we have used a Soft-Max function. This way, we can considerate to the outputs of the RNN as conditional probabilities, useful to train the language model and to obtain an entropy metric (score) for each of train and evaluation utterances comparing its probability with the corresponding model.

Then these scores are calibrated and fused [15] to obtain an overall score. Finally, the complete system is evaluated using the C_{avg} metric, which takes into account the False Acceptance and the False Rejection errors [11].

Figure 3 shows the procedure described using the phone-gram i_J_o from the sequence: $u\_n:\_i - n:\_i\_J - i\_J\_o - J\_o\_n$ as example. The referred Language Modeling has been called RNNLM-P since that phone-grams are used as features to train the RNN instead of phonemes.

2.5 Discriminative Language Information Applied to LID

The application of discriminative information can improve the performance of some language recognition systems [16]. To include it in the system, the idea proposed by Caraballo [17] has been used: To increase the score for the most discriminative units and

u_n:_i - n:_i_J - i_J_o - J_o_n

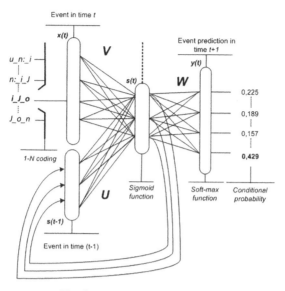

Fig. 3. Recurrent Neural Network

decrease it for the least discriminative ones, so that the recognizer will be more robust. Text categorization [18] has been used to this end.

Discriminative information is grouped into templates which contain the existing phone-grams in the training database and their discriminative score is to give more relevance to the phone-grams that exist in one language and do not exist (or with a low count) in competing languages. This way, language discrimination is reinforced.

In summary, in the training phase, the database is processed and the rankings for each language are generated. In the rankings, the top positions are occupied by the most frequent phone-grams of the current language and which have a low count in the rest of languages. This information is used to incorporate language knowledge in the RNN weights initialization.

2.6 Incorporation of Discriminative Information in RNNs

The objective of this work consists in the incorporation of the information contained in the discriminative ranking templates into the projection matrix of the Neural Network where the corresponding weights are initialized. This proposal is based in the fact of a good initialization of the weights of the Neural Network allows to define a better local minimum instead the weights are aleatory defined [19].

In practice, every phone-gram of the sequence obtained from the phoneme recognizer is presented, both, to the entry of the Neural Network and to the discriminative ranking template, the discriminative value is extracted from the template and it is multiplied to the vector in the projection matrix corresponding to the phone-gram examined, replacing it the previous value.

The discriminative values are between 0 and 1. Therefore, a phone-gram very discriminative for a language increase the corresponding values in the matrix while a phone-gram less discriminative for a language decreases the corresponding values in the matrix. The process is shown in Fig. 4.

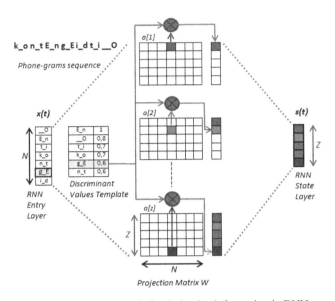

Fig. 4. Incorporation of discriminative information in RNN

To incorporate language discriminative information in RNNs, increasing the matrix values of the RNN for a language discriminative phone-gram as well as decreasing the matrix values for a less discriminative phone-gram, the next equation has been used:

$$x'(t) = \frac{x(t) + DiscrValue}{2}$$

Due to the lowest values obtained in the less discriminative phone-grams, a different ranges of discriminability has been evaluated. The ranges evaluated have been: (0.5, 1], (0.6, 1], (0.7, 1] y (0.9, 1].

2.7 Acoustic System Using MFCCs

We have fused the scores of the proposed techniques with the scores obtained from an acoustic system to check if they provide complementary information. The acoustic system has been generated as follows: from each speech utterance, 12 MFCC coefficients including C0 [20] are extracted for each frame. The silence and noise segments of the acoustic signal have been removed using a Voice Activity Detector. To reduce the noise perturbation, a RASTA filter has been used together with a cepstral mean and variance normalization (CMNV). We have a feature vector of dimension 56, generated from the concatenation of the SDC parameters using the 7-1-3-7 configuration. Feature vectors are used to train the total variability matrix, from which the i-vectors of dimension 400 with 512 Gaussians are extracted (optimal configuration).

2.8 Configuration of the RNN

In relation to the configuration of the RNN, the quantity of information recovered from the past (MEM) is required, after experimentation using MEM = 1 the best result has been obtained. Likewise, a definition of the number of classes used in the output layer is necessary. The value of 30 has offered the best result for 2phone-grams and 30k for 3phone-grams maintaining a good balance between accuracy and computational cost. Finally, the optimum number of neurons in the state layer has been determinate as 100 for 2phone-grams and 200 for 3phone-grams.

On other hand, it has been necessary to define the language modelling baseline to compare the results obtained, both, using the modelling of RNN and using the incorporation of discriminative information. Although the most well-known method to language modelling process is the "Kneser-Ney" [21] in our case it was not the best, probably because of some counts has a cero value generating probability values NA. To avoid the mentioned negative effect, the Ney method has been used, that considers the counts of the counts, minimizing the cited drawback.

3 Results

As described in Sect. 2.2, the Average Cost Function (C_{avg}) has been the metric used to quantify the application of the techniques described in this work.

The main idea of the C_{avg} is measuring the cost of making a decision, where both, the false acceptances (FA) and false alarms (miss) are included. To calculate the C_{avg}, the next equation has been used:

$$C_{avg} = \frac{1}{N_L} \sum_{L_T} c_{miss} P_{trgt} P_{miss}(L_T)$$
$$+ \sum_{L_N} C_{FA} P_{NONtrgt} P_{FA}(L_T, L_N) + C_{FA} P_{OutSet} P_{FA}(L_T, L_O)$$

Where:

N_L is the number of languages to be recognized
L_T is the target language and L_N is a non-target language.
L_o is "out-of-set" language (including both "unknown" languages and "known" but out-of-set languages.
$c_{miss} = C_{FA} = 1$. $P_{target} = 0.5$. $P_{out-of-set} = 0$. Because this work is related to the closed-set condition.

$$P_{Non-Target} = (1 - P_{Target} - P_{Out-of-Set})/(N_L - 1)$$

In Table 2, the results corresponding to the case of 2phone-grams are shown. The information relative to every ASR (Russ, Hung and Czech) is presented in the first three columns, the fusion result in the fourth column. The last column presents the relative improvement respect to the fusion results:

Table 2. Incorporation of discriminative information of RNNs – Case 2phone-grams.

Test-2phon-grams-C_{avg}	Russ	Hung	Czech	Fusion	Improve %
LM-ngram baseline	15,5	15,5	17,1	13,4	
RNNLM-P	15,6	16,3	19,4	14	
RNNLM-P + DiscRk(0:1)	16,6	17,4	24,7	14,3	−2,14
RNNLM-P + DiscRk(0,5:1)	16,3	17,3	19,9	12,6	10
RNNLM-P + DiscRk(0,6:1)	14,2	14,8	21	11.,9	16,67
RNNLM-P + DiscRk(0,7:1)	14,4	14,9	19,7	12,4	11,43
RNNLM-P + DiscRk(0,9:1)	15,9	16,8	17,4	12,82	8,43

As it can be seen in Table 2, considering the fusion results, the best performance of the system in presence of 2phone-grams in the phonetic sequences has been obtained with language discriminative templates whose limits are between 0,6 and 1. In this case, a relative improvement up to 17% of C_{avg} has been obtained compared to the C_{avg} of the RNNLM-P and up to 11, 19% of relative improvement when is compared to the LM-ngram baseline.

A comparative among the classical Language Modelling used as baseline, the Recurrent Neural Network Language Modelling and the application of the incorporation of Language Discriminative Information into the RNNLMs, all of them applied to improve the LID task, are shown in Fig. 5.

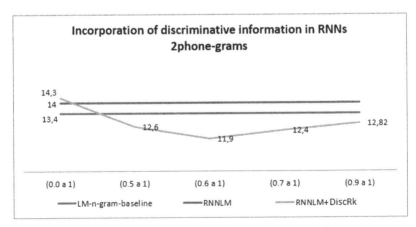

Fig. 5. Comparative among LMs, RNNLMs and RNNLM+Discriminative Information in 2phone-grams

In Fig. 5, the LM-ngram-baseline shows a better performance compared to the results obtained using RNNLM. The incorporation of Discriminative values in RNNLM improves the performance of the system in general when the Language Discriminative Templates are greater than 0, 4 approximately.

Table 3. Incorporation of discriminative information of RNNs – Case 3phone-grams.

Test-3phon-grams-C_{avg}	Russ	Hung	Czech	Fusion	Improve %
LM-ngram baseline	14,1	14,4	16,6	11,7	
RNNLM-P	15,2	16,8	18,5	13,6	
RNNLM-P + DiscRk(0:1)	14,9	15,8	23,3	12,5	8,09
RNNLM-P + DiscRk(0,5:1)	15,3	16,6	19,9	11,5	15,44
RNNLM-P + DiscRk(0,6:1)	13	14,9	19,4	11,4	16,18
RNNLM-P + DiscRk(0,7:1)	14,1	14,4	18,5	11,7	13,97
RNNLM-P + DiscRk(0,9:1)	14,9	15,8	17,4	12,02	11,62

In case of 3phone-grams, the results shown in the Table 3 has been obtained. The information relative to every ASR (Russ, Hung and Czech) is presented in the first three columns, the fusion result in the fourth column. The last column presents the relative improvement respect to the fusion results:

As it can be seen in Table 3, the trend of the result is similar to the obtained using 2phone-grams. The best results are obtained using the discriminate template limits between 0.6 and 1. Although the relative improvement is superior when comparing the RNNLM-P+DiscRk and the RNNLM (15.44%), the improvement is less good when comparing the RNNLM-P+DiscRk and the LM-ngram baseline (2.56%). The behavior of the complete system is described in the Fig. 6:

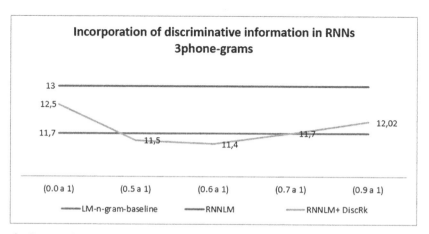

Fig. 6. Comparative among LMs, RNNLMs and RNNLM+Discriminative Information in 3phone-grams

As final step, the fusion results of the incorporation technique proposed in this paper described in Sect. 2.6 with the referential acoustic system described in Sect. 2.7 are shown in Table 4. Just for this Table 1phone-gram, 2phone-gram and 3phone-grams are referred as 1-gram, 2-gram and 3-gram respectively:

Table 4. Incorporation of discriminative information of RNNs – Case 3phone-grams.

	1-gram	2-gram	3-gram	1-2-3 g + acoustic	Improve %
Acoustic			7,60		
RNNLM-P	13,02	12,09	12,02	5,06	33,4
RNNLM-P + DiscRk (0,5:1)	13,00	12,60	11,50	5,01	34,1
RNNLM-P + DiscRk (0,6:1)	12,95	11,90	11,40	4,92	35,3
RNNLM-P + DiscRk (0,7:1)	13,52	12,40	11,70	5,09	33,0
RNNLM-P + DiscRk (0,9:1)	13,70	12,82	12,02	5,25	30,9

4   Conclusions

RNNs and their model languages have been adapted to work in a phonetic approach instead of lexical approach. For this purpose, parameters called "phone-grams" that include context information have been used. Hence, the phoneme sequences have been converted in larger sequences without reaching lexical level. Thought the results has not been better than the obtained using the classical language models PPRLM, the technique proposed in this work allowed improve the performance of the PPRLM, up to 11, 20% in 2phone-grams and up to 2, 56% in 3phone-grams.

The best results of this work has been obtained fusing the phonotactic techniques and the reference acoustic system that had been used as baseline. The relative improvement up to 35, 3% has been obtained when a language discriminative ranking between (0.6:1) was incorporated in the weight initialization of the RNN. This way, it can be demonstrated that context information provides complementary information into acoustic systems that improves the LID tasks.

In relation to the future lines, the use of different mathematical methods to define the ordering of the phone-grams in the ranking will be used to comparing among them. Further, analyzing of the behavior of the individual languages in the classification task could be useful to determinate the particular characteristic of the languages and their implication in the LID tasks.

References

1. Muthusamy, Y., Barnard, E., Cole, A.: Reviewing automatic language identification. IEEE Signal Process. Mag. **11**(4), 33–41 (1994)

2. D'Haro, L., Cordoba, R., Salamea, C., Echeverry, J.: Extended phone-likelihood ratio features and acoustic-based i-vectors for language recognition. In: Proceedings in Acoustics, Speech and Signal Processing, ICASSP, pp. 5342–5346 (2014)
3. Salamea, C., D'Haro, L., Córdoba, R., Caraballo, M.: Incorporation of discriminative ngrams to improve a phonotactic language recognizer based on i-vectors. Procesamiento del Lenguaje Natural **51**, 145–152 (2013)
4. Mikolov, T., Karafiát, M., Burget, L., Cernock, J., Khudanpur, S.: Recurrent neural net- work based language model. Interspeech **2010**, 1045–1048 (2010)
5. Brummer, N., et al.: Fusion of heterogeneous speaker recognition systems in the STBU submission for the NIST speaker recognition evaluation. IEEE Trans. Audio Speech Lang. Process. **15**(7), 2072–2084 (2007)
6. Mikolov, T., Kombrink, S., Deoras, A., Burget, L., Cernocky, J.: RNNLM-Recurrent neural network language modeling toolkit. In: Proceedings in ASRU Workshop, pp. 196 – 201 (2011). http://www.fit.vutbr.cz/~imikolov/rnnlm/
7. Zaremba, W., Sutskever I., Vinyals. O.: Recurrent neural network regularization. In: arXiv preprint arXiv:1409.2329 (2014)
8. Werbos, P.J.: Backpropagation through time: What it does and how to do it. In: Proceedings of the IEEE, vol. 78, no. 10, pp. 1550-1560 (1990)
9. Mikolov T.: Statistical language models based on neural networks. Ph.D. dissertation, Ph. D. thesis, Brno University of Technology (2012)
10. Rodriguez-Fuentes, L.J., Brümmer, N., Penagarikano, M., Varona, A., Bordel, G., Diez, M.: Kalaka-3: a database for the assessment of spoken language recognition technology on youtube audios. Lang. Resour. Eval. **50**(2), 221–243 (2016)
11. Martin, A., Greenberg C.: The 2009 NIST language recognition evaluation. In: Odyssey, p. 30 (2010)
12. D'Haro, L., Cordoba, R.: The gth-lid system for the albayzin LRE12 evaluation. In: Proceedings. Iberspeech, pp. 528–539 (2012)
13. Zissman, M., et al.: Comparison of four approaches to automatic language identification of telephone speech. IEEE Trans. Speech Audio Process. **4**(1), 31 (1996)
14. Ace, P., Schwarz, P., Ace, V.: Phoneme recognition based on long temporal context (2009)
15. Brummer, N., Van Leeuwen, D.: On calibration of language recognition scores. In: IEEE Odyssey Speaker and Language Recognition Workshop, pp. 1–8 (2006)
16. BenZeghiba, M., Gauvain J., Lamel, L.: Language score calibration using adapted Gaussian back-end. In: 10th Annual Conference of the International Speech Communication Association, pp. 2191–2194 (2009)
17. Caraballo, M., D'Haro, L., Cordoba, R., San-Segundo, R., Pardo, J.: A discriminative text categorization technique for language identification built into a PPRLM System. In: FALA 2010 VI Jornadas en Tecnología del Habla and II Iberian SLTech Workshop (2010)
18. Cavnar, W., Trenkle, J.: N-gram-based text categorization. In: 3rd annual Proceedings of SDAIR-94 (1994)
19. Duda, R., Hart, P., Stork, D.: Pattern Classification and scene analysis (1973)
20. Davis, S., Mermelstein, P.: Comparison of parametric representations for monosyllabic word recognition in continuously spoken sentences. In: Acoustics, Speech and Signal Processing, pp. 357–366 (1980)
21. Goodman, J.T.: A bit of progress in language modeling. Comput. Speech Lang. **15**(4), 403–434 (2001)

A Content-Based Multi Label Classification Model to Suggest Tags for Posts in Stack Overflow

Fredy A. Moreno and Jorge E. Camargo[✉]

Laboratory for Advanced Computational Science and Engineering Research,
Universidad Antonio Nariño, Bogota, Colombia
{fredymoreno,jorgecamargo}@uan.edu.co

Abstract. This paper presents a prediction model to automatically suggests tags when developers make a post in the Stack Overflow social network. The proposed model fuses the content of a post (text and code snippets) to build a multimodal representation that is used to find which are the most suitable words to be used as tags. The model was evaluated with a set of 20,000 posts extracted from Stack Overflow. Results show that the text modality reaches a higher performance compared to the code modality, whilst combining both modalities does not produce the best performance.

Keywords: Stack Overflow · Tag prediction · Word embedding · Multimodal learning

1 Introduction

Collaborative platforms are usually used for programmers in the process of software construction. Programmers typically address technical problems that other programmers have solved in the past. Specialized platforms for developers, a programmer commonly creates questions to ask other developers for solutions. These questions generate discussions around possible solutions that could be implemented. One of the most popular technical platforms for community developers is Stack Overflow, in which programmers help one another using a question and answers (Q&A). When programmers ask a question, other programmers are challenged to give a possible solution for that question. Answers are validated by the programmer who originated the question and also by other programmers in the platform. Questions are also rated by relevance, filtered by the community to prevent duplicated questions, and tagged by the user who asked. This process of Q&A creates a valuable repository that can be used by other programmers and for research purposes. When a question is formulated in Stack Overflow it is necessary to tag this question with a set of labels with the objective that they can be used to search and explore the repository. Selecting a good set of labels to tag a post produces an accurate search system, however, when the selected labels do not match well the content of the post decrease the quality of the retrieval system.

F. R. Narváez et al. (Eds.): SmartTech-IC 2019, CCIS 1154, pp. 176–187, 2020.
https://doi.org/10.1007/978-3-030-46785-2_15

This paper proposes a method to automatically predicts a set of labels to tag a post based on the content of a post. That is, when a programmer formulate a question, which can include text and code snippet, the model predicts which are the most suitable labels that describe the question.

The paper is structured as follows, Sect. 2 presents the state of the art and related works in the field, Sect. 3 shows the proposed method, Sect. 4 presents experimental evaluation, Sect. 5 present results, and finally, Sect. 6 concludes the paper.

2   Related Work

In previous works the problem of generate labels based on textual content has been addressed in different contexts. For instance, in [3] and [8] authors use methods such as Support Vector Machines (SVM) to train a classifier that is able to predict a set of tags based on the text of the post. In [14] authors also use SVM to predict labels but using code snippets to represent each post. In [2] labels are generated as a synonym expansion of words found in the text of the post. In [6] it is proposed a model based on SVM, K-NN y Fussy NNS. Authors in [4] propose a probabilistic model to predict labels using the title of the post. Snaket et al. [13] use TF-IDF to represent the textual content of the post. Tag prediction has been studied in other contexts such as social networks, blogs and websites to improve the user experience. For instance, in [1] authors propose a method to suggest labels based on user likes and preferences in the context of a social network. In [15] authors proposed a model that predicts labels to automatically tag images on *Facebook*. Hassanali et al. [5] propose a model to predict labels in a politician website. In the context of news, in [9] authors propose a model to suggest labels based on the textual content of a news. In [12] a tag system is proposed focusing in the impact of the representation of textual content. Wang et al. [7] use SVM and TF-IDF to select the best terms to be used as labels in the context of a website.

Most of the reviewed works focused on the extraction of features from text content and some of them on the extraction of features from code snippets. However, up to our knowledge, there no are works in which both modalities (text and code) are studied to determine the impact on the prediction of labels. In this paper both modalities are studied in order to determine what is the importance of each modality in label prediction.

3   Materials and Methods

The proposed method is composed of the following stages: (1) dataset building; (2) pre-processing of data; (3) feature extraction; (4) model learning and (4) prediction. Figure 1 shows an overall description of the method. In next subsections each stage will be presented in more detail.

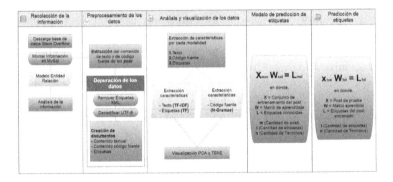

Fig. 1. Overview of the proposed method: (1) dataset building; (2) pre-processing of data; (3) feature extraction; (4) model learning and (4) prediction.

3.1   Dataset Building

In 2014 Stack Overflow released a dataset of posts that contains 7.9 millions of questions and 13.6 millions of answers. These two types of posts show the interaction between programmers that share text, snippets of source code, and a set of user tags (labels that programmers use to tag a question).

The dataset is about 25 Gb of text. Since we are interested in study the impact of text and code snippets, we selected questions posts with both modalities, as it is presented in Table 1. Figure 2 shows an example of the content of a post. Therefore, a set 5,549,458 posts were selected for our study.

Table 1. Composition of posts of type Question

Post composition	Number of posts	Percentage %
Only text	2,441,569	30.5%
Tex and code	5,549,458	69.4%
Total	7,991,027	100%

At the same time, in Fig. 3 text tokens is presented the distribution of text tokens in the dataset. Figure 4 shows the corresponding histogram for tags. It is worth nothing that 'C' and 'MongoDB' are the most frequent labels to tag the posts. On the other hand, 'second' and 'enter' the most common words in the posts.

3.2   Pre-processing of Data

Each post was processed to eliminate HTML tags and special characters. From each post three files were generated: text, code and tags. The NLTK (Natural Language Toolkit) library was used to perform some operations such as lower conversion, stop words removal and stemming.

▲

74

▼

☆

24

I am making extensive use of `boost:shared_ptr` in my code. In fact, most of the objects that are allocated on the heap are held by a `shared_ptr`. Unfortunately this means that I can't pass `this` into any function that takes a `shared_ptr`. Consider this code:

```
void bar(boost::shared_ptr<Foo> pFoo)
{
    ...
}

void Foo::someFunction()
{
    bar(this);
}
```

There are two problems here. First, this won't compile because the T* constructor for `shared_ptr` is explicit. Second, if I force it to build with `bar(boost::shared_ptr<Foo>(this))` I will have created a second shared pointer to my object that will eventually lead to a double-delete.

This brings me to my question: Is there any standard pattern for getting a copy of the existing shared pointer you know exists from inside a method on one of those objects? Is using intrusive reference counting my only option here?

c++   boost

Fig. 2. Example of a post: text and snippet of code.

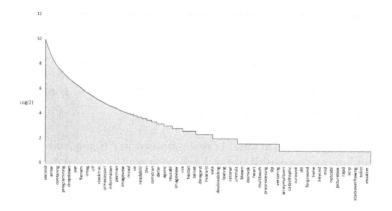

Fig. 3. Frequency of text tokens in the dataset.

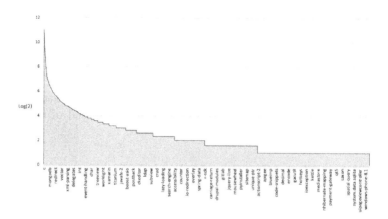

Fig. 4. Frequency of tags in the dataset.

3.3 Feature Extraction

Each post was processed to extract text and code features. Both modalities were fused to build a multimodal representation.

Text Representation. The text modality of a post is represented using the model proposed by [11], in which each term is weighted according to its frequency in a document as follows,

$$tf(w,d) = \frac{f(w,d)}{max\{f(w,d) : w \in d\}},$$ (1)

where w es el i-th term in document d, $f(w,d)$ is the frequency of w in document d, and max is the max function.

This term frequency is weighted by its inverse document frequency as follows,

$$idf(w,D) = \log \frac{|D|}{|\{d \in D : w \in d\}|},$$ (2)

where w is the i-th term, D is the total of documents in the dataset, and log is the logarithm function. This allows to penalize terms with high frequency and reward rare terms. Each document is represented as a vector with the frequency of each word in each document. At the end, the complete set of tokens is represented as a matrix X_t, where t represents the text modality.

Source-Code Representation. As it is proposed in [10] n-grams are an interesting way to extract tokens of size n. Each document is represented as a vector with the frequency of each n-gram in each document. At the end, the complete set of tokens is represented as a matrix X_c, where c represents the code modality.

Multimodal Representation. Each modality was fused for each post to build a vector in which text and code are represented at the same time. That is, a multimodal matrix X_m is built as the concatenation of X_c and X_c as follows,

$$X_m = X_t \frown X_c,$$ (3)

where $A \frown B$ is the concatenation between matrix A and matrix Y.

The concatenation of representations is known in the literature as 'early fusion', which produces a new representation space composed of two different modalities to be used in before the learning process.

3.4 Prediction Model Based on Multilabel Classification

We propose a new model to tag a post with multiple labels. This model can be categorized as a multilabel classification algorithm, which generates a set of possible labels for a post according to its content. The model uses the following definitions:

- Let X be the matrix representation of the post dataset.
- Let L be the matrix of labels, in which each column codifies 1 if a label is present in the post and 0 otherwise.
- Let W be the learning matrix, which will be learned after training.

Therefore, we can express the cost function as the following linear combination,

$$XW = L \tag{4}$$

We are interested in minimizing the cost function,

$$\underset{W}{\text{minimize}} \, ||XW - L|| \tag{5}$$

To find where this function is minimized, we derivate the cost function with respect to W as follows,

$$\frac{d}{dw} (XW - L)^2 = 0 \tag{6}$$

$$\frac{d}{dw} \left\{ (XW)^2 - 2 \, XWL + L^2 \right\} = 0 \tag{7}$$

$$\frac{d}{dw} \left\{ XX'WW' - XWL + L^2 \right\} = 0 \tag{8}$$

$$X'XW - X'L = 0 \tag{9}$$

$$(X'X) \, W - X'L + \lambda W = 0 \tag{10}$$

$$(X'X) \, W + \lambda W = X'L \tag{11}$$

$$W \, [(X'X) + \lambda I] = X'L \tag{12}$$

$$W \, [(X'X) + \lambda I] \, [(X'X) + \lambda I]^{-1} = (X'L) \, [(X'X) + \lambda I]^{-1} \tag{13}$$

$$W = [(X'X) + \lambda I]^{-1} \, (X'L) \tag{14}$$

This analytic process allows to find W, which learns the weights that can be used to predict labels for new posts. Therefore, W is used to predict as follows,

$$xW = l \tag{15}$$

where x the vector representation of the new post, W is the learning matrix, and l is the resulting vector of predicted labels.

4   Experimental Evaluation

This section presents details of the experimental evaluation conducted to evaluate the proposed method.

Training Data Set. A random sample of 0.3% of the 5,549,458 posts was used to train and test. That is, the resulting dataset is composed of 20, 23 posts. This dataset was divided into 90% for training and 10% for test in a configuration of 10-fold cross-validation.

Performance Measure Based on *recall*. The performance measure selected to evaluate the proposed model was *recall*. That is, for each post in the test set it was predicted the labels. The prediction model produces a vector l, in which each component is ranked by importance. Therefore, a set is created with the first k labels and is intersected with the set of real labels. The recall is calculated as the proportion of predicted labels with respect to the real labels. We experiment the impact of increase the number of labels between 1 and the maximum of possible labels.

Random Label Generation. As baseline a random label generation was performed, that is to say, a vector randomly generated was used as baseline to be compared with predicted labels by the proposed model.

5   Results

Performance Evaluation. Figure 5 shows the result obtained when it is measured the recall increasing the number of labels predicted. Each modality and its fusion were used independently to train the prediction model and are compared to the random baseline. Results show that text modality reaches the highest performance: in the first 10 labels an 80% of recall is reached for this modality. That can be attributed to the fact that text has a high semantic content in which there is a higher correlation between the language in which a question is formulated and its labels. It is worth nothing that code modality performs better than baseline but it is lower that text modality. It is worth also noting that multimodal representation reaches a lower performance compared to text modality, which can be interpreted that the code representation is not improving the representation of a post. This can be attributed to the fact that code snippets are in different programing languages such as Java, Javascript, Python, C'#, Visual Basic, PHP, among others, which makes it difficult to obtain a good representation of the code modality.

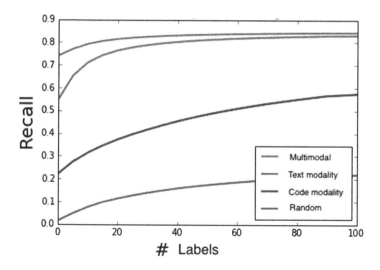

Fig. 5. Recall obtained when the number of generated labels is increased.

Qualitative Evaluation. Figure 6 shows a 2D visualization of the data set. Two posts are highlighted to show their content and how they are projected close each other in a 2D space. Note that both posts are related with Python. In Fig. 7 it is possible to note that both posts are related to questions about Python to generate HTML code. In Fig. 8 the highlighted posts are related to questions about the SQL language.

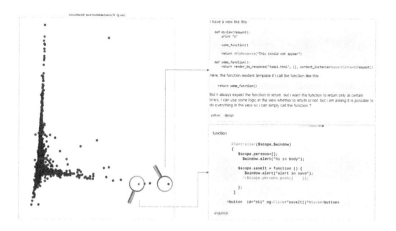

Fig. 6. 2D visualization of the dataset highlighting two posts related to Python.

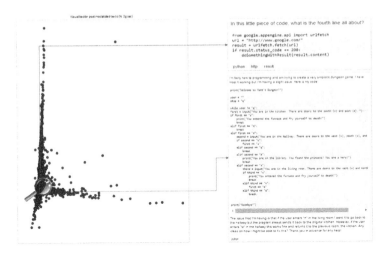

Fig. 7. 2D visualization of the dataset highlighting two posts about Python and HTML.

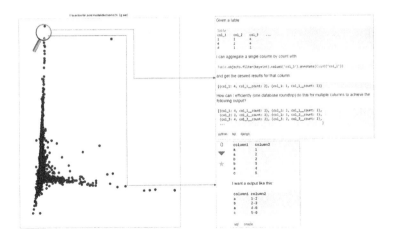

Fig. 8. 2D visualization of the dataset highlighting two posts related to SQL.

2D Visualization. We are interested in visualizing the impact of the dimensionality reduction method used to produce a 2D visualization of the dataset. Therefore, we evaluated PCA and t-SNE, two of the most used methods to do that. Figures 9 and 10 show the obtained results with PCA, and Figs. 9 and 10 show the obtained results with t-SNE. It is worth noting that t-SNE uses the space with less overlapping, whilst PCA generates more overlapping. This visualizations would be a good way to navigate the complete post dataset (Figs. 11 and 12).

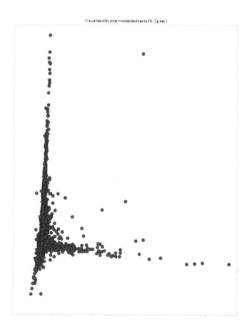

Fig. 9. 2D visualization of the complete dataset using PCA and text representation.

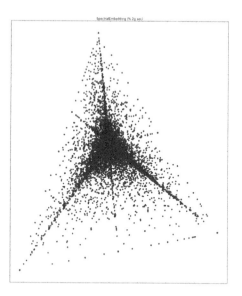

Fig. 10. 2D visualization of the complete dataset using PCA and code representation.

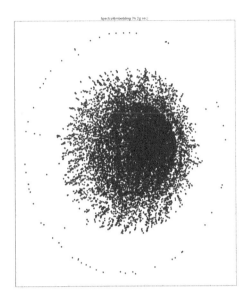

Fig. 11. 2D visualization of the complete dataset using t-SNE and text representation.

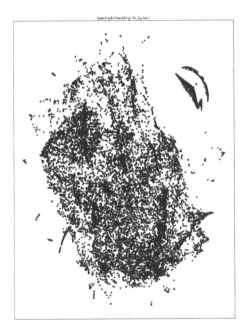

Fig. 12. 2D visualization of the complete dataset using t-SNE and code representation.

6 Conclusions and Future Work

This paper presented a method to predict labels based on the content of a post (text and code). The proposed model was evaluated in a set of posts of Stack Overflow. Results showed that text content of a post reaches the highest performance in terms of recall. The proposed model could be useful to suggest to developers the most suitable labels based on the content of the question reducing ambiguity in this process.

As future work we want to explore other feature extraction mechanisms to improve the representation of code snippets. We also want to propose a method that address the problem of training the model with larger datasets, which need an alternative to the analytic solution proposed when optimizing the cost function.

References

1. Adamic, L., Adar, E.: How to search a social network. Social Networks **27**(3), 187–203 (2005)
2. Beyer, S., Pinzger, M.: Synonym suggestion for tags on stack overflow. In: 2015 IEEE 23rd International Conference on Program Comprehension (2015)
3. Cedeño, J., Flores, J., Graff, M., Calderon, F.: Multi-class multi-tag classifier system for StackOverflow questions. In: 2015 IEEE International Autumn Meeting on Power, Electronics and Computing (ROPEC) (2015)
4. Clayton, S., Byrne, M.D.: Predicting tags for StackOverflow posts. In: 12th International Conference on Cognitive Modeling (2013)
5. Hassanali, K.N., Hatzivassiloglou, V.: Automatic detection of tags for political blogs. In: Proceedings of the NAACL HLT 2010 Workshop on Computational Linguistics in a World of Social Media, pp. 21–22, June 2010
6. James, H., Michael, F.: Keyword extraction and semantic tag prediction. Technical report (2012)
7. Wang, J., Davison, B.D.: Explorations in tag suggestion and query expansion. In: SSM 2008 (2008)
8. Moharana, M.K.: Tag recommender for StackOverflow questions. PhD thesis (2013)
9. Montanez, N., Brooks, C.H.: Improved annotation of the blogopshere via autotagging and hierarchical clustering. www2006 (2006)
10. Malhotra, N., Vij, A., Nandan, N., Dahlmeier, D.: SAP-RI: a constrained and supervised approach for aspect-based sentiment analysis. In: 8th International Workshop on Semantic Evaluation (SemEval 2014) (2014)
11. Salton, G., Fox, E.A., Wu, H.: Extended boolean information retrieval. Commun. ACM **26**(11), 1022–1036 (1983)
12. Birnbaum, L., Sood, S.C.: TagAssist: atomatic tag suggestion for blog posts. In: ICWSM (2007)
13. Mehta, S., Sodhani, S.: Stack exchange tagger (2015)
14. Schuster, S., Zhu, W., Cheng, Y.: Predicting tags for StackOverflow questions. cs229.stanford.edu
15. Stone, Z., Zickler, T., Darrell, T.: Autotagging facebook: social network context improves photo annotation. In: 2008 IEEE Computer Society Conference on Computer Vision and Pattern Recognition Workshops, pp. 1–8. IEEE, June 2008

Benchmarking of Classification Algorithms for Psychological Diagnosis

Jhony Llano, Vanessa Ramirez, and Paulina Morillo[(✉)]

Universidad Politécnica Salesiana,
Rumichaca y Morán Valverde s/n, Quito, Ecuador
{jllanot,vramirezp}@est.ups.edu.ec, pmorillo@ups.edu.ec,
https://www.ups.edu.ec/

Abstract. Generating a clinical diagnosis of a mental disorder is a complex process due to the variety of biological factors that affect this type of condition, so it is necessary that a professional performs a deep evaluation in order to identify and determine the type of disorder that affects the patient. This paper proposes the implementation and comparison of five machine learning algorithms (ML) to generate automatic diagnoses of mental disorders, through the set of symptoms present in a patient. The algorithms selected for comparison are: Support Vector Machine, Logistic Regression, Random Forest, Bayesian Networks, k-Nearest Neighbors (k-NN). The evaluation metrics used on the benchmarked were precision, accuracy, recall, error rate and also we analyzed the ROC curves and the AUC values. The general results show that the Logistic Regression algorithm obtained a better performance with 70.82% of accuracy. The Support Vector Machine model, on the other hand, showed a low performance reaching only 42.99% accuracy.

Keywords: Support Vector Machine · Logistic Regression · Random Forest · Bayesian Networks · k-Nearest Neighbors · Performance · ROC · Accuracy · Recall · Precision

1 Introduction

According to the World Health Organization 450 million people around the world suffer from some type of mental disorder, representing a total of 25% of global population. This condition is the cause of approximately one million suicides a year and "constitutes 20% of diseases, 24% of the prevalence and produce 43% of disabilities" [7], numbers that indicate the importance of making accurate diagnoses to issue an adequate treatment and reduce one of the main causes responsible for a series of referrals that alter the patient's well-being, their environment and their family [36].

This work was supported by IDEIAGEOCA Research Group of the Universidad Politécnica Salesiana.

© Springer Nature Switzerland AG 2020
F. R. Narváez et al. (Eds.): SmartTech-IC 2019, CCIS 1154, pp. 188–201, 2020.
https://doi.org/10.1007/978-3-030-46785-2_16

Generating a clinical diagnosis of a mental disorder is not a simple process, due to the absence of biologic markers that allow to accurately identify the neuronal abnormalities that afflict a patient [16]. Therefore, this process demands the integration of results from several evaluations which consider social, cognitive, personality and emotional aspects of the individual [10]. These aspects, as well as the characterizations of the disorders and their symptoms have been described in the DSM-5 manuals (Diagnostic and Statistical Manual of Mental Disorders) and the International Statistical Classification of Diseases and Related Health Problems (ICD-10) of the World Health Organization (WHO) [5].

Another aspect that makes it difficult to make a correct diagnosis is the large number and diversity of the symptoms associated with each type of disorder. Thus, this article proposes the implementation of Machine Learning techniques for the creation of an automatic diagnosis, a work that has been done in other studies for the prediction of mental disorders, such as [21,23,28]. These researches which although they use Machine Learning techniques to automatically predict clinical diagnoses require in the process the use of neuroimaging, that is obtained through magnetic resonance imaging. This type of exams can become a limitation for some patients, because of the cost and lack of equipment availability. Other studies focus their research on specific disorders such as categorized psychotic disorders (schizophrenia/bipolar disorder) [25,35]. In recent years the disorder of greatest interest has been depression, a disorder that according to WHO is among the six main causes of disability, affecting 300 million people around the world [34], leading to the development of the works as [17,20].

On the other hand, this work aims to make a comparative analysis of five classification algorithms: Support Vector Machine (SVM), Logistic Regression, Random Forest (RF), Bayesian Networks (BN) and k-Nearest Neighbors (k-NN) applied to this type of task, considering the main classes disorders with their symptoms of ICD-10. This article is structured as follows: Sect. 2 describes the methodology applied, including the description of data collection, operation, and setting of selected algorithms, and the evaluation metrics used in the analysis. Section 3 shows the experiments and results, and finally, Sect. 4 the conclusions.

2   Methodology

According to [11], a mental disorder is the alteration of emotional and/or behavioral type, so they are established under the concept of disease or condition where the first is based on a set of symptoms and the second based on subjective experiences and disability [33]. However most can be determined from the symptoms presented by the patient and therefore requires the issuance of a clinical diagnosis.

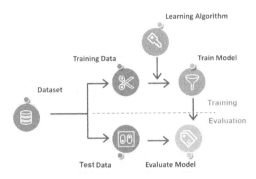

Fig. 1. Machine Learning process

This paper proposes the implementation of the automatic diagnosis of mental disorders, through machine learning algorithms. To achieve this objective, the diagnosis is analyzed as a supervised learning task, specifically classification. With this approach, each main disorder class in ICD-10 is a class to predict, and the symptom represent the attributes.

The used methodology follows the typical ML process Fig. 1 except for the k-NN algorithm. Once the dataset is constructed, two phases are defined: the training phase and the evaluation phase.

Subsequent subsections include the description of data and process of its acquisition, the explanation of selection criteria of ML algorithms, as well as their configuration, and finally, the description of evaluation metrics to compare the results.

2.1 Data Collection

The training data set was obtained from the clinical cases available in some psychological centers, cases entered by the Clinical Psychology students of the Salesian Polytechnic University, cases found on the web and from the theoretical basis of the ICD-10 classification (Chapter V), giving a total of 320 instances (cases), each with 185 attributes (symptoms), which were stored in a PostgreSQL database. Figure 2 shows in detail the number of cases obtained for the data-set of this study. The number of classes to be determined were eleven in total, corresponding to the main categories of ICD-10. On average each class has 29 instances, except class "Mood disorders" (F3) with 89 instances and class "Unspecified Mental Disorder" (F99) that it has only one instance.

We use website "Psico-web" [21] as a tool of data acquisition, this application was established under the CodeIgniter framework and Bootstrap to make it faster and adaptable to any device. It was hosted on a Centos virtual machine of "Google.cloud" with the web service "nginx" and php-fpm Composer.

The final dataset will be divided into a training dataset and a test dataset. Theoretical instances will always be considered within the training data, the rest will be divided randomly 70% for training, and 30% for test.

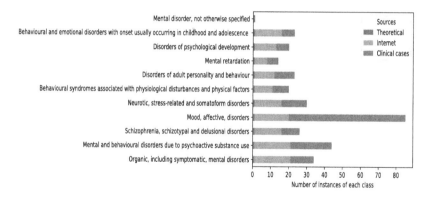

Fig. 2. Number of instance of each class and source

2.2   Algorithms Selection

The treatment and processing of the training set for obtaining the diagnosis were carried out with the use of five classification algorithms, selected for ease of implementation and availability in the Machine Learning library for PHP. Table 1 shows the names of algorithms and their acronyms.

Table 1. Machine Learning algorithms

Algorithm	Acronym
Support Vector Machine	SVM
Random Forest	RF
Logistic Regression	LR
Bayesian Network	BN
k-Nearest Neighbors	k-NN

The first algorithm considered in the analysis is called Support Vector Machine (SVM). It is used to solve classification and regression problems. It has had a high accuracy in solving several problems. So, it has been implemented in several studies in the area of mental health, where problems are addressed for the diagnosis of mental disorders, such as [8,24,27]. The high performance in the results of the mentioned studies is due to the mathematical foundation of the algorithm, the minimization of structural risk and the availability of tools that allow a fast execution with high-dimensionality data [9].

Random Forest (RF) is also an efficient algorithm for prediction and classification tasks since it is a noise-tolerant [4]. In [1,6], and [30], this algorithm was used for diagnostic tasks getting high precision results.

Another supervised learning algorithm is Logistic Regression (LR). It is a simple statistical technique, used specially in "predictive models for dichotomous or binarious problems" [32]. Its effectivity is high due to its stability [29], so it has been implemented in several medical studies [19,37]. Despite in this paper, we consider a multiclass task we use this algorithm for their high performance [14].

The fourth algorithm implemented is the Bayesian Network (BN). It allows us to model complex problems that involve knowledge under uncertainty, so they have been applied in various studies of engineering science and medicine [22] such as [31] and [3], where the implementation of the algorithm showed results with high accuracy.

The last algorithm is k-Nearest Neighbors (k-NN). It is one of a lazy learning method because it does not generate a model resulting from learning with training data, but the learning happens at the same moment in which the test data is tested [18]. This algorithm is widely used for its simple statistical conception [2], despite its low efficiency with large repositories. Works such as [13] have been carried out, where they successfully overcome their limitations, verifying that this technique can be very competitive in the prediction process.

2.3 Algorithms Setting

The algorithm will be configured in two stages: the training phase in which the models are created using the training dataset and the test phase in which the performance of the algorithms with the test dataset is evaluated.

The process followed by each of the classifiers to carry out the training phase is described in Algorithm 1 , Where, SE represents the training attribute matrix (symptoms), TE means the training class vector (main class disorders), n is the number of training instances, and m is the total number of symptoms for each disorder. The attribute matrix containing the symptoms is sent as inputs: assigning the value of "1" when the patient presents the symptom and "0" when

---

Algorithm 1. Training phase

Input:

$$SE_{n*m} = \begin{cases} se_{ij=0} & \text{if no symptom} \\ se_{ij=1} & \text{if there is symptom} \end{cases}$$

$$TE_{n*1} = \left\{ ti \in [1,2,3,...,78] \right.$$

Output Models{ $knn.php, lr.php, nb.php, rf.php, svc.php$}
Step 1: Model initialization
    $modelManager = newModelManager();$
Step 2: Model configuration
    $classifierknn = newKNearestNeighbors(k = 3);$
    $classifiernb = newNaiveBayes();$
    $classifierrf = newRandomForest();$
    $classifierlr = newLogisticRegression();$
    $classifiersvc = newSVC(Kernel :: RBF, cost = 1);$
Step 3: : Model training
    $classifierknn \rightarrow train(Ms, Mt);$
    $classifiernb \rightarrow train(Ms, Mt);$
    $classifierrf \rightarrow train(Ms, Mt);$
    $classifierlr \rightarrow train(Ms, Mt);$
    $classifiersvc \rightarrow train(Ms, Mt);$
Step 4: Model storage
    $modelManager- > saveToFile(classifiersvc, filepath);$

they does not have it and as a second entry the class vector containing the 11 main classes of disorders according to ICD-10. As output, the models to be trained are sent, followed by the initialization, configuration, training and storage steps of the models.

In the test phase, the process carried out is shown in Algorithm 2. Similarly, each instance of the test dataset is represented by a vector with binary attributes that represent the symptoms that the patient presents or not. Another entry is the vector that contains the models already trained and as output the vector of test classes containing the 11 main classes of disorders of the theoretical cases, followed by the initialization steps of the models, restoration of the models saved in the previous phase and finally the prediction of the results.

For the k-NN algorithm, the process is similar, however, this algorithm does not return a previous model but makes the predictions as the instances of test dataset are added. To make the predictions k-NN required an additional parameter related to distance. In this case, we used the Euclidean distance that was included in the default configuration of the algorithm. In this way, the algorithm calculates the distance between the new instance and each instance in the training dataset. Then, the predicted class is assigned based on the highest frequency class among the k closest instances. The k value was set to 3, to scan the three nearest neighbors of the instance with an unknown class.

In this case, SP is the matrix of test attributes (symptoms), TP is the vector of test classes (main classes disorders), r is the number of test instances.

Algorithm 2. Test phase

Input:

$$SP_{r*m} = \begin{cases} sp_{ij=0} & \text{if no symptom} \\ sp_{ij=1} & \text{if there is symptom} \end{cases}$$

$$Models = \Big\{ \text{knn.php,lr.php,nb.php,rf.php,svc.php} $$

Output

$$TP_{r*1} = \Big\{ \text{ti} \in [1,2,3,...,78]$$

Step 1: Model initialization
 $modelManager = newModelManager();$
Step 2: Restoration of models saved in the training phase
 $restoredClassifier = modelManager \rightarrow restoreFromFile(path);$
Step 3: Prediction
 $predictknn = restoredClassifier \rightarrow predict(Ms);$
 $predictnb = restoredClassifier \rightarrow predict(Ms);$
 $predictrf = restoredClassifier \rightarrow predict(Ms);$
 $predictlr = restoredClassifier \rightarrow predict(Ms);$
 $predictsvc = restoredClassifier \rightarrow predict(Ms);$

2.4 Evaluation Metrics

Based on literature [15], the metrics selected to evaluate the performance are shown in Table 2. An important tool to determine these metrics is the confusion matrix. In a binary classifier is common to use it to set the successes and the errors, in this way, the following concepts are defined: True Positives (TP) represents the number of instances labeled as positive that were really positive, True Negatives (TN) is the number of negatives that have been correctly labeled. On the other hand, False Positives (FP), represents the number of instances labeled as positive that were actually negative, False Negatives (FN) is the number of negatives that have actually been positive. These concepts can be generalized for multiclass tasks.

Table 2. Equations of selected metrics

Metric	Equation
Precision	$P = \frac{TP}{(TP+FP)}$
Recall	$R = \frac{TP}{(TP+FN)}$
Accuracy	$A = \frac{(TP+TN)}{(TP+TN+FN+FP)}$
Error rate	$Err = \frac{(FP+FN)}{(TP+TN+FN+FP)}$
F_Score	$F_1 = 2\frac{(Recall*Precision)}{(Recall+Precision)}$

In general, Precision is used to determine the positive instances that are correctly predicted from the total predicted instances in a positive class, Recall is the fraction o positive instances that are correctly classified, Accuracy is the ratio of correct predictions over the total number of instances evaluated, Misclassification error o Error rate is the proportion of incorrect predictions over the total number of instances evaluated, and finally, F_Score is defined as the weighted harmonic mean of the test's precision and recall.

Another tool used in the algorithm evaluation is the ROC (Receiver Operating Characteristic) curve. It is a graphical representation of sensitivity (fraction of positive instances that are correctly classified) versus specificity (fraction of negative instance that are correctly classified).

If the classifiers were perfect, that is, without overlap, there would be a region where any cut-off point has sensitivity and specificity equal to 1 which means that the curve has only the point $(0, 1)$. The worst classifier would be one where the sensitivity is equal to the proportion of false positives, the curve would be the diagonal of $(0, 0)$ to $(1, 1)$. Normally the curve of an acceptable classifier should approach the curve of the perfect classifier and move away from the diagonal.

From ROC curve we can obtain AUC (Area Under Curve) value. This metric shows the overall ranking performance of a classifier [12]. The AUC is convenient for the following two reasons: It is invariable concerning the scale since, measure how well the predictions are classified rather than their absolute values. The AUC is invariable to the classification threshold, it means that measure the quality of the model predictions, regardless of which classification threshold is chosen.

Higher the AUC, better the model is at predicting Negatives as Negatives and Positives as Positives. An excellent model has AUC near to the 1 which means it has good measure of separability. A poor model has AUC near to the 0 which means it has worst measure of separability. In fact it means it is reciprocating the result. It is predicting Negatives as Positives and Positives as Negatives. And when AUC is 0.5, it means model has no class separation capacity whatsoever.

3 Experiments and Results

This section shows the results obtained in the training and evaluation phase. To evaluate the models, the k-fold Cross Validation was implemented, and k was set to 10. This technique randomly separates the original data into two data sets, where the first corresponds to the training set and the second to the test set. This division is repeated k times (k-experiments) so that the training and the test model are carried out with a different set each time [26]. In each experiment the dataset of 320 instances was divided into 70% for the training phase, in this phase, the 78 theoretical cases were taken, and the remaining were randomly selected and for the testing phase, 30% of the total set of randomly selected instances was taken.

3.1 Training Phase

The measure considered to compare the algorithms in this section was the training time in seconds. The results of each experiment are shown in the Fig. 3. Without considering the K-NN algorithm, it can be seen that the algorithm that takes less time in its training is the Bayesian Networks as opposed to the Random Forest that takes more time in its training. Table 3 shows the average time it took for each experiment.

Table 3. Training time.

Classifier	Time (milliseconds)
SVM	14.1936
RF	23.6881
LR	7.79893
BN	2.49686
k-NN	1.19743

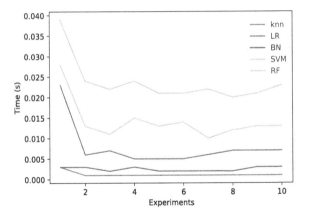

Fig. 3. Training time of each model

3.2 Testing Phase

In this phase the performance of the classifiers is evaluated according to the formulas described in Table 2.

The performance recorded in each test is described in Fig. 4. In general, it can be seen that the algorithm with the best performance was Logistic Regression, while the lowest performance was the Support Vector Machine. The average of the evaluation metrics are shown in Table 4. The range of Accuracy was between 42.99 and 70.82. The highest was obtained by LR, followed by the RF classifier. The confusion matrix of one of the experiments of LR is shown in Fig. 4.

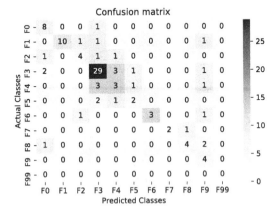

Fig. 4. LR confusion matrix

On the other hand, the lowest value was in SVM. In the same way, the highest recall and precision values both were obtained by LR with 64.91 and 70.30, respectively. The biggest error rate was 86.41 and corresponds to SVM.

Table 4. Performance results of the classifiers.

Classifier	Precision	Recall	Accuracy	Error rate
k-NN	47.86	47.29	58.09	55.80
LR	70.30	64.91	70.82	34.86
BN	59.03	52.70	61.13	47.72
SVM	13.19	17.23	42.99	86.41
RF	60.52	53.81	66.18	46.16

The results obtained by RF and BN are very similar, with RF being superior by a difference of less than 5%, in all metrics.

All models presented different results, but in general, the highest performance was obtained by Logistic Regression, also Random Forest had good results. Meanwhile, the classifier that obtained the lowest values in every evaluation measure was the SVM. In a brief comparison with other studies where Machine Learning techniques were implemented to predict some type of disorder, as in [20], it can be seen that the opposite happens with the SVM classifier, where it obtains results 0.93 of accuracy, 1.00 of precision, 0.63 of recall and 0.778 of F1Score. It shows highly performance, when there are only two classes, as the study in [27], achieves 90% accuracy and 88% of precision, but this process requires additional technology to complement the prediction (Fig. 5).

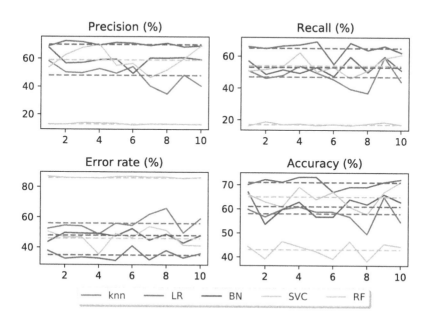

Fig. 5. Evaluation metrics for each experiment

In addition to comparing the metrics, the ROC curves were also used. The Fig. 6 shows the sensitivity versus the specificity for a different threshold in the five models. As can be seen Fig. 6, once again, the SVM algorithm had the worst performance, because the curve is very close to the diagonal, while the LR algorithm got a better curve. KNN also improved its performance as more instances were added.

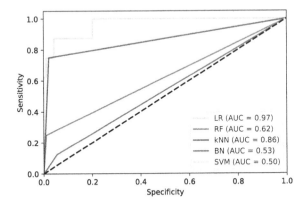

Fig. 6. ROC of each model

Regarding the results of the AUC, it is observed that the highest values correspond to LR, followed by KNN. In this case, BN and SVM got the worst values of AUC close to 0.5 which means that they are not models to have no class separation capacity whatsoever. Although this metric is used especially for binary classifiers. We can make this comparison taking into account the ability of the model to distinguish each class or not.

4   Conclusions

This work made a comparison of five Machine Learning algorithms applied in the automatic diagnosis of mental disorders, through the symptoms presented by the patients. The results show that not all the algorithms analyzed are adapted to multiclass tasks, which makes it difficult to solve problems in which there are more than two classes.

Further, the low performance of some algorithms such as SVM, KNN, and BN could be due to the lack of instances of each class, that is, the classes were unbalanced. This condition limited learning and the ability of algorithms to distinguish and separate classes.

On the other hand, despite the poor training dataset, the Logistic Regression algorithm achieved the best performance. Although it was not very high, it is evident that the model can distinguish between classes and it is likely that the model will improve considerably if the number of instances increases.

Another cause for poorly performed algorithms could be the large number of attributes of each instance. Future work could analyze the dependence of symptoms and their possible reduction, and also make tests with a bigger dataset.

References

1. Belgiu, M., Drăguţ, L.: Random forest in remote sensing: a review of applications and future directions. ISPRS J. Photogramm. Remote Sens. **114**, 24–31 (2016)
2. Bijalwan, V., Kumar, V., Kumari, P., Pascual, J.: KNN based machine learning approach for text and document mining. Int. J. Database Theory Appl. **7**(1), 61–70 (2014)
3. Bouzembrak, Y., Camenzuli, L., Janssen, E., Van der Fels-Klerx, H.: Application of Bayesian networks in the development of herbs and spices sampling monitoring system. Food Control **83**, 38–44 (2018)
4. Breiman, L.: Random forests. Mach. Learn. **45**(1), 5–32 (2001). https://doi.org/10.1023/A:1010933404324
5. Bzdok, D., Meyer-Lindenberg, A.: Machine learning for precision psychiatry: opportunities and challenges. Biol. Psychiatry Cogn. Neurosci. Neuroimaging **3**(3), 223–230 (2018)
6. Caruana, R., Niculescu-Mizil, A.: An empirical comparison of supervised learning algorithms. In: Proceedings of the 23rd International Conference on Machine Learning, pp. 161–168. ACM (2006)
7. Chávez-Oleas, H., Samaniego, N., Aguilar, E.: Manual de atención primaria en salud mental. Ministerio de Salud Pública (2019)
8. Crippa, A., et al.: Use of machine learning to identify children with autism and their motor abnormalities. J. Autism Dev. Disord. **45**(7), 2146–2156 (2015)
9. De la Hoz Manotas, A.K., Martínez-Palacio, U.J., Mendoza-Palechor, F.E.: Técnicas de ml en medicina cardiovascular. Memorias **11**(20), 41–46 (2013)
10. Dosen, A., Gardner, W., Griffiths, D., King, R., Lapoint, A.: Evaluación, diagnostivo, tratamiento y servicios de apoyo para personas con discapacidad intelectual y problemas de conducta (2010)
11. FEAFES: Salud Mental y Medios de Comunicación - Guía de Estilo
12. Ferri, C., Hernández-Orallo, J., Flach, P.A.: A coherent interpretation of AUC as a measure of aggregated classification performance. In: Proceedings of the 28th International Conference on Machine Learning (ICML-2011), pp. 657–664 (2011)
13. Guo, G., Wang, H., Bell, D., Bi, Y., Greer, K.: KNN model-based approach in classification. In: Meersman, R., Tari, Z., Schmidt, D.C. (eds.) OTM 2003. LNCS, vol. 2888, pp. 986–996. Springer, Heidelberg (2003). https://doi.org/10.1007/978-3-540-39964-3_62
14. Hanai, T., et al.: Prognostic models in patients with non-small-cell lung cancer using artificial neural networks in comparison with logistic regression. Cancer Sci. **94**(5), 473–477 (2003)
15. Hossin, M., Sulaiman, M.: A review on evaluation metrics for data classification evaluations. Int. J. Data Min. Knowl. Manag. Process **5**(2), 1 (2015)
16. Hyman, S.E.: Can neuroscience be integrated into the DSM-V? Nat. Rev. Neurosci. **8**(9), 725 (2007)

17. Kessler, R.C., et al.: Testing a machine-learning algorithm to predict the persistence and severity of major depressive disorder from baseline self-reports. Mol. Psychiatry **21**(10), 1366 (2016)
18. Kotsiantis, S.B., Zaharakis, I., Pintelas, P.: Supervised machine learning: a review of classification techniques. Emerg. Artif. Intell. Appl. Comput. Eng. **160**, 3–24 (2007)
19. Le Cessie, S., Van Houwelingen, J.C.: Ridge estimators in logistic regression. J. R. Stat. Soc. Ser. C (Appl. Stat.) **41**(1), 191–201 (1992)
20. Medina, O., Maybee, A.: Detección de depresión a través de análisis textual utilizando aprendizaje automático (2017)
21. Morillo, P., Ortega, H., Chauca, D., Proaño, J., Vallejo-Huanga, D., Cazares, M.: Psycho web: a machine learning platform for the diagnosis and classification of mental disorders. In: Ayaz, H. (ed.) AHFE 2019. AISC, vol. 953, pp. 399–410. Springer, Cham (2020). https://doi.org/10.1007/978-3-030-20473-0_39
22. Oniśko, A., Druzdzel, M.J., Wasyluk, H.: Learning Bayesian network parameters from small data sets: application of noisy-or gates. Int. J. Approx. Reason. **27**(2), 165–182 (2001)
23. Orru, G., Pettersson-Yeo, W., Marquand, A.F., Sartori, G., Mechelli, A.: Using support vector machine to identify imaging biomarkers of neurological and psychiatric disease: a critical review. Neurosci. Biobehav. Rev. **36**(4), 1140–1152 (2012)
24. Patel, M.J., Khalaf, A., Aizenstein, H.J.: Studying depression using imaging and machine learning methods. NeuroImage Clin. **10**, 115–123 (2016)
25. Salvador, R., et al.: Evaluation of machine learning algorithms and structural features for optimal MRI-based diagnostic prediction in psychosis. PLoS One **12**(4), e0175683 (2017)
26. Schaffer, C.: Selecting a classification method by cross-validation. Mach. Learn. **13**(1), 135–143 (1993)
27. Schnack, H.G., et al.: Can structural MRI aid in clinical classification? A machine learning study in two independent samples of patients with schizophrenia, bipolar disorder and healthy subjects. Neuroimage **84**, 299–306 (2014)
28. Stephan, K.E., et al.: Computational neuroimaging strategies for single patient predictions. Neuroimage **145**, 180–199 (2017)
29. Steyerberg, E.W., Harrell Jr., F.E., Borsboom, G.J., Eijkemans, M., Vergouwe, Y., Habbema, J.D.F.: Internal validation of predictive models: efficiency of some procedures for logistic regression analysis. J. Clin. Epidemiol. **54**(8), 774–781 (2001)
30. Svetnik, V., Liaw, A., Tong, C., Wang, T.: Application of Breiman's random forest to modeling structure-activity relationships of pharmaceutical molecules. In: Roli, F., Kittler, J., Windeatt, T. (eds.) MCS 2004. LNCS, vol. 3077, pp. 334–343. Springer, Heidelberg (2004). https://doi.org/10.1007/978-3-540-25966-4_33
31. Sýkora, M., Markova, J., Diamantidis, D.: Bayesian network application for the risk assessment of existing energy production units. Reliab. Eng. Syst. Saf. **169**, 312–320 (2018)
32. Tu, J.V.: Advantages and disadvantages of using artificial neural networks versus logistic regression for predicting medical outcomes. J. Clin. Epidemiol. **49**(11), 1225–1231 (1996)
33. Vidal, C.R.: Clasificación en paidoqsiquiatría. Conceptos y enfoques. Sistemas de clasificación: DSM.IV, ICD.10
34. WHO: Campaign for world health day (2017). https://www.who.int/campaigns/world-health-day/2017/en/

35. Wu, M.-J., et al.: Identification and individualized prediction of clinical phenotypes in bipolar disorders using neurocognitive data, neuroimaging scans and machine learning. Neuroimage **145**, 254–264 (2017)
36. Zelaya, M.G.R., Valladares, F.A.: Caracterización del trauma abdominal en pacientes geriátricos atendidos en el hospital escuela, tegucigalpa, 2000–2002. Urbana **50**, 89–92 (2003)
37. Zhou, X., Liu, K.-Y., Wong, S.T.: Cancer classification and prediction using logistic regression with Bayesian gene selection. J. Biomed. Inform. **37**(4), 249–259 (2004)

Proposal for an Integral System for Massive Open Online Courses (ISMOOC)

Lourdes Atiaja Atiaja[1][(✉)] [iD] and Andrés García Martínez[2][(✉)] [iD]

[1] Universidad de las Fuerzas Armadas ESPE, Sangolquí, Ecuador
lnatiaja@espe.edu.ec
[2] University of Havana, La Habana, Cuba
agarcia@cepes.uh.cu

Abstract. It is impossible to conceive of education without technology in this era of globalization, which make it imperative for Higher Education Institutions to diversify their academic offering and adopt continuous learning models to update the knowledge of their graduates. In response to this new mission, numerous institutions worldwide are adopting MOOCs (Massive Open Online Courses) as an option for inclusive education, thus satisfy the need for life-long learning, despite a series of doubts about these courses regarding aspects of pedagogy, credibility and lack of feedback, among others, which arise from its massive nature. The aim of this paper is to set out a benchmark for the design and development of a MOOC from the perspective of an integral system, which comprises a set of dimensions (pedagogical, technological, organizational and communicational), structured by levels, alongside a developmental teaching method based on Activity Theory and the principles of connectivism. An evaluation of this system was carried out by means of a quasi-experiment, with the implementation of a MOOC in which 324 students participated with very encouraging results 83.7% of the participants passed the course, which indicated that the usual high desertion rates of MOOC participants were minimized.

Keywords: Massive open online courses · MOOC · Inclusive education · Life-long learning · Integral system

1 Introduction

One of the main challenges facing the current education system is how to address the ongoing training needs of professionals who are aware that undergraduate university education is often insufficient to adapt with agility to the labor market.

Nowadays, this is possible as a result of advances in ICT (Information and Communication Technology), in particular emerging technologies[1], which have led to new modes of learning that are more accessible to the population, such as MOOCs (Massive Open Online Courses), an inclusive diversity-based training option, which have grown

---

[1] Emerging technologies are those tools, ideas, innovations and resources which will have an effect in the short-, medium-, and long-term in diverse educational contexts.

© Springer Nature Switzerland AG 2020
F. R. Narváez et al. (Eds.): SmartTech-IC 2019, CCIS 1154, pp. 202–214, 2020.
https://doi.org/10.1007/978-3-030-46785-2_17

in recent years as a way to access free courses, including programs offered by several prestigious universities from around the world.

MOOCs are the result of technology applied to education. They are online courses, which allow a massive, open participation, free or at a low cost. The components of these courses are generally as follows: a set of class videos recorded by a teacher, links to support material, automated assessment, discussion forums and peer evaluations, which offer greater access to flexible, ubiquitous education [1].

The most important aspect of this learning modality may be that it has appeared at a time when education, and in particular, university education, is under pressure to make changes to address the demands of a knowledge society, offering education for all and lifelong learning, which currently form part of Sustainable Development Goal No. 4 Agenda 2030 set out by CEPAL (Economic Commission for Latin America and the Caribbean), in which countries are urged to guarantee inclusive, fair and quality education, and to promote life-long learning opportunities [6].

However, from the onset these courses have been facing a series of questions with regarding the pedagogical quality, ethics and sustainability, among others. On the other hand the MOOCs must overcoming some important barriers (Internet, costs, language, Web content accessibility) if they really want to improve access to high-quality education for all [23].

Despite these inconveniences, many prestigious educational institutions in the world-wide are adopting this teaching method, with the aim of not only to satisfy the need for continuing education, but also of achieving the reconnection of professional graduates who seek to return to the university where they began their higher education, this flexible, ubiquitous and inclusive mode of learning enables professionals to train without having to leave either their job or their studies. This is achieved through a flexible, ubiquitous and inclusive learning modality.

In these circumstances, it is important to provide higher education institutions with a benchmark for the design and development of MOOCs, in which all the necessary elements for the production of this type of course are included and balanced. Hence, a proposal has been drawn up for an integral system for MOOCs, in which pedagogical, technological, organizational and communicational components are combined, organized into interconnected levels alongside a developmental teaching methodology, based on Activity Theory and the principles of connectivism.

2   MOOC Systems

The teaching-learning process involves the active participation of a range of actors and components, and more so nowadays in this knowledge society in which people talk of digital learning, online courses and the flipped classroom, etc. The technological component has become a mediational tool in education, which obliges higher education intuitions to reassess learning methods and adapt ICT appropriately in educational processes, that is to say, it implies an understanding of the activity of learning as a purely cooperative system [10].

Although many authors highlight that an interactive platform and instructional design are all that are required to produce MOOC courses, the authors of this paper consider that to develop these courses it is indispensable to consider the MOOC as a system with a structure, an environment or context, whose parts or components are inter-related, creating a new quality in the object.

For this reason, a connecting element of synergy should be incorporated into the system. In the MOOC system, **synergy** (from the Greek: syn meaning simultaneity, and ergon meaning work) is the integration of components which constitute a new object. It is the act of coordinating two or more of the parts or elements of a system, the effect of which is greater than the sum of the individual effects, enhancing the qualities of each part. In the case of the MOOC system, synergy can be seen between its four dimensions: pedagogical technological, organizational and communicational.

In a system, there are **three basic functional elements**: input or entry, process and output or product. Entry refers to the information received by the system, the resources, and the energy with which the system works initially; the process is the manner in which the system operates in an environment; and the output is the result or product of the process carried out within the system.

Additionally, there are four **components of the system:**

- Entities: These are all the participants in a system i.e. all those related to a system
- Attributes: These are the structural properties and features of the parts or components of a system.
- Relationships: These are the associations between entities or their attributes
- Environment: This is the environment in which the system operates

Based on the above, the MOOC System will be comprised of a set of components, principles and dimensions, mindful of the massive nature, in order to achieve improved quality and learning outcomes through the MOOC system.

The features of the MOOC System are as follows:

- **Openness and optimization.** Allows free access to the courses and educational material and is related to the use of open-source educational resources in order to reduce costs.
- **Massive and scalable:** Enables large scale enrollment of participants, without negatively affecting quality
- **Functional.** Allows the structuring of courses in a logical, systematic and organized fashion, aimed at achieving learning outcomes, with interactive material and assessment strategies, which guarantee learning.
- **Interactive.** Allows the development and integration of interactive educational materials and facilitates the connection between the actors in the teaching-learning process.
- **Flexible.** Facilitates the diversity of methods and resources used, allows adaptation to the characteristics, and needs of the students so that they can access the courses when required.
- **Feedback and control**. It includes monitoring tools for follow-up and checking students' progress, and tools to enable communication

- **Standardized**: It guarantees the functioning of content and other elements created independently (standard file format -SCORM) and allows courses created by third parties to be used and self-created courses to be exported.

3 Pedagogical and Technological Basis for the Design of a MOOC System

From its origins, the **teaching philosophy** of MOOCs brought with entailed changes in the traditional didactic model. The participants are those who generate knowledge and learning by means of the interaction, collaboration, participation and creation of networks between learners and teachers, the creation of content and contributions to forums and debates which comprise the teaching-learning process [24].

According to the first extended classification of MOOCs, different theories of learning can be identified: xMOOCs that have a behavioral tendency in which learning is linear, individualized, guided and focused on the information transmitted by the teacher [4], and cMOOCs have a constructivist tendency and are designed under the principles of connectivism, in which learning takes place through networks organized by the participants themselves, who create blogs or wikis regarding their own interpretations of the course materials (texts, videos, lectures, among others), at the same time making comments or contributing to the work of others to enhance their learning experience. iMOOCs are a combination of xMOOC and cMOOCs [12], and tend towards constructivist learning.

According to the works consulted, and from the personal experience of the authors of this paper of participating in MOOCs, one of the main problems of these courses was considered to be the high incidence of desertion. This is fundamentally due to lack of motivation, lack of support and feedback and poor teaching quality, among others, and highlights the need for the MOOC system proposed here to be based on pedagogical and psycho-pedagogical theories which motivate, and lead to improved communication and interaction between the various actors in the teaching-learning process [2].

As a result, the MOOC System has incorporated a didactic methodology based on the idea of developmental teaching, benchmarked by the concept of the Zone of Proximal Development (ZPD)[2].

The developmental nature of the teaching would suggest that the learning-teaching process should be organized not by the student's current level but rather taking into account potential for future development, that is to say, ZPD. It should be able to offer students the levels of support required to bring about the development of adequate motive toward the activity of learning, ensuring that the learner owns the learning process (learning to learn) and stimulating students' creativity, independence and reflection.

Other theories and pedagogical trends have been included within the concept of developmental teaching and form the pedagogical foundation of the MOOC System. These are as follows:

---

[2] This is the difference between two evolving levels in the individual's abilities: the real ability to complete a task and the potential ability to complete a task with help.

(a) Activity Theory

The inclusion of Activity Theory in the MOOC system is based on the learning, which takes place from understanding the activity itself, completing the task and the expected results. Thus, learning activities for the MOOC participants should be organized with reference to the functional components of this theory: orientation, execution, adjustment and correction or feedback

(b) Connectivism

Connectivism maintains that knowledge is disseminated by means of a network of connections, and as such learning consists in the capacity to build and move across these networks. It is no longer possible to personally experience and acquire the learning necessary to act, it is essential now to acquire competence from the formation of connections [19].

Learning networks may be then viewed as structures which are created in order to continuously acquire, experiment with, create and connect new knowledge. Connectivism implies putting emphasis on the individual as the subject of learning, but as part of a network. The ability to establish connections between different fields, ideas and concepts is an essential competency for a student.

Nodes are external entities which can be used to form a network. Nodes may be people, organizations, libraries, websites, books, magazines, databases or any other information source.

The starting point is the individual, whose personal knowledge is comprised of a network, which feeds into organizations and institutions, which in turn provide feedback to the network, providing new learning for the individuals, enabling them to remain updated in their field by means of the connections which have been formed. This is precisely what is required in a MOOC System.

(c) Collaborative learning

Collaborative learning is a carefully designed system of interactions, which organizes and leads to reciprocal influence between group members [13]. It is developed through a gradual process in which each of the members feels committed to the learning of the others, which creates a competition-free positive interdependence between them, which is acquired through the use of group work. It is characterized by the interaction of members and the contribution of everyone in generating knowledge, where authority is shared and responsibility accepted, respecting the point of view of others to jointly bring about new knowledge.

It is important to incorporate the collaborative learning strategy in the MOOC System, since this type of learning leads to a deeper level of learning, critical thinking, shared understanding, and longer-term recall of the learned material. Moreover, this type of learning is another contextual factor that influences students' educational achievement [18].

With regard to the technological foundations of the MOOCs, production of these courses are carried out by means of learning management systems or interactive platforms, whereby content is disseminated to hundreds, if not thousands of students, with synchronous and asynchronous communication between the actors in the teaching-learning process, tutoring, carrying out of tasks and learning activities, feedback, and peer and automatic assessment.

A number of authors have pointed out that in technological terms MOOCs are housed on a range of diverse platforms with different origins and focuses, which has led to terms such as xMOOCs and cMOOCs as two of the main types [5–8, 20] and a hybrid model of the foregoing, giving three basic categories [14–16, 24].

As a rule, to establish a teaching-learning platform for MOOCs the platform must include the following basic features: accessible, standardized, persuadable (functional, usable, ubiquitous and interactive), flexible and scalable. In a MOOC system use of an open-source LMS it is recommend as it permits personalization and creation of an identity, and facilitates the integration of other communication tools, such as learning analytics and augmented reality.

4 Design of a Massive Open Online Courses Integral System (ISMOOC)

The term "integral" can be seen as pointing to four: a model or framework, a methodology, a community, and/or a set of abilities or capabilities [15]. Hence, the authors of this research use the term integral and define the integral system of massive open online courses (ISMOOC) as the set of components organized by levels which interact with each other to produce the learning outcome in the student and their feelings with respect to these outcomes and the learning process developed. It is supported by the concept of developmental learning and draws on Activity Theory and connectivism, considering in the process the pedagogical, technological, organizational and communicational dimensions of the System, the results or products of which provide feedback to the system.

The design of an ISMOOC must be in line with the developmental level of the individuals who are to use it. If the real abilities of the student on entering the system are not considered, it will be rejected, since the designed activities will be outside the Zone of Proximal Development. This justifies the need for a diagnostic test to determine the students' level of development and what could potentially be developed in their learning with the help of others and the support of teaching means, in particular those related to ICT and emerging technologies. Thus, the diagnosis of knowledge, abilities, values and motivation of the students, teachers and other actors in the teaching-learning process is fundamental to the proper design of the ISMOOC. The findings of these diagnostic tests complement each other, because it must be appreciated that all the participants will communicate and work in virtual learning environments and will influence each other's learning.

The foundations, premises and principles encompassed in the design of the ISMOOC become the guiding component and should combine all the entry components of the system.

4.1 Levels of ISMOOC

The ISMOOC is organized into three levels:

Entry level. Comprised of actors in the teaching-learning process (students, teachers, directors, authorities, administrative personnel and other actors in the context who may influence the education of graduates and teachers); the demands of the Institution, national bodies, and the companies who will employ the graduates; the requirements of the teaching-learning process; and the diagnostic test carried out, all combined with the foundations of the System, the premises, principles and methodology to develop the courses.

Process Level. Established by the MOOC System dimensions: pedagogical, technological, organizational and communicational. At this level the strategies used by the students to learn and the methodology used by the teachers to develop the teaching-learning process are key.

Product or Output Level. Resulting from the learning achieved by students participating in the MOOC, their level of satisfaction, and degree of agreement of the experts with the MOOC system, where quality and quantity of learning will depend on the focus adopted. This level must respond additionally to the features and idiosyncrasies of the subject to be studied in the MOOC. The result of the product should provide feedback to the system.

4.2 The Dimensions of the MOOC System Are as Follows

- **Pedagogical Dimension**
  This dimension emphasizes course planning, taking into account the teaching methodology and the massive nature of the courses, student diversity and the dynamic, interactive nature of this type of course, that is to say, considering the principles of communication, diversity -thus, adaptation -and support materials highlighted by [3], as well as the possible reasons for participant demotivation and desertion of courses such as: Lack of time, lack of support, feelings of isolation, lack of prior knowledge and study skills, unchallenging course design and failure to understand course content [22]. However, a strategy of copying should not be adopted, as many universities have done, particularly in Europe, where the methodological and didactic structure is a "Spanish version" of the Anglo-Saxon methodological and teaching structure and quality is neglected [9].
  It is thus necessary to have a specific methodological strategy, which motivates students, and enhances and facilitates a learning network [21], in order that courses are completed. Learning should be student-centered and the learning process should arise from social interaction, in a concrete socio-historical environment, based on individual or group experience of the participants, contributing to their personal development.
- **Technological Dimension**
  In this dimension, the technological tools to be used in the learning management system (LMS) and the production of teaching material are defined. As far as possible, the use of open-source educational materials is recommended to achieve coherence with one of the features of MOOCs.

- **Organizational Dimension**
  This dimension refers to the formation of a multidisciplinary team of professionals (educators and technical personnel), who participate in the different activities of analysis, design, development and execution of the course. The technical personnel will be those responsible for defining and selecting the set of technological tools to be used for the implementation of the system and the design of the content and activities of the course, whereas teaching personnel will be entrusted with planning the course, designing teaching materials and providing follow-up tutoring and feedback to participants. The teaching personnel and the technical team will work in a coordinated fashion in order to achieve balance and a coherent and logical relationship between content and design of the course activities.

- **Communicational dimension**
  This dimension is indispensable since learning is a series of methods, paradigms and learning styles, based on transparent communication. Education is a process in which the communication around interaction and exchange of ideas, knowledge and experience must flow, and in which communicational tools are used. This dimension includes a series of resources and acts of social interaction which occur between students and teacher. Communication is produced using Web 2.0 tools such as forums, chats, intranet, email, videoconferencing or audio-conferencing, wikis and blogs. Each of these possesses a particular dynamic to facilitate communication, thus, it is necessary to plan when and how to use each of them during the teaching-learning process. The educational institution should establish different communication channels so that those participating in the MOOC activities have a range of alternatives at their disposal.

4.3 Principles of the MOOC System

- **Principle of the social nature of learning via a MOOC.** It is fundamental to understand learning in a social and cultural context, related to the concept of activity and integrating social, affective, intellectual, practical, and ethical aspects, among others. Collaborative learning facilitates the construction of knowledge from the "collective intelligence" produced, and leads to the exchange of knowledge and experience, in which the participants teach and learn from each other and develop a positive interdependence [7], also in its modern sense, collective intelligence requires diversity and the use of proper tools to gather as much knowledge, experiences and creativity as possible [11]. In addition, cooperative learning emphasizes the need for other people in order to understand what is learnt and thus exploit learning potentiality, fostering comprehensive development and enhancing feedback and motivation through constant interaction [17].

- **Principle of the integral nature of the MOOC System.** This integrates the main features of MOOCs, SPOCs (Small Private Online Courses) and NOOCs (Nano MOOCs), which are all free, open, online courses promoting democratization of knowledge. One difference between these courses is the number of units; in the case of NOOCs there is only one unit which permits the development of a specific competency, whereas SPOCs and MOOCs contain several units. Thus, these courses can easily be integrated as a system since they possess the same features: they are structured by module, each of which includes several open-source teaching resources (videos, downloadable documents, activities, online assessment, forums, and chats, among others). They vary only with regard to the number of modules, duration and the fact that these courses may or may not have tutor support. However, their construction requires the same components, structure and levels established in an ISMOOC.

- **Principle of unity of activity-communication- digital technology in a MOOC.** The inclusion of digital technology, communication and the identification of connections constitute learning activities to be carried out by students, but with freedom to choose methods, environments, digital tools, connections to networks and even learning tasks in some cases. Although it may be true that nowadays we find numerous MOOC platforms configured into course format, as a complement diverse free technological tools for the design of content or communication may be used. This is even more the case for open-source platforms where there is freedom to choose tools for the design of content and communication. These tools can easily be found on the World Wide Web.

- **Principle of the relationship between developmental teaching, Activity Theory and connective learning in the MOOC System.** The developmental nature of teaching, mediated through didactic material and the tools and technologies which support this process and guide, orient, enhance and enable participant control and assessment, emphasizes the need to create learning situations which not only guarantee students' assimilation of the contents of the subject, but also satisfy their interests and expectations, as well as leveraging their experience in the subject as a path to real affective engagement in the learning process. This fosters the creation of conditions focused on the integral development of the students and the assimilation of the content taught at the pace of the individual. It emphasizes learning as a social activity: that participants learn from each other through the activity being carried out while communicating with others via interactions, connections, learning networks or learning communities.

- **Principle of the relationship between pedagogical, technological, organizational and communicational dimensions in a MOOC System.** This is the harmonious combination of work carried out by the multidisciplinary team such as the selection and configuration of the technological tools based on the planning of the course in line with the specified teaching methodology. The process of incorporating emerging technologies should be carried out bearing in mind the need to configure new student-centered learning environments, but at the same time, teachers should be familiar with the resources and the tools which allow the creation of situations in which students are able to demonstrate what they have learnt and provide the teacher with data on progress and achievements. This is done within a developmental teaching-learning process, which starts from a diagnostic test and from this a Zone of Proximal Development will be calculated for each student. In the MOOC System, technology is a means to support student interaction with didactic materials, with the teacher, with the rest of the students in the training process and with the context. The organizational and communicational dimensions are concerned with institutional management as well as guiding criteria for the use of ICT and emerging technologies, and associated communicational processes.

5 Findings and Analysis

To validate the ISMOOC proposal the MOOC "Emerging technologies for Higher Education" (TEPIES) was delivered to graduates and teachers from the Universidad de las Fuerzas Armadas ESPE. The course had a duration of seven weeks, divided into five modules and required 40 h of study.

In order to implement the MOOC- TEPIES, a multidisciplinary team consisting of technical and teaching personnel was set up, comprised of four teachers with a Masters level degree (two in Educational Sciences and two in Information Technology). Additionally, an invitation was sent to colleagues at other universities, as a result of which three teachers from OpenInstitute joined (one has a PhD in Computer Science, one a Masters in Educational Technology and one a Masters in Multimedia design). The technical personnel who contributed to the development of the course were from the Catholic University of Cuenca, Ecuador, completing the technical-pedagogical multidisciplinary and interinstitutional team.

The commitment, creativity, collaboration and know-how of the technical-pedagogical team were key factors in the design and development of the MOOC. The team was made up of one academic coordinator, one pedagogical advisor, educator-tutors, one platform administrator and one multimedia resource designer. Each of the members had a specific role and following the implementation of the course all of them acted as tutors. Work meetings were generally held via mail or videoconferences.

After the team was set up, work began on the technological dimension. This mainly involved the selection of technological tools, with the proviso that these be open-source educational resources. The benchmark for the selection of LMS were the features established for the MOOC system and on this basis, Moodle was selected, particularly due to its range of tools, ease of installation and experience in its use.

The H5P tool was selected for the design of the learning objects of each of the modules. This is an open-source technology, completely free of charge, which is licensed by MIT (Massachusetts Institute of Technology). It enables Content Management Systems (CMS) and Learning Management Systems (LMS) to create more interactive and enriched content and has a learning objective approach which was of particular interest.

In addition, the tools Prezi, Youtube y Powtoon were used to create presentations and video tutorials; the Bigbluebotton tool was integrated into Moodle for scheduled videoconferences; AdobePhotoshop was used to personalize images; and for communication the platform's own tools were used (email, chats, blogs, wikis), as was Facebook.

The teaching methodology was then drawn up based on the pedagogical benchmarks analyzed previously, and the course activities and tasks were designed. Each of the modules included forums, deliverables from group work, online assessments and a scheduled videoconference. A learning path was designed to provide a clearer overview of the course in relation to the contents, activities and tasks to be completed by participants.

Initially, the participants were informed of the goals and guidelines of the course and were familiarized with the platform. In addition, a diagnostic questionnaire was sent out with the aim of gathering details of the participants (gender, age, nationality, province, knowledge of technological tool in the field of education, among others). Furthermore, a forum was opened online so that students could share experiences and expectations of the course with peers and tutors. On the basis of the results of the survey, some adjustments had to be made to the content, and more video tutorials on how to use the technological tools to be used on the course were incorporated since over 69% of participants had no experience in the use of technological tools for the design of teaching materials, which was one of the outcomes of the MOOC. In addition, some modifications were made to the content in response to the participants' interest in learning specific subject matter related to the MOOC TEPIES.

Throughout the course the active participation of the students was seen, as was empathy between tutors and participants, due to ongoing support and feedback from the tutors. There was bi-directional communication, vertical and horizontal, between the different actors in the MOOC via chats, mail and discussion forums.

With regard to the participation in the forums, more than simple responses were made, and tutors mediated interventions, motivating, congratulating and responding to these new expectations. In the tasks and deliverable products, participants' creativity and imagination were observed, which was due to the fact that the activities were set within a real-life context and students had to put their knowledge into practice in every module.

One of the group activities consisted in creating a wiki page about podcasts in education. The work submitted by each of the groups was of very high quality thanks to the intervention of tutors who noticed that the students in some groups were not participating. They thus contacted them via chat and email on the platform to motivate them and offer further explanation of the task to be completed. The scheduled videoconference was 45 min long (15 set aside for question and answer session), and 202 students managed to connect. For those who were not able to attend, a video of the conference was uploaded. According to the questionnaires, the participants did not experience any problems whatsoever.

In each of the activities in the course, support and feedback from tutors was permanent, which led to the building of academic confidence between participants and tutors, thanks to the level of motivation generated during the MOOC.

An analysis of the results showed that of 324 participants, 268 successfully completed and passed the MOOC, equivalent to 83.71%. In order to measure participants' level of satisfaction with the course a Likert scale survey was carried out. Overall, the findings of the survey indicate that over 72% of the participants rated their level of satisfaction (with organization, ease of access to content, motivation, timely feedback, among others) as excellent.

Overall, the success of the course was the result of the balanced interaction of each of the components of the ISMOOC, in addition to the excellent organization, coordination, tutor support and feedback, and the technical personnel responsible for platform support.

6 Conclusions

MOOCs have become an option for inclusive, flexible education which Higher Education Institutions are adopting in order to address the issue of continuous learning and updating the knowledge of professionals, who after graduating wish to continue training in the institution in which they studied.

The retrospective and prospective vision of MOOCs makes it necessary to reassess these courses from a pedagogical, technological, organizational and communicational perspective in order to reduce the high level of desertion, which has been one of the main challenges for MOOCs from the outset.

The best way in which to view a successful MOOC learning model is as a whole or as a system.

One of the key features of the ISMOOC is undoubtedly the developmental teaching methodology in which facilitators and participants play an active and dynamic role.

References

1. Atiaja, L., Guerrero, R.: The MOOCs: origin, characterization, principal problems and challenges in higher education. J. e-Learn. Knowl. Soc. **12**(1), 65–76 (2016)
2. Atiaja, L.A., Proenza, R.G., Yamba-Yugsi, M.: MOOCs: design of a teaching methodology from a humanist understanding. In: Proceeding of the International Conference on Future of Education, Bangkok, Tailandia, vol. 1, pp. 30–37 (2018)
3. Bates, T.: Comparing xMOOC and cMOOC: philosophy and practice (2014)
4. Bustamante, A.T., Jiménez, B.M.: Modelo de transferencia de conocimiento a través de la gamificación: Un gcMooc. Actualidades Investigativas en Educación **19**(2), 1–21 (2019)
5. Cabero Almenara, J., Llorente Cejudo, M.d.C., Vázquez Martínez, A.I.: Las tipologías de MOOC: su diseño e implicaciones educativas, Revista de Currículum y Profesorado, pp. 13–26 (2014)
6. CEPAL: Agenda 2030 y los Objetivos de Desarrollo Sostenible: una oportunidad para América Latina y el Caribe (2018)
7. Covey, S.: The Leader in Me: How Schools and Parents Around the World Are Inspiring Greatness. One Child at a Time. Free Press, New York (2008)
8. Downes, S.: Week2: The Quality of Massive Open Online (2013)
9. García Aretio, L.: Los MOOC están muy vivos. Respuestas a algunas preguntas. RIED. Revista Iberoamericana de Educación a Distancia **20**(1) (versión preprint) (2017)
10. García Romero, D., Lalueza, J.: Procesos de aprendizaje e identidad en aprendizaje servicio universitario: una revisión teórica. Educación XX1 **22**(2), 45–68 (2019)
11. Gee, J.P., Guitart, M.E.: El diseño para el aprendizaje profundo en los medios de comunicación sociales y digitales. Comunicar: Revista científica iberoamericana de comunicación y educación **58**, 9–18 (2019)
12. Hernández, R., Gütl, C., Amado-Salvatierra, H.: Cloud learning activities orchestration for MOOC environments. In: 3rd International Workshop on Learning Technology for Education in Cloud, Santiago (2014)
13. Johnson, D.W., Johnson, R.T.: Cooperative Learning, Values, and Culturally Plural Classrooms. Cooperative Learning Center at the University of Minnesota (1998). http://www.clcrc.com/pages/CLandD.html
14. Martí, J.: Tipos de MOOCs, Xarxatic (2012). http://www.xarxatic.com/tipos-de-moocs/
15. Murray, T.: What is the integral in integral education? From progressive pedagogy to integral pedagogy. Integral Rev. Transdiscipl. Transcult. J. New Thought Res. Praxis **5**(1), 96–134 (2009)
16. Pernías Peco, P., Luján-Mora, S.: Los MOOCS: Orígenes, historia y tipos. Comunicación y Pedagogía 269–270 (2014)
17. Pei, P., Shen, L.: Design and implementation for cMOOC-oriented online course learning community 2016. In: The 2nd International Conference on Education Science and Human Development (ESHD) (2016)
18. Pichardoa, C.M., Medina, M.A.G.: An overview of Mexican educational achievements in language, mathematics and science. Entreciencias **6**(17), 51–64 (2018)

19. Siemens, G.: Conectivismo: Una teoría de aprendizaje para la era digital (2004)
20. Siemens, G.: Learning analytics: envisioning a research discipline and a domain of practice. In: The 2nd International Conference on Learning Analytics and Knowledge, pp. 4–8. ACM, Vancouver (2012)
21. Teixeira, A., García-Cabot, A., García-López, E., Mota, J., De-Marcos, L.: A new competence-based approach for personalizing MOOCs in a mobile collaborative and networked environment. RIED Revista Iberoamericana de Educación a Distancia, **19**(1), (2016)
22. Topali, P., Ortega-Arranz, A., Er, E., Martínez-Monés, A., Villagrá-Sobrino, S.L., Dimitriadis, Y.: Exploring the problems experienced by learners in a MOOC implementing active learning pedagogies. In: Calise, M., Delgado, K.C., Reich, J., Ruiperez-Valiente, J., Wirsing, M. (eds.) European MOOCs Stakeholders. LNCS, vol. 11475, pp. 81–90. Springer, Cham (2019). https://doi.org/10.1007/978-3-030-19875-6_10
23. Sánchez-Gordon, S., Luján-Mora, S.: MOOCs gone wild. In: Proceedings of the 8th International Technology, Education and Development Conference (INTED 2014), Valencia, España (2014)
24. Vázquez, E., López, E., Sarasola, J.: La expansión del conocimiento en abierto: Los MOOC. Octaedro, Barcelona (2013)

Security Mechanisms in NoSQL DBMS's: A Technical Review

Irving L. Solsol[1], Héctor F. Vargas[2], and Gloria M. Díaz[1(✉)]

[1] Grupo de Investigación en Máquinas Inteligentes y Reconocimiento de Patrones,
Instituto Tecnológico Metropolitano, Medellín, Colombia
irvingsolsol260330@correo.itm.edu.co, gloriadiaz@itm.edu.co
[2] Grupo de Investigación Automática Electrónica y Ciencias Computacionales,
Instituto Tecnológico Metropolitano, Medellín, Colombia
hectorvargas@itm.edu.co

Abstract. The exponential growth of data in organizations, together with the success reported by large companies such as Facebook, Google or Twitter, has promoted to the migration of a large number of applications to the use of NoSQL databases, due to their scalability and performance to Big Data solutions. This phenomenon evidence the need to analyze these new databases from the information security point of view. This article presents a technical review of the controls that could be implemented to preserve security data in eight of the most used NoSQL Database Management Systems named MongoDB, Cassandra, Hbase, CouchDB, BigTable, DinamoDb, Neo4j, and GraphBD. Analysis is performed from the security mechanisms point of view, i.e, authentication, authorization, and encryption (in transit and at rest).

Keywords: NoSQL databases · Security mechanisms · Authentication · Authorization · Encryption

1 Introduction

At the last years, organizations have observed significant changes in their data, which are not only larger but also include images, signals, and other non-structured types. Those changes have increased the demanding in the applications and framework to store, analyzing, and administer it [1,2]. Aiming to deal with these requirements, emerged the NoSQL (Not Only SQL) databases [3], which offer many kinds of architectures according to the type of data to store [1]. Today, important companies such as Google, Facebook, and Twitter, have adopted these databases, which provide functionalities according to the needs of their clients [4,5]. This fact has promoted the development of several applications that use NoSQL databases such as e-health, e-commerce, e-learning, among others, which store confidential and sensitive information. Therefore, preserving

Supported by reciprocity grant Perú - Colombia and Instituto Tecnológico Metropolitano.

the security of data from malicious or accidental actions is one of the most challenging issues for developing those technologies [6].

Lack of security has been reported as one of the drawbacks of using NoSQL database models, due that most of the NoSQL DBMS's do not provide inbuilt security features itself; thus, developers need to insert security in the middleware [6]. Therefore, the preservation of data security requires the implementation of the security mechanisms according to the requirements of the specific NoSQL database solution.

In order to give developers information to decide what of the DBMS's is the most appropriated for preserving data security in a NoSQL database system, they require to know the main security controls provided by them and also the vulnerabilities that must be covered. In a previous work, Dindoliwala [7] presented a review of the security mechanisms offered by some NoSQL databases like MongoDB, Cassandra, GemStone, db4o and Objectivity/DB; this review is very general and left out some of the NoSQL databases that lead the actual market such as CouchDB, Hbase, BigTable, Neo4j and GraphDB. In this paper, a deeper technical review of those NoSQL databases is presented, which was performed from the security mechanisms point of view, i.e., authentication, authorization, and encryption (in transit and at rest).

2   NoSQL Databases

NoSQL (Not Only SQL) is a term defined by Carlo Strozzi in 1998 [8] that is currently used to refer to non-relational databases, which not necessarily guarantee compliance with the ACID property (Atomicity, Consistency, Isolation, Durability). Their main features include schema-less modeling, scalability, flexibility to support many data formats, sharding, high performance, and low maintenance costs. They allow to store structured and unstructured data such as images, audios, videos, emails, word processor files, spreadsheets, among others, and promised to be a solution to the problem of managing large volumes of data, queries, and daily transactions [3,4].

Many NoSQL database models have been proposed [1], being the most representative the Document Oriented (MongoDB, CouchDB, etc.), the Column Oriented (Hbase, Cassandra, etc.), the key-value (BigTable, DynamoDB, etc.) and the graph-based (Neo4j, GraphDB, etc.) [4,9]; therefore, this analysis included the most popular of them, according to the ranking of the portal DB-Engines[1].

MongoDB. It is one of the most popular NoSQL databases. It provides flexibility to users' mean of a distributed document store model that stores data in a schema-less document format. It is developed in C++, and documents are written in the binary JSON style. Open source distributions for many operating systems such as Windows, Linux, Mac OS, and Solaris are available. Among its main features are the ad-hoc queries, which support searches by fields, ranges,

---

[1] https://db-engines.com/en/ranking.

and expressions; the indexing, which allows any field in a database to be consulted; the load balancing, that allows horizontal scalability; and the execution of JavaScrip directly in the databases [10]. Regarding information security, on August 6, 2019, a critical vulnerability was found, which allows an attacker to erase the MongoDB server, which was registered with CVE-2019-2386, which implies establishing measures to reduce risks. There are others of a critical nature, such as CVE-2017-18381 (published on 07/31/2019) and CVE-2018-1784 (12/20/2018).

CouchDB. It is an open-source document-oriented database system that is distributed with Apache 2.0 license, which was initially released in April of 2005 by Damien Katz [11,12]. It is written in C++ and works with the JSON structure for free-schema data storage. It uses JavaScript as a query language to support the Map/Reduce data processing model, which allows stored data to be organized mean of views. CouchDB provides an ACID (Atomicity, Consistency, Isolation, Durability) semantics at document-level, and also provides the simplest form of replication, which allows synchronizing two or more copies of the same database hosted in the same or different servers, thanks to it implements a form of multi-version concurrency control (MVCC), and besides it has eventual consistency to offer availability and fault tolerance, [13]. For this database, medium type vulnerabilities such as CVE-2018-17188 (published on 01/02/2019) and CVE-2018-14889 (published on (21/09/2018) have been found.

Hbase. This database system was created in October of 2007 by Powerset [14] and is an Apache project distributed with the Apache 2.0 license. It is a column-oriented key-value distributed data store that runs on top of HDFS (Hadoop Distributed File System) [14] and supports Map/Reduce jobs. Hbase features include atomic and consistent reads and write, Scalability in both linear and modular form, Java API for programming access, data replication across clusters, among others [5]. A critical vulnerability was found (CVE-2019-9039 of 06/26/2019) and a high criticality (CVE-2019-0212, 03/28/2019).

Cassandra. It is a hybrid distributed database system (columns and key-value) that was created and released by Facebook in 2008 [15]. It is distributed with the Apache 2.0 license. It is written in java and works with a CQL (Cassandra Query Language) scheme. It implements a fault tolerance that allows data to be automatically replicated on multiple storage nodes, which communicate with a P2P protocol to offer a maximum redundancy this decentralized work, by which there is not a unique point of failure. Additionally, their scalability allows us to nerate queries and save data as the nodes grow[2] [16]. Critical vulnerabilities were found on 07/11/2018 (CVE-2018-0038); additionally, medium criticalities such as CVE-2018-8016 (06/28/2018).

---

[2] http://cassandra.apache.org/.

BigTable. It is a distributed key-value database that was created by Google and released in 2005 [12]. Although it is a proprietary database system, in 2015, a public version was made available as a service. It is developed using C and C++ and works with the file scheme GFS (Google File System). Bigtable functionality is within the Commodity Hardware environment that uses a lot of existing computer resources for simultaneous processing[3]. Among some of the applications that use this database are Google Analytics, Google Earth, Gmail [12,17].

DynamoDB. It is a proprietary NoSQL database service created by Amazon, which is offered as part of the Amazon Web Services (AWS) [18]. Dynamo is a hybrid database system (key-value and document), that does not have a defined scheme, and uses languages such as Java, .Net, Javascript, Perl, C#, and [19]. It is high availability and fully scalable by using the amazon hardware infrastructure. As was expected, data access is possible through its AWS administration console or AWS CLI, which allows making backup copies and restoration as needed[4] [19].

Neo4j. It is an open-source graph-oriented database system created by Neo Technology, which was developed in Java, and has its own language called Cypher based on declarative graphical queries, but supports Language Controllers for C#, Java, JavaScript, and Python [12]. It is considered the most used graph-oriented database; its architecture was designed to optimize the administration, storage, and rapid nodes path, and allows the integration of ACID properties [20]. It has horizontal scalability, which allows new nodes to be incorporated into the system, storage is disk-based through its own file system, and has an intuitive and easily accessible interface[5] [12,20]. For this database, critical type vulnerabilities such as CVE-2018-1000820 (published on 20/12/2018) and CVE-2018-18389 published on (16/10/2018) have been found.

GraphDB. It is a highly efficient semantic graph database, developed in java, that complies with W3C standards. It is supported on RDF (Resource Description Framework) and the SPARQL query language. It provides a centralized infrastructure and offers scalability that allows an efficient query performance according to the number of nodes. It supports data linking, which allows a geospatial indexing data for semantic searches, and generate knowledge graphs for advanced data analysis. It provides a Workbench interface that makes it easy to manage data from repositories, users, and access roles[6].

---

[3] https://cloud.google.com/bigtable/docs/overview?hl=en-419.
[4] https://aws.amazon.com/es/dynamodb/.
[5] https://neo4j.com/docs/operations-manual/3.5/.
[6] http://graphdb.ontotext.com/documentation/free/index.html.

3   Information Security Features

Information security is one of the most relevant issues in database implementation because of the necessity of reducing the risks of exposure to computer attacks, which may affect the privacy, confidentiality, and integrity of stored data. Previous works have identified. Security breaches and vulnerabilities of NoSQL databases have been described by some authors [6,21,22]. In this work, emphasis will be placed on the security mechanisms provided by these database systems due to its importance for developers [6,21,22].

Security Mechanisms are techniques used to implement security features in the information systems; among them, authentication, authorization, and encryption are valuable for controlling access and protecting information.

Authentication. The mechanisms in this category allow establishing the authenticity of something or someone for accessing information. These mechanisms include to identify and verify the users or processes linked to an information system. Some of them are credentials, authentication token, device identification, among others [7,23].

Authorization. They are mechanisms used to allow or deny access to an information resource by something or someone that attempts to link to a system. Authorization mechanisms define the information access level and use possibilities according to the assigned role and privileges of each user [7,23].

Encryption in Transit. Encryption is the process that converts readable data into illegible data (encrypted text), which aims to guarantee that only authorized parts can access and use the information. Encryption also provides mechanisms for validating integrity, authenticity, and non-repudiation of messages. Encryption in transit mechanisms seeks to protect the data confidentiality in a system that exchanges information or that is in communication through a connection [7,23].

Encryption at Rest. This feature seeks to protect the data confidentiality in the storage element, prevents possible exposure or theft of information, avoiding the data from being read or modified by unauthorized persons [7,23].

4   Information Security Mechanisms Provided by NoSQL Databases

Table 1 summarizes the security mechanisms available in the eight NoSQL database systems analyzed. They are grouped by security features, according to their technical documentation. As can be observed, different mechanisms are provided. Thus, below is a description of these mechanisms for each database system.

4.1 Authentication

MongoDB. MongoDB has two authentication mechanisms, Salted Challenge Response Authentication (SCRAM), it is implemented by default, and is based on password authentication; and the x.509 certificate protocol, which requires a public key infrastructure. On the other hand, MongoDB Enterprise Server supports two authentication mechanisms, LDAP (Lightweight Directory Access Protocol) and Kerberos, which allows taking advantage of existing authentication infrastructure and technologies.

CouchDB. It provides different authentication mechanisms: Admin Party, in which any user who has access to the database has the privilege of an administrator; Basic authentication, which allows authentication by user and password to differentiate between the administrator and other users, it can be implemented either through storage and encryption with PBKDF2, also the implementation of SSL/TLS certificates without the use of a proxy server; and authentication through cookies, which allows the user to login through a Web interface and the HTTP protocol, case in which, CouchDB generates a unique token for a defined time that can be adjusted to be authenticated in future connections. This last mechanism could cause some problems when this time is very long because it could allow attackers to obtain that information and carry out identity-theft attacks.

HBase. Default Hbase configuration not provides any security mechanism, so everyone is allowed to read and write to all tables in the database. However, HBase can be configured at the RPC level to provide User Authentication using additional mechanisms such as the Hadoop distributed system and Apache ZooKeeper, which can be integrated for allowing the implementation of Kerberos authentication to identify whether a host or client is who it claims to be.

Cassandra. This database system was designed to be easily accessed, reason by which it does not provides authentication mechanisms at default install. Thus, it is necessary to enable login/password user authentication. This mechanism can be reinforced by implementing the Authentication Standard Java Management Extensions (JMX) Auth, which validates the user identity previously registered on the JMX server, using a password; additionally, the Cassandra Integrated Auth functionality provides the most secure authentication control; however, it cannot be implemented until a node is integrated into the data center.

BigTable. As this database works within Google's infrastructure, the authentication is implemented in a centralized platform for the management of Cloud Identity identities, which is supported by the Google's security model known as BeyondCorp that is based on Zero trust networks, i.e., there is no confidence in any external system or user.

Table 1. Security mechanisms available in selected NoSQL database

	Authentication	Authorization	Data encryption in transit	Data encryption at rest
MongoDB[a] v4.2	- SCRAM (Salted Challenge Response Authentication Mechanism) - x.509 Certificate Authentication Note: LDAP proxy authentication and Kerberos authentication, available on MongoDB Enterprise	- Role-Based Access Control (RBAC) Note: - Not enabled by default	- Certificados TLS/SSL Note: - FIPS mode, available in MongoDB Enterprise - From version 4.0 onwards TLS 1.0 is disabled in systems where it is available TLS 1.1+	- Encrypted storage engine - Application Level Encryption Note: Available for Business
CouchDB[b] v2.3.1	- Admin Party - Basic - Cookies - Autenticación Proxy Note: - SSL/TSL certificates supported since version 1.1.0 - From version 1.3.0, uses the PBKDF2 encryption algorithm for stored passwords	- Role- and privilege-based	- TLS/SSL Certificates Note: Natively supports without the use of a proxy server	- Does not provide encryption for your data.
Hbase[c] v2.2.2	- HDFS, ZooKeeper - Kerberos - SASL Note: Does not check authentication by default	- Simple User Access (role-based) - Securing Access to HDFS and ZooKeeper - Access Control Labels (ACL) Note: - ACL is available from HBase 0.92 (CDH4) on-wards - It does not check for authorization by default	- SSL/TLS Note: - Must be configured to have a secure connection (HTTPS). - Kerberos SASL encrypted connection	- Transparent Data Encryption (TDE)
Cassandra[d] v4.0	- Username and password - Cassandra Integrated Auth - Standard JMX Authentication Note: Does not check authentication by default	- Internal Authorization - JMX access Note: It does not check for authorization by default	- TLS/SSL certificates	- Transparent Data Encryption (TDE).
BigTable[e]	- Cloud Identity Note: - Free service	- Access Management (Cloud IAM) - Role- and privilege-based	- TLS Certificates	- Default encryption - Client Managed Encryption Keys (CMEK) with Cloud KMS - Customer Provided Encryption Keys (CSEK).

(continued)

Table 1. (*continued*)

	Authentication	Authorization	Data encryption in transit	Data encryption at rest
DynamoDB[f]	- AWS Identity and Access Management (IAM) Note: - Free service	- Role-and privilege-based of AWS Identity and Access Management	- SSL/TLS Certificates Note: All data is encrypted except DAX data (indirect write caching service)	- CMK owned by AWS (predetermined) - CMK administered by AWS (paid) Note: - AWS KMS is the service that manages encryption.
Neo4j[g] v3.5	- Native Authentication Provider Note: Only for Bussines - LDAP Authentication Provider - Single sign-on Kerberos authentication - Custom plugin authentication providers	- Native roles Note: Only for Bussines - Role-based access control - Subgraph access control	- SSL/TLS certificates	- It only gives recommendations and does not specify any mechanism - Recommends the use of Bitlocker
GraphDB[h] v9.0.0	- Local - LDAP (standard x.500.) - Basic Authentication Note: The Local authentication generates access tokens	- Role-based (RBAC1) and privileges via Spring Security	- Selected SSL/TLS certificates with Tomcat server - HTTPS protocol on the server Note: - The certification settings must be enabled	- Does not provide encryption for your data Note: The data stored on the hard disk in binary

[a] https://docs.mongodb.com/manual/security/
[b] https://docs.couchdb.org/en/stable/intro/security.html
[c] https://hbase.apache.org/book.html#security
[d] http://cassandra.apache.org/doc/latest/operating/security.html
[e] https://cloud.google.com/bigtable/docs/
[f] https://docs.aws.amazon.com/es_es/amazondynamodb/latest/developerguide/dynamodb-dg.pdf#security
[g] https://neo4j.com/docs/operations-manual/3.5/
[h] http://graphdb.ontotext.com/documentation/free/security.html

DynamoDB. This database works within the Amazon Web Services (AWS) infrastructure; therefore, it uses AWS Identity and Access Management (IAM), which is a web service that allows access to all resources to be controlled through an account administration.

Neo4j. It provides various authentication mechanisms. First of them, Native Auth provider, which stores the information of all users on the disk, allowing for tracking and managing the identity of users in real-time. Also, It allows integrating LDAP auth provider, which works by implementing Active Directory or OpenLDAP. When these two mechanisms do not adapt to the application needs, it is possible to implement Custom-built plugin auth providers, which allows customizing the required authentication criteria. Finally, it is possible to implement Kerberos authentication and single sign-on, which can be integrated for more strict and unique network authentication.

GraphDB. Within the security mechanisms, this database count with local authentication as a default security provider, which store in the database username and passwords, which are stored through the SHA-256 integrity algorithm. Once users are validated, the database generates a JSON web token for access. It also allows implementing LDAP authentication server, which allows validating access to the database, as long as it is previously configured.

4.2   Authorization

MongoDB. Access control is not enabled in the default installation of MongoDB; however, it has the Role-Based Access Control (RBAC) for the access of any user, where one or more specific or inherited roles (privileges) can be assigned, allowing it access to the resources and operational functions of a database.

CouchDB. In this case, access control can only be implemented once the authentication mechanisms and controls have been defined, thus it is possible to establish restrictions, privileges and access roles to the database; To do this you must determine whether they are administrators or members (according to the need for privileges), then it can be changed, all these changes are recorded in a security document.

Hbase. Access control is not enabled by default. Simple User Access can be enabled to prevent users from making mistakes; it is an authorization mechanism based on roles that allow implementing access control without implementing Kerberos as an authentication mechanism; however, it provides very limited security. Alternatively, Securing Access to HDFS and ZooKeeper can be implemented. HDFS ensures that users do not access the system files and can not skip the security layer, and ZooKeeper allows access to authenticated and unauthenticated clients by implementing an access control list that contains the authentication and its security entity. Finally, Access Control Labels (ACL) is also available, which is an authorization mechanism based on the Hadoop group mapper that allows defining access levels according to operation (permission) and scope (privileges).

Cassandra. The authorization mechanism is not enabled by default; however, the Internal Authorization control can be implemented prior to configuration, which allows access through the registration and configuration of a white list. Additionally, the JMX access can be configurated hand in hand with the Authentication mechanism; although its initial configuration is only possible from the localhost, this control allows access based on roles and privileges.

BigTable. Authorization is supported by Access Management, a mechanism provided by Google that allows controlling user access to projects or instances based on a predefined function or a custom function through the Cloud Bigtable API.

DynamoDB. Authentication is supported by WS Identity and Access Management (IAM); it is a mechanism provided by Amazon Web Services (AWS) that allows control access based on roles and privileges.

Neo4j. It can implement an authorization mechanism based on native user roles. It provides only limited access control (change password, read, write, update, and delete data, among others) to the community. However, enterprise edition allows native and additional custom roles (assign/remove user roles, change other user passwords, activate/suspend users, among others). On the other hand, the Subgraph access control is also available, which restricts user access to actions such as reading, writing, access to specific nodes of the graph, among others.

GraphDB. This database implements Spring Security as a mechanism for user authorization is a framework that focuses on providing authentication and authorization to applications developed in Java. GraphDB performs a minimal implementation of role-based access control (RBAC1) and user-specific permissions.

4.3   Encryption in Transit

MongoDB. It supports TLS/SSL (Transport Layer Security/Secure Sockets Layer) protocol to encrypt both traffic and network connections. It provides powerful encryption with a minimum length of 128 bits and supports authority issued certificates to server identity validation. Moreover, self-signed certificates can be used, but it is not recommended due it does not validate the certificate's authenticity. Federal Information Processing Standard (FIPS) Mode is also available but only in the enterprise edition. It is a US government security standard that allows modules and libraries to be encrypted and decrypted using certificates according to the FIPS 140-2 standard for OpenSSL.

CouchDB. This database natively allows the implementation of TSL/SSL certificates once OpenSSL has been configurated. It supports any official certificate issued by an authority for allowing to make an HTTPS connection to the server. The use of self-signed certificates is also available, but it is not recommended due it cannot validate the authenticity of the certificate, which could make the system vulnerable to attacks such as phishing.

HBase. This database uses HTTP web connections for its user interface (UI) by default; However, the configuration of the webserver (Jetty) enables HTTPS connections for a secure connection between the client and the server using SSL/TLS encryption. Additionally, Kerberos SASL authentication can be implemented to allows an encrypted and confidential connection to the server.

Cassandra. This database allows encryption for the connection between a client and the server through TSL/SSL certificates, which can be client-node and node-node in a java virtual machine (JVM). Additionally, it can be configured and managed independently.

BigTable. This database handles the encryption of data in transit through a Framework called Google Front End (GFE), which allows to authenticate, encrypt, and authorize access to Google Cloud services. Additionally, the use of the HTTPS protocol through a TLS connection allows guaranteeing integrity and privacy in user connections by public/private keys and a certificate authorized by Google.

DynamoDB. This database encrypts data in transit by protecting connections through Amazon Web Services (AWS) APIs, with TLS certificates. Customers must enable encryption with full confidentiality offered by AWS and sign their ID with their access code, which must be associated with the Identity and Access Management (IAM) policies.

Neo4J. This database protects data in transit through the implementation of SSL/TLS certificates. For doing so, it first needs to be enabled on its platform, whereby certificates issued by an authority must be stored within the Neo4j configuration platform. Likewise, SSL policies must be defined manually, to allow the network connection provided by the Netty library to be secure.

GraphDB. This database incorporates SSL/TSL certificates signed by author-ity; it encrypts connections with HTTPS protocols and allows the implementa-tion of self-signed certificates; however, this can become a problem when a large number of nodes are implemented, since those nodes cant trust the certificate.

4.4 Encryption at Rest

MongoDB. It provides compliance with security and privacy standards, includ-ing HIPAA, PCI-DSS, and FERPA. Since version 3.2, it allows Encrypted Stor-age Engine (ESE), which works with the default WiredTiger storage engine, which aims data be decoded only by users who have the encryption key. Addi-tionally, from version 4.2., it also allows to implement Application Level Encryp-tion, which encrypts one or more specific fields of a document.

CouchDB. This database does not offer data encryption at rest, so the data stored on the disk can be exposed to any risk. Only recommendations of good security practices are given, such as secure storage and the execution of backups. However, the lack of encryption at rest exposes systems to emergent vulnerabilities. Additionally, if it is not configured properly, the stored information could be altered to impersonate identities and to escalate privileges.

HBase. This database allows the implementation of the Transparent Data Encryption (TDE) in its StoreFiles (HFiles) and also in the Write Ahead Log (WAL), as part of Hadoop Distributed File System (HDFS). This feature encrypts the data at writing and decrypts it when they are reading.

Cassandra. It also allows the TDE for encrypting data at rest, which is managed from a Java Cryptography Extension (JCE) store. Other key providers can be connected as long as those comply with the JCE style.

Bigtable. It allows encrypting all data through Google Cloud Platform solutions, which can be selected by the database administrator. Default encryption, encrypt data automatically using the Customer-Managed Encryption Keys (CMEK), which is accomplished using service accounts. It keeps the keys in the cloud so that Google Cloud services can be used; likewise, it provides Customer-Supplied Encryption Keys (CSEK), where the key is customized and handled by the user.

DynamoDB. Through AWS Key Management Service (AW KMS), DynamoDB encrypts all data at rest using a customer master key (CMK), as long as the table is stored on disk. For doing so, one of two customer master keys (CMK): AWS owned CMK, in which the key is owned by DynamoDB (no additional charge) or AWS managed CMK, case in which the key is stored in a client account and is managed by AWS KMS (charges apply).

Neo4J. This database does not provide encryption of data at rest. Therefore, the security of data stored on the disk must be supported with the execution of backups and good security practices such as the safe conservation of these backups.

GraphDB. In this database, all data are stored in binary; that is to say, it does not provide data encryption at rest. The lack of encryption at rest exposes stored data to be accessed or subtracted, also to be victims of accidental or intentional deletion and modification attacks. GraphDB recommends implementing some external tool that allows data encryption, which could be complex to integrate and even very expensive.

5   Conclusions

This work summarized the security mechanisms available by the NoSQL database management systems more used in the market; both open source and proprietary systems were included. Eight database systems were analyzed, two document-based (MongoDB and CouchDB), two column-based (HBase and Cassandra), two key-value (BigTable and DynamoDB), and two graph-based systems (Neo4j and GraphDB). Reported mechanisms were identified in the most recent technical documentation published by suppliers.

As was observed, information security seems to be a relevant aspect for the providers of these systems, as all of them have mechanisms to provide security features such as authentication, authorization, and data encryption. However, as some of them do not enable it in the default installation, developers must define they that will be implemented according to client requirements.

From a general point of view, proprietary systems (BigTable and DynamoDB) provide the easiest way to implement information security features, because they have their own support team and provide a catalog of security options, so the database administrator only must choose the controls to use. Conversely, other databases such as MongoDB, CouchDB, Neo4j, and GraphDB, require their own local server infrastructure and specific implementations to cover security issues. These implements **authentication and authorization** mechanisms by default, supported on user credentials and password, in terms of authorization, they are based on roles (user profiles) and privileges (access and user permissions). On the other hand, Cassandra and HBase were designed to be easily accessed; therefore, security mechanisms do not enable by default. Thus, it is very important to implement or integrate additional techniques that allow achieving at least one basic security control, previous to the initial configuration.

On the other hand, all database systems allow **data encryption in transit**, through the implementation of protocols and digital certificates that encrypt the connection between the user and the server, or between server and nodes so that confidentiality and privacy be obtained in the connection to the database server. Respect to the **data encryption at rest**, MongoDB stands out by its own disk encryption mechanism, in which no additional implementations are required. Hbase and Cassandra support the integration of additional tools for disk encryption, prior configuration. Finally, databases such as CouchDB, Neo4j, and GraphDB does not provide this encryption mechanism, which increases the risk of attacks.

References

1. Chen, J.-K., Lee, W.-Z.: An introduction of NoSQL databases based on their categories and application industries. Algorithms **12**(5), 106 (2019)
2. Hernández-Leal, E.J., Duque-Méndez, N.D., Moreno-Cadavid, J.: Big data: an exploration of research, technologies and application cases. TecnoLógicas **20**(39), 15–38 (2017)
3. Meier, A., Kaufmann, M.: SQL & NoSQL Databases: Models, Languages, Consistency Options and Architectures for Big Data Management, pp. 201–218. Springer, Wiesbaden (2019). https://doi.org/10.1007/978-3-658-24549-8

4. Li, Z.: NoSQL databases. The Geographic Information Science & Technology Body of Knowledge (2nd Quarter 2018 Edition), May 2018. https://doi.org/10.22224/gistbok/2018.2.10
5. Das, N., Paul, S., Sarkar, B.B., Chakrabarti, S.: NoSQL overview and performance testing of HBase over multiple nodes with MySQL. In: Abraham, A., Dutta, P., Mandal, J., Bhattacharya, A., Dutta, S. (eds.) Emerging Technologies in Data Mining and Information Security. AISC, vol. 813, pp. 269–279. Springer, Singapore (2019). https://doi.org/10.1007/978-981-13-1498-8_24
6. Gupta, N., Agrawal, R.: NoSQL security. In: Advances in Computers, vol. 109, pp. 101–132. Elsevier (2018)
7. Dindoliwala, V.J., Morena, R.D.: Survey on security mechanisms in NoSQL databases. Int. J. Adv. Res. Comput. Sci. 8(5), 333–338 (2017)
8. Strozzi, C.: NoSQL: a relational database management system. Lainattu 5, 2014 (1998)
9. Zaki, A.K.: NoSQL databases: new millennium database for big data, big users, cloud computing and its security challenges. Int. J. Res. Eng. Technol. (IJRET) 3(15), 403–409 (2014)
10. Abramova, V., Bernardino, J.: NoSQL databases: MongoDB vs Cassandra. In: Proceedings of the International C* Conference on Computer Science and Software Engineering, pp. 14–22. ACM (2013)
11. Lennon, J.: Introduction to CouchDB. In: Lennon, J. (ed.) Beginning CouchDB, pp. 3–9. Springer, Heidelberg (2009). https://doi.org/10.1007/978-1-4302-7236-6_1
12. Nayak, A., Poriya, A., Poojary, D.: Type of NoSQL databases and its comparison with relational databases. Int. J. Appl. Inf. Syst. 5(4), 16–19 (2013)
13. Boumahdi, A., El Majjodi, A., Baïna, K.: NoSQL-model quality assessment document-oriented databases, CouchDB
14. George, L.: HBase: the Definitive Guide: Random Access to Your Planet-Size Data. O'Reilly Media, Inc., Newton (2011)
15. Sharma, S., Shandilya, R., Patnaik, S., Mahapatra, A.: Leading NoSQL models for handling big data: a brief review. Int. J. Bus. Inf. Syst. 22(1), 1–25 (2016)
16. Wahid, A., Kashyap, K.: Cassandra–a distributed database system: an overview. In: Abraham, A., Dutta, P., Mandal, J.K., Bhattacharya, A., Dutta, S. (eds.) Emerging Technologies in Data Mining and Information Security. AISC, vol. 755, pp. 519–526. Springer, Singapore (2019). https://doi.org/10.1007/978-981-13-1951-8_47
17. Chang, F., et al.: Bigtable: a distributed storage system for structured data. ACM Trans. Comput. Syst. (TOCS) 26(2), 4 (2008)
18. Deshpande, T.: Mastering DynamoDB. Packt Publishing Ltd., Birmingham (2014)
19. Kalid, S., Syed, A., Mohammad, A., Halgamuge, M.N.: Big-data NoSQL databases: a comparison and analysis of "Big-table", "DynamoDB", and "Cassandra". In: 2017 IEEE 2nd International Conference on Big Data Analysis (ICBDA), pp. 89–93. IEEE (2017)
20. Guia, J., Soares, V.G., Bernardino, J.: Graph databases: Neo4j analysis. ICEIS 1, 351–356 (2017)
21. Mohamed, M.A., Altrafi, O.G., Ismail, M.O.: Relational vs. NoSQL databases: a survey. Int. J. Comput. Inf. Technol. 3(03), 598–601 (2014)
22. Li, L., Qian, K., Chen, Q., Hasan, R., Shao, G.: Developing hands-on labware for emerging database security. In: Proceedings of the 17th Annual Conference on Information Technology Education, pp. 60–64. ACM (2016)
23. Samaraweera, G.D., Chang, M.J.: Security and privacy implications on database systems in big data era: A survey. IEEE Trans. Knowl. Data Eng., 1 (2019). https://doi.org/10.1109/TKDE.2019.2929794

Corrective Feedback Through Mobile Apps for English Learning: A Review

Adriana Guanuche[1,2(✉)] ⓘ, Osana Eiriz[1] ⓘ, and Roberto Espí[1] ⓘ

[1] Universidad Politécnica Salesiana, UPS, 170146 Quito, Ecuador
aguanuche@ups.edu.ec
[2] Universidad de La Habana, 10200 La Habana, Cuba

Abstract. This paper aims to explore the influence of corrective feedback through mobile apps on smartphones, highlighting the benefits of its use in the English language learning process. To do this, the search and the analysis of the literature found were carried out taking into account the most relevant studies. The results of the research show that the use of corrective feedback contributes to the progress and improvement of student learning in more than 50% of the aforementioned foreign language. In the affective field, it increases the motivation, the belief in the individual capacities, the willingness to use the apps and therefore to be in contact with the language inside and outside the class. For professors, corrective feedback is a support that allows them to have individual and group monitoring of learning outcomes. This research reveals a review in which trends and challenges of mobile apps are evident.

Keywords: Corrective feedback · Mobile apps · English learning

1 Introduction

The development of the Internet and the appearance of new mobile technologies have created new learning opportunities that allow the interaction between teachers and students towards the use of tools that promote the improvement of English language skills [1–3]. At present learning English has become a very important tool because it is the most commonly used language worldwide in several aspects such as: education, health, business, technology, etc. [4].

Information and communication technology has been used a lot in the educational sector of the developed world. However, in developed countries, the use of ICTs, mainly in primary education is still in progress [5]. Mobile technology has contributed with new alternatives for English learning development. It is considerate an inevitable support in the classrooms and in general in the educative sector due to its multiple options and facilities [6–8].

Nowadays, iOS and Android domain the apps marketing. Since the third trimester of 2019, the Android users could choose between 2, 47 apps millions while App Store Apple was the second biggest app store with 1.8 million of available apps for iOs. In fact, this document is centered in this two platforms due to the high user request [9].

© Springer Nature Switzerland AG 2020
F. R. Narváez et al. (Eds.): SmartTech-IC 2019, CCIS 1154, pp. 229–242, 2020.
https://doi.org/10.1007/978-3-030-46785-2_19

Thus, having mobile resources makes it easier for students to have access to learning environments that are available anywhere, anytime, low cost, portability inside and outside the classroom, which makes it possible to be in contact with the foreign language in an effective manner and in accordance with the reality [2, 10]. This advantages allow remove many limitations inefficiencies form learning.

The evolution that technology and the rapid growth of telecommunication networks has had over time has allowed us to have smartphones for the learning process. The shift from the use of computers to mobile phones made English the official digital channel for foreign language students. Taking advantage of students' great dependence to use these devices encourages teachers to consider these resources for the progress of English learning [11, 12].

The advantages of mobile apps in smartphones are focused on being portable, useful, adaptable resources and most importantly, they are devices that the vast majority of young adult students from 18 to 29 have within easy reach [13, 14].

The immersion of apps represents a potential support in the teaching learning process in higher education. Thus, around the world, higher education is using these tools because of the impact of these devices on higher education. This influence is reflected in the advancement of learning methods and the development of specific skills in students [15, 16].

The disadvantages are related to programming environments sometimes are incompatible for smartphones. This happens because sometimes these apps are free or need to be paid [17].

Another disadvantage reveals that most mobile apps are designed, developed and used in English learning but not validated for a considerable period of time. There are a few apps that have been validated by developers. One of the techniques used to know the correct working of an app is through star grading and the user comments. Recent studies and surveys show that users trust a lot in star grading and of user comments given by another users. This feedback help students to decide which app they will download.

The moment to develop an app it is used to create multiplatform apps in this way getting more users, getting more incomes and accumulating more users [18]. Ideally a multiplatform app should provide the same availability in different platforms, but this does not happen at real time [19].

Learning through mobile devices maintains a complementary approach in the learning process whose objective is to motivate and encourage students to obtain results based on academic needs. The objective focuses on using mobile apps with exercises as support and complement of traditional learning [20, 21].

This challenge to update traditional learning brings much responsibility for Professor due to on the web there are many resources without relevant educational contents. So that it is important to find and select authentic apps to keep advantage of the benefits from technology [22]. Nowadays there are many mobile apps for vocabulary, writing, listening, speaking and grammar in the English language [23]. However, there are not mobile apps with an immediate corrective feedback that allows students to identify their errors.

An advantage of mobile apps is the corrective feedback in learning the foreign language. The correction of errors and the emission of comments to find the correct answer is a fundamental activity that teachers do in learning the foreign language. The learning opportunity through corrective feedback engage students' self-motivation to find the right answer [24]. The effectiveness of the corrective feedback is verified with the students' learning advances.

Currently, there are many mobile app search options that demonstrate that corrective feedback contributes to the improvement of students' production [25]. In addition, it becomes a support for the professor since it promulgates cooperative work, links students especially those with low performance and reduces the tension that students have to communicate in the foreign language [26].

The importance of corrective feedback is one of the most debated topics in the foreign language learning due to the lack of investigative data to establish whether or not there is a direct influence on written production [27].

The objective of this study is to get advantage of mobile apps as well as of corrective feedback benefits to join it and to develop in a mobile app that contributes to foreign language learning. Also this research aims to know what processes are used to validate mobile apps and analyze different criteria.

The paper is organized as follows: The second section presents the overview of corrective feedback and mobile apps the third section provides the methodology. In the fourth section, the results. The fifth section shows the discussion and finally the sixth section the conclusions and recommendations.

2 Overview of Corrective Feedback with Mobile Apps

2.1 Corrective Feedback

Corrective feedback refers to the information, comments or answers provided to students or professors for the error correction with a view to the linguistic precision of the foreign language [28–30].

For other authors it is the process of grammatical error correction of the foreign language that plays an important role in learning especially in written production. The effectiveness of corrective feedback is linked with content, attitude, motivation and the number of students focused on correcting grammatical errors. It is also referred to as any information, comment or response that is provided to students about their academic performance themselves that can be addressed to correct errors or to praise a correct answer for both students and professors [22, 31, 32]. Corrective feedback is a way of feedback that let students know about their linguistic errors made on oral and written production. In addition, it plays a fundamental role in the second language learning and teaching process [33]. The most important aspects in the analysis of written corrective feedback refer to error correction, that is which errors, when, by whom, how, first of all whether should be corrected and improved written production [34, 35].

In [36] one of the teachers' goals is to encourage students to self-correction due to the multiple activities to cover. Also mentions another type of corrective feedback that is in pairs. Peer feedback keeps a balance between teachers' talking time and student talk but it requires more attention to each student. This type of feedback promotes learners' talk, learn in a familiar context and the opportunity to learn each other. In [37] adds immediate feedback which increases motivation, independence and willingness for students no matter where they are.

In [30] the authors took a sample of 64 students to conduct a corrective feedback study using ICTs. They identified grammatical and lexical errors in English, and provided the opportunity for students to correct themselves. After feedback and self-correction, the learning results show more than the 50% of improvement in students' responses. In addition, it indicated students' motivation to analyze and find the correct answers to their mistakes by themselves.

In [25] a study with feedback through computers was conducted through three different groups. They chose more than 200 students to whom was used elaborated feedback. The results indicated that the use of technology influences in motivation and the improvement of learning outcomes, which are verified through the progress of assessments and grades.

In [38] 90 students participated in the research on the influence of corrective feedback on the grammatical English learning as a second language. We worked with three groups, the first employed direct corrective feedback, the second, corrective feedback with repetition and the third did not use feedback. The results revealed that the group with corrective feedback with repetition improved grammar knowledge to a greater extent, followed by the group with direct feedback and in a small proportion those who did not receive feedback.

More than seventy English as a foreign language (EFL) learners participated from ages ranged between 15 and 26 who had a B2 level. The study results showed the effectiveness of corrective feedback enhancing students to improve their learning [39].

In [40] some students participated within seven weeks using a platform, the results showed that the students became more collaborative in the English learning.

Another paper investigates the influence of English as foreign language so that this study applied a survey to 360 students to identify perceptions of grammar instruction and corrective feedback involving. The study applied two sets of already validated questionnaires to compare Persian and Azeri EFL learners. The results revealed that 70.1% learners have more positive views towards grammar instruction and corrective feedback learning experiences than the Azeri EFL. In the case of the corrective feedback learners presented significant relationship between language proficiency level and tendency to be benefited from corrective feedback [41].

2.2 Mobile Apps for English Learning

They are software programs developed for mobile devices such as smartphones that allow access from any place and time. Apps are small sets of programming statement that are available, easy to use and manage all the time [42, 43].

Some previous findings confirm that apps generate affirmative effects in English learning for instance it increases the motivation, improves learner performance in a specific language area, uses diversity of resources and promotes autonomy [13].

The wide variety of mobile devices and mobile apps are changing the way students improve their knowledge. M-learning gives students the opportunity to learn outside the classroom at anytime because it offers a flexible and easy ways to practice according to their convenience and at the same time improves the learning effectiveness and autonomy development [44, 45].

The use of smartphones and mobile applications have showed generation of positive effects regarding English learning. The results have revealed a significant impact in students' vocabulary retention [46]. Thus, they have become new support tools, easy to transport, save time, motivate and promote students' confidence in the academic field [47–50].

Exercises in mobile apps allow students to receive corrective feedback in a personalized way indicating their errors, motivating them to correct themselves and their progress in English learning [8]. Its popularity and acceptance in several countries has implemented its use by providing an enriching environment full of opportunities and challenges for students and professors [47].

Corrective feedback is presented through online exercises whose focus is the learning topic. Exercise types include: filling in the blanks, matching, images, and video, among others. The apps that work on the development of English language skills are Lexiway, Duolingo, Babbel and Busuu. Lexiway studies vocabulary, pronunciation and also provides virtual classes. Duolingo motivates students through games. Babbel builds on grammar and vocabulary and Busuu focuses on reading, conversation and writing. The organization of apps varies by levels, blocks, units and lessons [51].

In [52] a mobile app called Duolingo was developed and it allowed a study with 30 randomly chosen university students who study English as a foreign language. The research used the aforementioned mobile app to support the English language learning process. The results confirm that students who used the app improved by 57% accuracy in their translations from Indonesian to English and vice versa. The progress of learning is attributed to the ease of access and the flexibility of time provided by the app and leave open the possibility of studying the use of this instrument in other learning areas.

In [26] a mobile app was used for learning English vocabulary with students with low grades. This tool encouraged students to become interested, to believe in individual abilities, boosted cooperative learning, reflected a positive attitude and confirmed the validity of the usage of the mobile app as a support resource for academic progress. The results showed the use of the app enhanced English foreign language learning due to it encouraged students to move from individual to cooperative learning.

In [53] presents a case study which used an app platform to improve pronunciation in the English learning, the results showed that in fact this method helped students to practice and better in the spoken English pronunciation.

A total of 29 college students participated in a 6-week experiment. Data collected from a pre-assessment, a post- assessment, and a survey questionnaire on learning experience were adopted as the instruments and analyzed in this research. The results revealed the students have developed the capabilities in English spelling. This means a significant outcome in learning achievement of all the participants and a positive learning mood through App-based spelling learning and technology [54].

This quasi-experimental study investigated the significant influence of a mobile game installed on mobile devices in English learning. The sample comprised 38 high school students and the experimental period was 8 weeks. The results showed 72.82% students were more motivated and improve their English learning in relation to 63.9% [55].

This study investigated the influence of a mobile app in the Communication Skills on the learning outcomes of university students. The app was developed by students to work in a smartphone and lasted one semester. More than 100 students participated in the experimental and control group with a pre-test and a post-test. The results showed that the app influenced positively on the learning outcomes of the students. This improving in learning due to the "mobility effect" that means the app is available in anywhere, at any time and through any smartphone [56].

This work evaluated the effectiveness of a mobile application designed to facilitate student English learning as a foreign language. Ten seventh-graders were the participants who performed significantly below English grade level. The study collected student attitudes towards the learning experience, and perceptions regarding the design of the application. Interviews, observation, surveys, and exams showed indicated the use of the mobile application to enhance English learning and to work moving from individual to cooperative learning. The results showed that the mobile application increase confidence and promote positive attitudes toward English learning [26].

This work took into account six immigrant families in the United States from four countries to examine the parents' perceptions regarding young English learners in mobile-assisted language learning. Semi-structured interviews and a descriptive survey were applied to participants to explore about mobile apps. Results demonstrated that the parents were motivated to support English learning through mobile technology in spite of their diverse cultural backgrounds and socioeconomic status [57].

3   Methods

3.1   Searching Literature

This article proposes a methodology based on previous research recently, which is centered on different database such as Science Direct, Springer, IEEE Xplore Google Scholar, Redalyc, ACM and Scopus. The selection of these studies contributes to the analysis and optimal deployment of concepts on corrective feedback, mobile apps and learning English as a foreign language. The process of identifying articles began with broad queries into databases of: scholarly literature using a series of topically relevant keywords. The following keywords were used, typically in pairs but sometimes in groups of three or more: [corrective feedback], [mobile apps], [English learning], [mobile learning], [apps for English learning] and [error correction].

3.1.1   Searching Corrective Feedback with Mobile Apps

Some apps have been developed for English language learning which have been used for many students as a complementary learning tool. However, the apps verification and validation have not always been carried out by the authors. Therefore, the research focused on works and projects in which they have demonstrated the advantages of apps use. The second search strategy is center on getting the advantages and characteristics that have corrective feedback in English language learning. For this, we use search terms in combination with corrective feedback, for example: characteristics, classification, advantages and platforms. In this way, information was collected from January 2010 to May 2019. The search period was defined since the technology evolution in the last decade that leads with technological discovers, free internet access and 4G network development [58]. Also, this study took into account the increasing encouragement in digital interactive environments of the 21st century [59].

Finally, once all relevant articles and documents related to corrective feedback/EL Mobile Apps were identified, an inclusion/exclusion process was established based on criteria shown below.

3.2 Study Selection-Inclusion/Exclusion Criteria

Once scientific articles, documents about corrective feedback and apps for English learning were identified, a selective process was done through a systematic review, prima type.

So, a preliminary selection was done eliminating all the duplicated articles or related with the same app. Then, two inclusion and exclusion groups were defined: one for corrective feedback literature and other for English learning mobile app.

3.2.1 Inclusion Criteria Questions

1. Is the publication centered on the development of English learning through mobile apps?
2. Does the publication show results of English learning through mobile apps?
3. Is the publication centered on the development of English learning through corrective feedback in platforms?
4. Were searching publications published from 2010 to 2019?
5. Are there mobile apps delighted to improve English learning?
   If the answer was "yes" to the questions above, this study focused on the title and abstract on the selected article, that researching document was taken account in an eligibility review.

3.2.2 Exclusion Criteria Questions

1. Is the publication focused on the development of corrective feedback for other languages?
2. Does the publication show results of corrective feedback different form English learning?
3. Were searching publications published out from 2010 to 2019?
4. Were excluded searching publications different from English foreign language?
5. Is the publication a review, a degree project or a text book?

To conclude, the review process finishes with an eligibility review stage. While the review the full text was reviewed to establish eligibility criteria.

Once it has made the analysis of inclusion and exclusion criteria for the review process, it has followed some stages to get to the base papers that will be included in the overview as it is showed in Fig. 1.

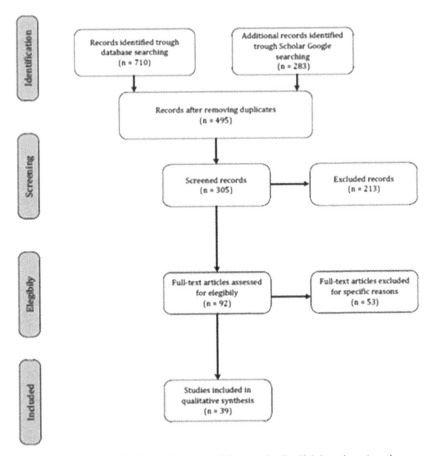

Fig. 1. Corrective feedback through mobile apps for English learning: A review

4   Results

The search started with 700 papers of which only 39 were chosen that met the selection criteria. Table 1 shows a general description of the distribution of the selected works by corrective feedback with online platforms, apps for learning the English language and the type of operating system they use. The studies focused on apps that have been validated by other authors for both mobile apps and corrective feedback respectively.

Table 2 shows a summary of the most relevant apps used in research and web platforms that obtained the best results in learning English as a second language.

4.1   Mobile Apps

In [13], this review analyzed the use of smartphones and apps, the results showed that using these devices enhance student English learning specially in the development of vocabulary. In [13], these studies demonstrated that through apps there is a big opportunity to be in contact with learning no matter where or what time.

Table 1. Number of projects of corrective feedback and mobile apps.

Topic	Number
Corrective feedback	18
Mobile apps for English learning	21

In [56], 106 students worked with a mobile app for speaking development, the results revealed students felt more confident in communicate their thoughts. In [26], students used mobile apps to improve their learning, the results engage learners to keep in contact with the academic process and reveal a positive attitude.

4.2   Corrective Feedback with Online Platforms

In [30], after the corrective feedback study using ICTs, results showed 53.6% chats through platforms improve students' accuracy responses, motivate learners and make them autonomous writers. In [25], 261 students used elaborated feedback in computers. The results indicated that the use of technology influences in intrinsic motivation and the improvement of learning results. The areas in which professors use written feedback to students focus 80% on correcting grammar and writing errors. Therefore, it is important to pay special attention to the way in which feedback is provided since students' motivation to correct errors depends on it [32]. In [39] 74 students participated in a corrective feedback study in which results revealed the superiority of clarification requests over recasts. This means that students improve their learning with corrective feedback that clarifies the learners' errors than recast that asked for structure again their answers.

In [40] some students participated in 10 sessions within seven weeks using an innovative platform with peer feedback, the results revealed students became more collaborative and felt more self-confident in the individual and the group English learning.

5   Discussion

The systematic review revealed that the use of mobile apps for English language learning shows new opportunities for students and teachers. The collected articles show the advantages and disadvantages of using mobile apps and the great growth that it has had in the last decade thanks to the development of new communication networks which has allowed internet access to be easier and cheaper for users.

In addition, documents show the current trend that users have when using Android or IOS as market leading operating systems each with its advantages and disadvantages. Free access to download and app development has been an advantage for the high growth of this app, although most of these applications have not been validated by experts, some are used and rated by the same users which does not show an exact acceptance data and validation. Another factor that users observe when installing an app is the amount of downloads and comments from other people. It should be considered that each brand of smartphone has its own operating system for which the app should be created, but there are also apps for multiple operating systems which is an advantage and therefore they are the most downloaded.

Table 2. Summary of corrective feedback with mobile apps.

Author(s)	Focus	Evaluation/participants
Fallah and Nazari [36]	L2 Teachers' Beliefs About Corrective Feedback: the Mediating Role of Experience	Not reported
Lucero et al. [32]	Studies in Educational Evaluation Teachers' written feedback comments on narrative texts in Elementary and Secondary Education	Not reported
Ene and Upton [30]	Journal of Second Language Writing Synchronous and asynchronous teacher electronic feedback and learner uptake in ESL composition	64 students
Maier et al. [25]	Computers & Education Effects of a computer-assisted formative assessment intervention based on multiple-tier diagnostic items and different feedback types	200 students
Hao and et al. [26]	Computers in Human Behavior An evaluative study of a mobile application for middle school students struggling with English vocabulary learning	Not reported
Daneshvar and Rahimi [38]	Written Corrective Feedback and Teaching Grammar	90 students
Khezrlou [39]	Task Repetition and Corrective Feedback: The Role of Feedback Types and Structure Saliency	41 students
Mohammadi and Yousefi [41]	Iranian EFL teachers and learners' perceptions of grammar instruction and corrective feedback	360 students
Rivera et al. [51]	Model-based approach to develop learning exercises in language-learning applications	Not reported
Luke [52]	The Effectiveness Level and Positive Values of Practicing Translation Using Mobile App DUOLINGO for Indonesian Freshmen Students	30 students
Shih [54]	Effects of English Spelling Learning Experience through a Mobile LINE APP for College Students	29 students
Tsai and Cheng [55]	Can learning motivation predict learning achievement ? A case study of a mobile game-based English learning approach	38 students
Ahmed et al. [56]	An analysis of the influence of a mobile learning application on the learning outcomes of higher education students	100 students
Chen et al. [57]	Learning, Culture and Social Interaction Parental perception and English Learners' mobile-assisted language learning: An ethnographic case study from a technology-based Funds of Knowledge approach	Not reported

On the other hand, the corrective feedback has been shown to have improvements in students' learning due to the additional information it shows, this allows students to be given feedback allowing them to know their mistakes. The information collected shows studies with corrective feedback only on web platforms and in all cases they show improvements in learning. So it would be interesting to develop a mobile app with corrective feedback which is validated by experts and students.

6 Conclusions

Having read previous studies allow conclude that the corrective feedback show learning improvement in students' learning process. Therefore, it is quite interesting to begin researching the possible influence of mobile apps in the English learning in accordance with pedagogy that focus on the different language abilities, where students be able to analyze their results, become collaborative entities of their learning process and be capable of correct their own mistakes. For professors, corrective feedback is a support that allows them to have individual and group monitoring of learning outcomes. Besides, it reduces the grading time.

The whole research that has been referred to confirm that the use of mobile apps in learning influences more than 50% in the improvement of English learning as a foreign language. This progress is verified through the results of evaluations. It is established that nowadays there are multiple kinds of apps for English learning, the majority are not validated by experts, and however they are available to be downloaded freely or by payment. On the emotional level, apps increase motivation, make learners believe in individual abilities and in the willingness to take advantage of apps inside and outside the class due to the feasibility of them to be used at any place and time. It would be important for future studies to follow apps validation processes to identify if the students learning improvement is because of the motivation influence or due to the app availability, also make a survey after using apps to receive student perceptions. To sum up, the study of new methodologies for English learning with mobile apps is a constantly developing field, so it would be necessary to make an app which uses corrective feedback to take advantage of it when joining the two techniques.

References

1. Tabuenca, B., Kalz, M., Ternier, S., Specht, M.: Mobile authoring of open educational resources for authentic learning scenarios. Univ. Access Inf. Soc. 15(3), 329–343 (2014). https://doi.org/10.1007/s10209-014-0391-y
2. Ding, J.: A study of English majors in a Chinese university as dictionary users. Lexicography 2(1), 5–34 (2015). https://doi.org/10.1007/s40607-015-0016-5
3. Song, Y., Wen, Y.: Integrating various apps on BYOD (Bring Your Own Device) into seamless inquiry-based learning to enhance primary students' science learning. J. Sci. Educ. Technol. 27(2), 165–176 (2017). https://doi.org/10.1007/s10956-017-9715-z
4. Aprendizaje, E.L., Idioma, D., Beltrán, M.: inglés como lengua extranjera (2017)
5. Hussain, N., Hussain, Z., Ali, B.: Assessing the usability of Urdu learning mobile apps for children. In: Zaphiris, P., Ioannou, A. (eds.) LCT 2018. LNCS, vol. 10924, pp. 117–126. Springer, Cham (2018). https://doi.org/10.1007/978-3-319-91743-6_8

6. Quan, Z.: Introducing "mobile DDL (data-driven learning)" for vocabulary learning: an experiment for academic English. J. Comput. Educ. **3**(3), 273–287 (2016). https://doi.org/10.1007/s40692-016-0067-0

7. Apolonius, L.E., Joseph, A.H., Thambu Raj, J.A.: Mobile phone app insights: L-Listen, I-Interact, R-Reflect, A-Act (LIRA). In: Luaran, J.E., Sardi, J., Aziz, A., Alias, N.A. (eds.) Envisioning the Future of Online Learning, pp. 413–421. Springer, Singapore (2016). https://doi.org/10.1007/978-981-10-0954-9_37

8. Wu, Q.: Designing a smartphone app to teach English (L2) vocabulary. Comput. Educ. **85**, 170–179 (2015)

9. Clement, J.: Number of apps available in leading app stores 2019, Statista (2019). https://www.statista.com/statistics/276623/number-of-appsavailable-in-leading-app-stores

10. Wong, L.-H., King, R.B., Chai, C.S., Liu, M.: *Seamlessly* learning Chinese: contextual meaning making and vocabulary growth in a seamless Chinese as a second language learning environment. Instr. Sci. **44**(5), 399–422 (2016). https://doi.org/10.1007/s11251-016-9383-z

11. Aunkon, M.W.B.K., Dipu, M.H., Moon, N.N., Saifuzzaman, M., Nur, F.N.: Enjoy and learn with educational game: Likhte Likhte Shikhi apps for child education. In: Abraham, A., Dutta, P., Mandal, J.K., Bhattacharya, A., Dutta, S. (eds.) Emerging Technologies in Data Mining and Information Security. AISC, vol. 755, pp. 409–417. Springer, Singapore (2019). https://doi.org/10.1007/978-981-13-1951-8_37

12. Karetsos, S., Ntaliani, M., Costopoulou, C.: Mobile learning: an android app using certified content. In: Sideridis, Alexander B., Kardasiadou, Z., Yialouris, Constantine P., Zorkadis, V. (eds.) E-Democracy 2013. CCIS, vol. 441, pp. 123–131. Springer, Cham (2014). https://doi.org/10.1007/978-3-319-11710-2_12

13. Klímová, B.: Mobile phones and/or smartphones and their apps for teaching English as a foreign language. Educ. Inf. Technol. **23**(3), 1091–1099 (2017). https://doi.org/10.1007/s10639-017-9655-5

14. Jurkovi, V.: Online informal learning of English through smartphones in Slovenia. System **80**, 27–37 (2019)

15. So, S.: Internet and higher education mobile instant messaging support for teaching and learning in higher education. Internet High. Educ. **31**, 32–42 (2016)

16. Al-Mashhadani, M.A., Al-Rawe, M.F.: The future role of mobile learning and smartphones applications in the Iraqi private universities. Smart Learn. Environ. **5**(1), 1–11 (2018). https://doi.org/10.1186/s40561-018-0077-7

17. Godwin-jones, R.: Emerging technologies mobile apps for language learning. Lang. Learn. Technol. **15**(2), 2–11 (2011)

18. Hu, H., Bezemer, C.-P., Hassan, A.E.: Studying the consistency of star ratings and the complaints in 1 & 2-star user reviews for top free cross-platform Android and iOS apps. Empirical Softw. Eng. **23**(6), 3442–3475 (2018). https://doi.org/10.1007/s10664-018-9604-y

19. Joorabchi, M.E., Mesbah, A.: Same app, different app stores: a comparative study (2016)

20. Berns, A., Isla-Montes, J.-L., Palomo-Duarte, M., Dodero, J.-M.: Motivation, students' needs and learning outcomes: a hybrid game-based app for enhanced language learning. SpringerPlus **5**(1), 1–23 (2016). https://doi.org/10.1186/s40064-016-2971-1

21. Northrop, L., Andrei, E.: More than just word of the day: vocabulary apps for English learners. Read. Teach. **72**(5), 623–630 (2019)

22. Montiel, I., Delgado, J., Natalia, C., De Mandojana, O., Antolin, R.: New ways of teaching: using technology and mobile apps to educate on societal grand challenges. J. Bus. Ethics **161**, 243–251 (2018)

23. Han, Y.: Written corrective feedback from an ecological perspective: the interaction between the context and individual learners. System **80**, 288–303 (2019)

24. Chen, S., Nassaji, H., Liu, Q.: EFL learners' perceptions and preferences of written corrective feedback: a case study of university students from Mainland China. Asian. J. Second Foreign Lang. Educ. **1**, 5 (2016). https://doi.org/10.1186/s40862-016-0010-y
25. Maier, U., Wolf, N., Randler, C.: Computers & education effects of a computer-assisted formative assessment intervention based on multiple-tier diagnostic items and different feedback types. Comput. Educ. **95**, 85–98 (2016)
26. Hao, Y., Lee, K.S., Chen, S., Chie, S.: Computers in human behavior an evaluative study of a mobile application for middle school students struggling with english vocabulary learning. Comput. Human Behav. **95**, 208–216 (2019)
27. Nemati, M., Alavi, S.M., Mohebbi, H., Masjedlou, A.P.: Teachers' writing proficiency and assessment ability: the missing link in teachers' written corrective feedback practice in an Iranian EFL context. Lang. Test. Asia **7**(1), 1–18 (2017). https://doi.org/10.1186/s40468-017-0053-0
28. Barron, A.B., Hebets, E.A., Cleland, T.A., Hauber, M., Stevens, J.R.: Embracing multiple definitions of learning. Trends Neurosci. **38**, 405–407 (2015)
29. Kerr, P.C.P.: Giving feedback on speaking. Giv. Feed. Speak. Part Cambridge, p. 92, December 2017
30. Ene, E., Upton, T.A.: Synchronous and asynchronous teacher electronic feedback and learner uptake in ESL composition. J. Second Lang. Writ. **41**(May), 1–13 (2018)
31. Guo, X., Yang, Y.: Effects of corrective feedback on EFL learners' acquisition of third-person singular form and the mediating role of cognitive style. J. Psycholinguist. Res. **47**(4), 841–858 (2018). https://doi.org/10.1007/s10936-018-9566-7
32. Lucero, M., Fernández, M.J., Montanero, M.: Studies in educational evaluation teachers' written feedback comments on narrative texts in elementary and secondary education. Stud. Educ. Eval. **59**, 158–167 (2018)
33. Yu, S., Zhang, Y., Zheng, Y., Lin, Z.: Written corrective feedback strategies in English-Chinese translation classrooms. Asia Educ. Res. **29**, 101–111 (2020). https://doi.org/10.1007/s40299-019-00456-2
34. Zabor, L., Rychlewska, A.: The effectiveness of written corrective feedback in the acquisition of the english article system by Polish learners in view of the counterbalance hypothesis. In: Piasecka, L., Adams-Tukiendorf, M., Wilk, P. (eds.) New Media and Perennial Problems in Foreign Language Learning and Teaching. SLLT, pp. 131–150. Springer, Cham (2015). https://doi.org/10.1007/978-3-319-07686-7_8
35. Bitchener, J.: Evidence in support of written corrective feedback. J. Second Lang. Writ. **17**, 102–118 (2008)
36. Fallah, N., Nazari, M.: L2 teachers' beliefs about corrective feedback: the mediating role of experience 第二外語教師對糾正回饋之信念：經驗的中介角色. Engl. Teach. Learn. **43**(2), 147–164 (2019). https://doi.org/10.1007/s42321-019-00020-7
37. Cho, M., Casta, D.A.: Motivational and affective engagement in learning Spanish with a mobile application. System **81**, 90–99 (2019)
38. Daneshvar, E., Rahimi, A.: Written corrective feedback and teaching grammar. Procedia Soc. Behav. Sci. **136**, 217–221 (2014)
39. Khezrlou, S.: Task repetition and corrective feedback: the role of feedback types and structure saliency. Engl. Teach. Learn. **43**(2), 213–233 (2019). https://doi.org/10.1007/s42321-019-00025-2
40. Selcuk, H., Jones, J., Vonkova, H.: The emergence and influence of group leaders in web-based collaborative writing: self-reported accounts of EFL learners. Comput. Assist. Lang. Learn. 1–21 (2019)
41. Mohammadi, M., Yousefi, M.H.: Iranian EFL teachers and learners' perceptions of grammar instruction and corrective feedback. Asian. J. Second Foreign Lang. Educ. **4**(1), 1–17 (2019). https://doi.org/10.1186/s40862-019-0068-4

42. Singh, A., Ranjan, J.: A framework for mobile apps in colleges and universities: data mining perspective. Educ. Inf. Technol. **21**(3), 643–654 (2014). https://doi.org/10.1007/s10639-014-9345-5
43. Enriquez, L., Isabel, S.: Usabilidad en aplicaciones móviles, pp. 25–47 (2013)
44. Teodorescu, A.: Mobile learning and its impact on business English learning. Procedia Soc. Behav. Sci. **180**, 1535–1540 (2015)
45. Yang, J.: Mobile assisted language learning : review of the recent applications of emerging mobile technologies. Engl. Lang. Teach. **6**(7), 19–25 (2013)
46. Klímová, B.: Mobile application as appropriate support for the retention of new english words and phrases in English-Language learning. In: Uskov, V.L., Howlett, R.J., Jain, L.C. (eds.) Smart Education and e-Learning 2019. SIST, vol. 144, pp. 325–333. Springer, Singapore (2019). https://doi.org/10.1007/978-981-13-8260-4_30
47. Mueller, J., Wood, E.: Examining mobile technology in higher education : handheld devices in and out of the classroom. Int. J. High. Educ. **1**(2), 43–54 (2012)
48. Aghaee, N., Larsson, K.: Students' perspectives on utility of mobile applications in higher education. In: Matera, M., Rossi, G. (eds.) MobiWIS 2013. CCIS, vol. 183, pp. 44–56. Springer, Cham (2013). https://doi.org/10.1007/978-3-319-03737-0_6
49. Zhang, Y.: Design of mobile teaching and learning in higher education, an introduction, pp. 1–6 (2015)
50. Zhang, Y.: Development of mobile application for higher education : an introduction, pp. 2–5 (2015)
51. Rivera, G.S., Tesoriero, R., Gallud, J.A.: Model-based approach to develop learning exercises in language-learning applications. IET Softw. **12**(3), 206–214 (2018)
52. Luke, J.Y.: The effectiveness level and positive values of practicing translation using mobile app DUOLINGO for Indonesian, pp. 26–29 (2018)
53. Yin, Z.: Training & evaluation system of intelligent oral phonics based on speech recognition technology. Int. J. Emerg. Technol. Learn. **13**(4), 45–57 (2018)
54. Shih, R.-C., Lee, C., Cheng, T.-F.: Effects of English spelling learning experience through a mobile LINE APP for college students. Procedia Soc. Behav. Sci. **174**, 2634–2638 (2015)
55. Tsai, C.-H., Cheng, C.-H., Yeh, D.-Y., Lin, S.-Y.: Can learning motivation predict learning achievement? A case study of a mobile game-based English learning approach. Educ. Inf. Technol. **22**(5), 2159–2173 (2016). https://doi.org/10.1007/s10639-016-9542-5
56. Arain, A.A., Hussain, Z., Rizvi, W.H., Vighio, M.S.: An analysis of the influence of a mobile learning application on the learning outcomes of higher education students. Univers. Access Inf. Soc. **17**, 325–334 (2017). https://doi.org/10.1007/s10209-017-0551-y
57. Chen, Y., Mayall, H., York, C.S., Smith, T.J.: Learning, culture and social interaction parental perception and English learners' mobile-assisted language learning. Learn Cult. Soc. Inter. **22**, 100325 (2019)
58. Jia, W.: Enlightenment from the innovative application of 4G communication technology in the mobile library, no. 3, pp. 153–156 (2016)
59. Mehran, P., Alizadeh, M., Koguchi, I., Takemura, H.: Are Japanese digital natives ready for learning English online? A preliminary case study at Osaka University. Int. J. Educ. Technol. High. Educ. **14**, 8 (2017)

Classification and Visualization of Web Attacks Using HTTP Headers and Machine Learning Techniques

Nicolás Ricardo Enciso(ID) and Jorge E. Camargo(✉)(ID)

Department of Systems and Industrial Engineering, Faculty of Engineering,
UNSecure Lab Research Group, Universidad Nacional de Colombia,
Bogotá, Colombia
{nricardoe,jecamargom}@unal.edu.co
http://www.unsecurelab.org

Abstract. This paper presents a methodology to identify web attacks such as XSS, CRLF and SQL injection using a data set that contains normal and anomalous items. The proposed methodology uses dimensional reduction techniques for visualization (PCA, t-SNE) and machine learning algorithms (SVM, Naive Bayes, random forest, logistic regression) to perform classification of URLs contained in HTTP headers. Results showed that visualization is useful to present a general overview of attacks and classification experiments showed an accuracy of 83% to detect attacks.

Keywords: Cybersecurity analytics · Cyber attacks · Feature engineering · Machine learning · Web attacks

1 Introduction

Web attacks are a growing problem worldwide, taking at the center of discussion security of information as a crucial part of the modern way of working from governments to private enterprises and industries [1,2]. With the increasing of new threats that are being discovered, it is necessary to build new tools that allow to automatically detect attacks at the same time that threats appear.

In order to address this challenging problem, machine learning algorithms are a powerful tool that offers the capacity to extract patterns from data, as the case of intrusion detection systems (IDS), which allow to get detection rates of anomalous behaviours or outlier cases in considerable high accuracy percentages on real time scenarios [3,4]. The same has been investigated using other techniques such as big data [5].

Nevertheless, to get high accuracy rates it is indispensable to apply a special previous treatment over data that will be used as input to the machine learning algorithms. Feature extraction is a key process, which defines success into his application. Besides the correct selection of characteristics from data, it is

© Springer Nature Switzerland AG 2020
F. R. Narváez et al. (Eds.): SmartTech-IC 2019, CCIS 1154, pp. 243–255, 2020.
https://doi.org/10.1007/978-3-030-46785-2_20

necessary to perform an analysis about the characteristics (features) that differentiate the target class from the other classes in the dataset. Additionally, when it is obtained a large number of extracted variables as features, the complexity of analysis raises (curse of dimensionality), which suggests to select a subset of such features to reduce complexity without lose of much information.

In the feature extraction process of URLs it is possible to detect web attacks such as CRLF (Carriage return line feed), XSS (Cross-site scripting), and SQL injection, even if they are used in the detection of phishing [6,7], catching the main characteristics with an analysis of different parts that forms an URL. This kind of web attacks are very usual and take advantage of bad software building, wrong configurations and naive mistakes from junior software engineers. According to OWASP [8], on the top 10 most common attacks appears injections and XSS as main types of attacks around the Internet.

In spite of visualization in high dimensional data presents difficulties, there are a variety of techniques that are able to reduce the number of dimensions on the data without lose of much information, as the case of non negative matrix factorization (NMF), which has been used with success detecting outliers in sensors [9] and anomalies in smart cards [10], and PCA, which has been used with success in the classification of anomalous cases in intrusion detection systems [11].

This paper presents a methodology to detect web attacks using visualization techniques and machine learning. The rest of the paper is organized as follows: Sect. 2 presents a brief description of web attacks; Sect. 3 discusses how dimensionality reduction techniques are used to visualize data; Sect. 4 presents the machine learning algorithms used to train a classification model; In Sect. 5 we present the proposed methodology to detect web attacks; Sect. 6 shows the obtained results; and Sect. 7 concludes the paper.

2   Web Attacks

2.1   Cross-Site Scripting

Basically this is an attack that consists in the injection of Javascript code or scripts into web applications. Typically scripts are injected into an HTML document, and take advantage of the fact that when a web browser reads an HTML document, it executes all the code, so, if there is Javascript code inside the HTML document, it will be executed compromising the target user device [16]. There is just one condition to execute the hidden script inside the HTML, it is turning on the execution of Javascript on the web browser, feature that is set on as default configuration in most of the popular web browsers. This attack is in the top 10 OWASP most common attacks through the Internet [8]. There are several types of XSS attacks, according to the OWASP project and guidelines about security on Internet [17].

2.2   Carriage Return Line Feed (CRLF)

This is a vulnerability exploited by attackers to introduce a code injection. An example of the attack consists in the introduction of a new line via URL, putting the hexadecimal %0d and %0a codes in the URL string [18]. These characters indicate a new line in the log of the server. The attacker puts for instance HTTP splitting code or phishing links on the new line. This take advantage of the characters that determine the end of a line depending on the operating system: Carriage return with ASCII 13 ($\backslash r$) and line feed with ASCII 10 ($\backslash n$).

2.3   SQL Injection

This is one of the most dangerous and popular along the history of web applications. This attack takes advantage of query languages used to access data bases. The main cause to be victim of an SQL injection attack is the absence of sanitization. Typically the attacker introduces in a text box special characters and reserved SQL words to be executed by the data base server [19]. Commonly, the attacker performs some tests to detect the types of user on the data base, if there is a direct connection with the data base, and others. To do that, true statements are always used, taking advantage of the obvious use of the "WHERE" statement on the SQL query, making the query true and returning a full error text directly from the data base, giving to the attacker important information. With the error log, the attacker can perform modifications on the data base, delete information, change user access, drop tables, get sensitive information, destroy data and many others.

3   Dimensionality Reduction for Data Visualization

3.1   Principal Component Analysis

Principal component analysis (PCA) is a method that uses matrix operations through linear algebra and statistics to get a projection in a lower dimensional space of the original data. This lower dimensional space allows to generate a trustful representation of the same data using the main components (2D or 3D representation). Such dimensions allow to plot data in a 2D/3D coordinates system highlighting the distribution of the data.

In this paper we use PCA to visually see the result of the performed analysis. Even though PCA could be used as a machine learning classifier, great results depends on the data itself and not on the learning method. This does not mean that the application of PCA as a classifier has not been performed with good results in the literature, but it needs of other methods to achieve good results [5].

3.2   t-SNE

t-Distributed Stochastic Neighbor Embedding (t-SNE) is a method that uses the student's t distribution to reduce a data set from a high dimensional space to a low dimensional space that retains the majority of the original information. It is a dimensionality reduction technique that preserves the local structure from the original data as well as learns the parametric mapping of which the data comes from. The method is described by the original author [15] as an unsupervised method that learns parametric mapping between the high dimensional space, to a low dimensional space. The main difference between PCA and this algorithm, is the different approach for measuring the distance between points, so the final dimensional reduction is another space with other representation of the same data.

4   Machine Learning Classifiers

4.1   Naive Bayes Classifier

It is based on a probability theory called the Bayes Theorem, that expresses the conditional probability of a random event, knowing previous probabilities. It shows how often the event A happens given that B happens. The probabilities of A and B alone are easily calculated, so the only condition is the probability given the other event. In the case of the classifier, it calculates the probabilities of every factor, then the algorithm gives as output the event with the highest score, in other words, the classifier shows as output the event that scores the higher number, meaning the higher probability to be of that class.

4.2   Support Vector Machine Classifier

It is a type of supervised machine learning like the other algorithms. Given labeled training data, the method creates a hyperplane that categorizes the classes, dividing the classes with the hyperplane: in a two dimensional space is a line, in three a plane and so on, the classifier is one dimension less than the data set. There are several ways to build this hyperplanes, this different types of classification building are called "kernels". On the present work, the kernels used are: lineal, sigmoid and gaussian.

4.3   Random Forest Classifier

Random forest is a machine learning algorithm that uses the decision trees theory to build classifiers. The main idea is apply queries that makes narrower the number of possibilities in which the entry data could be classify. The tree is a binary tree, driving the answer path through True or False statements. This use of binary trees and simple True or False question makes this algorithm $\text{Log}(n)$ on speed, taking advantage of the binary trees benefits. During the training, the random forest model builds a structure that makes the best queries that ends with a correct answer. The name random forest came from the fact that this technique builds some decision trees randomly, creating a "forest" of decision trees. The final result from a random forest, is the average of answers of all the decision trees, concluding with a unique output.

4.4   Logistic Regression Classifier

This method is based on the statistical origin of the logistic function and the traditional linear regression used for making predictions through the fit of a function across the points on the space. The method fits the logistic function "S" shape, dividing two classes, on True or False, so this method only works for binary types of data and can work with continues or not variables. The logistic function plotted on the dimensional space of the data set, determines probabilities, so an entry data can be classified using the projection on the logistic function curve to determinate the class that is most probably belongs to. The logistic curve is fitted using the maximum likelihood, that depends on the training data, so the curve is graphed according to the given data, the likelihood numbers of each point is multiplied, getting the likelihood of all the curve.

5   Methodology

5.1   Data Set

The data set that was used, comes from the Information Security Institute of CISC (Spanish Research National Council) from the Government of Spain [12]. It contains more than 60000 web request in form of HTTP headers generated automatically, containing the generated traffic targeted an e-commerce web application with GET and POST requests. The data set contains 36,000 normal requests and more than 25,000 anomalous requests, in which there are web attacks such as SQL injection, buffer overflow, files disclosure, CRLF injection, XSS and information gathering.

The data set was already used on other investigations, one of them on the building of intrusion detection systems (IDS) for WAFs (Web application frameworks), to detect web attacks [13]. Each HTTP header sample contains several fields. From all the fields, the URL was the one selected to be the object of analysis and feature extraction, due to the fact that the other fields on the HTTP headers didn't represent essential information that differentiate the anomalous cases from normal cases.

5.2   Feature Engineering Extraction

The goal for this part of the work, was the extraction of essential information from the URLs, taking relevant characteristics that represents faithfully the differences between the anomalous cases and the normal cases.

Uniform Resource Locator Structure "URL". As it is specified on the standard of the RFC, specifically the RFC 1738 [14], is a string of characters that represents a resource that is available through the Internet, and has a specific order to show the location of a resource on a server online. A URL has the following structure:

$$< scheme >:< scheme - specific - port >$$
(1)

The main focus was the characterization of the anomalous cases, that is, the features that an URL has when it is part of a web attack: SQL injection, CRLF injection or XSS. Some of the characteristics that were took into consideration, came from the techniques for detection of phishing from URLs in other paper work [7]. With that in mind, the characteristics extracted from the URLs are illustrated in Fig. 1.

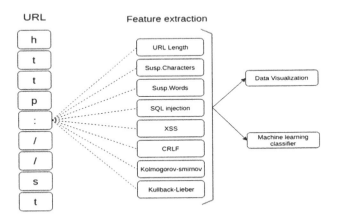

Fig. 1. Representation of the feature extraction performed on the URL given by each HTTP header. These 8 features are used as input to visualization and classification algorithms.

URL Length. This takes the URL's length. A long URL increases the probability that the URL comes from an attack, this is because the attackers typically want to confuse the user.

Suspicious Characters. A common characteristic on an URL that is part of a web attack, is the use of some characters, that confuse the user, who think that the URL is a trustful site when actually, this has minor differences from the original web site, using characters like "@", "#", "-" and so on.

Suspicious Words. Into the web attacks, is typical sign the use of reserved words commonly used on configuration of servers, network devices and login functions on web sites. Here some examples of the words: "confirm", "account", "secure", "webscr", "login", "admin", "password" etc.

SQL Injection Words. According to OWASP and the explanation given before about the SQL injection attack, the use of reserved words that come from the SQL language is used on this kind of attack. For this reason, words like "SELECT", "WHERE", "FROM", "DROP", "TABLE", "LIKE", are taking into consideration, counting each of this words on each URL.

XSS Attack Words. Following the guideline of OWASP about this kind of web attack, a cross site scripting injection uses scripts into the web browser to send malocious scripts. The typical way to do this, are the use of alerts and parameters into the HTML code. As a result, here are extracted words like: "alert", "script" and "param".

CRLF Injection Attack Words. Theoretically this is a vulnerability that is exploited by the attackers. Here they used two special characters, which confuses the end line signal on the ASCII end line character. The first character is the "%", which makes the rest of the string on the URL as a ignored part for the HTTP protocol, for that case, it is common the use of trustful domain names after the %, the user thinks that it is the original web site, but actually is the ignored part for the browser. The second one is the "0". This is used like the %. For that case, the "%" and "0" characters are capture as a feature on the URL.

Kolmogorov-Smirnov Test Score. This is a special statistic score, which wants to measure, through the non-parametric comparison of a list of values, determines a score if it comes from a determined probabilistic distribution. In other words, this want to measure how much a determined list of values are similar to pretend that all of it comes from the same distribution. At the present work, only the letters from the URL are compared to the distribution of characters on the Spanish language, because of the data set comes from Spain and uses Spanish as language, resulting on a score that could be a decimal number between 0 and 1, with 1 the score for the most similar to the language, meaning that the URL has a "logical" structure, with a possible lower "machine origin" or "random generated" URL that is commonly used by the attackers.

Kullback-Leibler Divergence. This is a measure that compares two distributions, and defines if this two are similar. This metric is very similar to the cross entropy, but in this case, it is measure how similar are the distribution A and the distribution B. For this work, it is compared the distribution of letter on the URL, with the distribution of letter on the Spanish language, giving the score of how much the URL is similar to the Spanish, so the URL has a logical language usage, meaning that the URL has a user friendly path, which could be took as a sign of trustful web sites.

Resulting Data Set. With the eight characteristic extracted, the data is putted on a new file with CSV format, because of the easy way to manage this kind of files with the Pandas Python library. In each HTTP header is so extracted the URL field, and later with the URL, the eight values captured, giving to the CSV file a vector of numbers, and a final one to the class it belongs to: 1 for anomalous and 0 for normal.

6 Results

6.1 Data Visualization

The data set was passed through the two visualization techniques. All the data set was visualized in a 2D coordinates system. On both cases, the original data set contains 8 variables in 8 columns, with more than 60,000 rows, each one a sample on the data set, getting as the output on both algorithms, a two dimensional graph with two variables, reducing the original dimensionality.

Table 1. Linear relationship between feature and principal component. Each coefficient represents correlation between a pair of feature and component.

Feature	PC1	PC2
URLlong	**0.4868**	0.1688
Characters	0.4669	0.0351
SuspWord	0.4404	0.0050
SQL	0.0497	0.0389
XSS	0.1086	0.5365
CRLF	0.2728	0.5070
Kolmogorov	0.4355	0.3168
Kullback	0.2693	**0.5685**

PCA Results. In Fig. 2 anomalous points form clusters in two regions making a clear identification of the anomalous cases, whilst normal cases are spread across the visualization space. The resulting PCA output graphic shows a clear classification and identification of the two classes that are on the data set, allowing to say that it is possible to identify the attacks on the data set on a graphic point of view using PCA. On the other hand, according with Table 1, the coefficients of each feature on both Principal Components, represents the eigenvalues, that were calculated on the process of dimensional reduction, as a linear relation. This numbers could be used as indicators of how much the feature contributes to explain the data with less dimensions, making this group of features with the most linear relation number (eigenvalue), candidates to be used on further works as principal features that captures the most relevant characteristics on the web attacks that had been studied here. On the Principal Component 1, the *URLlong* has the highest eigenvalue, followed by *Characters*, *SuspWord* and *Kolmogorov*. For Principal Component 2, *Kullback*, *XSS* and *CRLF* respectively, gather the majority of linear relation. It is important to point out that the *SQL* feature has the lowest coefficient value on both Principal Components, which is explained by the significant difference on the amount of samples that comes from the SQL injection malicious URLs, in comparison with the other attacks. As an overall result, the PCA visualization permits to determinate which data points could be part of a certain class (malicious or benign), opening the possibility to use this method as a previous unsupervised visual classifier, as a first filter follow by machine learning classifiers.

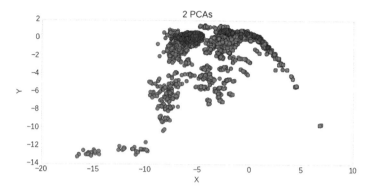

Fig. 2. PCA applied to the data set reducing from 8 dimensions to 2 dimensions (2 PCAs). On blue, the points correspond to anomalous cases, and red points to normal cases. (Color figure online)

t-SNE Results. As it can be seen in Fig. 3, the t-SNE shows clusters of both classes on the center, allowing to identify the two classes of data. The algorithm produces clusters of the same type on different zones, showing an easy way to

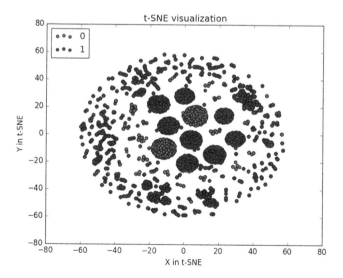

Fig. 3. t-SNE output on two dimensions. Blue points indicate anomalous cases and red points normal cases. Note that there are clusters of both classes on the center. (Color figure online)

identify the majority of points. In addition, the amount of malicious (0) outliers on Fig. 3 are just a few in comparison, which shows that the feature strategy performs well, according with the possibility to identify the cluster of malicious points, which could be used, combined with PCA, as an unsupervised identifier, or check method to determinate the quality of the features that were extracted. It is important to say that, in comparison with the PCA method, t-SNE is more computationally expensive than PCA, taking more than double the time of the PCA method, but continues to be efficient.

6.2   Machine Learning Classifiers

Classifiers Evaluation Method. For the evaluation of the machine learning classifiers, there were used 5 metrics to determinate the performance of each algorithm: Precision, Recall, F1-Score, Accuracy and AUC (area under the curve). Taking TP (True Positives), FP (False Positives), FN (False Negatives) and TN (True Negatives), the metrics for evaluation are:

$$Accuracy = \frac{TP + TN}{TP + FP + FN + TN} \tag{2}$$

$$Precision = \frac{TP}{TP + FP} \tag{3}$$

$$Recall = \frac{TP}{TP + FN} \tag{4}$$

$$F1Score = \frac{2 * (Precision * Recall)}{Precision + Recall} \tag{5}$$

Taking into consideration the fact that all the used algorithms were of the type supervised learning, the data used the labeled tag of each sample, and the training set was split on 30% for testing and 70% for training or fitting on the classifier model choosing randomly the samples to be used on the two sections of data (training and testing), using the Python Library Sklearn's standard Scaler and Train test split. All the classification algorithms perform binary classification, with label 1 for malicious types (CRLF, SQL injection, XSS) and 0 for the benign or normal ones (Table 2).

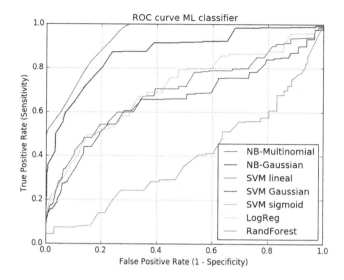

Fig. 4. Receiver Operating Characteristics - Area under the curve ROC-AUC graph that represents the overall performance of the machine learning classifiers, in this case seven types of them. The higher the curve, the better the performance.

Analysis and Results Classifiers. In the process of running the classifiers, the parameters were choose according to the results with certain values, as a proof and error cycle, until reach the best result for each algorithm. The process was manually performed due to computational costs related to run several times all the classifiers and better management of results. For the SVM Gaussian algorithm, there were used as parameters a C equal to 1.11 and a *gamma* equal to 0.09. For random forest, the number of estimator parameters was set to 100. According to Fig. 4, the best algorithm was the random forest, with 83.2% of accuracy and an area under the curve (AUC) of 93.3%, followed by SVM Gaussian with 79.4% and 87.09% of AUC. The others like Naive Bayes on both types, gave no concluding results with 65% of precision. A key idea that can be

Table 2. Performance evaluation on classification of anomalous cases

ML algorithm	Precision	Recall	F1-Score	Accuracy	AUC
NB + Gaussian	0.72	0.20	0.32	0.64	0.65
NB + Multinomial	0.75	0.23	0.35	0.65	0.65
SVM + Sigmoid	0.00	0.00	0.00	0.59	0.39
SVM + Linear	0.81	0.26	0.39	0.67	0.69
SVM + Gaussian	**0.83**	0.62	0.71	0.79	0.87
Logistic Regression	0.70	0.41	0.52	0.68	0.70
Random Forest	0.75	**0.88**	**0.81**	**0.83**	**0.93**

extracted from the results is the possibility to make combinations of algorithms to improve outputs, as a result, on a production environment, a real case could be classified accurately using a combination of the machine learning algorithms. In addition, the use of Random Forest as main classifier on a production environment, has the advantage of speed in which it runs, the times for training and classifying on Random Forest are the best overall, which gives the key combination of performance results and performance speed. Finally, the results as we can see on Fig. 4, show us that the mean of the classifiers are between 40 and 70%, with the exception of Random Forest and Support Vector Machine with Gaussian function. This results conclude that the features need to be combined with others to get a consistent results on all the classifiers. Nevertheless, the results of the two major ones, Random Forest and SVM Gaussian, indicate the possibility to continue using the 8 features of this work, to detect web attacks such as the ones used here.

7 Conclusions

Results show a good classification, precision and accuracy, especially on the random forest and SVM Gaussian cases. Nevertheless, the rates of classification are not too high so as to said that they are very precise and can be used on a production software environment. However, it is a general view on the potential of the usage of visualization techniques that works fine to determinate if the feature extraction was correct from a graphical point of view and the potential usage of other machine learning algorithms on the detection of web attacks, showing the previous results a possibility to use this kind of algorithms on a real environment on real users, with a good possibility to be improve and combined with other techniques, such as neural networks and deep learning.

The present work could be used as an approach of a practical use of reduction of dimensionality to visualize from a graphic if the distribution of the classes inside the data set are correctly characterized, including some other dimensional reduction algorithms such as ISOMAP could be useful. Although, on the machine learning classifiers, further works related should focus on the improvement of parameters on the algorithms used on this work. Even though the used classifier algorithms presented some good results, in future work we will use other machine learning algorithms such as neural networks and deep learning.

References

1. Verizon Data breach 2018 investigations report (2018). https://www.verizonenterprise.com/resources/reports. Accessed 2 Jan 2019
2. Kaspersky Labs: Security Bulletin 2018 - Threat Predictions for 2019 (2018). https://securelist.com/kaspersky-security-bulletin-threat-predictions-for-2019/88878/. Accessed 2 Jan 2019
3. Kumar, S., Viinikainen, A., Hamalainen, T.: Machine learning classification model for network based intrusion detection system. In: 11th International Conference for Internet Technology and Secured Transactions, ICITST 2016, pp. 242–249 (2017)

4. Kolias, C., Kambourakis, G., Stavrou, A., Gritzalis, S.: Intrusion detection in 802.11 networks: empirical evaluation of threats and a public dataset. IEEE Commun. Surv. Tutor. **18**(1), 184–208 (2016)
5. Veeramachaneni, K., Arnaldo, I., Korrapati, V., Bassias, C., Li, K.: AI2: training a big data machine to defend. In: Proceedings - 2nd IEEE International Conference on Big Data Security on Cloud, IEEE BigDataSecurity 2016, 2nd IEEE International Conference on High Performance and Smart Computing, IEEE HPSC 2016 and IEEE International Conference on Intelligent Data and Security (IDS), pp. 49–54 (2016)
6. Sahoo, D., Liu, C., Hoi, S.C.H.: Malicious URL detection using machine learning: a survey. ArXiv **1**(1), 1–37 (2017). http://arxiv.org/abs/1701.07179
7. Bahnsen, A. C., Bohorquez, E. C., Villegas, S., Vargas, J., Gonzalez, F.A.: Classifying phishing URLs using recurrent neural networks. In: ECrime Researchers Summit, ECrime, pp. 1–8 (2017)
8. OWASP top ten project 2017 (2017). https://www.owasp.org. Accessed 2 Jan 2019
9. Alshammari, H., Ghorbel, O., Aseeri, M., Abid, M.: Non-negative matrix factorization (NMF) for outlier detection in Wireless Sensor Networks. In: 14th International Wireless Communications and Mobile Computing Conference, IWCMC 2018, pp. 506–511 (2018)
10. Tonnelier, E., Baskiotis, N., Guigue, V., Gallinari, P.: Anomaly detection in smart card logs and distant evaluation with Twitter: a robust framework. Neurocomputing **298**, 109–121 (2018)
11. Shyu, M.L., Chen, S.C., Sarinnapakorn, K., Chang, L.: A Novel anomaly detection scheme based on principal component classifier. In: 3rd IEEE International Conference on Data Mining, pp. 353–365 (2003)
12. Torrano-Gimenez, C., Perez-Villegas, A., Alvarez, G.: HTTP DATASET CSIC 2010. National Investigation Conselour, Information security institute Spain Government (2010). http://www.isi.csic.es/dataset/. Accessed 4 Jan 2019
13. Torrano-Gimenez, C., Perez-Villegas, A., Alvarez, G.: An anomaly-based approach for intrusion detection in Web traffic. J. Inf. Assur. Secur. **5**(4), 446–454 (2010)
14. Berners-Lee, T., McCahill, M., Masinter, L.: RFC1738 - URL specification, pp. 1–25 (1994). https://www.ietf.org/rfc/rfc1738.txt
15. Van Der Maaten, L.: Learning a parametric embedding by preserving local structure. J. Mach. Learn. Res. **5**, 384–391 (2009)
16. OWASP Cross-site Scripting (XSS) (2017). https://www.owasp.org/index.php/Cross-site_Scripting_(XSS). Accessed 4 Jan 2019
17. OWASP Types of Cross-Site Scripting (2017). https://www.owasp.org/index.php/Types_of_Cross-Site_Scripting. Accessed 4 Jan 2019
18. OWASP CRLF Injection (2017). https://www.owasp.org/index.php/CRLF_Injection. Accessed 8 Jan 2019
19. OWASP Guide Project (2017). https://www.owasp.org/index.php/OWASP_Guide_Project. Accessed 8 Jan 2019
20. OWASP SQL injection (2017). https://www.owasp.org/index.php/SQL_Injection. Accessed 8 Jan 2019

Smart Trends and Applications

Fusion of 3D Radiomic Features from Multiparametric Magnetic Resonance Images for Breast Cancer Risk Classification

Diana M. Marín-Castrillón[1], Jaider Stiven Rincón[1],
Andrés E. Castro-Ospina[1], Liliana Hernández[2], and Gloria M. Díaz[1]([✉])

[1] Instituto Tecnológico Metropolitano, Medellín, Colombia
gloriadiaz@itm.edu.co
[2] Instituto de Alta Tecnología Médica, Medellín, Colombia

Abstract. Radiomics imaging technology refers to the computation of a large number of quantitative features to describe characteristics of medical images that specialists can not appreciate. The quality of Magnetic Resonance Images (MRI) allows capturing pathology features through different sequences acquired from the target tissue. The use of multiparametric MRI has shown to be useful in the diagnosis of breast cancer but is challenging to radiomic analysis by the fusion of information from different images. In this work, 3D radiomic features extracted from nine breast MRI sequences were used to train a model able to discriminate positive and negative breast masses in the region of interest manually identified. Two fusion strategies were here evaluated; in the first one, features from all sequences were concatenated, and Fisher-Score and Gini-Index feature selectors were used to identify the most discriminative features; in the second one, features were initially selected from each sequence and then were concatenated to be used for training a classification model; Random Forest and a Support Vector Machine learning models were also evaluated. To test both fusion strategies was used a database with 146 Interest volumes (VoIs) from which, 61 were positive and 85 negative findings. Although there are differences in the accuracy obtained by the two fusion strategies, these are not significant and it was clear that a small number of features provide better performance than using the whole set of them. The best performance was reached using Random Forest with the 20% of the computed features and selected by the Gini/index algorithm, With which an AUC of 73.6% was obtained.

Keywords: MRI sequences · Radiomics · Breast cancer · Fusion strategies

Supported by Colciencias, Instituto Tecnológico Metropolitano, and Instituto de Alta Tecnología Médica. Project RC740-2017.

F. R. Narváez et al. (Eds.): SmartTech-IC 2019, CCIS 1154, pp. 259–272, 2020.
https://doi.org/10.1007/978-3-030-46785-2_21

1   Introduction

Breast cancer is the most common cancer in females worldwide, with 2.1 million of new cases diagnosed in 2018 [2]. This pathology has a better prognosis and diagnosis if it is detected and treated on time [3]. Several strategies have been developed to increase early diagnosis. Mammography continues to be the standard method for early diagnosis in patients over 40 years, with a sensitivity of 70% and specificity of 92% in the general population [2]. However, It has been shown that some conditions affect the performance of mammography, for example regarding mutations such as BRCA-1 and BRCA-2, and dense breast tissue. Therefore, the use of complementary studies, such as ultrasound, Tomosynthesis, and Magnetic Resonance Images (MRI), is actually recommended.

Magnetic resonance is considered the most sensitive method in the detection of breast cancer. Its usefulness, not only includes screening but also in diagnosis and treatment response evaluation [15,20]. It provides images with high signal-to-noise ratio and spatial resolution and gets non-invasive multiple sequences, which provide complementary information about the analyzed tissue. A great benefit of MRI is its high detection sensitivity of breast cancer, and its usefulness to find tumors that are hidden in mammography, ultrasound and physical examination [22].

Despite the advantages of MRI for the diagnosis of breast cancer, the use of this study is limited by the high cost [14], since breast MRI studies are time-consuming to both the magnetic resonance device and the radiologist interpretation. Additionally, breast MRI analysis is very subjective, and it has reported a varied variability in the differentiation between positive (probably cancer) and negative (probably benign) findings, especially in novice radiologists [4,11,17].

A typical MRI study consists of at least nine image sequences, each of them exhibiting different visual characteristics that are relevant to the diagnosis. Figure 1 shows some examples of regions of interest (RoIS) extracted from lesion from four MRI studies, which are categorized using the *Breast and Imaging Report and Database System* (BI-RADS), a standard description for reporting breast studies, which allows categorizing findings according to their probability of malignancy [27]. It is used also to define the final assessment of the study and patient management. Table 1 describes the concordance between BI-RADS assessment categories and management recommendations. Note that, erroneous study categorization can affect the patient health, given that a false positive entails an unnecessary biopsy but a false negative prevents early detection of the tumor. Thus, one initial challenge in this interpretation task is distinguishing negative studies, which continue with the routine breast MRI screening from positive studies, which require a follow-up or biopsy probe for diagnosis confirmation. Note that category 6 is reserved for "Known Biopsy-Proven Malignancy". This category was not included in this study.

Computer-aided detection and diagnosis (CAD) systems have been proposed to assist radiologists in making more accurate interpretation of breast cancer related studies. At recent years, a new technique called radiomics has been used to develop CAD systems, since it allows to get quantitative features that describe patterns in medical images which can be analyzed to support decision making or to give a second opinion to radiologist [5]. The work-flow of radiomics-based CAD systems is commonly covered in four principal stages: segmentation, radiomics feature estimation, feature selection, and classification. Although works presented in the state of the art follow the mentioned steps, it is well known that in clinical practice specialists do not delineate findings because this is a time-consuming task and depends directly on the observer, which adds variability [16]. On the other hand, because the large number of computed features, dimensionality reduction has shown to be an important step for improving the classification performance. This step is the most relevant for developing computer systems for aiding the interpretation of breast MRI studies, because it requires to combine information from several image modalities.

Information from multiple medical images classically has been combined by concatenation of feature vectors, which are then processed using a feature selector algorithm that aims to found them that are more discriminative according to the classification stage. In this paper, we propose the use of first, second and higher order radiomic features for training a CAD system able to differentiate between positive and negative findings in Breast MRI studies. Proposed approach extracts features from Volumes of Interest (VoIs) containing radiological findings; which are not preprocessed, filtered or segmented. We evaluate two approaches for fusing features extracted from the different sequence that compose a full breast MRI protocol. In the former, features from each sequence were assembled into a unique vector and then reduced using a feature selection approach, while in the latter, features were firstly reduced and then fused.

2   Related Works

In-state of the art, research has been carried out to propose support systems to breast cancer diagnosis and prognosis, and different approaches to dimension reduction and classification have been put forward. In [6] was proposed an approach to predict lymph node metastasis in breast cancer, using 10962 3D features from pre-processed and segmented findings in T2 and Diffusion MRI sequences, applying dimension reduction with Gain function to obtain 25 features and finally feature selection training different logistic regression models of different orders to identify how many and which features give the highest performance. In this work, the best result was obtained (AUC = 0.80 in validation) when features from both sequences were used together for the classification task with an order 10 logistic regression model. In [30], also was proposed a work-flow with two steps to dimension reduction aiming to identify triple-negative breast cancer. The first step was a feature ranking using X^2 to later use a sequential forward search algorithm in order to identify optimal features from segmented VOIs from findings and background parenchymal, getting an AUC = 0.87 when the last one features were added.

Table 1. Concordance Between BI-RADS® Assessment Categories and Management Recommendations. Taken from [1].

Assessment	Management	Likelihood of cancer
Category 0: Incomplete — Need Additional Imaging Evaluation	Additional Imaging Evaluation Recommend additional imaging:mammogram or targeted US	N/A
Category 1: Negative	Routine breast MRI screening if cumulative lifetime risk 20%	Essentially 0% likelihood of malignancy
Category 2: Benign	Routine breast MRI screening if cumulative lifetime risk 20%	Essentially 0% likelihood of malignancy
Category 3: Probably Benign	Short-interval (6-month) follow-up	0% but 2 % likelihood of malignancy
Category 4: Suspicious	Tissue diagnosis	$> 2\%$ but $< 95\%$ likelihood of malignancy
Category 5: Highly Suggestive of Malignancy	Tissue diagnosis	95% likelihood of malignancy
Category 6: Known Biopsy-Proven Malignancy	Surgical excision when clinically appropriate	N/A

On the other hand, to distinguish malignant and benign lesions using multiparametric breast-MRI were used Dynamic contrast-enhanced (DCE), T2 and Diffusion (DWI) images in [18]. Performance analysis using features from each sequence separately was accomplished, getting $AUC = 0.89 \pm 0.06$, 0.86 ± 0.05 and 0.84 ± 0.06 for DCE, DWI, and T2, respectively. However, these results were improved when Radiomics features from all sequences were used together $(AUC = 0.88 \pm 0.04)$, which demonstrates the benefit of multimodality in CAD systems.

Recently, the performance of breast-MRI-based diagnosis systems using Radiomics features and the end-to-end deep neural network method was compared in the discrimination task of malignant and benign masses [29]. For the Radiomics approach, statistical, shape and textures features were estimated using T2, a Subtraction image between T1 pre-contrast and post-contrast, and four T1 post-contrast images, then, they applied feature selection.The architecture used to do prediction with deep learning entering a subset of three rectangular patches was a Convolutional Neural Network (CNN) called ResNet18, pretrained on RGB images [13]. As a result of the tests realized, was proved that unlike CNN, the performance of the Radiomics approach is not affected if the full or half dataset is used during training.

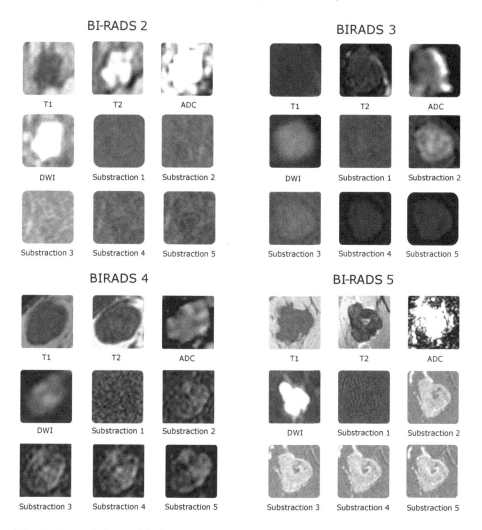

Fig. 1. Central slices of findings detected in MRI studies for different BI-RADS categories.

3   Materials and Methods

Figure 2 illustrates the framework used in this study. Briefly, volumes of interest extracted from the nine MRI sequences, are processed to extract a set of 3D radiomic features, which include first, second and higher-order features. Then, dimensionality reduction is performed by a feature selector algorithm. In this point, we evaluate two strategies for selecting discriminant features; in the first one, features are concatenated to generate a unique feature vector, and then the selector is applied; in the second one, the feature selector is applied for selecting the most discriminative features from each sequence, and then they are fused. In this study, two well-known feature selection algorithms were evaluated. Finally, selected features are used to train a classifier that discriminates the two kinds of findings (negative and positive).

3.1   Database

For this work, 88 studies were retrospectively included. Image acquisition was performed using an 1.5 Tesla Phillips Achieva scanner, according to the Breast MRI protocol defined by the Institution, which consists of the following MRI

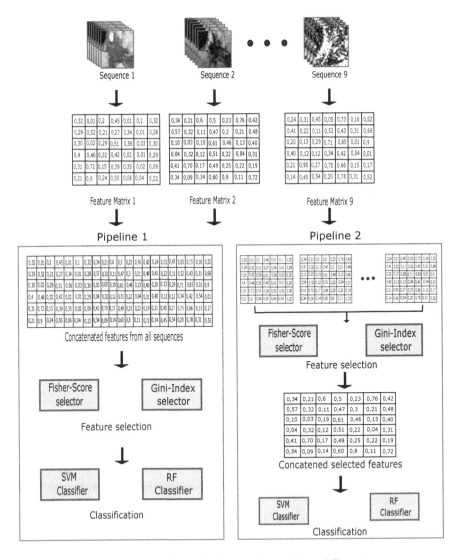

Fig. 2. Proposed pipelines for feature fusion from different sources

sequences: Axial T1 VISTA without flat fat saturation, FOV 280 × 368 × 180, matrix 352 × 459, TR 7.5 TE 4.6, axial DWI factor B0 and B 800, FOV 300 × 400 × 198 matrix 120 × 157, TR 7112, TE 70, 6 dynamic post-gadolinium 300 × 337 × 156, matrix 252 × 280, TR 6.8 TE 3.3, with initial sequence T1 fat suppression and after contrast injection, and 5 subsequent dynamics (DCE) of 60.1 seconds each, T2 VISTA without axial flat fat saturation, FOV 280 × 370 × 180, matrix 351 × 463, TR 2000 TE 211, coronal STIR FOV 299 × 372 × 200 matrix 232 × 241 TR 10000 TE 80. Contrast is an injection of meglumine gadoterate 376.9 mg/mL (Dotarem$^{®}$ Guerbert) dose 0.2 ml/kg (0.1 mmol/kg) body weight. The injection is performed with injector at a rate of 2.5 ml/s with venoclysis yelco No. 20. Additionally, the imaging technologist performs the dynamic sequence subtraction to generate 5 postprocessed sequences (F1, f2, f3, F4 and F5), and generate the ADC map by post processing the DWI image. Thus, nine sequences were considered in this study (T1, T2, DWI, ADC, and the five substraction images), original DCE images were discarded because they represent redundant information regarding subtraction.

Once studies are anonymized, radiologists with more than 6 years of experience in reading breast MRI images marked radiological findings in the most visible sequence, and then a trained technician projected it to the other sequences using the ROI tool of Horos software (https://horosproject.org/). Each finding was classified in a BI-RADS category between 2 and 5, which were then grouped as negative (BI-RADS 2), and positive (BI-RADS 3, 4, 5 and 6) groups, considering in the last one any possibility of malignancy in the finding. Taking into account that radiologists did not do fine segmentation, for the analysis, a cube was taken to get 3D information of each finding, using as reference the 2D rectangle that was drawn during reading in the central slice by radiologists to compute the number of slices needed to preserve the ratio in mm on each axis, as is shown in Eq. (1).

$$Slices\ number = \frac{Larger\ side\ of\ the\ rectangle}{(Thickness + space\ between\ slices)/2} \tag{1}$$

Finally, a total of 146 VoIs were used, from which, 61 belong to the negative findings and 85 to positive findings.

3.2 Feature Extraction

With the aim of representing information contained in different sequences of MRI, and obtain useful 3D features related to breast cancer probability, which allow a good performance during classification task, in this work were extracted 86 3D features of different nature over raw VoIs (first, second and superior order) using the Pyradiomics implementation [10]. These features were computed over the full finding, in order to get information from all of them in 3 dimensions, extracting symmetric cubes from the region of the image that contains the mass to avoid fine segmentation, since in clinical practice it is not performed because is a very time-consuming task.

First Order Features. These type of features are statistics measures taken from histograms of each VoI, in order to describe voxel intensities distribution present in these. In this case, a 64 bins histogram was computed, from which were computed 18 first-order features: minimum, maximum, mean, variance, standard deviation, kurtosis, skewness, energy, total energy, entropy, interquartile range, range, Mean Absolute Deviation, Robust Mean Absolute Deviation, Root Mean Squared, 10th percentile, 90th percentile, and uniformity [24].

Second Order Features. These type of features are measures computed directly from a Co-occurrence matrix, which describe the number of times that a couple of intensities levels appear in the VoI, separated by a distance δ and direction θ defined [12]. Aiming to obtain information about small changes in breast findings, in this work were computed Co-occurrence matrices with a distance equal to 1 in each possible direction for 3D images, obtaining 13 matrices, which were weighted to realize the features computing in the resulting matrix. Finally, a total of 22 texture features from the weighted Co-occurrence matrix were used.

Higher Order Features. Higher features are computed from different matrices, generated to describe the distribution of different grey levels in the VoI. Taking into account specific conditions or variations, such as grey levels repetition in connected voxels or separate for a δ distance chosen for analysis. To compute Higher-order features, three matrices were generated, namely, Gray Level Size Zone Matrix (GLSZM) [28], Gray Level Dependence Matrix (GLDM) [23] and Gray Level Run Length Matrix (GLRLM) [26]. From which were calculated 16, 16 and 14 features, respectively.

3.3   Feature Selection

With the aim to select relevant features to breast cancer probability prediction and reveal the relevant features from each MRI sequence for the classification task, in this work were carried out two tests, using two feature selectors, Fisher-score and Gini-Index.

Fisher-Score. This feature selector is a similarity-based supervised method, which evaluates the relevance of the features, taking into account its capacity to preserve data similarity [7]. The similarity of information from data is derived from the labels of each class. This method selects features that have similar values in one class and different regard to the other one, assigning a score o each feature, as it is shown in the Eq. (2).

$$fisher(f_i) = \frac{\sum_{j=1}^{c} n_j (u_{ij} - u_i)^2}{\sum_{j=1}^{c} n_j \sigma_{ij}^2} \tag{2}$$

where c is the number of classes, n_j the number of examples in class j, u_i is the mean value of feature f_i, u_{ij} the mean value of feature f_i to examples from class j and σ_{ij}^2 the variance of feature f_i to examples from class j.

Gini-Index. Gini-Index is a statistical feature selector, which for a given feature f_i with r different values separate dataset in two groups, taking W like a set of instances smaller or equal to the jth feature and $\bar{W}$ like the set larger than j^{th} feature value, giving a score to each feature using the Eq. (3) [9]

$$Gini\_index\_score = min(p(W)(1 - \sum_{s=1}^{c} p(C_s \mid W)^2) + p(\bar{W})(1 - \sum_{s=1}^{c} p(C_s \mid \bar{W}^2))$$

$$(3)$$

where $p(C_s \mid W)$ is the conditional probability of class s given W. When the classification task is binary, the maximum value that Gini-index can take is 0.5.

3.4   Classification

Considering the feature ranking provided by Gini-Index and Fisher Score feature selectors, the classification of negative and positive findings was carried out with two different approaches after this process. In the first approach, we concatenated radiomics features computed from each VoI on all sequences, obtaining a vector with 774 elements, which was used to apply dimension reduction with Gini-Index and Fisher Score independently. Finally, for classification, were trained four Random Forest (RF) [19] and four Support Vector Machine (SVM) [25] algorithms with the 10%, 20%, 50%, or 100% of ranked features sorted in ascending order by each feature selector independently. Parameters of each classifier were selected using a grid search during stratified cross-validation, taking values between 0.001 and 100 with an increase of 10 times the previous amount to adjust the γ and C for SVM, and values ranging in [10, 50, 100, 500] were used to select the number of estimators and max depth RF.

The second approach was performed to determine which features from each sequence are relevant and contribute more information to categorize positive and negative findings. Then, we made dimension reduction with both feature selectors independently again. Following 10%, 20%, or 50% of the relevant features of each sequence were selected to train RF or SVM classifier, adjusting its parameters with grid search as on the first approach. Finally, both pipelines were analyzed to determine the performance and relationship between features chosen as relevant in each one.

4   Results and Discussion

The evaluation study was performed using 5-stratified fold cross-validation strategy for the two fusion strategies described above, parameters of the SVM and RF classifiers were adjusted using the grid-search method [8], i.e., γ and C for SVM, and number of estimators (e) and max depth (max_d) for random forest. Results are presented in terms of area under ROC curve (AUC) since clinical applications is important considering a trade-off between sensitivity and specificity.

Tables 2 and 3 present the classification results of the SVM and RF classifiers respectively. Fisher Score and Gini Index feature selectors were used for selecting a subset of features from the two fusion strategies. The best performance (AUC = 73.6) was reported by the random forest classifier when a subset of 20% of features was selected by the Gini Index selector from each sequence, which was then combined in a unique vector. As can be observed, the performance classification is highly sensitive to feature selection in both SVM and RF classifiers, i.e, in both cases better performance was obtained when the feature selection process was performed.

Table 2. Classification performance regarding AUC for the two information fusion strategies using SVM as classifier and Fisher Score and Gini Index as feature selectors

	SVM Classifier			
	Fisher Score		Gini Index	
	Selection on all Features	Selection by sequence	Selection on all Features	Selection by sequence
10%	70.1 ± 11	71.9 ± 9	67.7 ± 14	69.4 ± 12
	$\gamma = 0.01,$ $C = 50$	$\gamma = 0.01,$ $C = 50$	$\gamma = 0.001,$ $C = 50$	$\gamma = 0.01,$ $C = 50$
20%	69.5 ± 10	67.1 ± 6	69.3 ± 13	68.0 ± 9
	$\gamma = 0.001,$ $C = 100$	$\gamma = 0.01,$ $C = 50$	$\gamma = 0.001,$ $C = 100$	$\gamma = 0.01,$ $C = 50$
50%	68.2 ± 5	69.9 ± 6	70.0 ± 11	71.1 ± 9
	$\gamma = 0.001,$ $C = 100$	$\gamma = 0.001,$ $C = 100$	$\gamma = 0.001,$ $C = 100$	$\gamma = 0.001,$ $C = 100$
100%	65.3 ± 6		65.2 ± 6	
	$\gamma = 0.001, C = 100$		$\gamma = 0.001, C = 100$	

Regarding fusion strategy, the results do not show a clear trend that supports the conclusion that one is better than the other. In some cases it is better to perform the feature selection and then to fuse them; and in others, better performance is reported by first performing the fusion and then the feature selection. However, it is recommended to evaluate this aspect due to the reported differences.

On the other hand, an important issue in the radiomic analysis is to identify the features related to the pathology on evaluation. Thus, Table 4 presents the first fifteen features selected by Fisher Score and Gini Index methods to the fusing-first strategy. Bold text denotes the eight features that are repeated in the two lists. This analysis shows that the most discriminative features were

Table 3. Classification performance regarding AUC for the two information fusion strategies using SVM as classifier and Fisher Score and Gini Index as feature selectors

	Random Forest Classifier			
	Fisher Score		Gini Index	
	Selection on all Features	Selection by sequence	Selection on all Features	Selection by sequence
10%	67.8 ± 13	66.7 ± 9	71.2 ± 10	72.3 ± 8
	$e = 100,$ $max\_d = 50$	$e = 10,$ $max\_d = 10$	$e = 50,$ $max\_d = 10$	$e = 500,$ $max\_d = 10$
20%	70.4 ± 12	67.9 ± 14	71.4 ± 10	73.6 ± 10
	$e = 50,$ $max\_d = 5$	$e = 100,$ $max\_d = 10$	$e = 500,$ $max\_d = 10$	$e = 500,$ $max\_d = 10$
50%	70.9 ± 11	68.4 ± 12	67.4 ± 14	66.5 ± 11
	$e = 50,$ $max\_d = 5$	$e = 50,$ $max\_d = 10$	$e = 500,$ $max\_d = 5$	$e = 100,$ $max\_d = 100$
100%	67.2 ± 9		66.7 ± 9	
	$e = 100, max\_d = 10$		$e = 100, max\_d = 5$	

Table 4. First fifteen features selected with Fisher Score and Gini Index using the first feature selection approach

Fisher Score	Gini Index
F3_glcm_Correlation	F2_glcm_ClusterShade
F4_glcm_Correlation	F3_glcm_ClusterShade
F3_glcm_Imc2	F4_glcm_ClusterShade
F4_glcm_Imc2	**F3_glcm_Correlation**
F5_glcm_Correlation	**F2_glcm_Imc2**
F2_glcm_Correlation	**F3_glcm_Imc2**
F5_glcm_Imc2	**F5_glcm_Correlation**
F3_glrlm_RunEntropy	F5_glcm_ClusterProminence
F2_glcm_Imc2	F5_glrlm_GrayLevelVariance
F3_glcm_Imc1	F4_glcm_ClusterProminence
F2_glrlm_RunEntropy	F5_glcm_SumSquares
F4_glrlm_RunEntropy	**F4_glcm_Correlation**
F5_glrlm_RunEntropy	**F4_glcm_Imc2**
F4_glcm_Imc1	**F2_glcm_Correlation**
F5_glcm_Imc1	**F5_glcm_Imc2**

those describing the texture of the subtraction sequences, in particular, those calculated from the co-occurrence matrix. These results can guide the development of more specific methods that take advantage of this information such as Wavelet-based descriptors.

5   Conclusions and Future Work

In this study, the fusion of radiomic features extracted from the image sequences that compose a breast MRI protocol was proposed for developing computer systems that aid the interpretation diagnosis process. Two fusion strategies were evaluated, in the first one features are fused in a unique vector for selecting then the most discriminative, in the second one, the most discriminative for each sequence are firstly selected to be later fused. Features used for describing findings were computed on a squared volume of interest avoiding manual or automatic lesion segmentation.

According to the results, we can conclude that dimensionality reduction is an important stage for fusing information from the different sequences used. However, results not allow to conclude that one of the two strategies be significantly better, although it is definitively important. Therefore, an analysis of the two strategies is recommended in a CAD development scenario. On the other hand, this study showed that texture features of substracted DCE images are the most discriminative features when the analysis is developed without a previous preprocessing or lesion segmentation. It is an encouraging result for developing CAD systems avoiding tumor delineation.

As future work, the use of image enhancement and filtering methods like Discrete Wavelet Transform (DWT) should be evaluated, as was proposed in [21]. Additionally, a similar study could be performed to evaluate the feasibility of predicting pathology results. For it, proven biopsy breast MRI studies are required.

References

1. American College of Radiology: ACR BI-RADS® Atlas fifth edition, quick reference (2013)
2. Bray, F., Ferlay, J., Soerjomataram, I., Siegel, R.L., Torre, L.A., Jemal, A.: Global cancer statistics 2018: Globocan estimates of incidence and mortality worldwide for 36 cancers in 185 countries. CA: Cancer J. Clinicians **68**(6), 394–424 (2018)
3. Caplan, L.: Delay in breast cancer: implications for stage at diagnosis and survival. Front. Public Health **2**, 87 (2014)
4. Dickinson, L., et al.: Scoring systems used for the interpretation and reporting of multiparametric MRI for prostate cancer detection, localization, and characterization: could standardization lead to improved utilization of imaging within the diagnostic pathway? J. Mag. Reson. Imag. **37**(1), 48–58 (2013)
5. Doi, K.: Computer-aided diagnosis in medical imaging: historical review, current status and future potential. Comput. Med. Imag. Graph. **31**(4–5), 198–211 (2007)
6. Dong, Y., et al.: Preoperative prediction of sentinel Lymph node metastasis in breast cancer based on radiomics of t2-weighted fat-suppression and diffusion-weighted MRI. Euro. Radiol. **28**(2), 582–591 (2018)
7. Duda, R.O., Hart, P.E., Stork, D.G.: Pattern Classification. Wiley, Hoboken (2012)
8. Ensor, K.B., Glynn, P.W.: Stochastic optimization via grid search. Lect. Appl. Math. Am. Math. Soc. **33**, 89–100 (1997)
9. Gini, C.: Variability and mutability, contribution to the study of statistical distribution and relaitons. Studi Economico-Giuricici della R (1912)

10. Griethuysen, J.J., et al.: Computational radiomics system to decode the radiographic phenotype. Cancer Res. **77**(21), e104–e107 (2017)
11. Grimm, L.J., et al.: Interobserver variability between breast imagers using the fifth edition of the BI-RADS MRI lexicon. Am. J. Roentgenol. **204**(5), 1120–1124 (2015)
12. Haralick, R.M.: Statistical and structural approaches to texture. Proc. IEEE **67**(5), 786–804 (1979)
13. He, K., Zhang, X., Ren, S., Sun, J.: Deep residual learning for image recognition. In: Proceedings of the IEEE Conference on Computer Vision and Pattern Recognition, pp. 770–778 (2016)
14. Heller, S.L., Moy, L.: Breast MRI screening: benefits and limitations. Curr. Breast Cancer Rep. **8**(4), 248–257 (2016). https://doi.org/10.1007/s12609-016-0230-7
15. Hochhegger, B., et al.: MRI in lung cancer: a pictorial essay. Br. J. Radiol. **84**(1003), 661–668 (2011)
16. Larue, R.T., Defraene, G., De Ruysscher, D., Lambin, P., Van Elmpt, W.: Quantitative radiomics studies for tissue characterization: a review of technology and methodological procedures. Br. J. Radiol. **90**(1070), 20160665 (2017)
17. Lunkiewicz, M., Forte, S., Freiwald, B., Singer, G., Leo, C., Kubik-Huch, R.A.: Interobserver variability and likelihood of malignancy for fifth edition BI-RADS MRI descriptors in non-mass breast lesions. European Radiology pp. 1–10 (2019)
18. Maforo, N., Li, H., Weiss, W., Lan, L., Giger, M.: Su-D-bra-02: radiomics of multiparametric breast MRI in breast cancer diagnosis: A quantitative investigation of diffusion weighted imaging, dynamic contrast-enhanced, and t2-weighted magnetic resonance imaging. Med. Phys. **42**(6 Part3), 3213–3213 (2015)
19. Pal, M.: Random forest classifier for remote sensing classification. Int. J. Remote Sens. **26**(1), 217–222 (2005)
20. Riedl, C.C., et al.: Triple-modality screening trial for familial breast cancer underlines the importance of magnetic resonance imaging and questions the role of mammography and ultrasound regardless of patient mutation status, age, and breast density. J. Clin. Oncol. **33**(10), 1128 (2015)
21. Rincon, J.S., Castro-Ospina, A.E., Narvaez, F.R., Diaz, G.M.: Machine learning methods for classifying mammographic regions using the wavelet transform and radiomic texture features. In: Botto-Tobar, M., Pizarro, G., Zuñiga-Prieto, M., DArmas, M., Zúñiga Sánchez, M. (eds.) CITT 2018. CCIS, vol. 895, pp. 617–629. Springer, Cham (2019). https://doi.org/10.1007/978-3-030-05532-5_47
22. Saslow, D., et al.: American cancer society guidelines for breast screening with MRI as an adjunct to mammography. CA Cancer J. Clinicians **57**(2), 75–89 (2007)
23. Sun, C., Wee, W.G.: Neighboring gray level dependence matrix for texture classification. Comput. Vis. Graph. Image Process. **23**(3), 341–352 (1983)
24. Sun, L., Zhang, S.: Pancreatic cancer survival prediction using CT scans and clinical variables. In: Stoyanov, D., et al. (eds.) POCUS/BIVPCS/CuRIOUS/CPM -2018. LNCS, vol. 11042, pp. 193–201. Springer, Cham (2018). https://doi.org/10.1007/978-3-030-01045-4_24
25. Suykens, J.A., Vandewalle, J.: Least squares support vector machine classifiers. Neural Process. Lett. **9**(3), 293–300 (1999)
26. Tang, X.: Texture information in run-length matrices. IEEE Trans. Image Process. **7**(11), 1602–1609 (1998)
27. Tardivon, A.A., Athanasiou, A., Thibault, F., El Khoury, C.: Breast imaging and reporting data system (birads): magnetic resonance imaging. Euro. J. Radiol. **61**(2), 212–215 (2007)

28. Thibault, G., Angulo, J., Meyer, F.: Advanced statistical matrices for texture characterization: application to cell classification. IEEE Trans. Biomed. Eng. **61**(3), 630–637 (2014)
29. Truhn, D., Schrading, S., Haarburger, C., Schneider, H., Merhof, D., Kuhl, C.: Radiomic versus convolutional neural networks analysis for classification of contrast-enhancing lesions at multiparametric breast MRI. Radiology **290**, 181352 (2018)
30. Wang, J., et al.: Identifying triple-negative breast cancer using background parenchymal enhancement heterogeneity on dynamic contrast-enhanced MRI: a pilot radiomics study. PloS One **10**(11), e0143308 (2015)

Evaluation of Learning Approaches Based on Convolutional Neural Networks for Mammogram Classification

Roberto Arias[1], Fabián Narváez[2], and Hugo Franco[1(✉)]

[1] Universidad Central, Bogotá 110321, Colombia
{rariasa,hfrancot}@ucentral.edu.co
[2] Universidad Politécnica Salesiana, Quito 111221, Ecuador
http://hpclab.ucentral.edu.co

Abstract. Mammography is still considered the best screening method for detection, diagnosis and follow-up of breast cancer. A correct classification of mammographic findings demands a high expertise level of the clinician observer. For this, different Computer-aided Diagnosis systems have been developed to support the diagnosis tasks and reduce the inter or intra-observer variability caused by the complex visual information contained in mammograms. However, the classification of some findings (masses, calcifications) is still a difficult task. This work presents a methodological approach to evaluate the performance of the training process for different convolutional neural network configurations of the VGG16 Convolutional Neural Network architecture, designed to perform mammographic classification. For doing that, the impact of different learning strategies (*focal loss*, to deal with highly unbalance datasets, gradient clipping and learning transfer) is evaluated.

The proposed method was two-fold evaluated. First, the performance for classifying between normal and abnormal Regions of Interest (ROIs) extracted from the DDSM and CBIS-DDSM datasets was explored. After that, a multi-class problem was addressed, for which a set of 5-class was included according to well-known BI-RADS classification. The obtained results reported an average accuracy of 0.92 for the binary classification and a rate of accuracy of 0.85 for the 5-class classification (with 30 epochs), reducing the convergence time (23 and 30 epochs for both binary and multi-class classification tasks, respectively).

Keywords: Mammogram · Convolutional Neural Network · Transfer learning · Focal loss · Gradient clipping · Class imbalance

1 Introduction

Breast cancer is frequently the most diagnosed cancer in women worldwide and is still considered the second cause of women death [38]. However, this neoplasia is curable if an early diagnosis is carried out – a clinical process that

© Springer Nature Switzerland AG 2020
F. R. Narváez et al. (Eds.): SmartTech-IC 2019, CCIS 1154, pp. 273–287, 2020.
https://doi.org/10.1007/978-3-030-46785-2_22

includes a mammography examination for determining radiologic signs suggestive of abnormal tissues. Among the different breast imaging modalities, mammography is still considered the best cost-effective technique for detecting abnormalities in early cancer stages [37]. Despite mammographic screening has demonstrated to be effective in reducing breast cancer mortality with percentages that vary from 30–70% [45], the sensitivity of the screening mammograms is strongly altered by the image quality and the experience level of the radiologist. In order to increase the mammography accuracy, specificity, and sensitivity, different Computer-aided diagnosis systems (CAD) have been developed to support the radiologist during the diagnosis process.

Those CAD systems consist of a set of computational tools and image processing methods for classifying some mammographic findings. However, their performance has been reported very variable when they are used to support different kind of abnormal findings [15], because of the large number of strategies proposed to improve CAD performance [29,30]. Among these strategies, some automatic segmentation techniques and characterization algorithms have been introduced in the literature for the task of classifying abnormal lesions as benign or malignant [29,31], reporting values for the area under the ROC curve above 0.8 when combining multiple features [31]. Among the approaches reported in the literature, there are different characterizations of the radiological properties of mammograms, such as textures, shapes and margins of relevant findings from regions of interest [33], mostly a handcraft process.

Additionally, a large variety of statistical, structural and spectral techniques have been used to analyze mammograms [10], including co-occurrence matrices [34], fractal dimensions [6], wavelets [7], curvelets [12] and contourlets [27], showing a very variable performance. All these approaches address the problem of classifying a mass as either malignant or benign. In contrast, the method proposed in this work is aimed to fully describe a mass following the Breast Imaging Reporting and Data System (BIRADS) lexicon standard, developed by the American College of Radiology (ACR).

As early as 1996, Sahiner et al. [36] reported a foundational CNN model to perform a binary classification of mammogram ROIs (normal tissue vs. masses) obtaining an accuracy of 0.87, a true positive rate of 0.90 and a false positive rate of 0.31. The application of early neural network models to medical images have been replaced by novel Deep Learning methods, reaching even better classification results. Different types of CNNs have been used in the literature [1], especially AlexNet, GoogleNet, ResNet and VGG16/19 models [25].

In 2015, Carneiro et al. [7] proved that a transfer learning method (from ImageNet [35] pre-trained CNNs) could be used to tackle computer vision problems in the scope of medical applications (s.a. diagnosis support); they also proved that unregistered images, no matter the projection of the mammogram (craniocaudal or mediolateral-oblique) the high level features imported from ImageNet are able to yield reliable results without ROI registration [7]. Dhungel et al. [9] proposed a method to detect masses in mammograms using cascading neural networks (Deep Belief Network + 2 CNN models) to feed with suspicious ROIs a two-step random forest classification process, significantly reducing the False Positive rate.

Jadoon et al. [22] proposed in 2017 a very complex CNN-based model for multiclass mammogram classification (three classes: normal, benign and malignant); to enhance the dataset, their approach used basic visual data augmentation techniques (rotation, flipping, etc.), then a Contrast Limited Adaptive Histogram Equalization (CLAHE) is performed. Using both the Two-Dimensional Discrete Wavelet Transform and the Discrete Curvelet Transform, the coefficients of each spectral representation were used as input for a CNN, obtaining an average accuracy of 0.81 for the standard wavelet representation and 0.82 for the curvelet representation. To overcome the issues of high model complexity and high computational resource consumption, several training-oriented techniques are being explored in recent works. Indeed, Basanth et al. [3] applied in 2017 a transfer learning approach to design a CNN-based method, specialized in benign and malignant mass classification for the DDSM dataset, obtaining an average accuracy of 0.82, a specificity of 0.86 and a precision of 0.85.

Recent CNN-based models in the literature report interesting results when tackling highly complex classification, detection and identification tasks in the scope of medical imaging, and, specifically, in CAD [14]. Nevertheless, model architecture, training regularization and optimization and class balancing, among other considerations, are required to enhance the applicability of this kind of models. This work presents an experimental evaluation of the performance of Convolutional Neural Network models for the binary and multiclass (5 class) mammogram classification problem, on the DDSM and CBIS-DDSM datasets, using different training strategies, specifically: (i) the focal loss approach (Lin et al. [24]) to implement the loss function in highly unbalanced datasets (s.a. DDSM and CBIS-DDSM); (ii) depth-wise separable convolution, such as the method proposed by Dumoulin et al. [11], to improve the resource consumption and the required iterations of the training process using a depth-wise separable convolution for similar target accuracy values [2] in comparison to standard convolution implementations; and (iii) the impact of methods preventing *gradient-explosion* artifacts, such as *gradient clipping* [32] is also evaluated. According to the obtained results, such methods provide noticeable improvements in the CNN-based model performance for both binary and 5-class classification.

2   Materials and Methods

2.1   Dataset Construction

Data Source. For this work, a 5-class annotated dataset was built using the ROIs and annotations from the DDSM and CBIS-DDSM dataset [39], according to the result of a visual examination by an specialist. The dataset consists of ROIs with no findings (0: negatives) extracted from the DDSM dataset and a set of *positive* ROIs (1: benign calcification, 2: benign mass, 3: malignant calcification and 4: malignant mass). The positive ROIs were extracted with a small of padding around the finding to provide context information (Fig. 1).

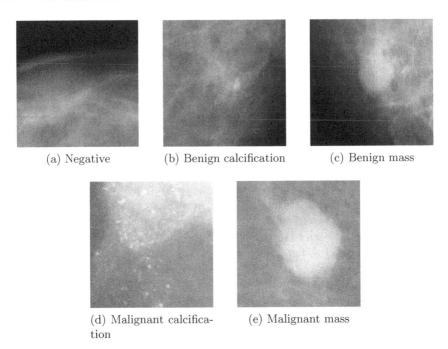

(a) Negative   (b) Benign calcification   (c) Benign mass

(d) Malignant calcifica-   (e) Malignant mass
tion

Fig. 1. Representative examples of mammogram ROIs from the DDSM and CBIS-DDSM datasets.

Data Preparation. Since the original datasets were split into training (`tfrecord` format) and validation/testing (`npy` format) subsets, it was necessary to convert all the data to one single format, in order to simplify the experimental data loading into the proposed Deep Learning classification framework (`tfrecord`).

After the extraction process, the entire imbalanced dataset contains $55,890$ samples (ROIs); 14% of them have annotated findings, while the remaining 86% were marked as *negative* by the specialists. Both *positive* (CBIS-DDSM) and *negative* (DDSM) ROIs were extracted by Scuccimarra [39] from previously labeled mammograms and resized to 299 pixels wide × 299 pixels high, in order to fit them to the standard input of a VGG16 model (Sect. 2.2). As far as the authors know, there are previous works using exactly the same dataset, so it is not possible to perform a result comparison with alternative methods in the literature, yet the reported results are in the range of those works approaching the same problem, and a comparison between alternative models is provided (Sect. 3.3).

Class Balancing. To address the high class imbalance in the resulting dataset, an oversampling method [13] was performed by generating new instances within the classes with a lower number of samples. This is performed using three histogram transformations (via the `skimage` library [41]), randomly applied onto the original ROIs:

Contrast stretching or normalization is an image enhancement method to improve the contrast in an image by *stretching* the intensity range, in order to span the histogram to a desired range of values [43].

Adaptive equalization or Contrast Limited Adaptive Histogram Equalization (CLAHE) is an algorithm for local contrast enhancement, that uses histograms computed over different tile regions of the image [43].

Histogram equalization, unlike contrast stretching, applies a monotonic, nonlinear mapping, such that the output image contains a uniform distribution of intensities.

A new instance is generated with probability of 0.5 for each of these histogram transform methods. To check if each histogram has a statistically significant difference with that of the original ROI (so it could be included in the final dataset for the training process) a Kolmogorov-Smirnov test is performed. If the KS statistic is greater than 0.05, the null hypothesis H_0 (original and transformed histograms are the same) is rejected and the new ROI is included [18].

2.2   CNN Configurations

The classification performance of three different VGG16-based CNN learning configurations is compared: (i) a standard convolutional layer model; (ii) a depthwise separable VGG16-based model [2]; and (iii) a VGG16-based standard model for transfer learning using the ImageNet weights [23]. The first two configurations are trained from-the-scratch. All models under study use data augmentation (i.e. rotation, zoom, width and height shift, shear and horizontal flip). The general architecture of the models under evaluation is shown in Fig. 2. Relevant details on each configuration are described as follows:

Standard Convolution Model. The standard CNN model is based on the VGG16 [25] network architecture. The input layer has a size of $299 \times 299 \times 1$ and transforms each input tensor to $224 \times 224 \times 1$ version; this output is fed into the first of four convolutional layer groups, each consisting of convolutional, activation function -ReLU- and max-pooling layers, which are followed by five fully conected and ReLU layers and an output soft-max layer.

Every convolutional group uses 3×3 filters, half padded [11]. Then, a nonlinear activation function (ReLU) is performed, and two regularization methods are applied: Batch Normalization [20] and Dropout [44] at 0.25. In turn, the reduction layer is based on a max-pooling process (window size: 2×2). The first fully connected layer has 256 nodes, while each of the remaining layers has 1024 units. Batch Normalization and Dropout regularization are also performed for the foward step in these layers. Finally, the output -softmax- layer corresponds to a probability vector whose size corresponds to the number of classes in the dataset. Figure 2 and Table 1 summarize the proposed general architecture, used to define the specific models under study in this work.

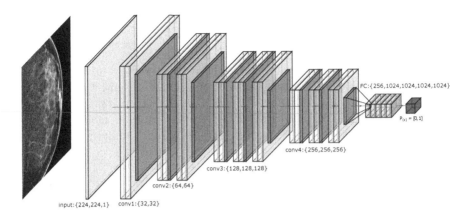

Fig. 2. Proposed CNN general architecture for this study. Source: own elaboration, using the *LATEX* scripts developed by Iqbal [21].

Table 1. Elements in each of the layer groups of the network trained from scratch

Layer	conv1	conv2	conv3	conv4
ConvNet	1	2	3	3
Activation function	1	2	3	3
Reduction (Max-Pooling)	1	2	3	3
Filters	32	64	128	256

CNN Model with Depth-Wise Separable Convolution. The second CNN-based configuration under evaluation in this study uses a depth-wise convolution strategy [40]. This approach, is known for reducing the number of parameters and operations of the neural network, with a noticeable impact in the training process resource and time consumption [40].

A convolutional depth-wise method works as follows: (i) separate the input data and the filters by channels (the number of filters for the corresponding tensors must match); (ii) perform a standard convolution per channel using the corresponding filter (the result of this process is usually a 2D tensor); (iii) regroup the resulting tensor; (iv) perform a 1×1 convolution to the channels per each output filter. A CNN model using depth-wise convolution will always require less parameters and less operations [4].

CNN Based on Transfer Learning. The third configuration consists of the application of Transfer Learning [3], using a previously trained model from a VGG16 network with the weights of ImageNet and using fine-tuning for the training of the fully connected layers and the classification layer.

The transfer learning through fine-tuning requires that the new part of the network be trained with small learning rates; therefore, the model uses gradient descent as an optimization function with a small learning rate. The main steps are summarized as follows: (i) remove fully connected nodes at the end of the network, those where class tag predictions are made; (ii) replace fully Connected nodes with the new nodes and load random weights to the new nodes; (iii) freeze the previous convolutional layers in the network to ensure that the previous robust characteristics learned by CNN are not destroyed; (iv) train the new fully connected layers; and (v) unfreeze the convolutional layers in the network and perform a second training step but applying a lower learning rate.

2.3   Performance Evaluation

To compare the performance provided by the three proposed VGG16-based configurations to classify oncological findings in mammogram ROIs, they are evaluated for both binary and multiclass (5-class) problems. For each configuration, the model reporting the best average accuracy and Mathews Correlation Coefficient, along with a lower number of epochs, is selected as representative, in accordance to the results of a standard cross–validation method. Once the representative model for each configuration is selected, the resulting models are compared in terms of the aforementioned performance metrics.

Model Implementation and Parameterization. The learning rate is the main hyper-parameter to tune in a deep learning model [42], and that tells the optimizer how far to move the weights in the direction opposite of the gradient for a mini-batch. In this work, the mini-batch Stochastic Gradient Descent (mini-batch SGD) method is used. The updates of the parameters is given by $\theta^t = \theta^{t-1} - \epsilon_t \frac{\partial L(x_t, \theta)}{\partial \theta}$ [5], where L is a loss function, z_t is a sample at the iteration t, and ϵ_t is the learning rate at the iteration t. It is well known that too small a learning rate will make a training algorithm converge slowly while too large a learning rate will make the training algorithm diverge [28]. Thus, it is necessary apply a higher learning rate during training and a lower one during the transfer learning process given that the fine-tuning process will require small learning steps to avoid the loss of generalization capacity provided by the convolutional layers of the base model.

On the other hand, the large weight updates during the training phase can exhibit the *exploding gradient* effect [32], making the learning algorithm unstable. A common solution to this problem (known as *gradient clipping* is to delimit the contribution of the error derivative before propagating it back to perform the weight update. This is usually carried out by (i) normalizing the gradient vector or (ii) clipping the gradient value to a predefined threshold.

For this work, the mini-batch SGD algorithm is parametrized using a learning rate of $1e-3$, a momentum of 0.9, and clip-value of 0.5, and a fine-tuning learning rate of $1e-4$, momentum equal to 0.9, and clipvalue equal to 0.5. Similarly, given the dataset has a noticeable class imbalance, the proposed models use focal loss [24] as loss function to reduce the relative loss for well-classified samples.

Finally, early stopping [28] is applied to finish the learning iterative process as soon as the validation loss reaches a stable plateau or when the loss function value starts increasing as a consequence of the potential overfitting.

Table 2. Commonly used evaluation metrics in CAD systems [14, 26].

Metric	Calculation formula
Accuracy	$accuracy = \frac{TP+TN}{TP+TN+FP+FN}$
Precision	$precision = \frac{TP}{TP+FP}$
Sensitivity	$sensitivity = \frac{TP}{TP+FN}$
Specificity	$specificity = \frac{TN}{TN+FP}$
F1-Score	$F1 - score = 2 * \frac{precison*recall}{precison+recall}$
MCC	$MCC = \frac{((TP*TN)-(FP*FN))}{\sqrt{((TP+FP)*(TP+FN)*(TN+FP)*(TN+FN))}}$

Data Segmentation. To train and test the selected configurations the DDSM and CBIS-DDSM samples were split into Training (80%) and Testing (20%) sets. In order to perform model selection, the training dataset was also split into a Training subset (90%) and a Validation subset (10%), according to the recommendations from Guyon et al. [16].

Metrics. The performance comparison of the CNN configurations under study is carried out by using a set of metrics described in Table 2, in order to assess the resulting classification and generalization capabilities of each model in the testing process. The training convergence time of the proposed models is also reported, in both epochs and seconds. Since the contingency matrix [14] is the basis of the performance metrics used in CAD systems [19], it will be also reported.

3   Results

3.1   Dataset

Class imbalance is a common problem in real-world datasets, which contributes to obtaining high accuracy values for the majority class and low performance of the models since it prevents convergence and the ability to generalize [8].

The DDSM and CBIS-DDSM datasets present a significant class imbalance; the greater class (negative ROIs) represents the 86% of the samples and the smaller class (positive ROIs) only the 14%. To reduce the imbalance, three image processing techniques were applied, as described in Sect. 2.1, resulting in an asymmetry reduction of the positive class from 36% to 12%. The dataset was segmented as described in Sect. 2.3 (Fig. 3).

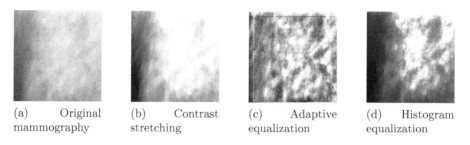

(a)   Original   (b)   Contrast   (c)   Adaptive   (d)   Histogram
mammography   stretching   equalization   equalization

Fig. 3. Result of applying the three image processing techniques in a mammogram.

3.2   CNN-Based Model Performance Comparison

The experiment consisted of performing two classifications, binary and multi-class (five classes). For each one, three ways to implement a deep learning model based on CNN networks are compared, from scratch using CNN-type networks with standard convolutional layers, depth-wise convolutional layers, and by transfer learning from a VGG16 network using fine-tuning. Also, the dataset was divided as it is shown in Table 3.

Table 4 shows that the configurations that use focal loss have low values in the loss function versus those that implement cross-entropy. Likewise, gradient clipping control reduces the values of the loss function. The model with separable convolutional layers converges in less than the time spent by the network with standard convolutional layers (Table 5). The methods based on transfer learning present better results in the relationship of time to converge versus performance measured with the MCC and the Accuracy in the testing phase.

Similarly, transfer learning reduces training time for the binary model by 71% versus a standard model trained from scratch. In the case of the multi-class model, the transfer learning method uses 87% less the time in comparison to a standard model trained from scratch. However, against the depth-wise convolution configuration, transfer learning required a training time 61% greater for the binary problem, and 76% greater for the multiclass problem, even it reached better classification performance.

An Early Stopping approach was used to estimate the training time for each configuration, i.e. train the model as long as the iteration -epoch- in which the model performace for the validation dataset starts to decline.

Table 3. Classes that each set of data contains for the comparison of the model.

Model	Classes
Binary	Negative, Positive
Multi-class	Negative, Benign calcification, Benign mass, Malignant calcification, and Malignant mass

Table 4. Evaluation of 24 configurations of the CNN network used for the evaluation of the effect of applying techniques, such as focal loss, for the reduction of the effect of class imbalance and control of gradient overflow through gradient clipping.

Dataset	CNN Type	Loss Function	Gradient clipping	Accuracy	Loss
Binary	Depth-wise	Cross-Entropy	Yes	0.93	0.15
			None	0.93	0.18
		Focal Loss	Yes	0.90	0.06
			None	0.91	0.05
	Standard	Cross-Entropy	Yes	0.92	0.18
			None	0.89	0.20
		Focal Loss	Yes	0.92	0.04
			None	0.92	0.05
	Transfer-Learning	Cross-Entropy	Yes	0.94	0.13
			None	0.88	0.28
		Focal Loss	Yes	0.92	0.09
			None	0.85	0.09
Multi-class	Depth-wise	Cross-Entropy	Yes	0.75	0.63
			None	0.75	0.66
		Focal Loss	Yes	0.75	0.35
			None	0.75	0.38
	Standard	Cross-Entropy	Yes	0.75	0.70
			None	0.75	0.64
		Focal Loss	Yes	0.75	0.36
			None	0.74	0.38
	Transfer-Learning	Cross-Entropy	Yes	0.90	0.29
			None	0.90	0.28
		Focal Loss	Yes	0.85	0.20
			None	0.84	0.26

3.3 Model with the Best Performance

The performance of the models was determined using two metrics from the Table 2; the Matthews Correlation Coefficient (MCC) [26] metric, which is a measure of the quality of a classifier and the Accuracy measure, which represents the dispersion of the set of values obtained from repeated measurements of the proportion between the number of correct predictions and the total predictions. The smaller the dispersion, the higher the accuracy value. A third performance metric is the training convergence time, related to computational complexity and resources, measured in epochs[1].

The model based on transfer learning (using fine-tuning) reported a better performance in both the binary case and the multi-class case, exhibiting a shorter

---

[1] One epoch is when an entire dataset is passed forward and backward through the neural network only once.

Table 5. Training convergence time for each of the best models.

Model	Epochs to converge	Epoch duration	Total time	MCC	Acc
Binary from scratch - standard	78	1052 sec	22.79 hr	0.78	0.87
Binary from scratch - depthwise	21	714 sec	04.16 hr	0.83	0.86
Binary transfer learning	23	1052 sec	06.72 hr	0.85	0.92
Multiclass from scratch - standard	217	827 sec	49.84 hr	0.48	0.74
Multiclass from scratch - depthwise	27	521 sec	03.95 hr	0.46	0.71
Multiclass transfer learning	30	827 sec	06.89 hr	0.52	0.85

convergence time (less epochs), yielding also higher values for average accuracy and MCC (Table 5).

Binary Classification. Table 7 summarizes the performance results of the binary classification problem for the configurations under study using 30 epochs. The transfer learning configuration reached an average accuracy of 0.92 with a loss value as small as 0.09. The configuration using Cross Entropy as loss function reported 0.94 as average accuracy, but its loss value rose up to 0.13.

Table 6. Performance metrics of the best CNN configuration for the binary classification problem. The table shows that two classes present similar probability since the values of their metrics are similar and therefore the imbalance of classes was controlled.

Class	Precision	Recall	F1-Score	Support
0 - Negative	0.90	0.96	0.93	7328
1 - Positive	0.95	0.89	0.92	7284

The best configuration for the binary problem exhibits a high value for the F1-Score metric, which represents the balance between precision (TPR) and recall (sensitivity) and is therefore an adequate metric when the dataset used presents class imbalance (Table 6). Such promising results support the potential use of this kind of CNN models in oncological finding detection/screening.

Table 7. Binary and multi-class classification evaluation.

Metric	Binary	Multi-class
Accuracy	0.92	0.85
Sensitivity	0.90	0.90
Specificity	0.95	0.77
MCC	0.85	0.53
F1 Score	0.92	0.95
AUC	0.98	0.92

Table 8. Multi-class classification metrics for negative, benign calcification, malignant calcification, benign mass and malignant mass classes.

Class	Precision	Recall	F1-Score	Support
0 - N	0.86	0.99	0.93	9729
1 - BC	0.52	0.10	0.16	521
2 - MC	0.72	0.05	0.09	525
3 - BM	0.33	0.01	0.01	374
4 - MM	0.68	0.30	0.42	429
Avg/total	0.82	0.86	0.81	11578

Multi-class Classification. The 5–class problem (Table 3) was addressed using the same configurations as those evaluated for the binary problem. Indeed, the labels of the ROIs are present in both the DDSM and the CBIS-DDSM (curated) datasets. Even the higher complexity of this classification task, the Transfer Learning model using Focal Loss and gradient clipping reported an average accuracy of 0.85, with a loss value of 0.20 (Table 4). However, the performance values could drop for individual classes, as it is shown in Table 8, possibly related to the class imbalance of the dataset and/or some confusion factors because of potential lack of separability according to the visual features.

4   Discussion

This work compared the performance of different configurations of a general model designed for both binary and multi-class classification of oncological findings in mammogram ROIs (DDSM and CBIS-DDSM datasets), using from-the-scratch training processes and transfer learning (through fine-tuning) on a VGG16 CNN model.

Beside the use of focal-loss, the re-sampling process applied to the smaller class (lowest number of samples) through image processing techniques (i.e. contrast stretching, adaptive equalization and histogram equalization) effectively reduces the imbalance without introducing exact duplicates, a frequent drawback in the case of standard over-sampling techniques.

CNN networks with separable convolutional layers (depth-wise convolution) reduces processing time, according to Table 5, with similar results to those obtained with CNN networks using standard convolutional layers and VGG networks applying transfer learning. Indeed, the depth-wise model is better than transfer learning if the dataset is large enough. However, this is not usually the case in medical imaging datasets, whose construction is quite demanding in most of the cases.

On the other hand, the gradient cropping method (intended to deal with the gradient explosion artifact) significantly reduces the convergence time of the model, decreases the values of the loss function and generates better quality models, according to the MCC metric.

Future steps in this field could involve the use of mammogram masks [17] to enhance the generalization abilities of CNN-based models. Beside the different nature of such available datasets in the literature, they exhibit some other problems, such as high class imbalance and small dataset sizes, usual in the medical imaging scope. Generative Adversarial Networks could be used to address such problems, complementing (and potentially replacing) the traditional State-of-the-Art resampling methods.

References

1. Abdelhafiz, D., Yang, C., Ammar, R., Nabavi, S.: Deep convolutional neural networks for mammography: advances, challenges and applications. BMC Bioinformatics **20**(11), 281 (2019)
2. Bai, L., Zhao, Y., Huang, X.: A CNN accelerator on FPGA using depthwise separable convolution. IEEE Trans. Circuits Syst. II Express Briefs **65**(10), 1415–1419 (2018)
3. Basanth, M., Shettar, R.: Transfer learning on pre-trained deep convolutional neural network for classification of masses in mammograms. IOSR J. Comput. Eng. **19**(50), e5 (2017)
4. Bendersky, E.: Depthwise separable convolutions for machine learning (2019). https://eli.thegreenplace.net/2018/depthwise-separable-convolutions-for-machine-learning/
5. Bengio, Y.: Practical recommendations for gradient-based training of deep architectures. In: Montavon, G., Orr, G.B., Müller, K.-R. (eds.) Neural Networks: Tricks of the Trade. LNCS, vol. 7700, pp. 437–478. Springer, Heidelberg (2012). https://doi.org/10.1007/978-3-642-35289-8_26
6. Bocchi, L., Coppini, G., Nori, J., Valli, G.: Detection of single and clustered microcalcifications in mammograms using fractals models and neural networks. Med. Eng. Phys. **26**(4), 303–312 (2004)
7. Carneiro, G., Nascimento, J., Bradley, A.P.: Unregistered multiview mammogram analysis with pre-trained deep learning models. In: Navab, N., Hornegger, J., Wells, W.M., Frangi, A.F. (eds.) MICCAI 2015. LNCS, vol. 9351, pp. 652–660. Springer, Cham (2015). https://doi.org/10.1007/978-3-319-24574-4_78
8. Chawla, N.V.: Data mining for imbalanced datasets: an overview. In: Maimon, O., Rokach, L. (eds.) Data Mining and Knowledge Discovery Handbook, pp. 875–886. Springer, Boston (2009). https://doi.org/10.1007/0-387-25465-X_40
9. Dhungel, N., Carneiro, G., Bradley, A.P.: Automated mass detection in mammograms using cascaded deep learning and random forests. In: 2015 International Conference on Digital Image Computing: Techniques and Applications (DICTA), pp. 1–8. IEEE (2015)
10. Dominguez, A.R., Nandi, A.K.: Detection of masses in mammograms via statistically based enhancement, multilevel-thresholding segmentation, and region selection. Comput. Med. Imaging Graph. **32**(4), 304–315 (2008)
11. Dumoulin, V., Visin, F.: A guide to convolution arithmetic for deep learning. arXiv preprint arXiv:1603.07285 (2016)
12. Eltoukhy, M.M., Faye, I., Samir, B.B.: Breast cancer diagnosis in digital mammogram using multiscale curvelet transform. Comput. Med. Imaging Graph. **34**(4), 269–276 (2010)

13. Estabrooks, A., Jo, T., Japkowicz, N.: A multiple resampling method for learning from imbalanced data sets. Comput. Intell. **20**(1), 18–36 (2004)
14. Gao, J., Jiang, Q., Zhou, B., Chen, D.: Convolutional neural networks for computer-aided detection or diagnosis in medical image analysis: an overview. Math. Biosci. Eng. **16**(6), 6536–6561 (2019)
15. Gur, D., et al.: Computer-aided detection performance in mammographic examination of masses: assessment. Radiology **233**(2), 418–423 (2004)
16. Guyon, I.: A scaling law for the validation-set training-set size ratio, pp. 1–11. AT&T Bell Laboratories (1997)
17. He, K., Gkioxari, G., Dollár, P., Girshick, R.: Mask R-CNN. In: Proceedings of the IEEE International Conference on Computer Vision, pp. 2961–2969 (2017)
18. Hodges, J.: The significance probability of the smirnov two-sample test. Arkiv för Matematik **3**(5), 469–486 (1958)
19. Hossin, M., Sulaiman, M.: A review on evaluation metrics for data classification evaluations. Int. J. Data Min. Knowl. Manage. Proc. **5**(2), 1 (2015)
20. Ioffe, S., Szegedy, C.: Batch normalization: accelerating deep network training by reducing internal covariate shift. arXiv preprint arXiv:1502.03167 (2015)
21. Iqbal, H.: PlotNeuralNet, December 2018. https://doi.org/10.5281/zenodo.2526396
22. Jadoon, M.M., Zhang, Q., Haq, I.U., Butt, S., Jadoon, A.: Three-class mammogram classification based on descriptive CNN features. Biomed. Res. Int. **2017**, 3640901 (2017)
23. Kornblith, S., Shlens, J., Le, Q.V.: Do better ImageNet models transfer better? In: Proceedings of the IEEE Conference on Computer Vision and Pattern Recognition, pp. 2661–2671 (2019)
24. Lin, T.Y., Goyal, P., Girshick, R., He, K., Dollár, P.: Focal loss for dense object detection. In: Proceedings of the IEEE International Conference on Computer Vision, pp. 2980–2988 (2017)
25. Ma, N., Zhang, X., Zheng, H.T., Sun, J.: Shufflenet V2: practical guidelines for efficient CNN architecture design. In: The European Conference on Computer Vision (ECCV), September 2018
26. Matthews, B.W.: Comparison of the predicted and observed secondary structure of T4 phage lysozyme. Biochimica et Biophysica Acta (BBA) Protein Struct. **405**(2), 442–451 (1975)
27. Moayedi, F., Azimifar, Z., Boostani, R., Katebi, S.: Contourlet-based mammography mass classification using the SVM family. Comput. Biol. Med. **40**(4), 373–383 (2010)
28. Montavon, G., Orr, G.B., Müller, K.-R. (eds.): Neural Networks: Tricks of the Trade. LNCS, vol. 7700. Springer, Heidelberg (2012). https://doi.org/10.1007/978-3-642-35289-8
29. Narváez, F., Díaz, G., Poveda, C., Romero, E.: An automatic BI-RADS description of mammographic masses by fusing multiresolution features. Expert Syst. Appl. **74**, 82–95 (2017)
30. Narváez, F., Romero, E.: Breast mass classification using orthogonal moments. In: Maidment, A.D.A., Bakic, P.R., Gavenonis, S. (eds.) IWDM 2012. LNCS, vol. 7361, pp. 64–71. Springer, Heidelberg (2012). https://doi.org/10.1007/978-3-642-31271-7_9
31. Oliver, A., et al.: A review of automatic mass detection and segmentation in mammographic images. Med. Image Anal. **14**(2), 87–110 (2010)
32. Pascanu, R., Mikolov, T., Bengio, Y.: Understanding the exploding gradient problem. CoRR, abs/1211.5063 (2012)

33. Qian, W., Sun, W., Zheng, B.: Improving the efficacy of mammography screening: the potential and challenge of developing new computer-aided detection approaches. Expert Rev. Med. Devices **12**(5), 497–499 (2015)
34. Ramos-Pollán, R., et al.: Discovering mammography-based machine learning classifiers for breast cancer diagnosis. J. Med. Syst. **36**(4), 2259–2269 (2012)
35. Russakovsky, O., et al.: Imagenet large scale visual recognition challenge. Int. J. Comput. Vision **115**(3), 211–252 (2015)
36. Sahiner, B., et al.: Classification of mass and normal breast tissue: a convolution neural network classifier with spatial domain and texture images. IEEE Trans. Med. Imaging **15**(5), 598–610 (1996)
37. Sarvazyan, A., Egorov, V., Son, J., Kaufman, C.: Article commentary: cost-effective screening for breast cancer worldwide: current state and future directions. Breast Cancer Basic Clin. Res. **1**, BCBCR1–S774 (2008)
38. Saslow, D., et al.: American cancer society guidelines for breast screening with MRI as an adjunct to mammography. CA Cancer J. Clin. **57**(2), 75–89 (2007)
39. Scuccimarra, E.A.: The Hypermedia Image Processing Reference (2018). https://www.kaggle.com/skooch/ddsm-mammography
40. Simonyan, K., Zisserman, A.: Very deep convolutional networks for large-scale image recognition. arXiv preprint arXiv:1409.1556 (2014)
41. Singh, H.: Basics of Python and Scikit image. Practical Machine Learning and Image Processing, pp. 29–61. Apress, Berkeley (2019). https://doi.org/10.1007/978-1-4842-4149-3_3
42. Smith, L.N.: Cyclical learning rates for training neural networks. In: 2017 IEEE Winter Conference on Applications of Computer Vision (WACV), pp. 464–472. IEEE (2017)
43. Solem, J.E.: Programming Computer Vision with Python: Tools and Algorithms for Analyzing Images. O'Reilly Media, Inc., Sebastopol (2012)
44. Srivastava, N., Hinton, G., Krizhevsky, A., Sutskever, I., Salakhutdinov, R.: Dropout: a simple way to prevent neural networks from overfitting. J. Mach. Learn. Res. **15**(1), 1929–1958 (2014)
45. Tabar, L., Yen, M.F., Vitak, B., Chen, H.H.T., Smith, R.A., Duffy, S.W.: Mammography service screening and mortality in breast cancer patients: 20-year follow-up before and after introduction of screening. The Lancet **361**(9367), 1405–1410 (2003)

Technological Platform for the Control of the Medication Supply to People with Diabetes

Mauro Callejas-Cuervo^(✉) , Juan Pablo Contreras Barrera ,
and David Leonardo Cárdenas Rengifo

Software Research Group, Engineering Faculty,
Universidad Pedagógica y Tecnológica de Colombia, Tunja, Colombia
mauro.callejas@uptc.edu.co

Abstract. This article presents the design of a technological platform called MedicHand, composed of a functional prototype of an electronic bracelet, and web system, elements which, together, allow for control the supply of medication to people who suffer from diabetes. In the first part, the problem Diabetes Mellitus (DM) for the immune system is discussed, as well as the situation of the medical treatments associated with this disease and the current medical trends. In the same way, the technologies involved in the construction of the device, the components that integrate the technological platform, the communication protocol and the design of the bracelet are described.

Keywords: Medication supply · Diabetes · Monitoring system · Electronic bracelet · API REST

1 Introduction

As a population gets older, the chances of developing multiple afflictions and illnesses increase. According to the World Health Organization (WHO), among the most common afflictions of old age, apart from coronary and cerebrovascular disease, are the problems caused by loss of hearing, cataracts, refractive error, back and neck pains, and osteoarthritis; in addition to chronic obstructive pulmonary disease, diabetes, depression and dementia, which produce the greatest number of deaths [1].

At number 7 among the 10 most common causes of death for the year 2016 [2], diabetes has been classified as the epidemic of the 21st century. In 2015, 415 million people suffered from diabetes and it is expected that by the year 2040, 642 million people will suffer from it. This will affect the world's economy and the cost in COP (Colombian Pesos) will be 1,639 trillion in health spending [3]. The costs associated with this illness are high, especially due to complications, hospitalizations and because patients should receive treatment throughout their whole lives. Today, it is known that when a patient is monitored effectively they do not present complications during the illness and inpatient treatment is not required, thus, the costs are reduced. However, around 70% to 80% of the people who suffer from diabetes do not reach the objectives set by a health professional, given that they refuse to change their eating habits and that they often forget to take their medication.

© Springer Nature Switzerland AG 2020
F. R. Narváez et al. (Eds.): SmartTech-IC 2019, CCIS 1154, pp. 288–296, 2020.
https://doi.org/10.1007/978-3-030-46785-2_23

As a consequence, the patient has to start new treatments with greater concentrations of medicines or a higher dose, which is translated into a higher cost. Thus, for example, for Colombia, in 2007, the annual cost of Melllitus Diabetes (MD), was 2,438,000 COP per monitored patient, which rose to 7,166,000 COP when the medication included insulin, while indirect costs and complications were higher than 12 million COP.

At present, the integration of technology offers tools and devices that detect the way in which a patient with diabetes [4–6] develops on a daily basis, performs tasks and how their body responds in order to reduce the negative impact caused by the illness. With that aim in mind, some researchers have focused their work on the development of non-invasive glucometers [7–11] using processes like NIR spectroscopy, devices which emit infrared light, the use of ultrasound, networks of sensors to monitor vital signs and free software. In commercial development, there are two devices that top the list in glucose measurement. The first is called Freestyle Libre [12] and is a monitoring system composed of a round sensor (the size of a coin) that is placed on the arm and a reader that measures and shows the result on a screen. The reader stores the sensor data for up to 90 days, providing a historical record of glucose levels. The other device is called K'Track [13]. It is a sport style watch which has a micro-pump used to extracted fluids from the skin and biosensors which analyse vital signs, thus, detecting the levels of glucose. The device can take a limitless amount of measurements for 30 days and the results are shown on a screen. It can also be synchronized with a dedicated mobile application.

The solutions described above help to improve the condition and quality of life of the diabetic patient, avoiding painful and uncomfortable blood samples. Despite that, it is necessary to mention that, in the case of the solutions with free hardware, most of them are not portable and they do not attain a high level of certainty or reliability in the glucose sample and, therefore, they have not been supported by the medical community. In contrast, commercial devices have the support of some medical organizations, but the cost is high and, on occasions, they are impossible to acquire in certain geographical areas.

This article presents a platform developed by the Software Research Group – (GIS, by its acronym in Spanish). It is called MedicHand and it is a low-cost solution, easy to use and accessible to the population of senior citizens who suffer from diabetes. Through the use of the electronic bracelet and web platform, the patient is guaranteed a medical treatment configuration that uses alerts for them to take their medication following the time intervals described by the doctor. Moreover, notifications are generated when a medication is close to being finished. For the health specialist, the platform will have the capacity to show statistics on the frequency of ingestion, the time intervals between doses, and the current status of the treatment, with the aim of making prompt decisions that benefit the health of the patient. These measurements have a social impact as they help to mitigate failures in treatment and, consequently, reduce the costs associated with the care of each patient.

2   Materials and Methods

2.1   Construction of the Electronic Device

The electronic device MedicHand was initially constructed with an electronic card, buttons, a led screen, a vibrating motor, a buzzer, a led light bulb and a battery. The organization and distribution of the electronic components are represented in Fig. 1.

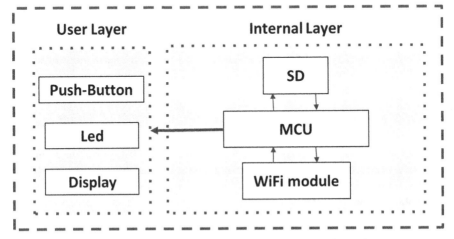

Fig. 1. Electronic components implemented in MedicHand.

Table 1. Descriptión of electrónic components

Components	Ref.	Function
Electronic card	Teensy 3.2	Development platform based on the 32-bit ARM Cortex M4. It records the integrated functioning of the components
Buttons	Generic	Capture high and low peaks for control: wi-fi configuration, data synchronization, confirmation of administering of medicine, postponing of medicine administration
Display	Teensy view	Shows the time. If there is an alarm, the screen will show the name of the medication as well as the dose
Vibrating motor	Servo motor	Vibrates when there is a notification that a medication has to be taken
Buzzer	Coin-shaped	Emits a sound while the medication notification is active
Led light bulb	Common anode	Provides light of a particular colour. The colour of the light bulb corresponds to an RGB code that will be associated with each medicine by the patient

Likewise, Table 1 presents the reference and function which each one of the components has.

2.2   Implementation of the Web Platform

When carrying out the selection of the development technology, a language with a low learning curve was sought, which would permit rapid development and was flexible or scalable over time. Aside from promoting these characteristics, NodeJS provides fluent and rapid communication between the back-end and the front-end; it can be executed in a variety of servers, making it multiplatform; it supports high concurrence; and is ideal for real-time applications. This is possible thanks to the architecture of the NodeJS, which is in fact the engine of JavaScript V8 with a superior layer of libraries of NodeJS, which are responsible for the communication between the NodeJS' API and Google's V8 Motor. Additionally, it is supported in the Libuy library, which is used for the processing of asynchronous inputs and outputs.

The web application has an interface that can be observed in Fig. 2. There, the registry section can be seen, which allows for entering basic information about the person who will be in control of the medication (it is preferable that it is someone different from the senior citizen who is undergoing treatment). It is possible to add more contacts to which an email will be sent to inform about the taking (or not) of any of the medications programmed for their application. It also has a module that is managed by the application administrator, who will be in charge of entering basic information about types of medication, dosage, configuration of the alarms for the medication (all this, supervised by a doctor, who is responsible for the patients' treatment) and other basic information regarding the functioning of the platform.

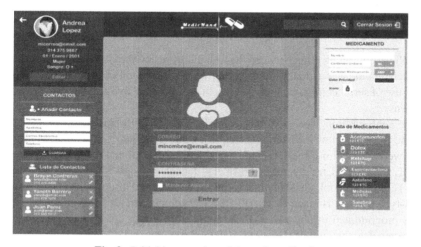

Fig. 2. Initial intervention of the web application

The interface shown in Fig. 3 allows for the configuration of alarms, the addition of medicines, and the management of the inventory of medications that have been prescribed by a doctor.

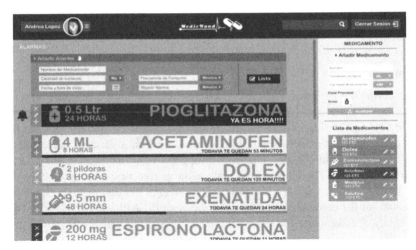

Fig. 3. Module – Alarms and medication management.

Coding with NodeJS allows for a web application oriented towards events and with an focus on the consumption of web services. The functions of MedicHand Web are:

- Registering medications
- Managing emergency contacts
- Managing ingestion reports
- Administering treatment according to the doctor's prescription.

2.3   Communication Description

To establish communication between the web platform and the electronic device, a Wi-fi ESP8266 module was added, which works with serial communication. This means that it makes use of serial communication TX/RX in order to send and receive buffers through the Teensy.

The configuration process of the technological platform presented in Fig. 4 starts with the registration of medications, frequency and quantity of ingestion, making use of the web application. These records are stored in a relational database managed by MySQL. Afterwards, the electronic bracelet is connected to a Wi-fi network, making use of the TCP/IP protocol. Once there is access to the internet, through the HTTP protocol a GET-type petition is made to an API REST developed exclusively for consulting the alarms programmed by the patient. The application server consults the database and sends some data that will be transformed in the server into a JSON-type object, which is sent to the electronic server. When the object is received, it is processed by the Teensy and the data is stored on a Micro SD memory, ensuring that the data will be available even when the device is not connected to the internet (offline).

Additionally, every time that the patient receives an alarm and pushes a buzzer, this will be taken as evidence that the medication has been taken, discounting the total amount (store) of the medication. These operations are recorded on the Micro SD and when the electronic bracelet is connected to the internet again (online), the data is sent to the API (through a POST petition) and from there, it goes to the database.

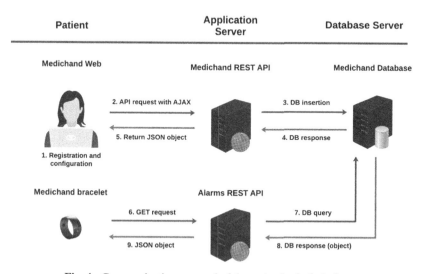

Fig. 4. Communication protocol of the technological platform

3   Results

The GIS Group has developed a functional prototype of the electronic bracelet with which it has been demonstrated that the protocol is suitable for the transmission, in real time as well as disconnected, of the data generated by the bracelet. For this, a map of an electronic circuit was made (see Fig. 5) and the model was built on a test plate.

The electronic components presented in Fig. 6 allowed for the realisation of the MedicHand device test of concept. It is equipped with the components described in Table 1, apart from having a Wi-fi module and a Micro SD slot. The tests carried out showed that real-time communication and the Micro SD storage allowed the web application to be fed without any difficulties and the veracity of the transferred data was verified.

The prototype was implemented in a circuit plate printed with a microcontroller and the necessary firmware, which will be installed in the bracelet as seen in Fig. 7.

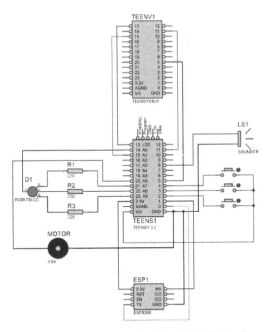

Fig. 5. Map of Electronic Circuit: MedicHand

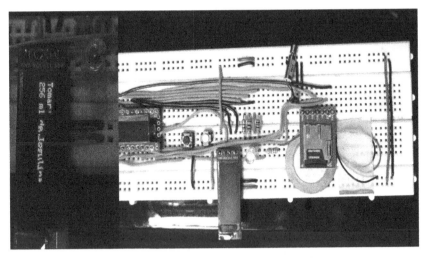

Fig. 6. MedicHand Bracelet: Hardware for test of concept

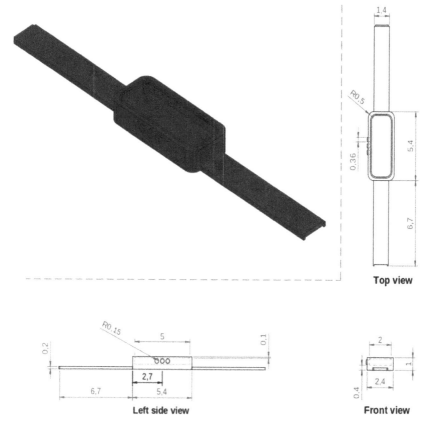

Fig. 7. Prototype bracelet

4 Conclusions

The platform developed in this research helps to control the taking of medicine by people diagnosed with diabetes, a problem that rose to 5.1% in the department of Boyacá, Colombia, in the year 2007 and pertained to the senior citizen category, those who are in rural areas or distant from the main cities, making access to and the use of technology in the control and follow-up of the disease impossible.

For its part, the technological platform (MedicHand) works in real time or delayed time, thanks to the incorporation of a secondary storage unit (Micro SD), which solves the problem of the loss of data in the case that the electronic device does not have internet access. Moreover, when using an API –working independently- to obtain the alarms and the synchronization of the medication storage, it is guaranteed that, in case the web application failed, this would not affect the control and the dosage notifications of the patient.

Finally, it is important to mention that, although it is a functional prototype, its size and layout do not correspond to an ergonomic design for the population studied. For that reason, it is a challenge for the research group to integrate the external design with the model presented in Fig. 6: a bracelet with a miniaturised electronic system without losing the present model. In fact, alternative investigations have been carried out, with the aim of integrating new functions into the platform, such as the taking of a pulse and measuring the levels of glucose in order to constantly monitor the patient.

Acknowledgements. The authors thank the participation of the other members of the Software Research Group of the Universidad Pedagógica y Tecnológica de Colombia, especially the members of the development of embedded devices line of investigation.

References

1. Organización Mundial de la Salud. Envejecimiento y Salud (2018)
2. Organización Mundial de la Salud. Las 10 principales causas de defunción (2018)
3. Fundación para la Diabetes. Diabetes una epidemia del siglo XXI (2015)
4. Brown, S., Raghinaru, D., Emory, E., Kovatchev, B.: First look at control-IQ: a new-generation automated insulin delivery system. Diab. Care **41**(12), 2634–2636 (2018). https://doi.org/10.2337/dc18-1249
5. Hannon, T.S., et al.: Advancing diabetes management in adolescents: comparative effectiveness of mobile self-monitoring blood glucose technology and family-centered goal setting. Pediatr. Diab. **19**(4), 776–781 (2018). https://doi.org/10.1111/pedi.12648
6. Sherwood, Z.: What factors influence glycaemic control in children aged under 11 years with type 1 diabetes? A literature review. J. Diab. Nurs. **20**(6), 213–217 (2016)
7. Vrba, J., Vrba, D., Díaz, L., Fišer, O.: Metamaterial sensor for microwave non-invasive blood glucose monitoring. In: Lhotska, L., Sukupova, L., Lacković, I., Ibbott, G.S. (eds.) World Congress on Medical Physics and Biomedical Engineering 2018. IP, vol. 68/3, pp. 789–792. Springer, Singapore (2019). https://doi.org/10.1007/978-981-10-9023-3_143
8. Huzooree, G., Khedo, K.K., Joonas, N.: Data reliability and quality in body area networks for diabetes monitoring. In: Maheswar, R., Kanagachidambaresan, G.R., Jayaparvathy, R., Thampi, S.M. (eds.) Body Area Network Challenges and Solutions. EICC, pp. 55–86. Springer, Cham (2019). https://doi.org/10.1007/978-3-030-00865-9_4
9. Shapovalov, V.V., Gurevich, B.S., Dudnikov, S.Y., Belyaev, A.V., Zagorsky, I.G.: Optical non-invasive methods for glucose determination in human blood. Int. J. Pharm. Res. **10**(1), 324–329 (2018)
10. Dinh, D.T.-M., Truong, V.A., Tran, A.N.-P., Le, H.X., Pham, H.T.-T.: Non-invasive glucose monitoring system utilizing near-infrared technology. IFMBE Proc. **69**, 401–405 (2020)
11. Wang, T.-T., et al.: A feasible image-based colorimetric assay using a smartphone RGB camera for point-of-care monitoring of diabetes. Talanta **206**, 120211 (2020)
12. Freestyle Libre. Abbott Diabetes Care Inc. (2019). https://www.freestylelibre.co.uk/libre/. Accessed 25 June
13. K'Track. PKVitality Inc. (2019). https://www.pkvitality.com/ktrack-glucose/. Accessed 25 July

Emotion Recognition from Time-Frequency Analysis in EEG Signals Using a Deep Learning Strategy

Ruben D. Fonnegra[1(⊠)], Pablo Campáz-Usuga[2], Kevin Osorno-Castillo[2], and Gloria M. Díaz[2]

[1] Institución Universitaria Pascual Bravo, Medellín, Colombia
ruben.fonnegra@pascualbravo.edu.co
[2] Instituto Tecnológico Metropolitano, Medellín, Colombia
{pablocampaz164292,kevinosorno220486}@correo.itm.edu.co,
gloriadiaz@itm.edu.co
http://www.pascualbravo.edu.co/
https://www.itm.edu.co/

Abstract. At recent years emerging technologies have experiences an exponential growing in the development of human computer interfaces with commercial or scientific purposes; in which is included the Affective computing. This area aims to develop computer interfaces to estimate human emotional states during an specific interaction environment with the goal of adapt itself to the users feelings in order to enhance their experience. In this paper a Deep learning based model is proposed to determine the emotional user state considering the Russell emotional model. This consist in determine high-low intensity (arousal) and positive-negative emotional intention (valence). The emotional recognition is based in time-frequency analysis through power spectral density and spectrogram features extracted from electroencephalography (EEG) signals in the well-known DEAP database. Besides, since Deep learning strategies require a significant amount of samples to effectively train their parameters; a volumetric framing consisting in signals windowing is employed. Finally, a non typical k-fold cross validation strategy is employed as most works in the state of the art; but a leave one subject group out (LOSGO) is used since it consist in a more suitable and reliable strategy for realistic interaction scenarios. Results for models to recognize emotional arousal and valence in EEG signals demonstrates efficiency to recognize emotions from different participants under different trials and affective stimuli.

Keywords: Emotion recognition · Electroencephalography · Deep learning

1 Introduction

The past years have experienced great growing in several working fields such as artificial intelligence and human computer interfaces; specially in research and

© Springer Nature Switzerland AG 2020
F. R. Narváez et al. (Eds.): SmartTech-IC 2019, CCIS 1154, pp. 297–311, 2020.
https://doi.org/10.1007/978-3-030-46785-2_24

commercial purposes since the 4th industrial revolution have impulse them in a world wide communities. This phenomenon have confirmed the interest of several institutions for contributing in several applications such as entertainment fields or gaming interaction [5], immersive, augmented or virtual environments [2,4], clinical applications [6,8], among others. Concerning this issue, a concurrently growing field of research known as Affective Computing has gained attention in several communities for creating interfaces which consider human emotional activity to adapt their systems with the aim of enhance the experience [1]. This, since human emotional states highly influences their decisions and perspectives during daily bases.

In affective computing, several strategies for the analysis of the emotions have been evaluated. First of all, the emotional model and characterization is an important fact for their analysis. This model determines the way to measure emotions and how they psychologically are expressed in humans [10]. In this sense, several emotional models have been conducted in the state of the art; and they are mainly classified as discrete and continuous emotional models [13]. The discrete emotional model is grounded in the fact that a group of emotional manifestations is easily recognizable indistinctly of race, cultural, social or economical aspects. Then, the emotions composing the discrete model are happiness, fear, anger, disgust, surprise and sadness [11]. On the other hand, the continuous models are developed considering different psychological variables to cast different emotions (besides the discrete ones) to create homogeneity and diversity among different emotional events. In this sense, several bidimensional and multidimensional models have been proposed in the state of the art, considering variables such as arousal, valence, positivity, negativity, liking, among others [25,28,29].

Second, the data source employed to recognize emotions is an important aspect, since the analysis and performance of the computational models must be based on it. In this sense, several data considerations have been used for the emotional problem such as facial expressions, voice recordings, physiological signals such as temperature, heart rate (HR), electroencephalography (EEG), among others. Between them, the physiological signals have been strongly studied since they have a great potential to physically describe the emotional events to characterize them in the human body. Besides, electroencephalography signals are the ones with a great potential of study since they can measure the electrical activity in the brain cortex. For this reason, their study in the emotional field could aid the characterization of the emotional activity to brain regions, to better understand their manifestation in the rest of the body.

Third, the computational algorithms to recognize the data is important fact according to the emotional application. So, machine learning strategies have been employed in this issue with the purpose of discriminating among different emotional events. For instance, Deep Learning strategies have been gaining attention in the scientific community since they have successfully outperformed several machine learning approaches in imaging analysis from 2012 to now [21]. Besides, several Deep Learning models have been proposed in the emotion recognition task obtaining promising results ([15–17]). These results suggest a deeper study on the strategy to continue implementing models aiming to the analysis of emotions for computational systems; besides their better understanding in a physiological and psychological manner.

In this work, an approach based on a Deep Learning strategy is developed to recognize emotions from EEG physiological signals. For this purpose, the well-known DEAP database is employed in which the signals are filtered and preprocessed including a volumetric framing strategy based on windowing segmentation and feature extraction based on the power spectral density (PSD) of each electrode is used in five frequency bands (delta: 0.5–4 Hz, theta: 4–8 Hz, alpha: 8–12 Hz, beta: 12–30 Hz, and gamma: 30–45 Hz). The extracted PSD and spectrogram features are fed to a three dimensional convolutional neural network to classify emotion content of signals according to the Russell bidimensional emotional model (arousal - valence) [29]. Besides, a Leave One Subject Group Out (LOSGO) experimental implementation for validation is employed conversely to conventional K-fold cross validation strategy since it can be more suitable to realistic scenarios of implementation. The model proposed in this approach shows promising results outperforming several approaches proposed in the state of the art, to recognize positive/negative valence and high/low arousal according to each emotions.

This paper is organized as follows: in the Sect. 2, a brief summary of the related works described in the literature, which use the DEAP database is presented using different experimental implementations. Section 3 describes the employed database, and proposed approach concerning the volumetric framing, the feature extraction and the deep neural network architectures. In Sect. 4 the experimental results and the discussion of the model are presented; and finally, in Sect. 5, the conclusions and future work are discussed.

2   Related Works

Approaches concerning emotion recognition for affective computing models have been an active research field in the last years, because of a large amount of applications, since humans behavior is highly influenced by their affective state. In this sense, the state of the art presents several characterization models to "measure" emotions with the aim of determining the physical and psychological causes of them. For this reason, these studies have been focused in the study of the brain as the center of thinking and feeling which manipulates physical reactions according to certain external stimuli [3]. From this point, a first model was proposed containing the emotions considered as recognizable indistinctly of cultural, social or other psychological aspects. This model is also known as universal emotional model [12]. However, the main limitation of these models lies in the vast diversity of emotional states that a human could experience including the universal emotions. For this reasons, research have been focused in the development of new models to effectively characterize emotions considering different variables and dimensions. Among them, an important and widely used bidimensional model is proposed by Russell [29] which is based in two dimensions: arousal/non-arousal as meaning of intensity and positive/negative as meaning of intention. Other emotional model is proposed by Plutchik [28], which is based in 2 main axes: unpleasant/pleasant as meaning of pleasure and acceptance/rejection as meaning of comfort. Another emotional model is proposed by Mehrabian called the PAD model [25], which is a three dimensional model based in arousal/non-arousal meaning of intensity; pleasure/displeasure as meaning of the intention; and dominance/submissiveness as meaning of self-control.

From the construction of the emotional model, several analysis from different kind of physiological changes have been employed. In this sense, several studies have been conducted to analyze emotions from facial expressions, temperature changes, electroencephalography (EEG), galvanic skin response (GSR), among others. Taking this into account, the EEG signals have been widely studied for the emotion characterization since the brain have been considered as the center of the humans behaviors and feelings. However, several factors which modify the brain structure change the way of how chemical reactions occur inside the brain; for instance, they modify the frequencies produced in brain signals when an external event is performed. This fact, complicates the recognition process since a personal characterization cannot be realized considering personal events. Instead, research have been focused in characterize the brain activity for the emotion recognition when an emotional event is produced in a population with specific features. However, results and strategies performed are still far away of finding a solution to this problem. A full review of the EEG analysis for emotion recognition can be found in [9].

For example, in works such as Lin et al. [24] is presented a computational model to recognize emotions in EEG signals during music playing in participants. They perform a short time Fourier transform (STFT) using hamming windows to compute the spectrogram of each signal, over five frequency bands (delta (δ: 1–3 Hz), theta (θ: 4–7 Hz), alpha (α: 8–13 Hz), beta (β: 14–30 Hz), and gamma (γ: 31–50 Hz)). After this feature extraction, a feature election process is employed using the F-score index for measuring the ratio of between- and within-class variance. Then, different number of features combinations are employed according to the F-score rank list to train a support vector machine (SVM) and a multilayer perceptron (MLP). The proposed approach shows feasibility for the emotion recognition; however, a great limitation of music elicitation strategy lies in the subjectivity of human perception of music since music likes and dislikes varies significantly from one each other. This aspect bias the distribution of the brain according to the participant perception.

Other works such as Yang et al. [32] present a framework to recognize emotions from EEG signals using high dimensional linear and non-linear features, including Hjorth activity, Hjorth mobility, Hjorth complexity, standard deviation, sample entropy (SampEn), wavelet entropy (WE) and PSD features. The characterization is then used to train a significance test, sequential backward selection, and support vector machine (ST-SBSSVM), which is the combination of relevance analysis, feature selection and classification. The model obtain a maximum accuracy of 0.68 in the DEAP database for the emotion recognition task.

On the other hand, deep learning strategies have been employed to determine the emotional state in participants to evaluate the ability of these models to learn patterns from EEG signals. For example, in Li et al. [22] is proposed an approach to investigate the relationships among different brain activations. Their strategy consist in using a feature fusion based algorithm to consider different feature joints and feature selection stage based in F-score values. Using the DEAP database they obtained an maximum accuracy of 0.62 by combining power spectral density (PSD) and features from EEG based network patterns (ENP).

Another work proposed by Pandey & Seeja [27] uses the EEG data for recognizing emotional activity in which a deep belief network (DBN) is employed for a semi-supervised learning from signal patterns. With this aim, discrete Wavelet coefficients are extracted using Daubechies 8 across all frequency bands to represent the degree of correlation between the signal under analysis and the wavelet function at different instances of time. Their approach obtained maximum value of accuracy of 0.64 in the recognition task using the DEAP database.

As it can be seen in previous state of the art works, emotion recognition in EEG is still a matter of study nowadays, so this problem is far to be completely solved. For this reason the research in this field could better understand the brain activity related to emotions for their better understanding. On the other hand, it is noteworthy that the mentioned works employed a similar validation strategy called leave one subject group out (LOSGO) in comparison to other works in the same field. These approaches are presented in this work since this strategy demonstrates a higher suitability for realistic scenarios in contrast to classical K-fold cross validation, since data will not be provided for a new subject in a model performing in real life applications.

3   Methodology

In this section is described the proposed methodology to recognize emotions from EEG data. First, a preprocessing stage is performed with the aim of filter signals to clean from noise and normalize. Then a windowing stage is perform as a volumetric framing with the purpose of perform an analysis in the changes of time-frequency features of each window in the deep learning model. At this point, power spectral density (PSD) features are estimated using the welch method and spectrogram using consecutive fast Fourier transforms. Features were extracted in 5 frequency bands (delta 0.5–4 Hz, theta 4–8 Hz, alpha 8–12 Hz, beta 12–30 Hz, and gamma 30–100 Hz). Finally, after features extraction samples are introduced to the model to perform recognition. An overview on the employed strategy to recognize emotions from EEG signals is shown in Fig. 1.

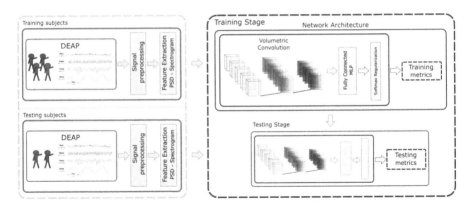

Fig. 1. Proposed strategy to perform emotion recognition in EEG signals.

3.1 Preprocessing Stage and Volumetric Framing

Before performing recognition from signals, a preprocessing stage is performed to clean up the signals from noise and undesirable frequencies added during the acquisition process. The preprocessing stage consist in down sampling original signals from 512 Hz to 128 Hz as in original work. Later, a band-pass filter from 0.5 to 45 Hz is employed, according to the five frequency bands used in which most brain activity is registered during an emotional event. Finally, the data was later segmented into 60 s per trial. The considered order of the acquired channels from the EEG device after segmented is shown in Table 1.

Table 1. Order of EEG channels considered for the experiments.

Num	Chan	Num	Chan	Num	Chan	Num	Chan
1	$Fp1$	9	$CP5$	17	$Fp2$	25	$C4$
2	$AF3$	10	$CP1$	18	$AF4$	26	$T8$
3	$F3$	11	$P3$	19	Fz	27	$CP6$
4	$F7$	12	$P7$	20	$F4$	28	$CP2$
5	$FC5$	13	$PO3$	21	$F8$	29	$P4$
6	$FC1$	14	$O1$	22	$FC6$	30	$P8$
7	$C3$	15	Oz	23	$FC2$	31	$PO4$
8	$T7$	16	Pz	24	Cz	32	$O2$

At this point, a windowing-based strategy is employed with the aim of generate a new dimension in which the cumulus of small window belonging to a signal create a volumetric space in which could be differentiated the changes among each consecutive frame. The windowing strategy consist in splitting each signal into 3 s windows with no overlapping percentage. For instance, in the case of 60 s signals, 20 sub-samples are extracted after the windowing strategy. Additionally, each sub-sample is considered as a novel dimension for the learning model; whereby, they are labeled according to the main sample the window is extracted from. After this procedure, features are extracted from each sub-sample before establish the learning model. It is noteworthy that the order of channels for the EEG signals is preserved after this stage and no mixtures are performed among channels during this phase.

3.2   Feature Extraction Using PSD and Spectrogram

With the aim of extracting features to effectively recognize significant differences among sub-samples extracted from signals in brain activity, two main strategies are performed for feature extraction in time and frequency domains. First, a power spectral density (PSD) from each sub-sample is performed using Welch's method based in averaging consecutive Fourier transform of small windows [30]. For the PSD features, the Welch method is selected since it improves the accuracy of the classic periodogram in the case that EEG signals are non-stationary and they are constantly varying over time according to brain activity. For instance, the classic periodogram extraction which is dependent of stationary signals will extract biased features containing a significant variance among them. However, the averaging of subsequent extracted periodograms, considered by the Welch's method for each window; reduces significantly the variance of the extracted density estimation, allowing to perform a more realistic spectral analysis for the signals.

Nevertheless, the averaging windows implies a cost in the signal analysis, concerning the frequency resolution employed to perform the Fourier transform. The frequency resolution for the Welch's method is defined as shown in Eq. 1, in which F_s is the sampling frequency of the signal, N the total number of samples and T the duration, in seconds, of the signal. However, as it can be seen in equation, despite the frequency resolution could be determined in terms of sampling frequency and number of samples; it can be reduced to the last term $(1/T)$. For instance the biggest the time of the window is perform, a lower frequency resolution would be achieved for the analysis. Therefore, an optimal window length must be considered to encompass enough information before PSD extraction. In our case, a window of length of the smallest interest frequency is selected $(0.5\,Hz)$, then a window of 2 s is employed. This configuration allowed to extract a 129 PSD features with their respective frequencies.

$$Freq\_resolution = \frac{F_s}{N} = \frac{F_s}{F_s T} = \frac{1}{T} \tag{1}$$

On the other hand, spectrogram is a bidimensional representation of a EEG signal in which is represented the change in the frequencies over time. This allows to represent whether there is more energy in an specific time interval. For instance, the relationships about variations among time-frequency in a window sub-sample in an EEG signal is spatially represented in a 2D space. The spectrogram is estimated taking small windows of the signal in which the discrete

Fourier transform (DFT) is performed. Taking the DFT of subsequent windows of the entire signal will show the frequency content over the entire time period. Besides, taking the DFT over a short period of will provide a local snapshot in time of the frequency content of the signal during that short time period. This process allowed the extraction of 129 features. After extracting PSD and spectrogram from sub-samples, they are merged and organized as three-dimensional arrays in which the first and second dimensions correspond to PSD and third one to spectrogram. The three-dimensional arrays are then, inputs to the learning model for recognition.

3.3   Recognizing Intensity and Intention of Emotions in EEG Signals

The recognition of intensity and intention of the affective content in the EEG signals means to identify their arousal and valence levels respectively, according to the Russell emotional model. This purpose, two learning models are proposed for each recognition problem. Both approaches are designed to perform using the same amount of data, and their difference lays in the labeling which depends on the arousal or valence quadrant they belong to. In this sense, as volumetric analysis from the extracted features is performed using 3D convolutions. The purpose of convolving the volume extracted from signals through the network layers is to analyze the data taking into account the time-frequency features between each window of the signal to find different recognition patterns. Similar to conventional neural networks, convolutional layers have also trainable weights and biases which are optimized across epochs in the network. The Eq. 2 describe the response for the volumetric convolution, of each signal $f(f[x, y, z])$ to a filter $h(h[x, y, z])$ when it is displaced $u([u, v, w])$ spaces. As it is described in Eq. 2, the displacement of the filter is performed in the three dimensions, which segments correspond to time-frequency features extracted. For instance, the volumetric convolution will preserve the most relevant components of each subsequent of features, corresponding to the same frequency range in different windows. Then, after fully displace the filter through all volume, this representation will contain the most relevant frequency patterns across all windows in a specific frequency range.

$$f[x, y, z] * h[x, y, z] = \sum_u \sum_v \sum_w f[u, v, w] \times h[x - u, y - v, z - w] \quad (2)$$

Considering this, in both cases the volumetric convolution is employed in a deep learning network to extract most significant representations of extracted features. After this, a conventional multilayer perceptron (MLP) is used to perform the classification of previous extracted representations. The proposed architecture for valence recognition in this work is composed by 4 convolutional layers with different kernel sizes (128, 32, 16, 8 subsequently), strides of 2 across all dimensions, zero padding ("same"), rectified liner activation ("relu") [26] and a Ridge Regression regularization ("l2") with 0.01 factor. After this, a MLP is employed with different number of units (512, 256, 128, 64, 32 subsequently) and rectified liner activation ("relu"). In both cases, Glorot Xavier initializer is used [18]. Same model architecture is used to recognize arousal in EEG signals.

Finally, the network parameters are optimized during the training stage using the stochastic gradient descent based algorithm, Adaptive Moment Estimation (Adam) [19]. Adam optimizer consists in momentum-based gradients updating (mean and variance) considering gradients initialization and small decaying rates during the training stage. These both considerations significantly improve parameters optimization, increase performance and avoid divergence in the network. In the case of the proposed model, the learning rate used is $1e^{-5}$.

3.4 The DEAP Database and Experimental Framework

For the implementation of the algorithms, a database is used that contains information extracted from EEG signals for the analysis of human affective states (the DEAP database [20]), provided by Queen Mary University in London. In this, EEG and other peripheral physiological signals of 32 participants are registered, of which fifty percent are women and the rest are men. In this dataset, 40 segments of a minute duration from music videos are used as visual stimuli to evoke the clearest emotional reactions, according to each of the quadrants of Russell's valence-arousal model, which has been widely used for the quantitative description of emotions. The 40 music videos were selected according to Last.fm emotional labels. In addition, the videos were also evaluated by at least 14 volunteers, qualifying on a discrete 9-point scale the valence, arousal and dominance each. The EEG signals were recorded using a Biosemi ActiveTwo system with a sampling frequency of 512 Hz with 32 active AgCl electrodes. Subsequently, at the end of each test the participants made a self-assessment of the level of arousal, valence, liking, and dominance that each video evoked.

From the original signals, preprocessing, volumetric framing and feature extraction stages are performed. After these stages, a total number of samples of 1280 were extracted. From these number of samples, a validation strategy called leave one subject group out (LOSGO) were considered. This strategy consist in separate a number of samples from the original total of samples considering the subject the signals are extracted from. This contrast to the classical bootstrap or K-fold cross validation since they considered random number of samples indistinct to the subject they belong to. This feature would produce a bias in the recognition task and an increase in the performance due to the train split could contain several segments (windows sub-samples) belonging to a signal of which other segments are also in the test split. Besides, it could be also possible to find signals from one subject in the train and test split; which could introduce other bias that increase overfitting in the model during the parameters optimization. The LOSGO validation ensures that the segments of signals extracted from a subject are not going to be mixed in the train and test splits; besides it also assures that none sample from the one subject is going to be present in both train and test splits. This validation strategy is more suitable for avoiding nonindependence in realistic scenarios, in which the models will have to perform recognition in data extracted from novel subjects or other data sources [14].

From the original number of samples (32 subjects), approximate 10% of them were separated for testing purposes (4 subjects), preserving the same gender distribution as described in the database (2 male and 2 females). The rest of the samples belonging to other subjects were taken for training the models. Additionally, in both learning models were considered the same data so there is no added bias for variability of the samples. Therefore, 1120 and 160 samples were taken as train and test sets respectively. After all the process samples of size (20, 32, 3, 129) were obtained. To organize the samples to analyze the changes among the 32 EEG signals, dimensions are squeezed so a final sample dimension is (32, 20, 3, 129) before volumetric convolution.

Finally, for the labeling process according to each experiment, samples were tagged considering the original continue label from the database. In case of valence recognition, all samples with a higher value of 5.0 are considered as high valence and all samples with a lower value of 5.0 are taken as low valence. In case of arousal, a similar process has been performed; however, when 5.0 value is used to bias high/low arousal a significant samples unbalance is introduced; which might conduct in overfitting for the learning model. For this reason, the mean value reported in the DEAP database paper for high arousal rating is employed (5.7), reducing the class unbalance.

4   Results and Discussion

In this section are presented the main results from the strategy employed in this work. First, results from both arousal and valence recognition models are presented in Tables 2 and 3 respectively. These values correspond to accuracy and $F1$-score obtained for each test subject. As it can be seen, best accuracy in both cases was obtained for participant 4 (female) in comparison with other subjects (0.85 and 0.75 for arousal and valence, respectively). Conversely, participant 2 (male) obtained the lowest accuracy scores (0.55 and 0.525 for arousal and valence, respectively). In this sense, it is also noteworthy that general performance is higher for female participants in comparison of male participants in both cases. This may lead in further studies considering gender dependency. Besides, for arousal and valence overall accuracy obtained was 0.6562 and 0.6375 respectively; besides the $F1$-scores of 0.64 and 0.62 respectively. It is noteworthy that in both cases, accuracy and $F1$-scores are closer to maximum values obtained per subject than lower values. On the other hand, in Fig. 2 is presented the confusion matrix for both valence (Fig. 2a) and arousal (Fig. 2b) recognition models. It can be seen that in both cases, best performance was obtained for recognizing low valence/arousal (0.77 and 0.83). Otherwise, in case of high valence/arousal, a high confusion rate is presented in valence model; however, in arousal model confusion rate is quite more balanced for same modality.

Additionally, in Table 4 is presented the performance comparison with other state of the art works. In this sense, the comparison metric employed was the overall accuracy for arousal/valence recognition. As it ca be seen, the proposed approach obtained better performance than other state of the art works

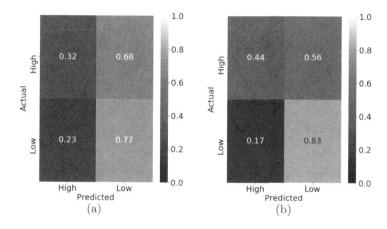

Fig. 2. Confusion matrix for valence

Table 2. Arousal scores for test group of participants (accuracy = 0.656, F1-score = 0.64)

	Accuracy	F1-score
Participant 1 (M)	0.575	0.57
Participant 2 (M)	0.55	0.55
Participant 3 (F)	0.65	0.64
Participant 4 (F)	0.85	0.80

[22,23,27,33]. However, in case of Yang et al. [32], performance comparison obtained was −0.034; nevertheless, this result was obtained using only 2 sub-joint of features (PSD and spectrogram) in comparison with the 10 sub-joint of features extracted in this work. This means that discriminative features obtained across the volumetric convolutional layers obtained a better representation of the signals using less non-linear features. Besides, Deep learning architectures allow to adapt their filters according to the input data. The adaptive features enable to obtain different representations depending on the network initialization, regulation and others. Therefore, an optimization stage for tuning these parameters could increase performance recognition in both models.

Finally, it is important to remark that performance comparison have been realized with these works, and other works such as [7,31]; which have obtained significant results have not been included since their performance is based in a different experimental conditions. In such works, the classical K-fold cross validation is employed, conversely to LOSGO validation used in this work. For instance; they have been excluded from comparison. As mentioned previously, the consideration of LOSGO validation has been taken into account since this validation is more suitable for avoiding non-independence in realistic scenarios in which models would have to perform recognition in EEG data extracted from novel data sources or completely unknown participants [14].

Table 3. Valence scores for test group of participants (accuracy = 0.637, $F1$-score = 0.62)

	Accuracy	F1-score
Participant 1 (M)	0.625	0.60
Participant 2 (M)	0.525	0.53
Participant 3 (F)	0.625	0.60
Participant 4 (F)	0.75	0.79

Table 4. Performance comparison of proposed approach with other state of the art works

Work	Accuracy
Yang et al. [32]	0.68
Pandey & Seeja [27]	0.637
Li et al. [22]	0.62
Li et al. [23]	0.61
Zhang et al. [33]	0.576
Proposed approach	0.646

5   Conclusions

In this work, an approach for emotion recognition from EEG signals have been proposed. The proposed strategy consist in a time-frequency analysis from PSD and spectrogram features extracted from original signals, in which a windowing approach is employed to generate a volumetric dimension to analyze changes across features in extracted windows of the full signal. After the volumetric implementation from original signals, two different deep learning models have been proposed to recognize arousal and valence; taking advantage of the volumetric feature generated. In all models have been employed a public, available and well known database (DEAP); and they were evaluated using a leave one subject group out (LOSGO). LOSGO validation was employed in this work, conversely to classical K-fold cross validation since LOSGO is more suitable for realistic scenarios in which EEG data from a new participant have never been seen for the model.

The results obtained for the arousal and valence models achieve significant performance in comparison with other recent state of the art works. Additionally, results have not surpass performance in a single work; however, the amount of features employed in this work in comparison is significantly less; which demonstrates the suitability of the model for the recognition problem. Besides, the adaptive filters from the deep learning model, which obtain adaptive features; adjust their parameters among different interactions and they could increase performance in the models.

As future works, several perspectives could be considered. First, a further study could be conducted considering a gender dependency. This, considered the differences between the results obtain for female and male, in which female participant obtained better performance in both arousal/valence cases. Second, an optimization strategy could be developed, considering different parameters such as initialization, batch size, learning rate, among others with the aim of increase performance. Third, the window length for generating the volumetric dimension of time-frequency features could be evaluated, in which different sizes are employed to outperform results. Fourth, a further study in the influence of the EEG channels ordering could be conducted with the aim of discovering the brain areas in which high/low arousal/valence activation is higher.

Acknoledgements. This work was supported by the Grupo de investigación e Innovación Ambiental (GIIAM) from the Institución Universitaria Pascual Bravo, under the research projects *RI201904* and *RI201903*.

References

1. Aranha, R.V., Corrêa, C.G., Nunes, F.L.: Adapting software with affective computing: a systematic review. IEEE Trans. Affect. Comput. (2019)
2. Balducci, F., Grana, C., Cucchiara, R.: Affective level design for a role-playing videogame evaluated by a brain-computer interface and machine learning methods. Vis. Comput. **33**(4), 413–427 (2017)
3. Barrett, L.F.: Solving the emotion paradox: categorization and the experience of emotion. Pers. Soc. Psychol. Rev. **10**(1), 20–46 (2006). https://doi.org/10.1207/s15327957pspr1001_2
4. Bartsch, A., Hartmann, T.: The role of cognitive and affective challenge in entertainment experience. Commun. Res. **44**(1), 29–53 (2017)
5. Blascovich, J., Bailenson, J.: Infinite Reality: Avatars, Eternal Life, New Worlds, and the Dawn of the Virtual Revolution. William Morrow & Co, New York (2011)
6. Bur, A.M., Shew, M., New, J.: Artificial intelligence for the otolaryngologist: a state of the art review. Otolaryngol. Head Neck Surg. **160**(4), 603–611 (2019)
7. Chen, J., Zhang, P., Mao, Z., Huang, Y., Jiang, D., Zhang, Y.: Accurate EEG-based emotion recognition on combined features using deep convolutional neural networks. IEEE Access **7**, 44317–44328 (2019)
8. Colling, R., et al.: Artificial intelligence in digital pathology: a roadmap to routine use in clinical practice. J. Pathol. **249**(2), 143–150 (2019)
9. Craik, A., He, Y., Contreras-Vidal, J.L.: Deep learning for electroencephalogram (EEG) classification tasks: a review. J. Neural Eng. **16**(3), 031001 (2019). https://doi.org/10.1088/1741-2552/ab0ab5. https://doi.org/10.1088%2F1741-2552%2Fab0ab5
10. Ekman, P.: An argument for basic emotions. Cogn. Emot. **6**(3–4), 169–200 (1992)
11. Ekman, P., Friesen, W.V.: Constants across cultures in the face and emotion. J. Pers. Soc. Psychol. **17**(2), 124 (1971)
12. Ekman, P., Friesen, W.V.: Unmasking the face: A guide to recognizing emotions from facial clues (1975)
13. Ekman, P., Friesen, W.V.: Measuring facial movement. Environ. Psychol. Nonverbal Behav. **1**(1), 56–75 (1976)

14. Esterman, M., Tamber-Rosenau, B.J., Chiu, Y.C., Yantis, S.: Avoiding non-independence in fMRI data analysis: leave one subject out. Neuroimage **50**(2), 572–576 (2010)
15. Fonnegra, R.D., Díaz, G.M.: Speech emotion recognition based on a recurrent neural network classification model. In: Cheok, A.D., Inami, M., Romão, T. (eds.) ACE 2017. LNCS, vol. 10714, pp. 882–892. Springer, Cham (2018). https://doi.org/10.1007/978-3-319-76270-8_59
16. Fonnegra, R.D., Díaz, G.M.: Deep learning based video spatio-temporal modeling for emotion recognition. In: Kurosu, M. (ed.) HCI 2018, Part I. LNCS, vol. 10901, pp. 397–408. Springer, Cham (2018). https://doi.org/10.1007/978-3-319-91238-7_32
17. Fonnegra, R.D., Díaz, G.M.: Speech emotion recognition integrating paralinguistic features and auto-encoders in a deep learning model. In: Kurosu, M. (ed.) HCI 2018, Part I. LNCS, vol. 10901, pp. 385–396. Springer, Cham (2018). https://doi.org/10.1007/978-3-319-91238-7_31
18. Glorot, X., Bengio, Y.: Understanding the difficulty of training deep feedforward neural networks. In: Proceedings of the Thirteenth International Conference on Artificial Intelligence and Statistics, pp. 249–256 (2010)
19. Kingma, D.P., Ba, J.: Adam: A method for stochastic optimization. arXiv preprint arXiv:1412.6980 (2014)
20. Koelstra, S., et al.: Deap: a database for emotion analysis; using physiological signals. IEEE Trans. Affect. Comput. **3**(1), 18–31 (2011)
21. Krizhevsky, A., Sutskever, I., Hinton, G.E.: Imagenet classification with deep convolutional neural networks. In: Advances in Neural Information Processing Systems, pp. 1097–1105 (2012)
22. Li, P., et al.: EEG based emotion recognition by combining functional connectivity network and local activations. IEEE Trans. Biomed. Eng. **66**(10), 2869–2881 (2019)
23. Li, X., Zhang, P., Song, D., Yu, G., Hou, Y., Hu, B.: EEG based emotion identification using unsupervised deep feature learning (2015)
24. Lin, Y., et al.: EEG-based emotion recognition in music listening. IEEE Trans. Biomed. Eng. **57**(7), 1798–1806 (2010). https://doi.org/10.1109/TBME.2010.2048568
25. Mehrabian, A.: Framework for a comprehensive description and measurement ofemotional states. Genetic, social, and general psychology monographs (1995)
26. Nair, V., Hinton, G.E.: Rectified linear units improve restricted boltzmann machines. In: Proceedings of the 27th International Conference on Machine Learning (ICML-10), pp. 807–814 (2010)
27. Pandey, P., Seeja, K.R.: Subject-independent emotion detection from EEG signals using deep neural network. In: Bhattacharyya, S., Hassanien, A.E., Gupta, D., Khanna, A., Pan, I. (eds.) International Conference on Innovative Computing and Communications. LNNS, vol. 56, pp. 41–46. Springer, Singapore (2019). https://doi.org/10.1007/978-981-13-2354-6_5
28. Plutchik, R.: The Circumplex as a General Model of the Structure of Emotions and Personality. American Psychological Association, Washington, DC (1997)
29. Russell, J.A.: A circumplex model of affect. J. Pers. Soc. Psychol. **39**(6), 1161 (1980)
30. Welch, P.: The use of fast fourier transform for the estimation of power spectra: a method based on time averaging over short, modified periodograms. IEEE Trans. Audio Electroacoust. **15**(2), 70–73 (1967). https://doi.org/10.1109/TAU.1967.1161901

31. Xu, H., Plataniotis, K.N.: Affective states classification using EEG and semi-supervised deep learning approaches. In: 2016 IEEE 18th International Workshop on Multimedia Signal Processing (MMSP), pp. 1–6. IEEE (2016)
32. Yang, F., Zhao, X., Jiang, W., Gao, P., Liu, G.: Cross-subject emotion recognition using multi-method fusion from high-dimensional features. Front. Comput. Neurosci. **13**, 53 (2019)
33. Zhang, J., Chen, M., Zhao, S., Hu, S., Shi, Z., Cao, Y.: Relieff-based EEG sensor selection methods for emotion recognition. Sensors **16**(10), 1558 (2016)

Automatic Exercise Recognition Based on Kinect Sensor for Telerehabilitation

Fernando Velasco[ID] and Fabián Narváez[(✉)][ID]

GIB&B Research Group, Department of Biomedicine,
Universidad Politécnica Salesiana, Quito, Ecuador
fnarvaeze@ups.edu.ec

Abstract. Telerehabilitation is considered an alternative to traditional therapeutic rehabilitation process for restoring some human functional movements from long distances by using a spectrum of emerging technologies, such as telecommunication technologies and Kinect-based exergames strategies, among others. Its efficacy and clinical usefulness depend on different tools introduced for monitoring and executing exercise sessions for the user. However, these telerehabilitation systems are limited to act as videogames without a quantitative analysis of the rehabilitation progress, in real-time. In this paper, a novel kinect-based exercises recognition strategy is presented, which allows a proper execution of the rehabilitation routines based on clinical measures of the joints of body, in real-time. For doing that, a skeleton-based human action recognition scheme is introduced using a Kinect sensor. The proposed method is composed of two stages: First one, it allows to identify both defined postures, the initial and final pose, respectively, which are established during an exercise execution. The second one, it compares trajectories of body segments involved in the same exercise. Our proposed method was two-fold validated using both, the posture and exercise recognition strategies, respectively. For our evaluation process, a set of 25 healthy volunteers was used. The obtained results demonstrate that the estimated joint orientations from each body segment are effective to represent clinical measures, allowing to improve the efficiency for monitoring the user's performance during the execution of defined exercises and reducing the required computational cost in these kind of strategies. Therefore, the proposed method could be used in clinical applications and rehabilitation analysis of impaired persons.

Keywords: Telerehabilitation · Exercise recognition · Posture classification · Kinect sensor

1 Introduction

In the last years, telerehabilitation has emerged as a technological alternative to traditional face-to-face therapy among the patient and physicians [5,10,18]. Particularly, these telerehabilitation strategies are applied to people who have been

© Springer Nature Switzerland AG 2020
F. R. Narváez et al. (Eds.): SmartTech-IC 2019, CCIS 1154, pp. 312–324, 2020.
https://doi.org/10.1007/978-3-030-46785-2_25

affected with some kind of locomotor impairment caused by different physical or neurological pathologies, but they present difficulties for accessing to functional rehabilitation programs in specialized clinics [3,14,18]. Hence, telerehabilitation system have been developed by including several emerging technologies for capturing, monitoring and visualizing relevant information related to the patient's movements from long distances. For which, some motion capture strategies have been introduced for acquiring the patient's movements, which are based on either technologies, computer vision and wearable sensors approaches, respectively [1,16]. Several efforts have been conducted for developing approaches to guarantee a suitable exercises execution by the telerehabilitation users, among these, interactive interfaces with graphical environments in 3D, allowing to visualize how an exercise must be executed and how the patient execute it. Basically, telerehabilitation systems provide different sequence of human movements, which are integrated on 3D avatars (graphical human models), which are design to be mimic by the patients. These movements are recorded and stored by therapists and they are used as an execution guide for motivating patients to perform exercises (eg. exergames). Currently, some low-cost technologies for human motion capture have been included such as, Kinect cameras [2,20,23], WII sensors [11] and inertial movement unities (IMUs) [8,14,15], which have shown to be more feasibility and a cost-effective option. Among these, Kinect-based telerehabilitation systems are the most common in the state-of-the-art [7,16,23] and these have been applied with several kind of physical disabilities, due to its easy integration with programming technologies [1]. However, these systems not quantify the performance and rehabilitation progress according to some kinematic aspects related to the patient's movements during the exercises execution. This fundamental problem have limited the use of these kinect-based system in real clinic applications. Therefore, there exist a widely research area focused on the development of suitable computational tools for estimating the progress of exercise sessions during the use of telerehabiltation platforms.

2   Related Works

Several computational strategies have been proposed to solve this fundamental problem [6,9,22,24], by attempting to recognize the human exercise carried out by the user respect to some exercises defined by the rehabilitation schemes. Basically, this problem has been addressed as a comparison between movements captured from the user respect to the avatar's movements [3]. For which, several human activity recognition techniques have been included and reported in the literature [7,17,23], some strategies have been based on silhouette information extracted from the user by using Kinect cameras [19]. The human silhouette is extracted from depth maps generated of each video frame from the Kinect, then, different algorithms for pose estimation have been applied by using machine learning approaches [13]. However, these strategies require high computational costs, reducing their usefulness in real time applications [13]. On the other hand, several skeleton tracking approaches have been introduced for human exercises recognition [6]. In the same way, these strategies capture skeleton information from depth maps, which is defined by each joint's position captured by Kinect sensor [24]. Once, the joints skeleton are defined, a feature extraction process is carried out, finding to describe any kinematic aspects from human joint such as: joint angles, joint positions and its orientations, among other. Thus, skeleton data are classified by specialized algorithms to recognize and categorize human poses [13]. In order to determine human exercises recognition, some works have included also information related to specific trajectories extracted from both, body joints and the limbs involved in an exercise routine. Accordingly, these schemes have combined both approaches based on pose estimation and skeleton tracking schemes, respectively, which have shown promising results in real time applications [3].

This paper presents a novel Kinect-based strategy for automatic exercises recognition during rehabilitation routines, for which some clinical measures of the joints of body are described, such as flexion, extension, adduction and abduction, respectively. The proposed method involve two strategies: a human pose classification and a trajectories recognition strategy, respectively. The first one, it allows to identify the initial and final pose during an specific exercise routine, and the second one, it compares the trajectories of joint based on quaternion information by extracting from body segments involved in the same exercise. Unlike others approaches, we do not only attempt to exactly compare the patient's poses in each video frame, instead we estimated the trajectories of each limb by using its position and orientation, allowing to improve the efficiency for monitoring the user's performance during the execution of exercises. This paper is organized as follows: after this introduction and related works, next section presents the proposed methods, then results are shown and last section discusses conclusions.

3   Methods

An overview of the proposed method is shown in Fig. 1. The method starts by assuming that a defined routine of exercise is associated to a 3D graphical model, namely the Avatar, which has been defined by therapists and stored in a database of exercises, previously. Then, the proposed method aims is to compare the patient's exercise respect to the defined routine by the avatar, providing a success level (score) as result of it. For doing that, a Kinect sensor captures the human skeleton from the patient as an structured chain of body segments, connecting the most important consecutive body joints, so, a features extraction process is carried out by using a quaternion representation. Once, skeleton data are obtained and characterized, the method herein proposed is able to identify both the beginning and end of the routine of an exercise, as well as the routine itself, for which it combines two strategies: a posture classification and a trajectory recognition strategies, respectively, as described below:

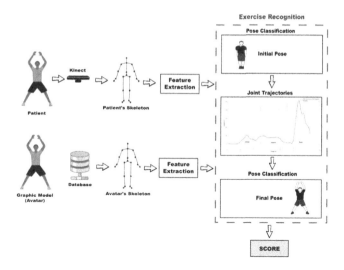

Fig. 1. Method overview.

3.1 Skeleton Features Extraction

Firstly, patient movements are captured using a Kinect camera, a low-cost RGB-Depth sensor introduced by Microsoft for human-computer interface applications. This technology provides videos based on depth imaging information with a resolution of 320 × 240 pixels and captured to a maximum frequency of 30 Hz, approximately. Then, a skeleton extraction process is applied by using a distance map approach from the displayed silhouette of each video frame [19]. Thus, a skeletal structure is defined, in which each node is a body joint, obtaining a skeleton with a total of 20 joints described by 3D joints and these are referenced in a coordinate system (x, y and z axes), whose origin is considered the center of the plane parallel to the captured image and intersecting with the Kinect, as is described in [22]. In order to extract some features invariant to both location (translation-rotation) and body size (scale) of patients, information related to joint orientation, more than its position, is used for feature extraction process. For doing this, our feature extraction process uses joint orientation of each joint relative to user's coordinate for describing human movements. Thus, the coordinate system obtained by Kinect camera are translated into another coordinate system, whose origin is in the center of the patient's hip. So, a rotational representation based on quaternion information is carried out. This rotational representation defines joint orientation using quaternions, which are a compact representation of rotations in 3D space respect to Euler angles. In general terms, a quaternion q_0 is a 4 dimensions tuples defined as $q_0 = (w, x, y, z)$, with a norm of 1, where w represents one real dimension and (x, y, z) represent three imaginary dimensions with unit length i, j, k and orthogonal one another. Then, a quaternion is shown as:

$$q_0 = w + x_i + y_j + z_k \tag{1}$$
$$|q_0| = w^2 + x^2 + y^2 + z^2 = 1 \tag{2}$$

Usually, quaternions show a rotation about the (x, y, z) axis by an angle α defined as: $\alpha = 2cos^{-1}w = 2sin^{-1}\sqrt{x^2 + y^2 + z^2}$. Therefore, positions of each body joint obtained as a representation based on Euler angles by the Kinect SDK, are converted to quaternion using method described in [12]. In the same way, these obtained quaternions are used to compute some anatomical angles (eg. flexion angle and extension angles, among others) of the limbs, which are defined by connecting consecutive joint on the skeletal segments. These angles are computed as following:

Given two connected joints defined by quaternions q_0 and q_1, which are represented as $q_0 = (w_0, x_0, y_0, z_0)$ and $q_1 = (w_1, x_1, y_1, z_1)$, the angle between these quaternion is computed as: $\theta = 2cos^{-1}(q_0.q_1^*)$, where (*) is its complex conjugate. Finally, a feature vector is constructed by concatenating 19 quaternions extracted from the most relevant joint from skeleton, as well as, 13 joint angles computed from connected joints of body, which correspond to both left and right legs, as well as, to both left and right hands, and the Spine. Therefore, this feature vector constitutes our human pose description.

3.2   Human Posture Classification

Once that pose descriptor is obtained, this is used as input data for a classifier scheme. This classification approach compares the obtained descriptor respect to previously annotated pose descriptors stored in a database of exercises. In order to compare two pose descriptors, V_i and V_2, a similarity measurement based on the distance between them is used, for which both pose features, quaternions and anatomical angles of the limb, are included in this metric defined as:

$$dist(V_1, V_2) = quaterdist(V_1, V_2) + angdist(V_1, V_2) \tag{3}$$

where $quaterdist(V_i, V_2)$ are quaternions extracted from the joints, and $angdist(V_i, V_2)$ correspond to the angles between connected joints in the pose. Finally, these metrics are computed independently. In the case of the distance between quaternions, it corresponds to distance between orientations provided that the quaternions are fairly close to each other. This is because that comparing quaternions, q and $-q$, always represent the same orientation, even though the distance between them is any value. Therefore, the angle θ of rotation required to get from one orientation to another is given by the formula:

$$\theta = cos^{-1}(2\langle q_1, q_2 \rangle^2 - 1) \tag{4}$$

where $\langle q_1, q_2 \rangle$ denotes the inner product of the quaternions. This formula is obtained from the double-angle cosine, where the angle between orientations is twice the angle between unit quaternions. In this work, the similarity measurement between quaternions is based on the concept related to difference between rotations, defined as:

$$dist(q_1, q_2) = 1 - \langle q_1, q_2 \rangle^2 = (1 - cos\theta)/2 \tag{5}$$

where q_1 and q_2 are quaternions of the same joint but from two different postures undergo comparison. In particular, this metric gives 0 whenever the quaternions represent the same orientation, and it gives 1 whenever the two orientations are 180° apart. Therefore, the similarity metric for joint orientation between two feature vectors is defined as:

$$quaterdist(V_i, V_j) = \sqrt{\sum_{k=1}^{20} |V_1(q_k) - V_2(q_k)|} \tag{6}$$

where (q_k) is the quaternion k of descriptor V_x. On the other hand, similarity measurement for joint angles, as features of human pose, is computed by:

$$angdist(V_i, V_j) = \sum_{k=21}^{33} |V_1(q_k) - V_2(q_k)| \tag{7}$$

Once these similarity metrics are computed, these are added to provide a general similarity measurement, which is finally normalized between 0 and 1, respectively. In order to classify a pose descriptor as a appropriate or not, a level of acceptance is defined using a (t_h) threshold value, which is applied during a sequential search of postures previously annotated in the database. In addition, these annotated postures define the beginning and end of an exercise routine. Therefore, this classification strategy has been implemented to run during the whole exercise routine for classifying the initial and final poses during an exercise.

3.3 Trajectory Recognition

In this stage, the proposed method aims to recognize if the exercise itself is well performed. Thus, the trajectories defined by joint angles of the limbs involved in an exercise routine are analyzed and compared to the angular trajectories of the same limbs stored in the database for that exercise. In order to compare trajectories in real time, this strategy allows to periodically compare performed and stored angular trajectories for each limb. In fact, this angular trajectory comparison is carried out until the user have not finished the exercise completely. A strategy that besides it allows to determine how a limb performed the movement. So, the angular trajectory of each limb involved in an exercise is computed by applying Eq. (4) as it is above described. Figure 2 illustrates angular trajectories of both, upper and lower limbs, respectively, which are involved in an exercise routine. In this case, the graphs are drawing by starting the user's movement from a T-pose. In order to compare the performed and stored angular trajectory of limb i, a similarity value w_i is obtained based on distance between them.

Then, a threshold value (T_{thd}) is used to define if this trajectory is correct or not. The distance between trajectories is obtained by using a similarity measurement which is based on the dynamic time warping (DTW) approach, as is described in [21].

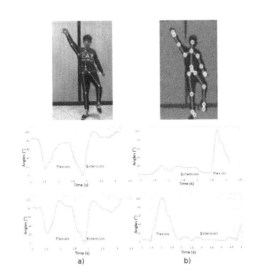

Fig. 2. Example of trajectories of body joint during an exercise routine. Panel (a) illustrates the trajectory for flexion-extension angle of left limbs. Panel (b) illustrates the trajectory for flexion-extension angle of right limbs.

DTW is a well-known algorithm, which has been used in areas such as speech recognition, it has shown being efficient in the time-series similarity measure, minimizing the effects of shifting and distortion in time by applying a warp path to detect similar shapes with different phases [21]. Then, a partial distance (k) into trajectories i and j, is represents by $dist(s_i, s_j)$, which is defined into a warp path $w_{k_{i,j}} = dist(s_{ik}, s_{jk})$, So a global DTW metric is obtained, as is shown in [21]:

$$dist(w) = \sum_{k=1}^{n} dist(s_{ik}, s_{jk}) \tag{8}$$

where n is the number of partial trajectories into a specific trajectory of a limb undergo comparison. On the other hand, to detect when an exercise is finished, the pose classification is again applied for detect the final pose associated to the end of movements. This strategy is also periodically applied during each trajectory recognition. Finally, our proposed method provide a success level or score by adding all distances computed of the trajectory recognition process for each limb involved in the exercise, which is defined by: $score = \sqrt{w_1^2 + w_2^2 + ... + w_n^2}$, where n is the number of analyzed limbs.

4   Experimental Results

The performance of our proposed method was two-fold evaluated. First evaluation allows to determine its ability for classifying both the initial and final postures during an exercise sequence, which were previously annotated and stored in the database. Second evaluation allows to validate the ability for recognizing limbs trajectories when an exercise is executed, respectively. For doing that, our proposed method was implemented in a 3D graphic environment adapting two avatar, which were built using the well-known graphical tool, Blender software[1]. These graphical models were adapted to our motion capture strategy was based on a Kinect camera, as is illustrates in Fig. 3. Kinect data were captured to a sampling rate of 30 Hz. The experimental evaluation process was implemented on OpenFramework (C++ language) V10, running on a Linux PC with 2 Intel Quad Core i7 at 3.07 GHz and 8 GB of RAM.

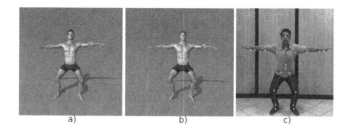

Fig. 3. Example of our motion capture scheme using 3D graphical environments (Avatar). Panel (a) corresponds to the avatar used to recreate exercises annotated and stored in database. Panel (b) illustrates the user's avatar used to duplicate the movements captured from the user. Panel (c) illustrates the user's skeleton captured by Kinect.

4.1   Posture Classification Assessment

For this evaluation, a training dataset of 600 postures was selected, annotated and stored in a database. These postures were extracted from 5 different kind of exercises, selecting 100 postures for each class of exercise, respectively. Thus, we defined 5 classes of posture according to the relevant position of limbs such as: (ExS) Upper limbs extended above of head, (InT) trunk leaned to a side, (SBH) Squats with the arms in horizontal position, (FBPo) Flexion of opposite arm and leg, respectively, (Fx-ExS) flexion and extension of upper limbs. Finally, another 100 different postures to the 5 exercises class were annotates as "unknown" posture to determine whether a posture is classified as correct or incorrect. Examples of our posture classes are illustrate in Fig. 4.

---

[1] www.blender.org.

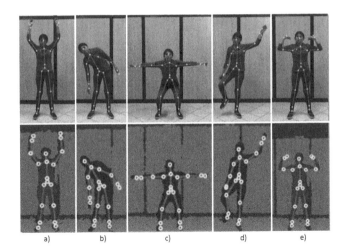

Fig. 4. Different kind of exercises with their corresponding positions. The panel (a) corresponds to the (ExS) exercise. Panel (b) corresponds to the (InT) exercise. Panel (c) illustrates the (SBH) exercise, Panel (c) illustrates (FBPo) exercise, and Panel (e) corresponds to (Fx-ExS) exercise

Firstly, training dataset was used to determine the best threshold value (t_h) for classifying postures, which was determined by applying a 10-fold cross-validation scheme for classifying the training dataset, reporting an average accuracy of 97%, approximately, with a normalized threshold value of $(t_h = 0.7)$ between 0 and 1. Table 1 presents the best results obtained for classifying the training set by using the normalized threshold value of $(t_h = 0.7)$.

Table 1. Confusion matrix for threshold value $(t_h = 0.7)$

	Unknown	ExS	InT	SBH	FBPo	Fx-ExS
Unknown	**91**	2	4	2	0	1
ExS	2	**96**	1	1	0	0
InT	0	0	**100**	0	0	0
SBH	1	2	0	**96**	0	1
FBPo	2	0	0	2	**93**	3
Fx-ExS	0	0	2	0	0	**98**

Once, the threshold value was established, it is used to classify a new dataset with 60 postures, which is used as the dataset for testing. In the same way, these postures were extracted from the same kind of exercises above defined and annotated, which were executed by 5 volunteers. This test dataset include 10 postures for each exercise classes, including the class defined as unknown posture, respectively. The results obtained can be evidenced in Table 2, reporting an accuracy rate of 87%, approximately, for classifying the test dataset.

Table 2. Confusion matrix of the test dataset (60 postures)

	Unknown	ExS	InT	SBH	FBPo	Fx-ExS
Unknown	**7**	1	1	0	0	1
ExS	1	**8**	0	1	0	0
InT	0	0	**10**	0	0	0
SBH	0	1	0	**9**	0	0
FBPo	0	0	1	0	**8**	1
Fx-ExS	0	0	0	0	0	**10**

These obtained results show the discriminative capacity of our posture descriptor for classification tasks, reporting a suitable performance for the (InT) posture with an accuracy rate of 100%. However, its performance for classifying the (FBPo) posture decrease up to an accuracy rate of 80%, approximately.

4.2   Trajectory Recognition Assessment

For this evaluation task, a training set of trajectories was extracted and annotated for each class of exercise. This training dataset contains 10 trajectories by each exercise, obtaining an entire dataset with 50 trajectories, which were extracted from the 5 exercises above defined as: the (ExS), (InT), (SBH), (FBPo) and (Fx-ExS) exercises, respectively. Each trajectory correspond to values of joint angles measured each joint of body involved during a routine of exercise. Therefore, the complete trajectory information of each exercise was stored in the database, as .csv files. In order to determine if a trajectory is recognized as correct or incorrect, a threshold value (T_{thd}) was also computed by applying our proposed trajectory recognition scheme. For which, the well-known 10-fold cross validation strategy was used over our training dataset. This approach split the dataset into groups of 10 subsets, where a subset is used as test dataset and the remainder subsets are used to obtain the best parameter of any model. In our particular case, the model parameter is the (T_{thd}) threshold value. The obtained results present an average accuracy of 96%, approximately, for a normalized threshold value of $(T_{thd} = 0.8)$, as is shown in Table 3.

The obtained results shown the ability of the method to recognize different trajectories defined by joint angle values from the limbs associated to any routine of exercise. In the same way, this results shown the performance for recognizing trajectories as an incorrect execution of movements. Thus, the threshold value was established, which is used to completely evaluate our exercise recognition scheme, such as is defined below:

Table 3. Confusion matrix of trajectory recognition for threshold of $(T_{thd} = 0.8)$

	Defined as correct	Defined as incorrect
Correct trajectories	96.83%	3.17%
Incorrect trajectories	8.50%	91.50%

4.3 Exercise Recognition Evaluation

Finally, the performance for recognizing exercises was evaluated. For doing that, a group of 25 volunteers were evaluated. These volunteers did not report any musculoskeletal problems. The group of volunteers was constituted for 7 men and 8 women (among 22 and 27 years old). Their limbs trajectories corresponded to flexion-extension angles of joints. Each subject performed 5 repetitions of each exercise (from the 5 exercise above defined as: (ExS) Upper limbs extended above of head, (InT) trunk leaned to a side, (SBH) Squats with the arms in horizontal position, (FBPo) Flexion of opposite arm and leg, respectively, (Fx-ExS)). In order to establish the beginning of an exercise routine, a standard T-position was defined for each exercise, aligning the feet respect to shoulder in biped position, with the arms in horizontal position. So, a periodic comparison between the avatar and the volunteer descriptors was carried out and analyzing to a frequency of 30 frames per second, respectively. This is due to intrinsic characteristics of the Kinect sensor. Once, the beginning of the exercise was identified, sagittal plane was used for capturing flexion-extension angle of joints from both upper and lower limbs involved during the exercise routine. Finally, for ending the same exercise execution a final posture was defined for each exercise. The obtained results are shown in Table 4, reporting an average of accuracy of 100% for identifying exercises that involve movements of the patient's trunk. This is because that the our skeleton descriptor is built using its reference system located at the user's hip.

Table 4. Performance of exercise recognition for defined exercises

Exercises	Ident. as correct	Ident. as incorrect
ExS	93.8%	6.2%
InT	100%	0%
SBH	98.6%	1.4%
FBPo	93.9%	6.1%
Fx-ExS	98.4%	1.6%
General accuracy	**96.92%**	**3.08%**

5   Conclusions

This paper has shown a Kinect-based algorithm for monitoring rehabilitation exercises, which was based on two fundamental strategies for recognizing exercises, a pose classification scheme combined with a trajectory recognition approach, respectively. This proposed method allowed to identify the beginning and the end of a routine of exercise, as well as the movements, for which some anatomical angles from the limbs were used, breaking any traditional scheme based on a subjective evaluation by physiotherapists. In order to motivate the users of our rehabilitation scheme, the proposed method included 3D avatars to simulate rehabilitation sessions, making more enjoyable it use in each exercise execution and allowing the users to be aware of their rehabilitation progress. The results shown a discriminative capacity of the proposed pose descriptor when a classification task was carried out. Therefore, the feasibility of the entire method was validated in a real scenario with 25 healthy volunteers, reporting an accuracy rate of 96%, which evidence that the method could be adequate for using in real clinical applications. In future works, we hope to implement our algorithm using specific rehabilitation programs for a particular locomotor disability, and validate its performance, as well as the users progress during the rehabilitation program.

References

1. Altilio, R., Liparulo, L., Panella, M., Proietti, A., Paoloni, M.: Multimedia and gaming technologies for telerehabilitation of motor disabilities. IEEE Technol. Soc. Mag. **34**(4), 23–30 (2015)
2. Antón, D., Goñi, A., Illarramendi, A., Torres-Unda, J.J., Seco, J.: KiReS: a Kinect-based telerehabilitation system. In: IEEE 15th International Conference on e-Health Networking, Applications and Services, pp. 444–448 (2013)
3. Antón, D., Goñi, A., Illarramendi, A.: Exercise recognition for Kinect-based telerehabilitation. Methods Inf. Med. **54**(02), 145–155 (2015)
4. Chen, L., Wei, H., Ferryman, J.: ReadingAct RGB-D action dataset and human action recognition from local features. Pattern Recogn. Lett. **50**, 159–169 (2014)
5. Chumbler, N.R., et al.: A home-based telerehabilitation randomized trial for stroke care: effects on falls self-efficacy and satisfaction with care. In: 2014 International Conference on Collaboration Technologies and Systems (CTS), pp. 436–440 (2014)
6. Cippitelli, E., Gasparrini, S., Gambi, E., Spinsante, S.: A human activity recognition system using skeleton data from RGBD sensors. Comput. Intell. Neurosci. **2016**, 1–14 (2016)
7. Da Gama, A., Fallavollita, P., Teichrieb, V., Navab, N.: Motor rehabilitation using Kinect: a systematic review. Games Health J. **4**(2), 123–135 (2015)
8. Deng, W., Papavasileiou, I., Qiao, Z., Zhang, W., Lam, K.Y., Han, S.: Advances in automation technologies for lower extremity neurorehabilitation: a review and future challenges. IEEE Rev. Biomed. Eng. **11**, 289–305 (2018)
9. Gal, N., Andrei, D., Nemes, D.I., Nadasan, E., Stoicu-Tivadar, V.: A Kinect based intelligent e-rehabilitation system in physical therapy. Stud. Health Technol. Inform. **210**, 489–493 (2015)

10. Jeong, I.C., Finkelstein, J.: Introducing telerehabilitation in patients with multiple sclerosis with significant mobility disability: pilot feasibility study. In: International Conference on Healthcare Informatics, pp. 69–75 (2015)
11. Li, K.F., Sevcenco, A.M.: A feasibility study on using low-cost gaming devices for rehabilitation. In: 27th International Conference on Advanced Information Networking and Applications Workshops, pp. 219–224 (2013)
12. Liu, X., Feng, X., Pan, S., Peng, J., Zhao, X.: Skeleton tracking based on Kinect camera and the application in virtual reality system. In: Proceedings of the 4th International Conference on Virtual Reality, ICVR 2018, pp. 21–25 (2018)
13. Liu, Y.S., Xu, Y., Li, S.: 2-D human pose estimation from images based on deep learning: a review. In: IEEE Advanced Information Management, Communicates, Electronic and Automation Control Conference (IMCEC), pp. 462–465 (2018)
14. Narváez, F., Arbito, F., Luna, C., Merchán, C., Cuenca, M.C., Díaz, G.M.: Kushkalla: a web-based platform to improve functional movement rehabilitation. In: Valencia-García, R., Lagos-Ortiz, K., Alcaraz-Mármol, G., Del Cioppo, J., Vera-Lucio, N., Bucaram-Leverone, M. (eds.) CITI 2017. CCIS, vol. 749, pp. 194–208. Springer, Cham (2017). https://doi.org/10.1007/978-3-319-67283-0_15
15. Narváez, F., Árbito, F., Proaño, R.: A quaternion-based method to IMU-to-body alignment for gait analysis. In: Duffy, V.G. (ed.) DHM 2018. LNCS, vol. 10917, pp. 217–231. Springer, Cham (2018). https://doi.org/10.1007/978-3-319-91397-1_19
16. Narváez, F., Marín-Castrillón, D.M., Cuenca, M.C., Latta, M.A.: Development and implementation of technologies for physical telerehabilitation in Latin America: a systematic review of literature, programs and projects. TecnoLógicas 20(40), 155–176 (2017)
17. Papadopoulos, G.T., Axenopoulos, A., Daras, P.: Real-time skeleton-tracking-based human action recognition using Kinect data. In: Gurrin, C., Hopfgartner, F., Hurst, W., Johansen, H., Lee, H., O'Connor, N. (eds.) MMM 2014. LNCS, vol. 8325, pp. 473–483. Springer, Cham (2014). https://doi.org/10.1007/978-3-319-04114-8_40
18. Perry, J.C., Ruiz-Ruano, J.A., Keller, T.: Telerehabilitation: toward a cost-efficient platform for post-stroke neurorehabilitation. In: IEEE International Conference on Rehabilitation Robotics, pp. 1–6 (2011)
19. Plantard, P., Auvinet, E., Pierres, A.S.L., Multon, F.: Pose estimation with a Kinect for ergonomic studies: evaluation of the accuracy using a virtual mannequin. Sensors 15, 1785–1803 (2015)
20. Rybarczyk, Y., Deters, J.K., Gonzalvo, A.A., Gonzalez, M., Villarreal, S., Esparza, D.: ePHoRt project: a web-based platform for home motor rehabilitation. In: Rocha, Á., Correia, A.M., Adeli, H., Reis, L.P., Costanzo, S. (eds.) WorldCIST 2017. AISC, vol. 570, pp. 609–618. Springer, Cham (2017). https://doi.org/10.1007/978-3-319-56538-5_62
21. Salvador, S., Chan, P.: FastDTW: toward accurate dynamic time warping in linear time and space. Intell. Data Anal. 11(5), 70–80 (2003)
22. Tupa, O., et al.: Motion tracking and gait feature estimation for recognising Parkinson's disease using MS Kinect. Biomed. Eng. Online 14(1), 97 (2015)
23. Webster, D., Celik, O.: Systematic review of Kinect applications in elderly care and stroke rehabilitation. J. NeuroEng. Rehabil. 11(1), 108 (2014)
24. Zhu, H., Pun, C.: Human action recognition with skeletal information from depth camera. In: 2013 IEEE International Conference on Information and Automation (ICIA), pp. 1082–1085 (2013)

Hand Angle Estimation Based on sEMG and Inertial Sensor Fusion

Alfredo Lobaina Delgado[1(✉)], César Quinayás[2(✉)], Andrés Ruiz[2],
Adson F. da Rocha[3(✉)], and Alberto López Delis[4(✉)]

[1] Department of Biomedical, Universidad de Oriente, Santiago de Cuba, Cuba
alobainad@gmail.com
[2] Antonio Nariño University, Bogotá, Colombia
cquinayas@uan.edu.co
[3] Department Electrical Engineering, University of Brasilia, Brasilia, Brazil
adsonr@gmail.com
[4] Center of Medical Biophysics, Universidad de Oriente, Santiago de Cuba, Cuba
lopez.delis69@gmail.com

Abstract. Continuous kinematics estimation based systems from surface electromyographic (sEMG) signals can predict movement intention to drive upper-limb prostheses in a more natural and intuitive way. Recently studies about inertial sensors combined with this kind of biosignal have improved the regression algorithms performance significantly. The goal of this work is to propose and evaluate strategies to control prostheses that can be applied in a virtual hand training platform during the training phase of amputee patients. This work presented strategies based on MLP neural networks to estimate 18 DoFs across hand joint angles using sEMG and Inertial Sensor Fusion (ISF). The dataset used was obtained of the seventh Ninapro database. The regression algorithms applied are based on time-domain features, such as auto-regressive model using recursive least squares, slope-sign changes and waveform length. The sEMG and ISF based strategy showed equivalent performance compared to strategy based exclusively on sEMG signals. The results suggest the usability of inertial sensors as a source signal in multi-modal control of upper-limb prostheses.

Keywords: Continuous estimation · Upper-limb protheses · Inertial Sensor Fusion · Surface electromyographic signals · Neural networks

1 Introduction

The sEMG signals can be used as a neural interface to command electric-powered prostheses. This approach can help amputees to perform everyday activities of daily living [7,19]. Currently, commercial myoelectric prostheses of upper limbs operate using the direct control paradigm. Even so, the scientific community has developed other pattern recognition based strategies that are more advantageous than conventional control. These paradigms respond to the current demands of

© Springer Nature Switzerland AG 2020
F. R. Narváez et al. (Eds.): SmartTech-IC 2019, CCIS 1154, pp. 325–336, 2020.
https://doi.org/10.1007/978-3-030-46785-2_26

prostheses: that they should be more articulated, robust, and multifunctional. [7]. EMG based on pattern recognition has provided frameworks that achieve a high classification accuracy, but the selection of motion classes is discrete, sequential, and unnatural [1]. However, human movements are more intuitive and naturally based on the simultaneous and continuous control of multiple degrees of freedom (DoFs). The design of algorithms with characteristics close to natural control involves regression-based methods to estimate movement information from sEMG signals [7,9,22]. An alternative to improve such methods, can be the use of other sources of information [7,9]. The application of additional sensory modalities is relatively recent in the field of robotic hand prostheses. sEMG sensors combined with inertial sensors have been employed to predict the joint angle, angular velocity and other kinematic variables [21]. This modality is also referred to as multi-modal control [10] and have many advantages. The inertial sensors usually integrate a wide spectrum of biomedical sensors, such as, gyroscopes, accelerometers, and magnetometers. Integrated versions of these sensors are the inertial measurement units (IMUs). They are cost-effective and can be successfully used for accurate, non-invasive, and portable motion tracking [8]. These devices can also be used to minimize the number of sEMG electrodes used by the prostheses without compromising performance [6,14]. Furthermore, although the IMU measurements cannot predict the intent of movement, the sEMG signals can do it [7,21]. Despite this, the most of control strategies are only based in myoelectric signals. Nevertheless, some estimation methods have been improved with multi-modal approach. Krasoulis et al. used sEMG and accelerometry data to achieve highly-accurate in the mapping of finger movements [13]. Blana *et al.* evaluated a transhumeral prosthesis controller. This device predicted the movement of the forearm from six proximal EMG signals, humeral angular velocity and linear acceleration. This scheme was evaluated offline with able-bodied subjects, as well as in a target-reaching task presented in a virtual reality environment [5].

López *et al.* proposed three algorithms from sEMG and gyroscope sensors using Kalman filters [17]. Their methods showed an improved performance in the accuracy of knee joint angle estimation compared with methods exclusively based on sEMG data. Recently, Zhang *et al.* also presented regression-based methods, including single-/multi-variable linear regression and support vector regression framework for quantitative assessment of muscle spasticity from wearable sEMG and IMUs [23].

In [14], Krasoulis *et al.* suggested that IMUs can form an excellent complementary source signal for upper-limb myoelectric prostheses. This researches provided evidence supporting the hypothesis that multi-modal combinations outperformed the algorithms based only on sEMG. In [14], an interesting alternative concerning Inertial Sensor Fusion (ISF) was also suggested to determine orientation.

The sensor fusion technique enables to fuse data read from an IMU without compromising useful information. Moreover, the ISF can be recommended to extract features from multiple sensors, including magnetometers.

The goal of the present study is to estimate hand joint angles from ISF using Multilayer-perceptron (MLP) networks based methods. A comparison between the two proposals is carried out. The first one is based on only sEMG signals, and the second one, these signals are combined with fused IMU signals. In this work, we argue that if joint angles can be mapped from sEMG and ISF, then it would be possible to improve the performance of algorithms based on sEMG only. The employed methodology in this work will contribute to the development of a virtual hand training platform for the training of patients to improve prostheses control. The virtual hand can obtain information from IMU and sEMG signals and will be configured to perform three types of movements: hand open, power grip, and tripod grip; the rest state is also included.

2 Methodology

The methodology applied in this work is based on the continuous estimation of hand joint angles that is validated with basic and coordinated hand movements during daily activities in healthy subjects. The proposed algorithm consists of preprocessing, feature extraction and regression algorithm. This study proposes non-linear models based on MLP neural networks to estimate angles from sEMG signals and joint orientation from ISF. The general scheme of the proposed methodology is presented in Fig. 1.

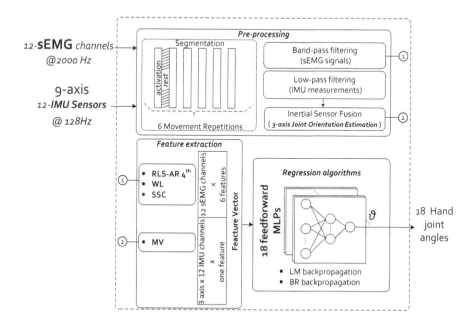

Fig. 1. General block diagram of the estimation method based on sEMG and IMU data. The movement labels were refined a-posteriori

In this work, neural networks were trained using Levenberg-Marquardt (LM) backpropagation algorithms and their variant with Bayesian Regularization (BR). Both algorithms were selected by their particular characteristics during the optimization process in the training of multilayer perceptrons. First, models based exclusively on characteristics extracted from sEMG signals were evaluated. Then the same models were trained from the combination of the sEMG and IMUs data. Subsequently, a comparison was made to answer the hypothesis.

3 Materials

3.1 sEMG DataBase Ninaweb 7

Ninapro databases have been used for comparison of regression or classification performances obtained from computational techniques by providing sEMG, as well as hand/arm kinematic, dynamic, and clinical parameters [10,13,20]. They aim at helping the development of non-invasive, naturally controlled robotic hand prostheses for trans-radial amputees, but the databases can also be used to study hand kinematics and dynamics in non-amputated subjects (for example, in research involving the control of robotic hands or exoskeletons) [3].

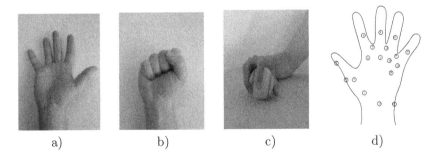

Fig. 2. Selected hand movements from *Ninapro* database: (a) open hand (**M1**), (b) close hand (**M2**), (c) Tripod grasp (**M3**) and (d) 18-DOF model used for performing the regression based methods in this work. Photographs showing movements have been reproduced from [2].

The dataset used were obtained from the seventh *Ninapro* database, described in [14], which is online available for use in research on EMG controlled prostheses. Their data are similar to data acquired in real-life conditions. This database includes data of twenty able-bodied subjects and two right-hand transradial amputee participants, which were collected by using a *Delsys*® *Trigno^{TM} IM Wireless System*. The protocol included six repetitions of 40 different movements, including isometric, isotonic hand configurations, basic movements of the wrist, grasp and functional movements, and rest. Each movement repetition lasted 3 s and was followed by 5 s of rest. Each sEMG electrode incorporated an IMU (a tri-axial accelerometer, gyroscope, and magnetometer measuring acceleration, angular velocity, and local magnetic field, respectively). An example of the sEMG and IMU data is depicted in Fig. 3. For sensor placement, was followed the *NinaPro* protocol and used 12 sensors. The sampling frequency was set at 2 kHz for sEMG and 128 Hz per axis for IMU data according to the configuration of the acquisition system referred previously [3,14].

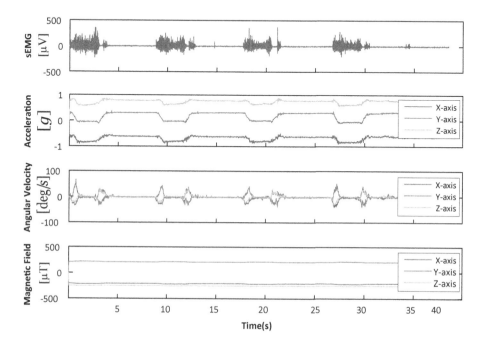

Fig. 3. Traces of the filtered signals associated with a single sEMG-IMU sensor. These readings are shown for movement Tripod grasp.

The data used in this work were obtained during three basic movements of the hand in five able-bodied subjects (see Fig. 2a, b and c) selected randomly (subjects 3, 5, 6, 11, 13). Hand joint angle measurements correspond to data from the 18 cyber glove sensors placed in the positions shown in Fig. 2(d). The raw data are assumed to be proportional to the angles of the hand joints [3].

3.2   Data Processing and Featuring Extraction

To remove the movement artifact, the sEMG signals were bandpass-filtered (4th Butterworth with 20–500 Hz cutoff frequencies). The IMU data were filtered by a 2nd Butterworth low pass filter set at 6 Hz. In this research, the following feature set from sEMG has been used: coefficients of a fourth-order forgetting-factor autoregressive model using recursive least squares (AR-RLS), slope-sign changes (SSC) and waveform length (WL). This feature set was applied or referred to in previous works [4,9,14,15,17,18]. SSC is associated to the number of times that slope of the sEMG signal changes sign, and WL is a measure of the complexity of the sEMG signal [9,17]. For estimating the autoregressive coefficients, the forgetting factor was set at 0.98. Therefore, it was assumed that the system remains approximately constant 50 samples or 25 ms. These estimation parameters were only considered in the time domain because a system for upper-limb prosthesis control should have low computational requirements during real-time control [7,14]. The selection of these parameters was based on previous studies demonstrating their efficacy in decoding motion intention [17,18].

The IMU data consist of raw values from IMUs, which measured acceleration, angular velocity, and magnetic field. ISF was employed as an alternative for extracting features from IMU signals. In most of these techniques, the unknown variables, such as Euler angles, are estimated. ISF uses algorithms based on Kalman filters to estimate joint orientation over time. An object's orientation describes its rotation relative to the body coordinate system in three dimensions. The mean value (MV) from Euler angle representation (in degree) of orientation was used as a feature for IMU information; this feature has been applied in [4, 13,15]. Euler angles have an intuitive physical meaning: it is a representation of the roll-pitch-yaw angles that is compatible with the anatomy (DoFs) of human limbs [8]. All signals were processed using moving windows for data analysis (according to a forgetting-factor).

3.3   Regression Algorithms

MLP was used to predict hand joint angles from the sEMG and IMU features. These feedforward networks have been widely used as a supervised nonlinear approach to predict joint angles [11,12,16,22]. Although several methods have produced better results in contrast to the MLP neural networks [4], this continues to be a universal nonlinear regression model for mapping input-output problems.

Different input data were used for training and testing of the estimation model, including rest, which made to algorithm more robust. One-third of the movement repetitions were randomly selected to create the test set (repetition 1 and 2 or 5 and 6), while the remaining repetitions were used to create the training set. In each training, the neural networks, there were three layers. The dimensionality of the input layer was assumed according to the feature space (i.e., 108 for the sEMG-IMU channel-set). The hidden layer contains twelve neurons, and the output layer, a single neuron.

The neurons in the hidden layer had a tangent sigmoid transfer function and the output layer, a linear transfer function. Eighteen separate MLPs were trained for estimating the joint angles; each MLP network corresponds to one joint angle in order to obtain accurate estimates for each joint angle.

The networks were trained through the LM or BR backpropagation algorithms. LM is a fast backpropagation algorithm and is highly recommended.

BR allows updating the weight values according to Levenberg-Marquardt optimization but minimizes them with a combination of squared errors and weights. All the estimations were performed on the data recorded from five able-bodied subjects for the movements showed in Fig. 2.

3.4   Performance Evaluation

For performance evaluation, we have, among the most frequently applied metrics: coefficient of determination R^2, root mean square error (RMSE), mean squared error (MSE), and Pearson correlation coefficient (CC). The performance of networks with MSE was evaluated to select the dimensionality of the hidden layer, which allowed us to define 12 neurons for this layer, ensuring the lowest MSE value. CC and global R^2 was considered in order to evaluate and to compare the regression performance between the methods based solely on sEMG signals and the proposed method in this study based on sEMG and IMU. CC quantifies the strength of a linear relationship between two variables, in this case between the predicted joint angle output, $f(t)$, for a single DoF and the measured hand joint angle, $\widehat{f(t)}$, by the cyberglove sensors for the same DoF. This metric is defined in terms of the covariance of A and B as:

$$CC = \frac{cov(\widehat{f(t)}, f(t))}{\sigma_{\widehat{f(t)}} \sigma_{f(t)}} \tag{3.1}$$

where $\sigma_{f(t)}$ is the standard deviation of $f(t)$. The correlation function can range from -1 to 1, with -1 representing a negative correlation, 0 representing no correlation, values close to 1 representing a high correlation.

Global R^2 was calculated across all the DoF as follows:

$$R^2 = 1 - \frac{\sum_{i=1}^{D} \sum_{j=1}^{N} (\widehat{f_j(t)} - f_j(t))^2}{\sum_{i=1}^{D} \sum_{j=1}^{N} (f(t) - \overline{f_j(t)})^2} \tag{3.2}$$

where D refers to the number of DoF, N refers to the number of samples used during the corresponding test set, $f_j(t)$ refers to the measured joint angle of the jth sample, $\widehat{f_j(t)}$ refers to the estimated joint angle of the jth sample, $\overline{f_j(t)}$ refers to the average value of the measured joint angle in one test set. The R^2 coefficient can range from $-\infty$ to 1. The value of R2 closer to 1 indicates a better accuracy in the estimation. These statistics were evaluated and computed for each method, movement and subject.

4   Results and Discussion

In the evaluation of the proposed methods, we compared the joint angle measurements of a large number of DOFs of the human hand, with the estimates attained with solely sEMG signals and with combined data from sEMG and ISF, for LM and BR neural networks.

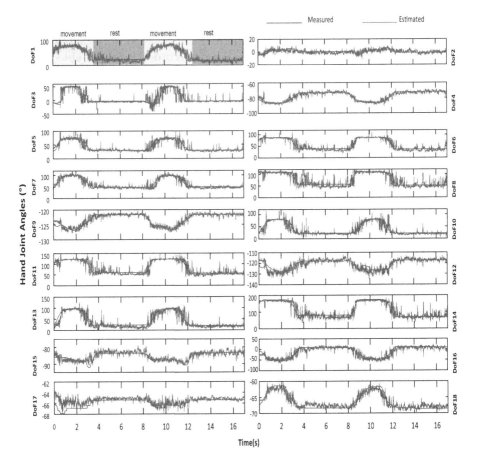

Fig. 4. Example of reconstruction of the 18-DoF hand joint angles through LM algorithm during the test phase from sEMG and ISF fusion. The data corresponds to Subject 2 during two repetitions of the class (Close hand (**M2**): fingers flexed together in fist). The blue lines indicate the filtered measurements from cyberglove system, considered as the real joint angles. The red lines indicate the predicted joint angles. In this case, the R^2 coefficient was 0.84. (Color figure online)

For validating the hypothesis about the possibility of reconstruction of kinematic variables using sEMG and IMU fusion, we present, in Fig. 4, a representative study of 18 DoF across joint angle estimation during the test phase for each DoF. These data show that the estimated hand joint angles follow the real measurements in the remaining proposals.

Figure 4 also shows the presence of random noise in the output targets. This noise can be minimized by using a Kalman filter or another low pass filter for this type of noise. The possible cause of this noise may be the requirements for solving the optimization problem, to get the weight adjustments. Besides, the feature vector is still large, so the use of feature reduction methods is recommended.

One of the advantages of using inertial sensors is that fewer electromyography channels could be used, which can be investigated. Even so, BR based proposed methods reduced in some cases this noise, when compared to LM.

The estimation accuracies from Global R^2 of each motion and strategy across all the subjects were averaged and they are summarized in Fig. 5. Both algorithms, either with sEMG only or sEMG-ISF multimodal strategy shown similar results. Tripod grasp (**M3**) showed the lowest performance during the evaluation of the algorithms. The cause may be due to that the movement of daily life have more kinematic variability than the basic movements. An alternative to obtain better results would be to increase training data, which requires more repetitions of these types of movement. This approach would make the implemented proposal more robust. The estimation performance was a little better with sEMG-ISF-LM, except for the motion **M3** where sEMG-LM presents apparent advantages comparing with multi-modal approach.

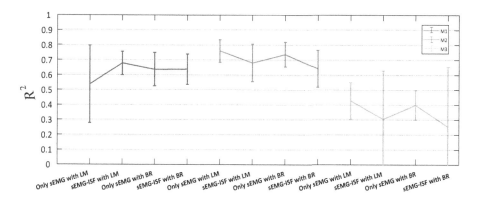

Fig. 5. Performance comparison between different MLP algorithms and different proposed strategies (mean ± std).

Figure 6 illustrates the differences among the proposed strategies having in mind the subject specifics. The figure shows the behavior of the averaged CC indicator for each DoF, different movements, different subjects. In the majority of cases, CCs corresponding to different strategies were equivalent. The reconstruction of the 18-DoF hand joint angles presented in Fig. 4 provides qualitative evidence of the better performance of this indicator. It is noticeable that the reconstruction from sEMG signal without IMU data, presented the best accuracy in most of the DoFs, but similar results were obtained with a combination of sEMG and IMU features. For the most of DoFs, correlation coefficient of above 80% were achievable. The results of the proposed algorithms showed a reasonable correlation (>75.1%) between the estimated and real angles in each strategy.

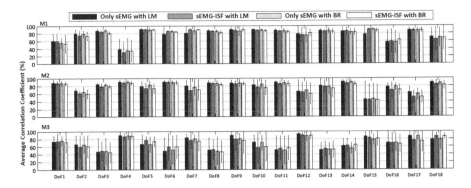

Fig. 6. Performance comparison of different MLP algorithms and different strategies for each DoF of the presented model Fig. 2(d).

5   Conclusion

In this study, we applied two strategies for estimating hand joint angles from sEMG signals and the Inertial Sensor Fusion technique. The dataset from able-bodied subjects was used to train the neural networks and validate the performance of the joint angle estimation in the following movements: open hand, close hand, and Tripod grasp (rest included). The continuous estimation of these movements will contribute to the development of a virtual hand training platform for subjects with amputations or defects in their upper limbs. The comparison used in this work indicates a reasonable correlation between the estimated joint angles with the measured joint angles by *Ninapro* protocol, it follows that the results suggest that sEMG and ISF combination can improve the performance as well as algorithms based only on sEMG. In future works, we intend to improve the proposal herein presented, in view of the fact that the sEMG-IFS multimodal approach outperformes the control based solely on sEMG, especially in the estimation of functional movements.

References

1. Atzori, M., Gijsberts, A., Caputo, B., Maller, H.: Natural control capabilities of robotic hands by hand amputated subjects. In: 2014 36th Annual International Conference of the IEEE Engineering in Medicine and Biology Society, 26–30 August 2014, pp. 4362–4365 (2014)
2. Atzori, M., et al.: Building the ninapro database: a resource for the biorobotics community. In: 2012 4th IEEE RAS & EMBS International Conference on Biomedical Robotics and Biomechatronics (BioRob), 24–27 June 2012, pp. 1258–1265 (2012)
3. Atzori, M., et al.: Electromyography data for non-invasive naturally-controlled robotic hand prostheses. Sci. Data **1**, 140053 (2014). https://doi.org/10.1038/sdata.2014.53

4. Bakshi, K., Manjunatha, M., Kumar, C.: Estimation of continuous and constraint-free 3 dof wrist movements from surface electromyogram signal using kernel recursive least square tracker. Biomed. Signal Process. Control **46**, 104–115 (2018). https://doi.org/10.1016/j.bspc.2018.06.012
5. Blana, D., Kyriacou, T., Lambrecht, J.M., Chadwick, E.K.: Feasibility of using combined emg and kinematic signals for prosthesis control: a simulation study using a virtual reality environment. J. Electromyogr. Kinesiol. **29**, 21–27 (2016)
6. Brenna, D.A.: Autonomy in rehabilitation robotics: an intersection. Ann. Rev. Control Rob. Auton. Syst. **1**, 441–464 (2018)
7. Farina, D., et al.: The extraction of neural information from the surface emg for the control of upper-limb prostheses: emerging avenues and challenges. IEEE Trans. Neural Syst. Rehab. Eng. **22**(4), 797–809 (2014). https://doi.org/10.1109/TNSRE.2014.2305111
8. Filippeschi, A., Schmitz, N., Miezal, M., Bleser, G., Ruffaldi, E., Stricker, D.: Survey of motion tracking methods based on inertial sensors: a focus on upper limb human motion. Sensors **17**, 1257 (2017). https://doi.org/10.3390/s17061257
9. Fougner, A., Stavdahl, Ø., Kyberd, P.J., Losier, Y.G., Parker, P.A.: Control of upper limb prostheses: terminology and proportional myoelectric control: a review. IEEE Trans. Neural Syst. Rehab. Eng. **20**(5), 663–677 (2012)
10. Ghaderi, P., Karimimehr, S., Emadi A., Mehran Reza M.H.: Hand kinematics estimation to control prosthetic devices: a nonlinear approach for simultaneous and proportional estimation of 15 dofs. In: 22nd Iranian Conference on Biomedical Engineering(ICBME 2015), Iranian Research Organization for Science and Technology (IROST), pp. 233–238, November 2015
11. Grech, C., Camilleri, T., Bugeja, M.: Using neural networks for simultaneous and proportional estimation of upper arm kinematics. In: 25th Mediterranean Conference on Control and Automation (MED), pp. 247–252 (2017)
12. Hahne, J.M., et al.: Linear and nonlinear regression techniques for simultaneous and proportional myoelectric control. IEEE Trans. Neural Syst. Rehab. Eng. **16**, 269–279 (2014)
13. Krasoulis, A., Vijayakumar, S., Nazarpour, K.: Evaluation of regression methods for the continuous decoding of finger movement from surface EMG and accelerometry. In: 2015 7th International IEEE/EMBS Conference on Neural Engineering (NER), 22–24 April 2015, pp. 631–634 (2015)
14. Krasoulis, A., Kyranou, I., Erden, M.S., Nazarpour, K., Vijayakumar, S.: Improved prosthetic hand control with concurrent use of myoelectric and inertial measurements. J. NeuroEng. Rehabil. **14**(1), 71 (2017). https://doi.org/10.1186/s12984-017-0284-4
15. Kyranou, I., Krasoulis, A., Suphi Erden, M., Nazarpour, K., Vijayakumar, S.: Real-time classification of multi-modal sensory data for prosthetic hand control. In: 6th IEEE International Conference on Biomedical Robotics and Biomechatronics (BioRob) (2016). https://doi.org/10.1109/BIOROB.2016.7523681
16. Liu, J., Kang, S., Xu, D., Ren, Y.L.S., Zhang, L.Q.: Emg-based continuous and simultaneous estimation of arm kinematics in able-bodied individuals and stroke survivors. Front. Neurosci. **11**, 480 (2017). https://doi.org/10.3389/fnins.2017.00480
17. López, D.A., Miosso, C.J.A., Carvalho, J.A.L., da Rocha, A.F., Borges, G.A.: Continuous estimation prediction of knee joint angles using fusion of electromyographic and inertial sensors for active transfemoral leg protheses. World Sci. **10**(2), 1840008 (2018). https://doi.org/10.1142/S242422X18400089

18. López Delis, A.: Propuesta de métodos para la estimación del ángulo de la rodilla en la detección de la intención de movimiento. Ph.D. thesis, Universidad de Oriente (2011)
19. Merletti, R., Botter, A., Troiano, A., Merlo, E., Minetto, M.A.: Technology and instrumentation for detection and conditioning of the surface electromyographic signal: State of the art. Clin. Biomech. **24**(2), 122–134 (2009). https://doi.org/10.1016/j.clinbiomech.2008.08.006
20. Stival, F., Michieletto, S., Pagello, E.: Online subject-independent modeling of semg signals for the motion of a single robot joint. In: 6th IEEE RAS/EMBS International Conference on Biomedical Robotics and Biomechatronics (BioRob), pp. 1110–1116, June 2016
21. Zhang, K.W., de Silva, C., Fu, C.: Sensor fusion for predictive control of human-prosthesis-environment dynamics in assistive walking: a survey. arXiv (2019)
22. Zhang, Q., Liu, R., Chen, W., Xiong, C.: Simultaneous and continuous estimation of shoulder and elbow kinematics from surface EMG signals. Front. Neurosci. **11**, 280 (2017)
23. Zhang, X., Tang, X., Zhu, X., Gao, X., Chen, X., Chen, X.: A regression- based framework for quantitative assessment of muscle spasticity using combined emgand inertial data from wearable sensors. Front. Neurosci. **13**, 398 (2019)

Estimation of Spatio-temporal Parameters of Gait Using an Inertial Sensor Network

Marcelo Bosmediano⬤ and Fabián Narváez(✉)⬤

GIB&B Research Group, Department of Biomedicine,
Universidad Politécnica Salesiana, Quito, Ecuador
fnarvaeze@ups.edu.ec

Abstract. Gait analysis is clinically used as a diagnostic tool to quantify gait issues associated with neuromuscular or locomotion disorders. The variability of different spatio-temporal parameters during the gait cycles provides clinical information related to state of patients and the progress of certain diseases. Usually, gait analysis based on spatio-temporal parameters requires costly-instrumented walkways and video-based motion capture systems, which are only available in specialized clinical scenarios. Hence, Inertial sensors-based gait analysis has been proposed with promising results, but it is still considered a challenging task. In this paper, a novel method for estimating spatio-temporal parameters of gait by using an inertial sensor network is proposed. For doing that, a set of 7 inertial sensors are setting into a biomechanical model to capture both position and rotation of body segments of lower limbs. Then, gait cycles are segmented by including information from angles of the hip, knee and ankle joints, respectively. So, a quaternion-based motion analysis is carried out for defining gait phases by detecting gait events. The proposed method was validated using a camera-based motion system, respectively. The obtained results demonstrate that the estimated spatio-temporal parameters are equal to the expected values obtained by camera motion system widely used in real clinical scenarios. Therefore, the proposed method could be used in clinical applications.

Keywords: Gait analysis · Spatio-temporal gait parameters · Inertia sensor network · Quaternion-based motion analysis

1 Introduction

Gait analysis is widely used as a clinical tool for providing a quantitative description of gait patterns associated to different locomotive, neurological and musculoskeletal disorders, among others [7,20]. In clinical scenarios, it is important to characterize pathological gait patterns, showing to be useful for prescription of rehabilitation therapies, treatments as well as for evaluating these treatments [4,10,12]. Gait analysis based on spatio-temporal parameters has been established as a common way to understand some kinetic and kinematic aspects of

© Springer Nature Switzerland AG 2020
F. R. Narváez et al. (Eds.): SmartTech-IC 2019, CCIS 1154, pp. 337–350, 2020.
https://doi.org/10.1007/978-3-030-46785-2_27

human gait. However, estimation of spatio-temporal parameters demands the use of specialized technological devices for detecting gait phases such as: stance phase, swing phase and support phases, which are caused by foots position during the walking [5,21]. Currently, video-based motion capture systems have been considered as a gold-standard technique for clinical gait analysis [4,12]. However, this technology is quite expensive and requires specialized video cameras, advanced video processing techniques and an appropriate position of optical markers on the human body according to its anatomical landmarks. In order to detect the gait phases, some automatic systems have been developed by using emerging technologies such as: systems based on shoe-integrated sensors [15], systems based on electromyography signals and systems based on force platforms (e.g., embedded metal plates with force sensors). These systems find to determine the beginning and end of each gait phase during a complete cycle of it [8,16]. Currently, gait analysis based on inertial sensor technology has emerged as an alternative to traditional computer vision motion capture systems. Its low cost and usability in internal/external environments allows a wide range of remote applications [10,20]. This portable technology combines multi-axial accelerometers, gyroscopes and eventually magnetometers, which are contained in a single inertial measurement unit (IMU). Basically, IMUs provide inertial measurements such as: linear acceleration, angular velocity and magnetic field strength measurements [1,19], which are obtained by placing different sensors on specific segments of the body. However, its use in clinical real scenarios is limited due to its measurements are directly affected by sensors position and orientation at the body segments, by its coordinate reference system, as well as, it is affected by the number of IMU-sensors used during the gait analysis, a fundamental problem that directly affect for estimating some spatio-temporal parameters of the gait [11,19].

2   Related Works

Several strategies have been proposed to solve this fundamental problem by attempting to estimate some spatio-temporal parameters of the gait using inertial sensors [13,14]. Some strategies have agreed to segment the complete cycle of the gait into two main gait phases, the stance and swing phases, respectively [5,9,14], which occur when the foot is on the ground (contact phase) followed by a movement of the same foot forward through the air (swing phase). For which, several IMUs systems have been used to calculated the joint movements in different settings [3,13,17]. These strategies are based on gyroscopes information for measuring the spatial parameters of gait, as well as, temporal parameters of gait are calculated by using the accelerometers information from IMUs. Basically, these previous works find to detect the gait events during a complete gait cycle, such as: heel contact (HC) and toe-off (TO), which define the beginning and ending of each phase during a successive two-step sequence. However, gait phase detection process with automatic adaptation to gait velocity changes from the both feet allow to define spatial parameters of the gait, such as stride length, step length and step width. In the same way, these spatial information between both feet have been used to calculated temporal parameters such as: stride time, stance time or swing time, respectively. For which, some configurations based on 6-IMUs or 7-IMUS have been used for estimating the gait parameters by attaching the IMUs at the lower limbs [14, 17]. Finally, the joint kinematics have been calculated by processing its angular velocity in the sagittal plane. However, it has been well-established that the performance of the obtained measures can be improved by including clinical angles of the joints involved during gait analysis [19]. Therefore, analysis of spatio-temporal parameters of the gait demands three important aspects: a suitable location of the IMUs placed at the lower limbs, an accurate detection of the gait events and an accurate definition of anatomical planes respect to reference coordinate system of IMUs to avoid the accumulative error produced by processing the acceleration signals from IMUs, making of the estimation of gait spatio-temporal parameters, a challenging task.

This paper presents a novel strategy to automatically estimate the spatial-temporal parameters of gait by using an inertial sensor network. For doing that, a set of 7 inertial sensors are setting into a biomechanical model to capture both position and rotation of body segments of lower limbs respect to its anatomical planes. So, a quaternion-based method to IMU-to-body calibration is carried out for defining anatomical planes of body and for accurately detecting gait phases and some gait events. Then, gait cycles are segmented by including rotational information from angles of the knee and ankle joints, respectively. Thus, gait events such as heel strike and toe-off are detected, allowing to calculate spatial parameters such as the stride length and step length, respectively. Finally, temporal parameters such as: stride time, stance time and swing time were calculated by integrating information obtained from accelerometers and gyroscopes sensors contained into the IMUs sensors. Unlike other approaches, we do not attempt to exactly obtain certain inertial data of motion sensors placed at the body limbs, but instead, a biomechanical model calibrated respect to body frames is applied using rotational angle information from the motion of lower limbs. This paper is organized as follows: after this introduction and related works, next section presents the proposed methodology, then experimental results are shown and last section discusses conclusions.

3   Methodology

An overview of the proposed framework is illustrated in Fig. 1. The proposed method starts defining a biomechanical model by setting an inertial sensors network located on lower limbs, for which a set of seven IMU-sensors structured as a rigid body model is used. Then, a process for calibrating and aligning the IMUs to body is carried out by using a strategy based on its quaternions information. Once biomechanical model has been aligned, a gait event detection scheme is applied for segmenting the gait into both stance and swing phases. These gait phases are used to estimate its spatial-temporal parameters. Thus, the proposed method consists of three stages: a stage to IMU-to-body calibration, a gait events detection process and a stage for estimating spatio-temporal parameters.

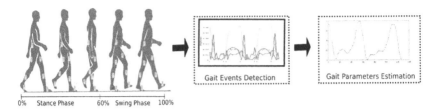

0%   Stance Phase   60%   Swing Phase   100%

Fig. 1. Method overview

3.1   Biomechanical Model Configuration

Firstly, an inertial sensors network is setting by using six IMUs arranged on each segment of the lower limbs and defining a rigid body model. For doing that, each IMU is attached to the lateral position of segments of each limb, as well as, at superior position of the mid-foot. This biomechanical model involves an additional IMU sensor located over the pelvis, at the L5S1 joint, approximately, as is illustrates in Fig. 2. Finally, in this work, the inertial sensor network is constituted by an IMU-based motion capture system developed by the well-known XSens Technology, namely, the MVN AWINDA system, a commercial motion capture system for motion tracking applications in real time [2]. The used IMUs measure accelerations, angular velocities and the magnetic field vector in its own three-dimensional local coordinate system, representing an orthonormal base that is well aligned with the outer casing of the IMU. In addition, each IMU includes algorithms for estimating sensor's orientation respect to a global fixed coordinate system. The orientation information is provided in a quaternion format (q). Finally, inertial sensor data are collected at a sampling frequency of 60 Hz and it processed in MATLAB R17 software, running on a Linux PC with 2 Intel Quad Core i7 at 3.07 GHz and 16 GB of RAM.

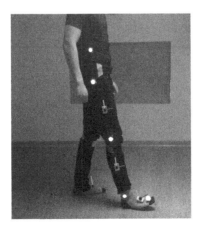

Fig. 2. Setting IMU sensors to body limbs respect to the body coordinate system

3.2   IMUs-to-Body Calibration Algorithm

Once our biomechanical model is established, it requires to align and calibrate its local coordinate system respect to anatomical coordinate system of each body segments for avoiding wrong measure of the joint angles. For doing that, we define a new reference coordinate system from the sensor placed at Pelvis, which is used as reference system for the rest of sensors placed on the body segments. For achieving this, a calibration algorithm based on orientation information, in quaternion format (q), from each IMU is applied. This strategy was developed in our previous work, as is described in [11], where this problem is formulated as the decomposition into quaternion factors from a quaternion associated with a rotation in R^3, which provide meaningful and useful rotation about to their principal axes defined as $i, j, k = 1, 2, 3$. Thus, it is consider that any two independent coordinate systems can be related by a sequence of rotations about its coordinate axis. Therefore, the quaternion (q) from the pelvis is assumed as a rotation operator related by a sequence of rotations defined by (abc), as is described in [11], then:

$$q = a^i \otimes b^j \otimes c^k \tag{1}$$

where the sequence of rotation corresponds to $a^3 b^2 c^1$ according to the importance of movements at the pelvis [18]. So, the proposed rotation operator is established as: $q = a^3 \otimes b^2 \otimes c^1$. Hence, their quaternion factors are obtained by a factorizing operation according to quaternion algebra [6], defining the principal axes according to their unit vector for each rotation as:

$$c^1 = c_0 + \hat{i}c_1 = \cos\frac{\phi}{2} + \hat{i}\sin\frac{\phi}{2} \tag{2}$$

$$b^2 = b_0 + \hat{j}b_2 = \cos\frac{\theta}{2} + \hat{j}\sin\frac{\theta}{2} \tag{3}$$

$$a^3 = a_0 + \hat{k}a_3 = \cos\frac{\psi}{2} + \hat{k}\sin\frac{\psi}{2} \tag{4}$$

where c^1 is the rotation respect to $X\hat{i}$-axis, b^2 is the rotation respect to $Y\hat{j}$-axis, a^3 is the rotation respect to $Z\hat{k}$-axis, c_0, c_1, b_0, b_2, a_0 and a_3 are the components of each sequence of rotation, a, b, c, respectively. Hence, each angle of rotation is obtained by:

$$\tan\phi = \frac{-2(q_0q_1 + q_2q_3)}{-q_0^2 + q_2^2 + q_1^2 - q_3^2} \tag{5}$$

where, q quaternion is also depicted as: $q = q_0 + \hat{i}q_1 + \hat{j}q_2 + \hat{k}q_3$ and ϕ angle is used to obtain the factor c^1 from Eq. 2. Therefore, the initial orientation of sensor placed at pelvis allows to estimate ϕ, θ and ψ angles. Finally, these rotation angles and each quaternion factors are used as correction factors for calibrating and adjusting the new reference coordinate of sensor according to Earth's coordinate system. Once the new reference coordinate systems is established at the pelvis, each inertial sensor is aligned to its body segment. This problem is solved by implementing the sensor-to-body alignment algorithm, as is described in [11] by:

$$^0q'_n = p_0 \otimes {}^0q_0^* \otimes {}^0q_n^* \tag{6}$$

where $^0q'_n$ corresponds to the corrected quaternion of any n−IMU, at a time $t = 0$ respect to general sensor coordinate system. $p_0 \otimes {}^0q_0^*$ depicts the improved rotation of the pelvis' coordinate system. So, body coordinate references are aligned to the principal axis of body segments by using the corrected quaternion $^0q'_n$, which allows to define a common body coordinate system, the anatomical coordinate system. Finally, the body segment rotations are estimated respect to our proposed rigid body model, as follow:

$$R_n = p_0^* \otimes {}^0q_0^* \otimes q_n \otimes p_n \tag{7}$$

where R_n is the rotation of any n−IMU. Therefore, the joint rotation between two continuous body segments is computed by:

$$\Theta_n = R_{n-1} \otimes R_n \tag{8}$$

where Θ_n is the joint angle of limbs, which allows to compute the angles from hip, knee and ankle joints, such as: flexion/extension, internal/external rotation and abduction/adduction, respectively. In this work, flexion/extension angles are used to estimate the gait parameters, which are defined respect to sagittal plane.

3.3   Gait Events Detection

Human gait is considered a periodic motion of lower limbs and is defined from foot contacts the ground and the same foot contacts the ground again, a sequence that is known as a complete gait cycle. So, a gait cycle includes two phases, both the stance and swing phases, respectively, which are defined by the foot heel contact (HC) following of the toe-off (TO) of the same foot, as is illustrated in Fig. 3.

In order to segment the gait, we propose a gait event detection strategy based on peak-peak detector from accelerometer data captured by the IMUs attached at the mid-foot of each foot. For doing that, the magnitude of acceleration signal is obtained, such as:

$$Acc(t) = \sqrt{Acc_x^2(t) + Acc_y^2(t) + Acc_z^2(t)} \tag{9}$$

then, the local maximum and minimum (eg. critical points) are computed using the well-known zero-derivate method, defined by:

$$\{max, min\} = \frac{d(Acc)}{dt} = 0 \tag{10}$$

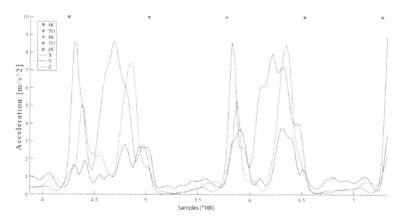

Fig. 3. Example of 3D signals captured from an accelerometer sensor during a sequence of two gait cycles from a IMU placed in the mid-foot of the right legs. HC and TO marks define the gait events associated to the 3D acceleration signals

where max and min values correspond to critical points of $Acc(t)$ function. However, in order to accurately establish the gait events from periodic gait cycles, an threshold value is established by including the rotation angles of the joints involved in the gait cycles in sagittal plane (eg. flexion-extension angles). For doing that, rotation angles are estimated using Eq. 5 from the hip and knee joints contained on the right limb, respectively. Then, a weighting factor based on range of movements from the hip and knee joint during the gait is established, which is defined by:

$$\lambda_{Tho} = (\phi_H * \lambda_H) + (\phi_K * \lambda_K), \{\lambda_H, \lambda_K\} \in (0, 1) \tag{11}$$

where ϕ_H and ϕ_K correspond to flexion-extension angles of the hip joint and knee joint, respectively. λ_H and λ_K correspond to the normalized weighting factor according the range of movements of the hip joint and knee joint during a gait cycle. Finally, the threshold values for detecting local maximum and minimum values from the acceleration signal are defined by:

$$max_{Tho} = max * \lambda_{Tho} \tag{12}$$

These values allow to detect the events such as: heel contact and toe-off during a gait cycle, as is illustrated in Fig. 4, defining the beginning and the end of the stance phase. For avoiding a wrong detection of two consecutive events, the average time of stride is included for detecting sequential gait events.

3.4 Spatial Parameters Estimation

Once the stance and swing phases are segmented from a gait cycle. The next stage consists to estimate some spatial parameters of gait. The most important gait

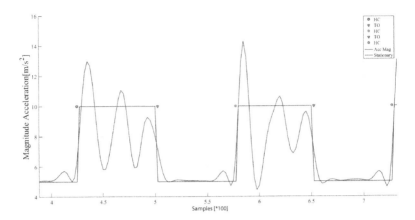

Fig. 4. Illustration of our gait event detection algorithm using threshold values by including normalized weighting factor according to the range of movements of the hip joint and knee joint, respectively. Signal corresponds to acceleration modulus from the right leg during two complete gait cycles

parameter is strike length for both medical and robotic fields, which is defined as the distance between the two successive contacts of the same foot with the ground. For estimating strike length, a double integration of acceleration signal is computed, which is delimited by two successive (HC) events. Then, a single integration operator defines the linear velocity of the strike by:

$$v_N(t) = \int_{T_{HC_{N-1}}}^{T_{HC_N}} Acc_N(t)dt \qquad (13)$$

where $[T_{HC_{N-1}}, T_{HC_N}]$ define a time interval occurred from two successive (HC) events. Finally, strike length is computed by

$$SL(N) = \int_{T_{HC_{N-1}}}^{T_{HC_N}} v_N(t)dt \qquad (14)$$

On the other hand, step length parameter is estimated by:

$$S_{tep}L(N) = \frac{SL(N)}{2} \qquad (15)$$

3.5 Temporal Parameters Estimation

Gait temporal parameters constitute the time intervals of duration of repetitive events during the walking. For instance, gait cycle time, step time, stance time and swing time, among others. For which, it is convenient to use the instant in which gait events (HC and TO, respectively) are carried out. In order to estimate these gait temporal parameters, we measure the time slice when each event occurs for the right limb. Firstly, the gait cycle time (GTC) corresponds to the duration of a complete gait cycle, which is obtained by adding stance time and swing time, respectively. However, stance phase and swing phase are defined by both (HC) and (TO) events for the same foot. Hence, the gait cycle time (GTC) is calculated by:

$$GTC(N) = R_{HC}(N+1) - R_{HC}(N) \tag{16}$$

where $R_{HC}(N)$ represents the heel contact (HC) of the right limb during a Nth-gait cycle. In the same way, the stance time (ST) is obtained by

$$ST(N) = \frac{[R_{HC}(N) - R_{HC}(N)]}{GTC(N) * 100} \tag{17}$$

Therefore, the swing time is obtained such as: $S_wT(N) = GTC(N) - ST(N)$. Finally, step time (S_tT) is defined as: $S_tT(N) = GTC(N)/2$.

4   Experimental Results

The performance of our proposed method was two-fold evaluated. A first evaluation was carried out for determining the ability of our calibrated biomechanical model for measuring the joint angles of the lower limbs during the gait. Finally, a second evaluation was carried out for determining the efficacy of our proposed method for estimating gait spatial-temporal parameters. In both cases, a comparative analysis respect to clinical measures obtained by a camera-based motion system was carried out. In this case, the joint angles of lower limbs, as well as the gait parameters were recorded by using a set of six passive markers located at anatomical landmark of the right leg at lateral plane. Its recorded data were analyzed by using Kinovea software[1], an open-source tool, well-known for clinical applications. This comparative analysis is illustrated in Fig. 5.

For these two evaluations, a group of 5 healthy subjects (age range of 20–28 years, 3 males and 2 females), with no previous history of locomotive disorders, were evaluated. Their gait data were collected from a consecutive sequence of 6 gait cycles, walking a straight line about 8–10 m at normal speed. Each subjects was evaluated three times for claiming the repeatability of gait data. In addition, each subject was evaluated with both the IMUs system and camera-based motion system, at the same time. The IMUs data were collected at a sampling frequency of 60 Hz and it processed in MATLAB R17, running on a Linux PC with 2 Intel Quad Core i7 at 3.07 GHz and 16GB of RAM.

4.1   Evaluating the Joint Angles Estimation

For this first evaluation, flexion-extension angles of the hip, knee and ankle joints were estimated during the sequence of six gait cycles respect to sagittal

---

[1] https://www.kinovea.org/.

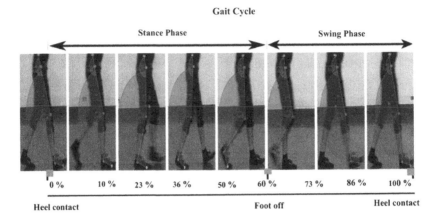

Fig. 5. Example of comparative analysis between the measurements obtained by the IMU sensors respect to camera-based motion system processed by Kinovea software during a complete gait cycle.

plane. The sagittal plane was considered due to the position of the optical markers at lateral view used with camera-based motion capture system. For which, six optical markers were placed and configured on the right limb according to the anatomical landmarks [18], in the same way, the IMUs were placed and unaligned in each body segments of the subject. Then, both IMUs and video information were captured together for comparative purpose. The camera-based motion system captured sequences of videos to a rate of 30 frames per second. For comparing the joint angle trajectories during the complete gait cycle, a similarity metric, defined as coefficient of multiple correlation (CMC), was calculated, which allows to quantify the similarity between angular trajectories (curves), this coefficient can take values between 0 and 1; being 1 an exact similarity. CMC was computed as is shown in [11]:

$$CMC = \sqrt{1 - \frac{\sum_{g=1}^{G}[\sum_{p=1}^{P}\sum_{f=1}^{F}(\theta_{gp}(f) - \bar{\theta}_{gf})^2/GF_g(P-1)]}{\sum_{g=1}^{G}[\sum_{p=1}^{P}\sum_{f=1}^{F}(\theta_{gp}(f) - \bar{\theta}_g)^2/G(PF_g-1)]}} \tag{18}$$

where θ_{gpf} depicts the joint angle at frame f and measured by method p (whatever IMUs or camera systems) during a complete gait cycle g; $\bar{\theta}_{gf}$ is the mean angle at frame f between angles measured by the two systems. $\bar{\theta}_g$ is the grand mean for the gait cycles g among these two methods. Finally, $P = 2$ is the number of methods evaluated, $F = 150$ corresponds to the total number of video frames and $G = 6$ is the number of gait cycles used during this evaluation.

The obtained results report an average of $CMC = 0.99$, $CMC = 0.70$ and $CMC = 0.89$ for the knee, hip, and ankle joints, respectively. Figure 6 shows the average trajectories of Flexion-Extension angle vs. (%) percentage of gait cycle. Overall, the average of angular trajectories show how our aligned biomechanical model with the IMU-based motion capture (green line) system coincide when knee-angles and ankle-angles are estimated by the optical tracking system (blue line) during the swing phase of the foot (from 60% of the gait cycle, approximately).

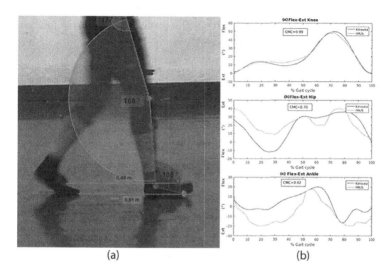

(a)   (b)

Fig. 6. Average of angular trajectories of flexion-extension during a complete gait cycle. Panel (a) illustrates the angular measurements obtained for the hip, knee and ankle joints by using Kinovea software. Panel (b) corresponds to the obtained angular trajectories for the knee, hip and ankle joints by applied both IMUs and camera systems, respectively (Color figure online).

However, Fig. 6(b) evinces that the measurements of hip-angles are the most variable when the stance phases was carried out, this is to say, when the foot contacts the ground, the displacements of hip angles depend perhaps of the anthropometric measures of lower limbs of subjects undergo analysis, requiring to use more anatomical markers at the right leg. Therefore, the obtained results shown that knee and hip-angles may be considered for estimating the spatio-temporal parameters of the gait.

4.2   Evaluating the Gait Spatio-Temporal Parameters Estimation

For this evaluation, the group of 5 healthy subjects conducted a consecutive sequence of 6 gait cycles, walking a straight line about 8–10 m at normal speed. Then, the threshold values were estimated by segmenting each gait cycle using our proposed peak-peak detector. Each subjects was evaluated three times for claiming the repeatability of gait data, obtained the normalized weighting factors of $\lambda_H = 0,78$ and , $\lambda_K = 0.4$ according to range of movements from the hip and knee joint during this experiment. So, these values were used by our proposed method to estimate the gait spatio-temporal parameters. In the same way, the spatio-temporal parameters of gait where measured using the Kinovea software, which were analyzed according to gait events detected during the gait cycles. For doing this, each video frame was analyzed to find the relevant gait events such as: HC and TC from the lower limbs, as is illustrated in Fig. 6(a). The obtained results are shown in Table 1, where the mean, standard deviation and root mean square error (RMSE) were obtained from the group of volunteers for both IMUs and Camera systems, respectively.

Table 1. Average of obtained spatio-temporal parameters of the gait (with $\lambda_H = 0,78$ and, $\lambda_K = 0.4$) respect to camera system (Kinovea software)

Gait parameters	IMUs system			Camera system		
	Mean	±SD	±RMSE	Mean	±SD	±RMSE
Gait speed (m/s)	1.13	0.17	0.09	1.16	0.11	0.10
Strike Length (m)	1.31	0.13	0.25	1.24	0.19	0.22
Step Length (m)	0.65	0.07	0.10	0.61	0.18	0.11
Gait cycle Time (s)	1.06	0.03	0.19	1.07	0.06	0.17
Step Time (s)	0.53	0.09	0.18	0.85	0.03	0.16
Stance Time (%)	61.02	0.05	0.06	60.40	0.11	0.06
Swing Time (%)	39.79	0.04	0.46	39.50	0.06	0.50

The obtained results report an accurate estimation of the spatial and its temporal parameters despite of error that it can occur due to variability of the gait cycles carried out during the consecutive sequence of six gait cycles. This obtained results show the effectiveness of our proposed method in spite of both orientation and position problems of inertial sensors when its are attached in the body segments of lower limbs. In addition, this means that our proposed method allows to accurately estimate temporal parameters of gait by using its spatial parameters. On the other hand, the gait cycle time reports an average rate of 1.5 s, approximately, with the stance and swing time of the 60% and 40%, respectively, which confirm a suitable gait segmentation process according to percentages reported in the literature.

5   Conclusions and Future Work

The herein proposed method provides an easy and fast strategy for estimating some gait spatio-temporal parameters applying a calibrated biomechanical model based on a setting of 7 inertial sensors. The obtained results demonstrate that the estimated joint angles are equivalent to the expected values obtained by camera-based motion system widely used as gold-standard in real clinical applications. In addition, the obtained results indicate that the method is suitable to estimate gait parameters including the angular rotations from the hip and knee joints during the gait events detection. Therefore, the proposed method could be used in clinical applications that requires gait analysis of impaired persons. However, in a future work is expected to validate our proposed method during the running of subjects, or with experiments that include different gait speeds, for instance physical activity under free living conditions.

References

1. Al-Amri, M., Nicholas, K., Button, K., Sparkes, V., Sheeran, L., Davies, J.L.: Inertial measurement units for clinical movement analysis: reliability and concurrent validity. Sensors **18**(3), 719 (2018)
2. Bellusci, G., Dijkstra, F., Slycke, P.: Xsens MTw: miniature wireless inertial motion tracker for highly accurate 3d kinematic applications. Technical report, April, Xsens Technologies (2013)
3. Bugané, F., et al.: Estimation of spatial-temporal gait parameters in level walking based on a single accelerometer: validation on normal subjects by standard gait analysis. Comput. Meth. Prog. Biomed. **108**(1), 129–137 (2012)
4. Muro-de-la Herran, A., García-Zapirain, B., Méndez-Zorrilla, A.: Gait analysis methods: an overview of wearable and non-wearable systems, highlighting clinical applications. Sensors **14**(2), 3362–3394 (2014)
5. Kluge, F., Gaßner, H., Hannink, J., Pasluosta, C., Klucken, J., Eskofier, B.M.: Towards mobile gait analysis: concurrent validity and test-retest reliability of an inertial measurement system for the assessment of spatio-temporal gait parameters. Sensors **17**(7), 1522 (2017)
6. Kuipers, J.B.: Quaternions and Rotation Sequences: A Primer With Applications to Orbits, Aerospace, and Virtual Reality. Princeton University Press, New Jersey, princenton edn. (1999). https://doi.org/10.5860/choice.37-0370
7. Li, J., Wang, Z., Shi, X., Qiu, S., Zhao, H., Guo, M.: Quantitative analysis of abnormal and normal gait based on inertial sensors. In: IEEE 22nd International Conference on Computer Supported Cooperative Work in Design, pp. 365–370 (2018)
8. Mazzetta, I., Zampogna, A., Suppa, A., Gumiero, A., Pessione, M., Irrera, F.: Wearable sensors system for an improved analysis of freezing of gait in Parkinson's disease using electromyography and inertial signals. Sensors **19**(4), 20 (2019)
9. Meng, X., Yu, H., Tham, M.P.: Gait phase detection in able-bodied subjects and dementia patients. In: Proceedings of the Annual International Conference of the IEEE Engineering in Medicine and Biology Society, EMBS, pp. 4907–4910 (2013)
10. Narváez, F., Arbito, F., Luna, C., Merchán, C., Cuenca, M.C., Díaz, G.M.: Kushkalla: A web-based platform to improve functional movement rehabilitation. In: Technologies and Innovation, pp. 194–208 (2017)
11. Narváez, F., Árbito, F., Proaño, R.: A Quaternion-based method to IMU-to-body alignment for gait analysis. In: Digital Human Modeling. Applications in Health, Safety, Ergonomics, and Risk Management, pp. 217–231 (2018)
12. Narváez, F., Marín-Castrillón, D.M., Cuenca, M.C., Latta, M.A.: Development and implementation of technologies for physical telerehabilitation in Latin America: a systematic review of literature, programs and projects. TecnoLógicas **20**(40), 155–176 (2017)

13. Nüesch, C., Roos, E., Pagenstert, G., Mündermann, A.: Measuring joint kinematics of treadmill walking and running: comparison between an inertial sensor based system and a camera-based system. J. Biomech. **57**, 32–38 (2017)
14. Teufl, W., Lorenz, M., Miezal, M., Taetz, B., Fröhlich, M., Bleser, G.: Towards inertial sensor based mobile gait analysis: event-detection and spatio-temporal parameters. Sensors **19**(1), 1–20 (2018)
15. Trojaniello, D., et al.: Estimation of step-by-step spatio-temporal parameters of normal and impaired gait using shank-mounted magneto-inertial sensors: application to elderly, hemiparetic, parkinsonian and choreic gait. J. NeuroEng. Rehabilit. **11**(1), 1–12 (2014)
16. Wang, C., et al.: Estimation of spatial-temporal gait parameters based on the fusion of inertial and film-pressure signals. In: IEEE International Conference on Bioinformatics and Biomedicine (BIBM), pp. 1232–1239 (2018)
17. Wang, Z., Ji, R.: Estimate spatial-temporal parameters of human Gait using inertial sensors. In: IEEE International Conference on Cyber Technology in Automation, Control and Intelligent Systems, pp. 1883–1888 (2015)
18. Wu, G., et al.: ISB recommendation on definitions of joint coordinate system of various joints for the reporting of human joint motion–part I: ankle, hip, and spine. J. Biomech. **35**(4), 543–548 (2002)
19. Zhang, J.T., Novak, A.C., Brouwer, B., Li, Q.: Concurrent validation of Xsens MVN measurement of lower limb joint angular kinematics. Physiol. Measure. **34**(8), 1 (2013)
20. Zhao, H., Wang, Z., Qiu, S., Shen, Y., Wang, J.: IMU-based gait analysis for rehabilitation assessment of patients with gait disorders. In: 4th International Conference on Systems and Informatics (ICSAI), pp. 622–626 (2017)
21. Zijlstra, W., Hof, A.L.: Assessment of spatio-temporal gait parameters from trunk accelerations during human walking. Gait Post. **18**(2), 1–10 (2003)

A Genetic Algorithm for BAP + QCAP with Imprecision in the Arrival of Vessels

Flabio Gutierrez[1(✉)], Edwar Lujan[2], Jose Rodríguez-Melquiades[2], and Miguel Jimenez-Carrion[1]

[1] National University of Piura, Campus Universitario, Urb. Miraflores S/N, Piura, Peru
{flabio,mjimenezc}@unp.edu.pe
[2] National University of Trujillo, Campus Universitario, Av. Juan Pablo II S/N, Trujillo, Peru
{elujans,jrodriguez}@unitru.edu.pe

Abstract. In this work we present a genetic algorithm (GA), to address the imprecision occurring in the berth allocation problem (BAP) and the quay crane assignment problem (QCAP). The BAP + QCAP is an NP-hard problem of combinatorial optimization. The arrival imprecision in the vessels are represented by fuzzy triangular numbers. The fuzzy model and the GA obtain robust berthing plans, which assign quay cranes to each incoming vessel. Also, the plans support early and late arrivals of vessels. To compare the efficiency of the fuzzy model and GA, instances of 5 to 50 vessels were used. The fuzzy model implemented in CPLEX, obtained optimal and non-optimal solutions for small and medium instances, respectively whereas for large instances, solutions were not found in the defined runtime period. In contrast, the GA implemented in C++ obtained a good solution for all the instances in less time.

Keywords: Berth Allocation Problem · Quay Crane Assignment Problem · FFLP model · Genetic Algorithm

1 Introduction

International maritime trade improved in 2017. The best connected economy to the global shipping network was China, followed by, Singapore, the Republic of Korea, Hong Kong and Malaysia, regarding subregional leaders such Panama, Colombia and Mexico in Latin America and the Caribbean; Morocco, Egypt and South Africa in Africa; and Sri Lanka in South Asia. Ukraine has surpassed the Russian Federation as the best connected transition economy. The goods that go by sea, are mostly transported in containers, which are large metal boxes with standard measures in multiples of 20 feet called "twenty-foot equivalent units" (TEU). 753 million TEUs were handled in ports around the world. The global performance of maritime container terminals increased by 6% between 2016 and 2017. Currently the ports of China are the ones with the highest traffic, for example, the Shanghai port moved 40.23 million TEUs [1].

As points of entry and exit of goods in the worldwide, Maritime Container Terminals (MCT) are vital elements of the global supply chain. Due to the increase in global

© Springer Nature Switzerland AG 2020
F. R. Narváez et al. (Eds.): SmartTech-IC 2019, CCIS 1154, pp. 351–363, 2020.
https://doi.org/10.1007/978-3-030-46785-2_28

maritime trade in many ports resource restrictions occur such as space, time, quay cranes. The problems that exist in a TMC are different. In this work we focus on the BAP (Berth Allocation Problem) and the QCAP (Quay Crane Assignment Problem). The BAP is an NP-hard combinatorial optimization problem [2], which consists of assigning to each incoming vessel a berthing position at the quay; the QCAP tries to assign a number of quay cranes (QC) to each berthed vessel, so that all movements can be made to unload or load the containers to or from the vehicles. The QCs are giant cranes that are mounted on rails, therefore, they cannot be passed one from another.

On the other hand, another problem is the arrival times of the vessels that are uncertain, this uncertainty depends on factors such as, other MTC that the vessel must visit, weather conditions (winds, storms), technical problems, or other reasons. Vessels can arrive before or after their expected arrival time [3, 4], this influences other MTC activities.

The BAP and the QCAP have been treated independently there are few jobs that treat the BAP + QCAP together and with imprecise data [5].

A fuzzy MILP (Mixed Integer Linear Programming) model for the discrete and dynamic BAP was proposed in [6], the imprecise time of the arrival of the vessels are represented by triangular fuzzy numbers, this model does not treat the continuous BAP. For the dynamic and continuous BAP + QCAP an MILP model and a GA were developed [7], time spaces are added to the departure times of the vessels to mitigate the effect of the imprecision and give it robustness; however, it does not take into account the possibility of early or late arrivals of vessels.

A Fully Fuzzy Linear Programming (FFLP) model for continuous and dynamic BAP + QCAP is presented in [8]; this model assumes the vessel arrivals are imprecise (fuzzy). The resulting berthing plans supports possible early or late. In this work, a small instance of eight vessels is resolved in CPLEX to show the applicability of the model, but they do not solve the model for real cases, that is, the work does not show the efficiency of the model for different instances.

In this paper, we present a Genetic Algorithm (GA) that solves the BAP + QCAP problem presented in [8]. The GA and FFLP model are compared in small, medium and large instances.

This research paper is structured as follows: Sect. 2, describes the basic concepts of fuzzy sets. Section 3, details the BAP + QCAP problem, the used notation is also described. In Sect. 4, the fuzzy optimization model is presented. Section 5, details the GA implementation. In Sect. 6, the model and the GA are evaluated and compared. Finally, Sect. 7 presents the conclusions and future research work.

2   Introductory Items of Fuzzy Set Theory

Fuzzy sets are used to represent and model the imprecision of systems. Fuzzy set definitions were obtained from [9].

Definition 1. A fuzzy set $\tilde{A}$ in X is a set of pairs:

$$\tilde{A} = \left\{ \left(x, \mu_{\tilde{A}}(x) \right), x \in X \right\}$$

Where, X is the universe of discourse; $\mu_{\tilde{A}} : X \rightarrow [0, 1]$ is the membership function, $\mu_{\tilde{A}}(x)$ represents the degree of x belonging to the set $\tilde{A}$. In this work, we use fuzzy sets defined on real numbers $\mathbb{R}$.

Definition 2. A fuzzy number is a normal and convex fuzzy set in $\mathbb{R}$.

Definition 3. A triangular fuzzy number is represented by $\tilde{A} = (a1, a2, a3)$.

3 Problem Description and Notation

In this work, we consider two known problems in the literature as BAP and QCAP. In addition, it is considered that the vessels have imprecise arrival times; that is to say, they can arrive early or delay. BAP focuses on the moment and positions to berth at the MTC for each arriving vessel. On the other hand, in the QCAP, a number of quay cranes has to be assigned to each vessel to be served. Thus, the research objective focuses on minimizing the waiting (w) and the service times (h). BAP can be represented bi-dimensionally, see Fig. 1, where the horizontal axis represents time and the vertical axis, the quay length.

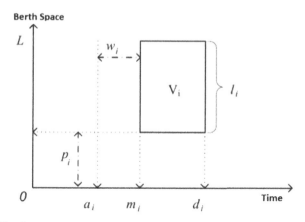

Fig. 1. Representation of a vessel according the time and position.

In this research work we use the next notation [7]:

H: Planning horizon.
QC: Quay cranes available in the container terminal. All QCs carry out the same number of movements per unit of time $(movs\,QC)$, given by the terminal.
L: Length of the quay in the TMC.

Let V is the set of vessels arriving, the data for each vessel $i \in V$ are given by:

a_i: Arrival time to the port.

l_i: Vessel length.
c_i: Required number of movements to load and unload containers of the vessel i.

With the data described above, the following decision variables must be obtained:

m_i: Mooring time of vessel i in the quay. Thus, the service time (w_i) of i is calculated as $(w_i = m_i - a_i)$.
p_i: Berthing position on the berth for the vessel.
q_i: Assigned number of QCs to vessel i.

With these data the following decision variables are defined:

h_i: Service time of the vessel i. This time depends on q_i and c_i, this is: $c_i/(q_i * movs\,QC)$.
t_{ik}: Working time of the QC, k assigned to vessel i.
d_i: Departure time of the vessel i : $(d_i = m_i + h_i)$.
s_i; e_i: Indexes for the first and last QC used in the vessel i, respectively.

We consider the following assumptions: all related information regarding the waiting vessels is known in advance. Each vessel has a draft less than or equal to the quay. Also, simultaneous berthing is allowed. In addition to the safety distance one vessel and another is not considered. Finally, the berthing and departures are not time consuming. And also set the following limitations: the quay length is 700 m, and the available QCs number is 6. The maximum QCs number assigned to a vessel depends on its length. There must also be a safety distance of 35 m among them.

Furthermore, the maximum number of assigned QC is 5. Finally, the number of movements made for a crane in a given time is 2.5.

4   FFLP Model for the BAP + QCAP

In [8], a fuzzy optimization model for BAP + QCAP is presented, where the vessel arrival parameter $\tilde{a}$ and the decision variables: $\tilde{m}$, $\tilde{d}$, $\tilde{h}$, are considered imprecise and represented by fuzzy numbers.

$$min \sum_{i \in V} (\tilde{w}_i + \tilde{h}_i) \tag{1}$$

Subject to:

$$\tilde{m}_i \geq \tilde{a}_i, \ \forall i \in V \tag{2}$$

$$\tilde{w}_i = \tilde{m}_i - \tilde{a}_i, \ \forall i \in V \tag{3}$$

$$\tilde{d}_i = \tilde{m}_i + \tilde{h}_i, \ \forall i \in V \tag{4}$$

$$p_i + l_i \leq L, \ \forall i \in V \tag{5}$$

$$q_i = \sum\nolimits_{k \in QC} \tilde{u}_{ik}, \; \forall i \in V \tag{6}$$

$$1 \leq q_i \leq QC_i^+, \; \forall i \in V \tag{7}$$

$$1 \leq s_i, e_i \leq |QC|, \; \forall i \in V \tag{8}$$

$$s_i \geq e_i, \; \forall i \in V \tag{9}$$

$$q_i = \tilde{e}_i - \tilde{s}_i + 1, \; \forall i \in V \tag{10}$$

$$\sum\nolimits_{k \in QC} t_{iqk} * movQC \geq c_i, \forall i \in V \tag{11}$$

$$\tilde{h}_i = max_{k \in QC} t_{ik}, \; \forall i \in V \tag{12}$$

$$t_{ik} - M * ul_i \leq 0, \forall i \in V \tag{13}$$

$$\tilde{h}_i - M(1 - u_{ik}) - t_{ik} \leq 0, \forall i \in V \tag{14}$$

$$u_{ik} + u_{jk} + z_{ij}^x < 2, \forall i, j \in V, i \neq j \tag{15}$$

$$M(1 - u_{ik}) + (e_i - k) \geq 0, \forall i \in V \tag{16}$$

$$M(1 - u_{ik}) + (k - s_i) \geq 0, \forall i \in V \tag{17}$$

$$p_i + l_i \leq p_j + M\left(1 - z_{ij}^x\right) \quad \forall i, j \in V, i \neq j \tag{18}$$

$$e_i + 1 \leq s_j + M\left(1 - z_{ij}^x\right), \forall i \in V, i \neq j \tag{19}$$

$$\tilde{d}_i \leq \tilde{m}_j + M\left(1 - z_{ij}^y\right), \forall i \in V, i \neq j \tag{20}$$

$$\tilde{m}_i + \tilde{h}_i \leq H \quad \forall i \in V \tag{21}$$

$$z_{ij}^x + z_{ji}^x + z_{ij}^y + z_{ji}^y \geq 1 \quad \forall i, j \in V, i \neq j \tag{22}$$

$$z_{ij}^x, z_{ij}^y \in \{0, 1\} \quad \forall i, j \in V, i \neq j \tag{23}$$

In the proposed model, the objective is the allocation of all vessels according to several constraints, which minimize the total weighted time (waiting and service), for all vessels. The explanation of the meaning of the restrictions can be reviewed in [8].

It is assumed that all parameters and decision variables are linear and some of them are fuzzy thus we are facing a FFLP problem. The imprecision arrival time of vessels are represented by triangular fuzzy numbers $\tilde{a} = (a1, a2, a3)$, the berthing time $\tilde{m} = (m1, m2, m3)$, $\tilde{h} = (h1, h2, h3)$ is considered a singleton, $\tilde{d} = (d1, d2, d3)$. The Nasseri method [10], was used to transform the FFLP model into a classical Linear Programming (LP) model, see [8]. The restrictions of the PL model are used in the proposed AG to solve the BAP + QCAP.

5   Genetic Algorithm

In this section, we described the used GA to solve the problem. We first designed the structure of an individual (chromosome), and then generated the initial population. The chromosome is composed by n genes (n: number of vessels). The gene position indicates the vessel number, i.e., gene 1 represents vessel 1, each gene contains the number of cranes assigned to each vessel, see Table 1.

Table 1. Example of chromosome

G1	G2	G3	G4	...	Gn
2	3	4	5	...	2

The following activities were performed: The size population was defined and individuals that integrated the population were generated. Each individual represents a valid schedule, i.e., the chromosome values fit the problem conditions and the decision maker could be used. In order to have more diversity, these individuals are randomly generated, this allows us to find better solutions and avoid local minimums or maximums. The population size was set to 100 individuals. Then, when assigning the berthing time and position, all the restrictions of the problem are verified, which are represented in Eqs. (2) to (23).

In order to know which individuals represent the best solutions. The adaptation function (fitness) of each individual is evaluated (Eq. 24). This function seeks to minimize the waiting and service time.

$$fa = \sum_{i \in V} \left(\frac{(m1_i - a3_i) + (m2_i - a2_i) + (m1_i - a3_i)}{3} \right) + h_i \qquad (24)$$

Parent 1 (Individual 1):

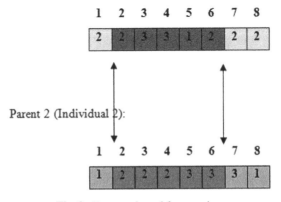

Fig. 2. Parent selected for crossing.

The next steps are the selection of the crossing and mutation operators, which are applied in each generation of the GA. The selection method used was a random selection. Once the individuals had been selected, the crossover operator was applied to obtain the children (new individuals). We applied the two points crossing method which randomly generates two points to cross them; new individuals replace their parents, as long as they overcome them in adaptation. Figure 2, shows an example, where the parents will be crossed using the two-point method. Likewise, Fig. 3 shows the resulting children created from the parents.

After crossing the two points, a random number is generated for each individual then this number is compared to the mutation probability. If the probability is less, mutation can be carried out. The process of mutation consists of choosing a gene at random so the gene value is replaced by another randomly generated value (see Fig. 4). This value represents the number of quay cranes assigned to the vessel. One of the main advantages of the mutation is the creation of individuals that explore other possible solutions. This creation allows to escape from the minimum and maximum local.

Children 1 (New Individual 1):

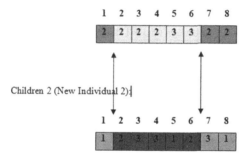

Children 2 (New Individual 2):

Fig. 3. Generated children (new individuals).

This process is repeated over and over until the number of generations is completed. The best individual is the best plan for the BAP + QCAP.

Individual:

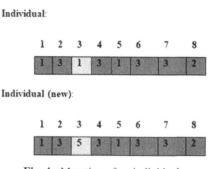

Individual (new):

Fig. 4. Mutation of an individual.

Next, we present the genetic algorithm pseudocode (Algorithm 1).

INPUT: $V, L, QCs, \tilde{a} = (a1, a2, a3), movQC, c, l, iterations$
OUPUT: Best individual: $\tilde{m} = (m1, m2, m3)$ and p.

Step 1. Calculate: $h_i = \left(\frac{c_i}{q_i * movsQC}\right)$

Step 2. Generate population with n individuals.

Step 3. Assign time and berthing position, verifying that for each individual. The following restrictions are met:

$$m1_i \geq a1_i, m2_i \geq a2_i, m3_i \geq a3_i$$
$$p_i + l_i \leq L$$
$$m1_j \geq m1_i + h_i$$
$$m2_j \geq m2_i + h_i$$
$$m3_j \geq m3_i + h_i$$
$$p_j \geq p_i + l_i$$
$$donde\ i, j \in V,\ i \neq j$$

And all other model restrictions are met (Eq. (3) to (24))

Step 4. WHILE iterations > 0 **DO**

Step 4.1. Evaluate the adaptation function of each individual in the population:

$$fa = \sum_{i \in V} \left(\frac{(m1_i - a3_i) + (m2_i - a2_i) + (m1_i - a3_i)}{3}\right) + h_i$$

Step 4.2. Select individuals for crossing (crossing probability of 0.5)

Step 4.3. Cross selected individuals (apply two-point method).

Step 4.4. IF children do not meet the restrictions presented in step 3 **THEN** correct the children.

Step 4.5. IF children have a better adaptation than parents **THEN** eliminate parents **ELSE** eliminate children

Step 4.6. Mutate individuals with a mutation probability of 0.1.

Step 4.7. IF the mutated individual does not meet the restrictions presented in step 3 **THEN** correct individual.

Step 4.8. Find the best individual.

Step 4.9. Calculate the average adaptation of the Population.

Step 4.10. Decrease iterations in 1.

Step 5. Show better Individual.

Step 6. End

The restrictions that must be met in step 3 and the adaptation function of step 4.1 are obtained from the FFLP model solution process presented in Sect. 4. For a more detailed explanation, please review the work [8].

6 Evaluation

The two approaches developed in this paper, the FFLP model and the GA, were coded using CPLEX solver and C++, respectively. For the evaluation process, we used a personal computer equipped with an i5 Core (TM) - 4210U CPU 2.4 Ghz, with 8.00 Gb of RAM. The experiments were performed within a 60 min "timeout".

In the GA, the population size was 100. Crossover and mutation probabilities were 0.5 and 0.1, respectively.

6.1 Case Study

To evaluate the GA we use the data from Table 2. The input data for each vessel were composed by the imprecise arrival time (early, on time, and delay), service time (h), length (L), number of QCs movements (Movs) and other data mentioned in the problem description. In Fig. 5, we show the imprecise arrival of vessel as a triangular fuzzy number. For example, to the vessel V3, the most possible arrival is at 68 units of time, but it could be early or late up to 56 and 85 units of time, respectively.

Table 2. Instance with 8 vessels.

Vessel	a1	a2	a3	h	L	Movs
V1	14	16	20	83	260	4160
V2	18	31	48	96	232	9680
V3	56	68	86	29	139	3640
V4	81	82	97	60	193	7610
V5	92	105	119	54	287	6860
V6	106	116	133	63	318	6300
V7	126	138	147	162	366	8110
V8	155	167	176	12	166	1560

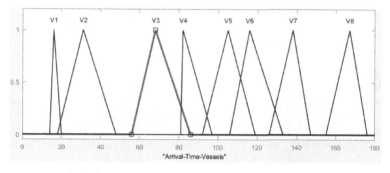

Fig. 5. Imprecise arrival of vessels showed in Table 2

The fuzzy berthing plan obtained with the AG is shown in Table 3; for example, the vessel 4; it can berth between 115 and 145 units of time, with more possibility at 128 units; the departure time can be between 175 units of time and 205 units of time, with more possibility at 188 units; it must berth at position 0; and is assigned 5 cranes. The AG obtains fuzzy berthing plans similar to the FFLP model.

Table 3. Fuzzy berthing plan for study case

Vessel	m1	m2	m3	h	d1	d2	d3	L	p	QCs
V1	14	16	20	83	97	99	103	260	0	2
V2	18	31	48	96	114	127	144	232	261	4
V3	98	100	104	29	127	129	133	139	0	5
V4	115	128	145	60	175	188	205	193	0	5
V5	176	189	206	54	230	243	260	287	0	5
V6	231	244	261	63	294	307	324	318	0	4
V7	176	189	206	162	338	351	368	366	319	2
V8	295	308	325	12	307	320	337	166	0	5

In order to check the robustness of the plan, we simulate incidents (See Table 4), with these incidents, a feasible final berthing plan is obtained (see Table 5).

Table 4. Incidences in vessel arrival times

Vessel	Incidence	Time
V1	Early	2
V2	Delay	17
V3	On time	0
V4	On time	0
V5	Delay	11
V6	On time	0
V7	Early	10
V8	On time	0

In Fig. 6, in the fuzzy berthing plan, the vessels are represented in polygon form, instead of rectangles as shown before in Fig. 1. The red line represents the advance, the green line represents the delay; for a more detailed explanation, please review the work [11], note that the final berthing plan (rectangles) is part of the fuzzy plan initially obtained.

Table 5. Final berthing plan including incidences

Vessel	m	h	D	L	p	QCs
V1	14	83	97	260	0	2
V2	48	96	144	232	261	4
V3	98	29	127	139	0	5
V4	127	60	187	193	0	5
V5	187	54	241	287	0	5
V6	241	63	304	318	0	4
V7	176	162	338	366	319	2
V8	304	12	316	166	0	5

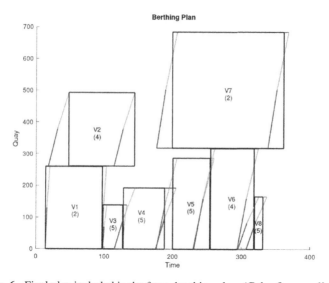

Fig. 6. Final plan included in the fuzzy berthing plan. (Color figure online)

6.2 Instance Set and Results

In order to compare the efficiency of the FFLP model and GA, a benchmark containing instances of 5 to 50 vessels was used (see Table 6).

From results in Table 6, obviously, in all cases, the objective function increases as the number of incoming vessels increases. To the given timeout, CPLEX found the optimum solution of the instances from 5 to 8 vessels, a non-optimum of the instances from 9 to 25 vessels; and for a number of vessels greater or equal to 30 no solution was founded. Instead, the AG obtains a solution in all of them. In instances where CPLEX gets a solution, this is better than the AG. In all instances, the AG get a solution in less time than CPLEX.

Table 6. Results of the FFLP model and GA.

Vessels	CPLEX			GA	
	Objective function	Time (s)	Optimal	Objective function	Time (s)
5	538.3	8.7	Yes	563.4	0.124
6	722.3	22.7	Yes	762.4	0.140
7	953.3	267.4	Yes	1150.4	0.144
8	1038.3	2589.1	Yes	1204.8	0.172
9	1335.7	3600	No	1668.6	0.192
10	1515.	3600	No	1883.0	0.207
11	1825.3	3600	No	2052.0	0.218
12	2375.0	3600	No	2642.4	0.234
13	2810.3	3600	No	2924.3	0.56
14	3370.7	3600	No	3746.4	0.296
15	3668	3600	No	3922.2	0.321
20	6851	3600	No	7255.0	0.573
25	9397.7	3600	No	9814.2	0.709
30	–	–	–	13572.3	0.916
35	–	–	–	16842.2	1.589
40	–	–	–	19341.5	2.262
45	–	–	–	27381.1	2.867
50	–	–	–	29698.3	4.884

7 Conclusions and Future Work

The implementations of the FFLP model and the GA for the BAP + QCAP give as results the planning of the berths and the appropriate allocation of the quay resources.

From the obtained results, we can assure that the FFLP model obtained optimal solutions only for small instances, non-optimal solutions were obtained for medium instances, for large instances any solutions were obtained; in all cases the AG got good solutions in shorter times.

The solution of the BAP + QCAP by AG can be used to obtain berthing plans and quay crane allocation for TMC that receives a large number of vessels and the plans support possible early or delayed arrival of the vessels.

Considering the inherent complexity of the studied problem BAP + QCAP (Non-polynomial complexity), we can observe the importance of the metaheuristics, in this case the AG since it allows us to find schedules in shorter times.

Finally, from this research work there are open problems for future researches. For example, one can extend the model in order that it also considers multiple quays. Also, heuristic can be applied, alongside with genetic algorithms to get better solutions.

References

1. UNCTAD: World seaborne trade, 15 June 2019. https://stats.unctad.org/handbook/MaritimeTransport/WorldSeaborneTrade.html
2. Lim, A.: The berth planning problem. Oper. Res. Lett. **22**(2), 105–110 (1998)
3. Bruggeling, M., Verbraeck, A., Honig, H.: Decision support for container terminal berth planning: integration and visualization of terminal information. In: Proceedings of the Van de Vervoers logistieke Werkdagen (VLW 2011), pp. 263–283. University Press, Zelzate (2011)
4. Laumanns, M.: Robust adaptive resource allocation in container terminals. In: Proceedings of the 25th Mini-EURO Conference Uncertainty and Robustness in Planning and Decision Making, Coimbra, Portugal, pp. 501–517 (2010)
5. Bierwirth, C., Meisel, F.: A survey of berth allocation and quay crane scheduling problems in container terminals. Eur. J. Oper. Res. **202**(3), 615–627 (2010)
6. Expósito-Izquiero, C., Lalla-Ruiz, E., Lamata, T., Melián-Batista, B., Moreno-Vega, J.M.: Fuzzy optimization models for seaside port logistics: berthing and quay crane scheduling. In: Madani, K., Dourado, A., Rosa, A., Filipe, J., Kacprzyk, J. (eds.) Computational Intelligence. SCI, vol. 613, pp. 323–343. Springer, Cham (2016). https://doi.org/10.1007/978-3-319-23392-5_18
7. Rodriguez, M., Ingolotti, L., Barber, F., Salido, M., Puente, J.: A genetic algorithm for robust berth allocation and quay crane assignment. Prog. Artif. Intell. **2**(4), 177–192 (2014). https://doi.org/10.1007/s13748-014-0056-3
8. Gutierrez, F., Lujan, E., Asmat, R., Vergara, E.: A fully fuzzy linear programming model for berth allocation and quay crane assignment. In: Simari, G.R., Fermé, E., Gutiérrez Segura, F., Rodríguez Melquiades, J.A. (eds.) IBERAMIA 2018. LNCS (LNAI), vol. 11238, pp. 302–313. Springer, Cham (2018). https://doi.org/10.1007/978-3-030-03928-8_25
9. Young-Jou, L., Hwang, C.: Fuzzy Mathematical Programming: Methods and Applications. LNE, vol. 394. Springer, Heidelberg (2012). https://doi.org/10.1007/978-3-642-48753-8
10. Nasseri, S.: Fully fuzzy linear programming with inequality constraints. Int. J. Ind. Math. **5**(4), 309–316 (2013)
11. Gutierrez, F., Lujan, E., Vergara, E., Asmat, R.: A fully fuzzy linear programming model to the berth allocation problem. Ann. Comput. Sci. Inf. Syst. **11**, 453–458 (2017)

Data Analysis of Particle Physics Experiments Based on Machine Learning and the Mitchell's Criteria

Huber Nieto-Chaupis[✉]

Dirección de Investigación, Universidad Autonoma del Peru,
Km.16.3 Villa el Salvador, Lima, Peru
huber.nieto@gmail.com

Abstract. Commonly the searching and identification of new particles, requires to reach highest efficiencies and purities as well. It demands to apply a chain of cuts that reject the background substantially. In most cases the processes to extract signal from the background is carried out by hand with some assistance of well designed and intelligent codes that save time and resources in high energy physics experiments. In this paper we present one application of the Mitchell's criteria to extract efficiently beyond Standard Model signal events yielding an error of order of 1.22%. The usage of Machine Learning schemes appears to be advantageous when large volumes of data need to be scrutinized.

1 Introduction

1.1 Motivation

Clearly, one of the most successful theories that has been tested in large and international experiments, is the Standard Model inside of high energy physics. The most prominent example was that of the discovery of the Higgs boson as achieved by the ATLAS and CMS experiments in CERN in 2012. In fact, the precision of measuring the mass of Higgs boson was in fully according to the predicted theory. Furthermore, these experiments still do continue in the searching of new particles as predicted by advanced theories. With the arrival of novel computational technologies, the exercise of finding new particles or measuring physics properties becomes automatized. In fact, one example is the implementation of sophisticated algorithms entirely based on the so-called Machine Learning. One os these well sustained algorithms is the derived by Mitchell and it is well-known as the Mitchell's criteria by which has strong features whose applicability reaches the territory of the high energy physics where there is a mandatory policy on the disentangle between signal and background. So that one expects that the application of the Mitchell's criteria can be seen as an alternative but powerful methodology to extract signal of new physics at the level of one per mile.

© Springer Nature Switzerland AG 2020
F. R. Narváez et al. (Eds.): SmartTech-IC 2019, CCIS 1154, pp. 364–374, 2020.
https://doi.org/10.1007/978-3-030-46785-2_29

1.2   Identification of Problem

Among the different ways to claim a discovery, we identified the fact that the signal should be visible and presenting a large ratio against the background. To accomplish this, experimental particle physicists have systematized computational methodologies that aims to reject huge amount of noise data [1].

For instance, the purity and efficiency are defined as follows:

$$\mathcal{P} = \frac{N_S}{N_S + N_B} \tag{1}$$

$$\mathcal{E} = \frac{N_{S,A}}{N_{S,N}} \tag{2}$$

where N_S and N_B denote the number of signal and background events, whereas $N_{S,A}$ and $N_{S,N}$ the remaining number of signal events after cuts and the number of signal events without any cut. Often the product $\mathcal{E} \otimes \mathcal{P}$ if of great interest in the claiming of identifying new particles.

Although in most cases has been coined definitions inside the framework of Advanced Statistics, nowadays is used Bayesian theories, maximum likelihood tests and parameters estimation [2]. Equation (1) and (2) represent to certain extent a manner to assess the quality of signal. These relations have extensively used in the field of Monte Carlo simulation in the studies of future colliders. Although for studies of signal identification, the usage of (1) and (2) might sound rather empirical, however both have been of importance to assess real capabilities of prospective experiments in future colliders.

This can be applied to the case where the mass of any new particle can be measured. Thus $N(E)$ the number of events with respect to the energy after cuts is commonly employed to test mass's models. In this manner the main task is to identify $N(E) = S(E) + B(E)$ the signal and background respectively. Unfortunately, both are observed together so one needs to apply advanced techniques to identify substantially the signal to proceed with the fitting procedures that constitutes the final computational strategy to extract any physical observable with the highest statistics.

1.3   What's Done in This Paper?

In this paper, based on the Eq. (1) and Eq. (2), we perform an analysis of signal extraction from its background but using the criteria of Mitchell inside the framework of Machine Learning. We aim to systematize the searching of new symmetries in ongoing and prospective experiments where the main task is to (i) identify and (ii) measure properties of new states in scenarios of abundance of data [3].

Following the heuristic mechanisms of the experimental high energy (HEP) physics where diverse schemes of flow of cuts are applied, we fusion the Mitchell's ideas [4] to the ones of standard usage in HEP. In this manner, the coherent inclusion of a cutflow in a Machine Learning algorithm should be done under the basis of effective collaboration, targeting to minimize those signal events that might be rejected along the operations of signal-background separation. It demands to incorporate well-known algorithms such as the Metropolis scheme that in essence can be summarized as follows

```
IF EVENT X(K,J)>X(K,J-1) THEN
ACCEPT
OTHERWISE REJECTS
K → K+1
```

where X(K,J) the signal distribution for the K-th cut variable and the J-th bin. Actually, the lines shown above appear to be of common use in HEP, and despite that the master code targets to extract the signal events with a relative error, mostly of this error is adjudicated to inaccuracy of the human decision to accept or reject events. We postulated that this might be inhibited when a sophisticated algorithm as the one following the Mitchell's criteria and yielding an optimized statistics that allows us to claim the existence of events belonging to new physics, for example. The remaining of this paper is structured as follows: in second section we reviewed the HEP statistical concepts in order to engage with the well-known Mitchell's algorithm. In third section we apply the theoretical ideas of the proposed scheme to study the properties of Supersymmetric particles [5] that might be observed in an electron-positron collider beyond the LHC-era. In fourth part we present the results wheres last section presents the conclusion of paper.

2   The FlowCuts-Mitchell Algorithm

2.1   Basic Definitions

Consider a certain experiment where after a time T it was collected a data consisting in a large amount of events. The data acquisition system has the capability of save the physics properties per event. In this manner it is possible the reconstruction of M variables that are needed to identify new physics events. Therefore, we have initially the variable "Q" that is the focus of analysis and initially there are N events in a given range. Therefore considering Eq. (2) we define the efficiency when a first cut is applied:

$$\mathcal{E}(Q,1) = \frac{N(Q,1)}{N(Q,0)} \tag{3}$$

where $N(Q,1)$ and $N(Q,0)$ the number of events of the variable Q after and before the application of the first cut. We illustrate this operation in Fig. 1 below.

As seen in Fig. 1 the imposition of the cuts affects in high degree to the background than the signal. Thus, after of L cuts:

$$\mathcal{E}(Q,L) = \frac{N(Q,L)}{N(Q,0)} \tag{4}$$

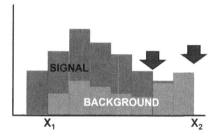

Fig. 1. Illustration of the application of cut to reject away evident background events. Red arrows indicate the position of cuts of maximum convenience to the signal events. (Color figure online)

By following the logic of (4), the purity can be written below as:

$$\mathcal{P}(Q, L) = \frac{S(Q, L)}{S(Q, L) + B(Q, L)} \tag{5}$$

We can also impose the condition after each cut that is a necessary condition to pass to next cut. It can be simplified with then definition of the vector $\mathcal{C}(Q, L)$,

$$\text{Max}\left[\mathcal{C}(Q, L)\right] = \text{Max}\left[\mathcal{P}(Q, L) \otimes \mathcal{E}(Q, L)\right] \tag{6}$$

It should be noted that per each cut there is a specific range in the variable Q that has also a concrete binning by which the applied cut should be done with a particular careful in order to optimize and care the signal events.

Commonly the choice of cuts is done by hand. For example consider the value ℓ if the variable Q, then the signal variable has N_ℓ events while the background $B_{(\ell)}$.

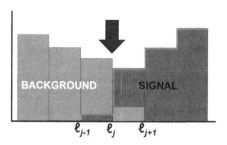

Fig. 2. The application of cut with a care on the bin that do not has implications on the number of signal events but it does on the background ones.

In Fig. 2 is sketched the importance of binning for the choice of any cut along the variable Q. While the cut is applied on the point ℓ where signal surpasses to the background, the acceptance for all those values $>\ell$ is guaranteeing still an acceptable signal efficiency with a substantial decreasing of the background events.

As seen there, the application of the cut on ℓ only would affect a few amount of signal events but it is rejecting noise events. In according to Fig. 2 the other two possibilities are fully discarded:

- $\ell > \ell_j$: this scenario cannot be contemplated because beyond ℓ_j is pure signal events.
- $\ell < \ell_j$: this scenario is a bit questionable in the sense that there is still some signal events belonging to the bin ℓ_{j-1} however the number of the background ones surpasses largely to signal.

In this way appears relevant to compare the number of events both signal and background along the bins of the variable under study previous to the application of the cut. In terms of computing it demands to implement a successive comparison of the number of events, but emphasizing that the signal would have to be biggest than the background ones.

So that, once that it has been identified the value along the variable, then the subsequent step would consist in the application of the cut. With this step, the efficiency and purity are calculated.

Again, the transition to the next cut requires to employ once more the procedure that optimizes the application of the cut. In general, experience tell us that there are actually various values along the variable which might exist interesting candidates where the cut turns out to be applicable.

The application of cuts allows to measure properties of new particles [5] such as the branching ratio of decay. In fact, for this case, the final number of signal events after of all applied cuts is mandatory to estimate the error on the measurement of the main channel decay of the scalar supersymmetric particles. In all these simulations the target was that for reaching a Max $[\mathcal{C}(Q, L)]$ of order of 90%. Klaemke [6] has implemented a novel statistical error formulation based on efficiencies and purities from the remaining statistics after of the application of cuts.

2.2   The Implementation of the Mitchell's Criteria

For Mitchell, any system can improve its history of actions in according to three aspects: (A) **Task** any simple or complex system has a kind of task along the time as part of the intrinsic existence, (B) **Performance** that is quality by which the task is accomplished. Clearly, this can be successful or fail, and (C) **Experience** that express the fact by which the system has learned to improve its future actions.

Now we turned to use these criteria to the computational analysis of signal reconstruction through a flowcut algorithm. Consider

```
TASK
1 MEASUREMENT OF PROPERTIES
2 DO Q = 1, MAX ! VARIABLES
3 S(Q) = INITIAL SIGNAL EVENTS
4 B(Q) = INITIAL BACKGROUND EVENTS
```

```
 5 MAX = NUMBER OF CUTS
 6 DO L = 1, MAX ! CUTS
 7 DO J = 1, MAX ! RANGES
PERFORMANCE
 8 SETS A BEST RANGE = R(Q,J)
 9 APPLY CUT C(L,J)
10 S(Q,L,J) = SIGNAL
11 B(Q,L,J) = BACKGROUND
12 C(Q,L,J) = S(Q,L,J) ⊗ B(Q,L,J)
13 IF C(Q,L,J)< 0.5 THEN
14 GOTO 8 SEARCH NEW RANGES
15 END IF
16 END DO
17 IF L = MAX THEN
18 ESTIMATE OBSERVABLES
19 BR(L,J) BRANCHING RATIO
20 MINV(L,J) INVARIANT MASS
21 E(Q,L,J) ERROR
EXPERIENCE
22 IF E(Q,L)>15% THEN METROPOLIS
23 GOTO 5 SEARCH FOR NEW AND MORE CUTS
24 END IF
25 END IF
26 END DO
27 END DO
28 END
```

3   Simulations and Results

We have applied the previous algorithm with simulated data to test the efficiency of the Mitchell's criteria. It is noteworthy that in contrast to those ordinary analysis done by hand, we have executed the algorithm in a FORTRAN code inside of a Makefile script that do the following:

- ask for the specific reactions
- assign the background reactions
- enter luminosity collider
- calculates number of events
- compiles and run algorithm
- creates histograms
- apply algorithm
- when $\mathcal{P}(Q,L) \otimes \mathcal{E}(Q,L) > 0.9$
- display best scenario

To achieve the simulations we have used well-known codes such as PYTHIA, ISAJET, CIRCE, SHERPA, and finally a fast detector simulator inspired on the well-known

SIMDET [6]. For instance in Fig. 3 left side is plotted the resulting histograms corresponding to the case of $\gamma\gamma \to \tilde{\tau}^+\tilde{\tau}^-$ with the staus decaying into tau leptons and subsequently into charged pions. For this exercise it was employed a cone-finder that provides a best identification of the tau lepton. In effect, in photon collisions is characterized by having pile-up events by which it produces million of final state hadrons that mimic the signal in the case that one is searching by supersymmetric scalar taus particles. As shown in the final histogram, the energy of final state pions has resulted in a very low efficiency and purity as displayed: 0.204 and 0.27 respectively. Certainly, one need to apply more robust kinematic cuts in order to defeat the pile-up ones but substantially. In right side of Fig. 3, is shown the resulting histogram after the application of the Mitchell's algorithm resulting in an efficiency and purity of order of 0.63 and 0.73. Although these numbers are actually above the 50% still the final spectrum of the 3-muons invariant mass still contains some background events along the tail of spectrum. In Fig. 4 are plotted the resulting histograms in the scenario of photon collisions. For this, we have simulated the reactions $\gamma\gamma \to \tilde{\ell}_L^+\tilde{\ell}_L^-$ emphasizing the pair of charged muons at the final state. In top left and right panels, the reconstructed invariant mass of μ^+ and μ^-. While magenta and green colours denote the background and signal respectively. In both cases the preselection has as result efficiencies below 25%. While the Mitchell's algorithm measures the efficiencies as seen in line 22, for those low values the estimation of the product $\mathcal{P}(Q,L) \otimes \mathcal{E}(Q,L)$ is canceled and new scenarios with different and effective cuts are searched.

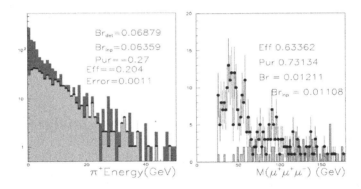

Fig. 3. (Left) Energy pion spectrum after cuts. (Right) The invariant mass for 3 muons in slepton production in $\gamma\gamma$ collisions.

In fact, the new searching of efficient cuts that provides a better performance is seen in the bottom left and right panels where the efficiency and purity of order of 0.70, 075 and 0.91 and 0.86 respectively, are shown. Clearly the right panel is an interesting example of how the Mitchell's criteria might be employed as a computational tool that works out through the best set of cuts in an independent manner without a direct human intervention. There can be seen that the background has been defeated substantially to perform further measurements such as the branching ratio of the main channel decays.

3.1 Measuring Slepton Decays with the Mitchell's Criteria

Photon collisions can offer an interesting arena to measure branching ratios of the so-called scalar leptons with a high statistical despite of the fact of the presence of the pile-up events that might be a factor that would degrade the kinematic spectra that is a factor that makes impossible to measure the mass of these supersymmetric particles. Sophisticated schemes of background discrimination have been proposed in the past for test of precision [7]. With a sample 100K signal events and 5M background events, we have applied the Mitchell ideas resulting in the Fig. 5 for the right-handed Smuon production [8]. For instance the relative statistical error of $\mathrm{Br}(\tilde{\mu}_R \to \tilde{\chi}_2^0 \mu)$ we start with the relation

$$2 \cdot \mathcal{L} \cdot \sigma_{\mathrm{eff}} \cdot \mathrm{Br}(\tilde{\mu}_R \to \mu \tilde{\chi}_1^0) \cdot \mathrm{Br}(\tilde{\mu}_R \to \mu \tilde{\chi}_2^0) = N_{\mathrm{ML}} \frac{\mathrm{p}}{\epsilon}, \tag{7}$$

where $\mathcal{L}$ and σ_{eff} the machine luminosity and the effective cross section. Once the signal has been disentangled from the background as seen in Fig. 5 for the scenarios top and bottom, being the bottom panel the one that by which was possible to get a high efficiency of order of 75% after of applying the Mitchell's criteria. With this we write down the statistical errors as $\frac{\Delta \mathrm{Br}(\tilde{\mu}_R \to \mu \tilde{\chi}_2^0)}{\mathrm{Br}(\tilde{\mu}_R \to \mu \tilde{\chi}_2^0)}$, that for the case where not any machine learning is applied and only the experience is employed and the cut procedure is through by hand without any computational strategy one gets

$$\sqrt{\left(\frac{\Delta N_{\mathrm{HAND}}}{N_{\mathrm{HAND}}}\right)^2 + \left(\frac{\Delta \mathcal{L}}{\mathcal{L}}\right)^2 + \left(\frac{\Delta \sigma}{\sigma}\right)^2} = 3.79\%, \tag{8}$$

with N_{HAND} the number of final signal events after the cut application when not any Machine Learning technique is used. The case when the algorithm above is applied with the highest efficiencies as seen in bottom panel of Fig. 5 the error can be written and calculated as:

$$\sqrt{\left(\frac{\Delta N_{\mathrm{ML}}}{N_{\mathrm{ML}}}\right)^2 + \left(\frac{\Delta \mathcal{L}}{\mathcal{L}}\right)^2 + \left(\frac{\Delta \sigma}{\sigma}\right)^2} = 1.22\%, \tag{9}$$

that is approximately one third of the one when not any Machine Learning algorithm is used. In both cases the errors of the luminosity and cross section might be critic in a fully scenario of precision measurements. This demonstrates to some extent the possible relevant impact of the implementation of the Mitchell's criteria to a pretty efficient extraction of the signal from the background events.

3.2 The Machine Learning Error

The algorithm of Machine Learning might be subject to errors of decisions so one should include an extra error $\frac{Q}{q}$ therefore we arrived to $\mathcal{S}$ the expected error from the signal in a entire Machine Learning scenario:

$$S = \frac{\sqrt{\left(\frac{\Delta N_{\mathrm{ML}}}{N_{\mathrm{ML}}}\right)^2 + \left(\frac{\Delta \mathcal{L}}{\mathcal{L}}\right)^2 + \left(\frac{\Delta \sigma}{\sigma}\right)^2}}{\sqrt{\left(\frac{\Delta N_{\mathrm{ML}}}{N_{\mathrm{ML}}}\right)^2 + \left(\frac{\Delta \mathcal{L}}{\mathcal{L}}\right)^2 + \left(\frac{\Delta \sigma}{\sigma}\right)^2 + \left(\frac{\Delta Q}{q}\right)^2}} = 7.62\%, \tag{10}$$

Now we can define the union of the efficiencies in both experimental and from Machine Learning where only signal and background enters into the analysis:

$$\mathcal{U} = \frac{\left(\frac{\Delta N}{N+B}\right)^2}{\sqrt{\left(\frac{\Delta \mathcal{L}}{\mathcal{L}}\right)^2 + \left(\frac{\Delta \sigma}{\sigma}\right)^2 + \left(\frac{\Delta N}{N+B}\right)^2}} = 3.79\%, \tag{11}$$

and finally we define the total error that is actually the combination of the Machine Learning and the obtained with Monte Carlo yielding:

$$\mathcal{T} = \frac{\sqrt{\left(\frac{\Delta N_{\mathrm{ML}}}{N_{\mathrm{ML}}}\right)^2 + \left(\frac{\Delta \sigma}{\sigma}\right)^2}}{\sqrt{\left(\frac{\Delta N_{\mathrm{ML}}}{N_{\mathrm{ML}}}\right)^2 + \left(\frac{\Delta \mathcal{L}}{\mathcal{L}}\right)^2 + \left(\frac{\Delta \sigma}{\sigma}\right)^2 + \left(\frac{\Delta Q}{q}\right)^2}} + \frac{\sqrt{\left(\frac{\Delta N}{N+B}\right)^2}}{\sqrt{\left(\frac{\Delta \mathcal{L}}{\mathcal{L}}\right)^2 + \left(\frac{\Delta \sigma}{\sigma}\right)^2 + \left(\frac{\Delta N}{N+B}\right)^2}}$$

$$+ \frac{\sqrt{\left(\frac{\Delta S}{S}\right)^2}}{\sqrt{\left(\frac{\Delta \mathcal{L}}{\mathcal{L}}\right)^2 + \left(\frac{\Delta \sigma}{\sigma}\right)^2 + \left(\frac{\Delta N}{N+B}\right)^2}} + \frac{\sqrt{\left(\frac{\Delta B}{B}\right)^2 + \left(\frac{\Delta S}{S}\right)^2}}{\sqrt{\left(\frac{\Delta \mathcal{L}}{\mathcal{L}}\right)^2 + \left(\frac{\Delta \sigma}{\sigma}\right)^2}} = 12.93\%, \tag{12}$$

Below we presented the total errors pure Machine Learning $\mathcal{ML}$ and the full $\mathcal{F}_{\mathrm{ML+MC}}$ that is the sum of the Machine Learning and Monte Carlo resulting in the highest error since the parametrization of the random number generator is fully independent from the Machine Learning algorithm.

$$\mathcal{ML} = \frac{\sqrt{\left(\frac{\Delta N_{\mathrm{ML}}}{N_{\mathrm{ML}}}\right)^2 + \left(\frac{\Delta \mathcal{L}}{\mathcal{L}}\right)^2 + \left(\frac{\Delta \sigma}{\sigma}\right)^2}}{\sqrt{\left(\frac{\Delta N_{\mathrm{ML}}}{N_{\mathrm{ML}}}\right)^2 + \left(\frac{\Delta \mathcal{L}}{\mathcal{L}}\right)^2 + \left(\frac{\Delta \sigma}{\sigma}\right)^2 + \left(\frac{\Delta Q}{q}\right)^2}}$$

$$+ \frac{\sqrt{\left(\frac{\Delta B}{B}\right)^2 + \left(\frac{\Delta S}{S}\right)^2}}{\sqrt{\left(\frac{\Delta \mathcal{L}}{\mathcal{L}}\right)^2 + \left(\frac{\Delta \sigma}{\sigma}\right)^2 + \left(\frac{\Delta N}{N+B}\right)^2}} + \frac{\sqrt{\left(\frac{\Delta B}{B}\right)^2 + \left(\frac{\Delta S}{S}\right)^2}}{\sqrt{\left(\frac{\Delta \mathcal{L}}{\mathcal{L}}\right)^2 + \left(\frac{\Delta \sigma}{\sigma}\right)^2 + \left(\frac{\Delta N}{N+B}\right)^2}} = 14.25\%, \tag{13}$$

$$\mathcal{F}_{\mathrm{ML+MC}} = \beta_1 \frac{\sqrt{\left(\frac{\Delta N_{\mathrm{ML}}}{N_{\mathrm{ML}}}\right)^2 + \left(\frac{\Delta \mathcal{L}}{\mathcal{L}}\right)^2}}{\left(\frac{\Delta \mathcal{L}}{\mathcal{L}}\right)} + \beta_2 \frac{\left(\frac{\Delta N}{N+B}\right)}{\sqrt{\left(\frac{\Delta \mathcal{L}}{\mathcal{L}}\right)^2 + \left(\frac{\Delta \sigma}{\sigma}\right)^2 + \left(\frac{\Delta N}{N+B}\right)^2}}$$

$$+ \beta_3 \sqrt{\left(\frac{\Delta N_{\mathrm{ML}}}{N_{\mathrm{ML}}}\right) + \left(\frac{\Delta \sigma}{\sigma}\right)^2 + \left(\frac{\Delta Q}{q}\right)^2} + \beta_4 \frac{\left(\frac{\Delta S}{S}\right)}{\sqrt{\left(\frac{\Delta \mathcal{L}}{\mathcal{L}}\right)^2 + \left(\frac{\Delta \sigma}{\sigma}\right)^2 + \left(\frac{\Delta N}{N+B}\right)^2}} =$$

$$19.68\%.$$

The fact why $\mathcal{F}_{\mathrm{ML+MC}}$ reaches 19.68% is due to the high uncertainty from $\frac{\Delta Q}{q}$ as stated above it appears from the decisions and undecisions in the correct application of the Mitchell's criteria. While more decisions are applied onto the measurements of N_{ML} and ΔN through a pure process of Machine Learning. Thus, the usage of Machine Learning would induce to large errors if variables under analysis are not well correlated to experimental observables. In other words: **The application of the Mitchell's criteria would have to be well correlated to the collider and detector uncertainties**.

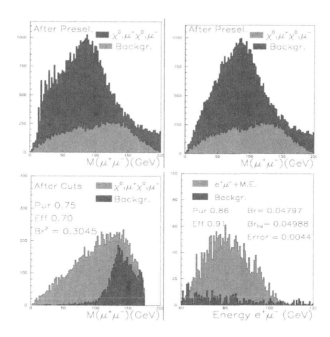

Fig. 4. Top left and right panels: the case of slepton pair production in a photon collider yielding pretty low efficiencies. Bottom left and right: the Mitchell criteria have increased substantially the statistics.

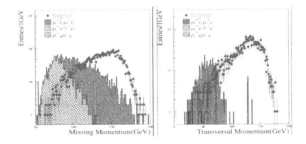

Fig. 5. Final missing momentum spectra when a cutflow has been applied. Right side plot has yielded an efficiency of 75% in accordance to [10].

4   Conclusion

In this paper, we have presented a study of the application of the Mitchell's criteria inside the Machine Learning algorithm to assess its potential advantageous as to extract signal events with the highest efficiencies, that is crucially needed to perform precision measurements in particular in these scenarios of new physics such as supersymmetry. The main channel decay of the right-handed scalar muon was measured to be of order of 1.22%. However the usage of Mitchell's criteria might be subject to decisions that increases the error as estimated in this paper being it of order of 19.68%. It is because the presence of extra variables that demands the implementation of the algorithms of Machine Learning and would establish a scenario by which makes fully coherent for a measurement given a data and their intrinsic uncertainties.

References

1. Knuteson, B., Padley, P.: Statistical challenges with massive datasets in particle physics. J. Comput. Graph. Stat. **12**(4), 808–828 (2003). Published Online 01 Jan 2012
2. Kalmus, P.I.P.: Experimental techniques in particle physics. Contemp. Phys. **26**(3), 217–239 (1985). Published Online 20 Aug 2006
3. Coniavitis, E.: Higgs Boson decays to leptons with the ATLAS detector. Nucl. Part. Phys. Proc. **273–275**, 901–906 (2016). ATLAS Collaboration
4. Schwab, D.J.: A high-bias, low-variance introduction to machine learning for physicists. Phys. Rep. **810**(30), 1–124 (2019)
5. Ren, J., Wu, L., Yang, J.M., Zhao, J.: Exploring supersymmetry with machine learning. Nucl. Phys. B **943** (2019). Article 114613
6. Klaemke, G., Moenig, K.: Studies on Chargino production and decay at a photon collider. arXiv:hep-ph/0503191
7. Diaconis, P., Neuberger, J.W.: Numerical results for the metropolis algorithm. Exp. Math. **13**(2), 207–213 (2004). Published Online 03 Apr 2012
8. Nieto-Chaupis, H.: Study of scalar leptons at the TESLA photon collider. Mathematisch-Naturwissenschaftliche Fakultät I, edoc-Server Open-Access-Publikationsserver der Humboldt-Universitat

Quantum Mechanics Formalism
for Modeling the Flux of BitCoins

Huber Nieto-Chaupis[✉]

Universidad Autonoma del Peru, Dirección de Investigación,
Km. 16.3 Villa el Salvador, Lima, Peru
huber.nieto@gmail.com

Abstract. Because bitcoins processes depend on Internet transactions, one can argue that the dynamics of flux and volume of bitcoins might be subject to stochastic instead of a pure determinism event. By knowing that Quantum Mechanics describes well physics in the microscopic level and it is capable to calculate exact measurements of physical observables, we apply the concept of amplitude of probability to model the success probability of any transaction involving the new monetary unit so-called bitcoins. In this manner we focus on the description of the potential transactions using entirely the formalism of quantum mechanics. In addition we use also the concept of Green's function that appear along the construction of the amplitude. Although not any direct correspondence can exist between the dynamics of flux of bitcoins and the purpose of a quantum theory, the modeling is limited to the extent of the interpretation of the success probability to complete any bitcoin-based transaction. For a transaction of $\mathcal{N}$ US dollars, we found that the bitcoin flux might reach up to a 90% of the completion of the transaction.

1 Introduction

With the apparition of the so-called bitcoins [1], a diversity of applications to be used to acquire objects either to sell or buy is foreseen [2]. Certainly one of the more critic properties of these bitcoins is the anonymous path, in other words for an external observer, there is not any track where the transaction begins and not any information about the end. It is also assumed that the route goes through the Internet network. Thus, whatever is the path taken by the flux of bitcoins is believed that is highly secured. In this manner one can argue that the bitcoin transaction would give rise to a new world economy. However, this pseudo economy might be subject of instabilities and stochastic fluctuations as inherently linked to semi random processes. In fact, we can coin the term semi in the sense that although the purpose of the customer is clear, the Internet and true routing of the transaction might be unclear and random so this only can assure the success of any operation that is acquiring products employing bitcoins. Furthermore, bitcoin are known because these unit of currency has attained a random number that makes it non-vulnerable to attacks of a third party or eavesdropper. In this manner, a critic point of the Cryptocurrency [3] is

© Springer Nature Switzerland AG 2020
F. R. Narváez et al. (Eds.): SmartTech-IC 2019, CCIS 1154, pp. 375–388, 2020.
https://doi.org/10.1007/978-3-030-46785-2_30

the usage of the technology to carry out the encryption, thus whom are involved in the transaction do know about any one [3].

2   The Quantum Mechanics of Bra and Ket Formalism

In Quantum Mechanics [4], it is well-known that the state of any system can be represented by a vector of a $\mathcal{N}$-dimension Hilbert space. By using the Dirac notation this non-physical state is written as $|\Psi\rangle$. In addition, the existence of an orthogonal basis makes possible to work out in real problems, so that often one can define the completeness relation for the discrete and continuous case as is written below:

$$\mathbb{I} = \sum_q |\phi_q\rangle \langle\phi_q|, \tag{1}$$

$$\mathbb{I} = \int dx\, |x\rangle \langle x|. \tag{2}$$

In this manner we can write down the physical state through the projection of the general state $|\Psi\rangle$ onto the unitary operator $\mathbb{I}$,

$$\mathbb{I}|\Psi\rangle = \int dx\, |x\rangle \langle x|\Psi\rangle \tag{3}$$

in addition we can multiply by the left side with the same state so one gets

$$\langle\Psi|\,\mathbb{I}\,|\Psi\rangle = \int dx\, \langle\Psi|x\rangle \langle x|\Psi\rangle \tag{4}$$

denoting the Quantum Mechanics probability of finding any physical object in x [5]:

$$\langle\Psi|\Psi\rangle = \int dx\, ||\Psi(x)||^2. \tag{5}$$

However, we can combine the cases discrete and continuous for a better description of the event. In this way we have that any state can be described by the linear superposition of orthogonal vectors,

$$|\Psi\rangle = a_1 |\phi_1\rangle + a_2 |\phi_2\rangle + a_3 |\phi_3\rangle ... + ...a_{N-1} |\phi_{N-1}\rangle + a_N |\phi_N\rangle$$

$$|\Psi\rangle = \sum_q^N a_q |\phi_q\rangle, \tag{6}$$

that defines the initial or final state of any event. For instance, we consider the product of two arbitrary states: $\langle A|$ and $|B\rangle$ the through the combination of the orthogonal states in their discrete and continuous versions, we arrived to

$$\langle B|A\rangle = \sum_J a_J \langle\phi_J| \sum_K a_K |\phi_K\rangle \tag{7}$$

and with the implementation of up to two continuous variables, thus

$$\langle B|A \rangle = \sum_J a_J \langle \phi_J | \int dx \, |x\rangle \langle x| \sum_K a_K \int dz \, |z\rangle \langle z| \, |\phi_K\rangle \tag{8}$$

that finally can be written as

$$\langle B|A \rangle = \int dx \int dz \sum_J \sum_K a_J a_K \delta(x - z) \phi_J(x) \phi_K(z) \tag{9}$$

where it was used that $\langle x|z \rangle = \delta(x - z)$.

3 Full Modeling of an End-to-End Bitcoin Transaction

With Eqs. 1–9 is possible to derive a model that accounts the probabilities of flux of bitcoins in any market [6]. Thus we should define the following considerations:

- The initial state models the volume of bitcoins to be used for a concrete transaction.
- The propagation of the flux has a probabilistic character.
- The final state is the desired end of the flux, so it involves the result of the transaction [7].
- The error on the transaction is given by the deviation between is expected and the tangible results of the transaction.
- The transaction can be canceled only in those cases where the initial state lacks of capabilities to flux through the defined route.

We consider the following end-to-end process modeled by

$$\langle F|H \rangle = \sum_{j,q}^{J,Q} \langle F|q \rangle \langle q|j \rangle \langle j|H \rangle . \tag{10}$$

where the discrete case of the completeness relationship was inserted. The flux should has dependence on the time so for an initial and final time, (10) can be rewritten as:

$$\langle F(t_2)|H(t_1) \rangle = \sum_{j,q}^{J,Q} \langle F(t_2)|q \rangle \langle q|j \rangle \langle j|H(t_1) \rangle . \tag{11}$$

and the subsequent insertion of the completeness in the continuous case we have then that:

$$\langle F(t_2)|H(t_1) \rangle = \sum_{j,q}^{J,Q} \langle F(t_2)| \int dx \, |x\rangle \langle x| |q\rangle \langle q|j\rangle \langle j| \int dx' \, |x'\rangle \langle x'| |H(t_1)\rangle , \tag{12}$$

by changing the notation $|j\rangle \to \phi_j$ and $|q\rangle \to \phi_q$ we rewrite (12) as:

$$\langle F(t_2)|H(t_1)\rangle = \sum_{j,q}^{J,Q} \int dx \int dx' F(t_2, x) H(t_1, x') \delta(x - x') \delta_{j,q} \phi_j(x') \phi_q(x). \quad (13)$$

In this manner we have written above an expression that can be interpreted as the probability of carry out a transition of flux from the state H to the F. This transition has a time of duration given by the difference $t_2 - t_1$.

3.1   Separability of the States

As seen in (13) it is plausible to appeal to the separability of the states G and H in the sense that each one can be written as the product of their parts of both the dependence on x, x' and the times t, t', in order for acquiring a better manage on the calculation of the full amplitude of probability $\langle F(t_2)|H(t_1)\rangle$ [8]. It also can gives us a better comprehension of the flux of the volume of bitcoins along the trajectory and the time that it takes. Under this view we have that:

$$\langle F(t_2)|H(t_1)\rangle = f(t_2)h(t_1) \sum_{j,q}^{J,Q} \int \int dxdx' F(x) H(x') \delta(x - x') \delta_{j,q} \phi_j(x') \phi_q(x).$$
$$(14)$$

The usage of the Dirac-Delta function allows us to simplify (14) as follows:

$$\langle F(t_2)|H(t_1)\rangle = f(t_2)h(t_1) \sum_{j,q}^{J,Q} \int dx F(x) H(x) \delta_{j,q} \phi_j(x) \phi_q(x). \quad (15)$$

As will be discussed later, the morphology of the functions $f(t_2)$ and $h(t_1)$ is going to depend of how has been established the states and particularly on the desired outcomes of the transaction. It allows us to define the success probability in the sense that for given the times of the request of a bitcoin-based transaction, and the time that the system would yields a concrete result: either the transaction was approved or canceled, the probability is therefore a number and it is written as

$$\mathcal{P}(T) = \int_{T_0+T_B}^{T} \int_{T_0}^{T_B} \langle F(t_2)|H(t_1)\rangle \, dt_1 dt_2 \quad (16)$$

depending on the time that takes the approval the transaction namely T. The probabilities will have their maximum values if only

$$\frac{d\mathcal{P}(T)}{dT}\Big|_{T=\text{TMAX}} = 0 \quad (17)$$

by which there is an unique value that the probability acquires its best value towards to a successful completion of the transaction. Thus when the optimal value is found, there is range where the probability can acquire the best values, so that

$$\mathcal{P}(\text{TMAX}) = \int_{T_0+T_B}^{\text{TMAX}} \int_{T_0}^{T_B} \langle F(t_2)|H(t_1)\rangle \, dt_1 dt_2 > 0.9. \tag{18}$$

The why our choice is 0.9 (for example) is due to the fact that the full transaction is subject to stochastic fluctuations that is entirely governed by the Internet network. Under this view, it is plausible to incorporate operators that would modify the state of the flux of bitcoins for a concrete operation [9]. A tentative operation would be that of $\mathbf{D}\,|H(t_1)\rangle = |H(t_1 + \Delta t)\rangle$ that states the action of the unitary operator in the sense that $\mathbf{D}\mathbf{D}^{-1} = \mathbb{I}$.

3.2   Canceling a Transaction

As we can see in (14) the fact of the existence of the product of two orthogonal basis, it gives rise to th so-called Delta of Kronecker function defined as $\delta_{I,J} = 1$ either $I = J$ or $\delta_{I,J} = 0$ for $I \neq J$. So that, whatever the algorithm that is running, there is always a possibility to cancel the full transaction when two different states appear in the product [10]. Therefore, the derived relationship makes only sense for equals orthogonal polynomials. A portion of a more general algorithm reads below as: According to (14) the canceling of the transaction

---

CANCELING ANY TRANSACTION

---

1   **DEFINE ORTHOGONAL FUNCTIONS**
2   **DEFINE INTEGER NUMBERS**
3   **IF INTEGER ARE DIFERENT**
4   **AMPLITUDE = 0**
5   **ENDIF**
6   **UPDATES ORTHOGONALITY**

---

obeys also to the small values of the $f(t_2)$ and $h(t_1)$ as given by the usage of separability. It is clear that on these values can be the case where $\langle F(t_2)|H(t_1)\rangle$ acquires too small values that the full algorithm makes the question whether there still sense to continue with the running of the software attained to the operation associated. Thus, it is implemented in the following lines below: In the case shown above one can see that the values of the times t_1 as well as t_2 can be shifted appealing to the employ of the operator $\mathbf{D}$ so that a tentative possibility to surpass possible cases of canceling the operation is the implementation of the unitary property of these operators as follows: $\langle F(t_2)|\mathbf{D}\mathbf{D}^{-1}|H(t_1)\rangle$ that can shift the times in the sense as $\langle F(t_2 + \Delta t)|H(t_1 - \Delta t)\rangle$ thus although asymmetry in the time displacements can be anticipated, the values of the product might

RECOVERY OF TRANSACTION

---

1 **FINDING VALUES FOR F(t_2) AND H(t_1)**
2 **IF F(t_2)⊗H(t_1) > 0**
3 **CALL RANDOM Γ**
4 **F(t_2) ⊗ H(t_1) ¡ Γ**
5 **BACK AGAIN TO FIND NEW VALUES**
6 **UPDATES F(t_2) AND H(t_1)**

---

be high enough to cancel the full transaction. Under this approach (15) reads as

$$\langle F(t_2 + \Delta t)|H(t_1 - \Delta t)\rangle$$
$$= f(t_2 + \Delta t)h(t_1 - \Delta t)\sum_{j,q}^{J,Q}\int dx F(x)H(x)\delta_{j,q}\phi_j(x)\phi_q(x). \qquad (19)$$

From (19) clearly only the diagonal elements are contributing to the full amplitude, thus for $I = J$ one easily gets:

$$\langle F(t_2 + \Delta t)|H(t_1 - \Delta t)\rangle = f(t_2 + \Delta t)h(t_1 - \Delta t)\sum_{j}^{J}\int dx F(x)H(x)||\phi_j(x)||^2,$$
$$(20)$$

in this manner the amplitude depending on the times and their respective displacements in according to the action of the operator **D** one gets:

$$\mathcal{A}(t_1, t_2, \Delta t) = f(t_2 + \Delta t)h(t_1 - \Delta t)\sum_{j}^{J}\int dx F(x)H(x)||\phi_j(x)||^2. \qquad (21)$$

3.3   Interpretation of Eq. 21

We can now to describe the potential modeling of any flux of bitcoins through the Eq. (21). We can associate a meaning to the ingredients as follows [11,12]:

- x is the amount of bitcoins.
- x can also depend on the time $x(t)$.
- there is a uncertainty linked to the choice of the functions F and H.
- The full probability for carry out a complete bitcoins-based transaction is given by the square of $\mathcal{A}$.
- The flux stops when the time derivate of $\mathcal{A} = 0$.

Finally we can write the amplitude as the ratio between $\mathcal{A}$ and the amount of bitcoins:

$$\frac{d\mathcal{A}(t_1, t_2, \Delta t, x(t))}{dx(t)} = f(t_2 + \Delta t)h(t_1 - \Delta t)\sum_{j}^{J}F(x)H(x)||\phi_j(x)||^2. \qquad (22)$$

even though we can disentangle the x-dependent functions to arrive to a much more compact expression:

$$\frac{1}{f(t_2 + \Delta t)h(t_1 - \Delta t)} \frac{d\mathcal{A}(t_1, t_2, \Delta t, x(t))}{dx(t)} = \sum_{j}^{J} F(x)H(x)||\phi_j(x)||^2. \quad (23)$$

4 The Full Transaction: Sellers and Buyers

The main purpose of the usage of a bitcoin currency is the anonymous character [13,14]: no one knows who is buying or selling. Thus the transaction is only known by the two parties: buyers and sellers. Consider for instance that exists a seller labeled by U and its corresponding customer W that is selling a product Z in the cost of γ bitcoins. Thus the first task of W is change its amount of standard currency (euros or US dollars, for instance) in bitcoins. Thus W transfer their local currency to an universal change machine that returns only bitcoins. It clearly implies that a state is defined, it is $|H(t)\rangle$ and it can be written as $\langle x|H(t)\rangle = H(x,t)$. Only the full operation to acquire the product with a cost of γ bitcoins is going to end when the amplitude $\langle F|H\rangle$ is near to 1.

Random Serial
The initial state is the projection of the ket $|H(t)\rangle$ over a basis $|u_m\rangle$. So that the dimension of the basis is a random number, thus

$$|H(x,t)\rangle = \sum_{m}^{R} |u_m\rangle \langle u_m|H(x,t)\rangle \quad (24)$$

with R and random number. Clearly the target that is understood as the acquisition of product offered by the seller U requires that the amplitude of probability given by

$$\langle F(t')|H(x,t)\rangle = \sum_{m}^{R} \langle F(t')|u_m\rangle \langle u_m|H(x,t)\rangle. \quad (25)$$

The Arrival of Bitcoins and Acquisition of Product
One of the questionable facts of a currency entirely based on bitcoins is the lack of any mechanism that applies taxes along the transaction. Although this point goes beyond the scope of this paper, we only paid attention to the physical propagation of the bitcoins and how the sent volume converted in a random number has capabilities to acquire any product over the Internet network. From (25) the arrival to the amount of bitcoins to acquire the desired product is translated in terms of bra and kets. Thus, we need to implement additional intermediate states as follows

$$\langle F(t')|H(x,t)\rangle = \sum_{m}^{R} \langle F(t')| \int dx' |x'\rangle \langle x'| |u_m\rangle \langle u_m| \int ds |s\rangle \langle s| |H(x,t)\rangle \quad (26)$$

operating the bras and kets we arrived to:

$$\mathcal{A} = \langle F(t')|H(x,t)\rangle = \sum_m^R \int dx' \int ds F(x',t')u_m(x')u_m(s)H(x,s,t), \quad (27)$$

thus we can define a function $\mathbf{G}(s,x') \in \mathbb{R}$ that absorbs the characteristics of the pseudo propagation of the volume of bitcoins. From this (27) can be rewritten as

$$\mathcal{A} = \langle F(t')|H(x,t)\rangle = \sum_m^R \int dx' \int ds F(x',t')\mathbf{G}(s,x')H(x,s,t), \quad (28)$$

The implementation of a quantum mechanics propagator appears from the necessity of justify the physical flux of bitcoins through encrypted keys made of purely random numbers. It actually comes from the fact that commonly in Quantum Mechanics any space-time translation can be expressed as a path that is in general subject to the interpretation of Feynman that states [15] that any space-time displacement is governed by the propagator that encloses the characteristics of system. In effect, the analysis of these quantum paths require the assumption of the Hamiltonian in accordance to the definition of the evolution operator:

$$G(s,x') = \langle s| \mathrm{Exp}\left\{\frac{\mathbf{H}(\Delta t)}{\hbar}\right\} |x'\rangle \quad (29)$$

where $\mathbf{H}$ the Hamiltonian that gives account of energy of system. The analogue to our case becomes the function that manages the flux of bitcoin so in the same view of any quantum mechanics Green function, the zeros of this function either on the numerator or denominator, would be account of the success to complete the transaction otherwise would denote the full fail or cancellation of the transaction. So we propose an universal propagator equation given by

$$\left\{\beta\frac{d^2}{ds^2} + \lambda\frac{d^2}{dx'^2}\right\} \mathbf{G}(s,x') = \sum_\ell^L B_\ell(s)C_\ell(x'). \quad (30)$$

We assume that $\sum_\ell^L B_\ell(s)C_\ell(x') = \Delta(s - x')$ in order that claim that actually (30) is a propagator-like function. The why we are using a second derivate is because the stochastic flux might follow a physics that obeys in part to the well-known diffusion equation that implements a scenario merely deterministic. For instance $\frac{\partial\rho(x,t)}{\partial t} = D\frac{\partial^2\rho(x,t)}{\partial x^2}$ and its generalization given by $\frac{\partial\rho(x,t)}{\partial t} = D\Delta^{(d)}\rho(x,t)$, where D the diffusion equation. Thus one can define a full solution for the propagator inspired on the solutions of the diffusion equation. Under this view the constants λ and β would denote the weight of the flux.

Testing Green Functions

Independently of the coordinate system we can test the product $\mathbf{G}(s, x') = u_m(x')u_m(s)$ as one of periodical character. Thus we implement this through a simple product, and it reads as

$$\mathbf{G}(s, x') = \mathrm{Sin}\left(\frac{\beta s}{\beta_{\mathrm{OP}}}\right)\mathrm{Cos}\left(\frac{\lambda x'}{\lambda_{\mathrm{OP}}}\right), \tag{31}$$

where β_{OP} and λ_{OP} denoting their optimal values, in other words those values that provides the highest values to $\mathbf{G}(\mathbf{s}, \mathbf{x}')$. These solution are far of getting infinite values, fact that it is unrealistic for any transaction consisting in bitcoins. Below is presented the central algorithm of bitcoins flux.

5   Computational Simulation and Results

In order to estimate numerical predictions, we define the full flux of bitcoins along the Internet network and it reads as:

$$\frac{d^2\mathcal{A}}{dx'^2 ds^2} = \sum_m^R F(x', t')\mathbf{G}(s, x')H(x, s, t), \tag{32}$$

when the input and output functions are modeled by simple Gaussian functions based on the fact that both functions are derived from a Hermite equation, i.e.,

$$\frac{d^2[F, H]}{dx^2} - 2x\frac{d[F, H]}{dx} + 2n[F, H] = 0, \tag{33}$$

where the symbol $[F, H]$ denotes either F or H. In this manner the full flux of any volume of bitcoins that target to acquire any product can be written as:

$$\frac{d^2\mathcal{A}}{dx'ds} = \sum_m^R \mathrm{Exp}\left[\left(\frac{x'\beta t'}{\Delta x'}\right)^2\right]\mathrm{Sin}\left(\frac{m\beta s}{\beta_{\mathrm{OP}}}\right)\mathrm{Cos}\left(\frac{m\lambda x'}{\lambda_{\mathrm{OP}}}\right)\mathrm{Exp}\left[\left(\frac{s\lambda t}{\Delta s}\right)^2\right] \tag{34}$$

and its corresponding integration of square would be interpreted as the probability of achieving a end-to-end flux of bitcoins to acquire a certain product,

$$\mathcal{P}(t) = \int_{x_A}^{x_B}\sum_m^R \mathrm{Exp}\left[\left(\frac{x'\beta t'}{\Delta x'}\right)^2\right]\mathrm{Cos}\left(\frac{m\lambda x'}{\lambda_{\mathrm{OP}}}\right)dx' \times$$
$$\times \int_{s_A}^{s_B}\mathrm{Sin}\left(\frac{m\beta s}{\beta_{\mathrm{OP}}}\right)\mathrm{Exp}\left[\left(\frac{s\lambda t}{\Delta s}\right)^2\right]ds \tag{35}$$

This has been implemented in the algorithm below. In the following are given in details the algorithm that estimate the amplitude as written in Eq. (34). The algorithm appeals to the Metropolis step that accepts or rejects any value that is far from the desired outcomes. Between lines 1–12 all parameters are given in ad-hoc manner. So it actually represents the deterministic part of the algorithm. Nevertheless, the random extraction of the the parameters β and λ is attributed to the fact that these quantities models the network performance. Clearly those small values might to influence on the values of (34). In line-15 the amplitude is estimated. Because it is a finite sum over M until R, with R being a random integer, in (16) the full flux is estimated. We can interpret that sum as the contribution of various segments where the flux is running. These segments can be the reboot from a server to another. The Internet provider manages the physical location of the servers. Depending on the level of risk, the finite contribution of these segments has as main purpose to guarantee an unstoppable flux until the transaction has ended. While network can be under attacks of unexpected eavesdroppers, the continuous monitoring of each segment would guarantee a reliable flux of bitcoins towards their end. Once the limit has been reached as seen in line-17, the configuration is accepted. Herein we proceed to extract the optimal values of β and λ seen in line-17. The flux would continuous unless that there is a strong difference of amplitudes among two consecutive values. The identification of these events is seen as a sudden collapse of the flux. However, the flux can be recovered as seen between lines 23–28. To accomplish this new random values are needed. The transaction ends when the amplitude have reached a high value so it would be of confidence for both seller and buyer.

FLUX OF A VOLUME OF BITCOINS

1 INITIAL VALUES β, λ
2 **DO** M = 1, R (R=RANDOM)
3 **PREPARATION OF STATES**
4 **DO** J = 1, JMAX
5 **DO** K= 1, KMAX
6 **T** $+$ $\varDelta$ **T** $\times$ **K**
7 **T'** $+$ $\varDelta$ **T'** $\times$ **K**
8 **X** $+$ $\varDelta$ **X** $\times$ **J**
9 **X'** $+$ $\varDelta$ **X'** $\times$ **J**
10 **S** $+$ $\varDelta$ **S** $\times$ **K**
11 $\varDelta S = \varDelta(\text{K-1})S$
12 $\varDelta X' = \varDelta(\text{J-1})X'$
13 **CALL RANDOM** β
14 **CALL RANDOM** λ
15 $\mathbf{A}(\text{J,K,M}) = \frac{d^2 \mathcal{A}(J,K,M)}{dX'dS}$
16 $\mathbf{A}(\text{J,K,M+1}) = \mathbf{A}(\text{J,K,M-1}) + \mathbf{A}(\text{J,K,M})$
17 **IF** M $= R$ **THEN**
18 **ACCEPT CONFIGURATION**
19 EXTRACTION $\beta_{\text{OP}}, \lambda_{\text{OP}}$

CONTINUATION

```
20      GIVEN A INTEGER Q
21      IF A(J,K,M-Q)>> A(J,K,M+Q) THEN
22      BITCOINS FLUX COLLAPSE
23        CALL RANDOM β
24      CALL RANDOM λ
25      GOTO LINE-6
26      GIVEN A INTEGER P
27   IF A(J,K,M-P)<< A(J,K,M+P) THEN
28   BITCOINS FLUX RECOVERY 29     ENDIF
30   ENDIF
31   ENDIF
32   ENDDO
33   ENDDO
34   ENDDO
35   IF T=TMAX THEN
36   IFA(J,K,M)>>0 THEN
37   TRANSACTION DONE
38   ENDIF
39   ENDIF
40   END
```

---

6   Curves of Probability Amplitude and Stability of Flux

In Fig. 1 we have plotted up to three different scenarios for the pair of parameters β and λ. In top left the case where β is four times the value of λ. This has as effect the rapid fail of the curves. Based on the Eq. (30) where the role of β and λ in view of their analogue to quantum theory that to certain extent are perceived as coupling constants, the highest values as plotted in top left where the colors denote the integer numbers of the sum over m Eq. (34). As seen in all cases, the amplitude falls down in time. Same phenomenology is perceived in top right where β is twice λ. Although the values have changed to be smallest with respect to the previous ones, again the amplitude is well-correlated with time. In bottom plot are seen that amplitudes would increase with time but the cost is that β turns out to be around the half of λ. Being x a variable that is analogue to D the diffusion but with a meaning of coupling constant as stated above. In fact, the fact of this increasing is due to the flux of volume of bitcoins is growing is keeps stable along the times that it would take the whole transaction. In this manner, all three plots reflects the fact that the flux has not acquire instabilities during the transaction. Because the Hilbert space is reduced to one of 5 dimension as seen in the colors of the plots, this low-dimensional space turns out to be enough to a solid flux of the volume. Clearly this supports the fact about the confidence on the completion on the bitcoins-based transaction.

6.1   Collapse of Flux

The sin and cos as seen in (34) can be approximated as function of integer-order of Bessel functions, $\mathrm{Cos}(x) = J_0(x) + 2\sum_n^\infty (-1)^n J_{2n}(x)$ and $\mathrm{Sin}(x) = 2\sum_n^\infty$ $(-1)^n J_{2n+1}(x)$ in the sense of providing an interpretation of (34) the density of probability of success because we proceed with the sums as is given in (43) being each order a normalized (to unity) limited contribution to the total density of probability. Thus, in Fig. 2 are plotted up to three different scenarios with random values for β and λ describing the possible events along the bitcoins-based transaction. In top left panel we can see the rupture of the continuity between two different events belonging to same transaction. The fact that the success probability acquires a null value is due to the collapse of the transaction as cause either (i) the Internet network or (ii) the failed encryption system. Although the recovery is seen a while after, the further values might not reach the desired high values of probability. In other words, even the transaction is recovered the end of the transaction might not be reached so that it is not guaranteed the acquisition of product. Actually, a prospective bitcoin-based process would have to operate with certain limitations to avoid fraud or another abnormality that disrupts the interaction buyer-seller. The random assignation of the pair β and λ can be also optimistic as seen in top right plot where after the collapse the probability back again to each high values of probability. Finally in bottom panel the case where the transaction is collapsed and therefore is canceled is seen as the lack of capability to restore its evolution to the completion of the transaction.

Curves of Full Probability. In Fig. 3 are presented different results since the usage of Eq. (35) that is closed-form integrations [16,17]. From top to bottom we have assigned best values to the pair β and λ. The curves denote the full probability to complete the bitcoin-based transaction. In top left panel, all contributions coincides in the time for which $|\mathcal{A}(t)|^2$ gets a maximum. Here, β and λ would share a values around a time $= 2.4$ in arbitrary units. This coincidence do not continue in top right where clearly is seen that the initial Gaussian state appears from the critic time and the full probability finally acquires lowest values beyond that time. In bottom plot is seen that would exist a kind of separation between the states given by continue and reestablished. Because each color denotes a different integer m, the plot exhibits that for a certain integer or state orthogonal,

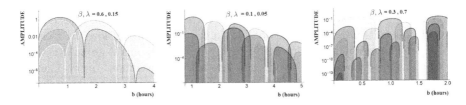

Fig. 1. Plots of amplitude of probability showing in the top panels the decreasing behavior in time in contrast to the bottom panel where a rapid increasing in time is observed.

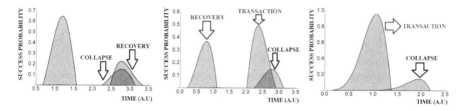

Fig. 2. Scenarios of collapse and recovery of the amplitude of probability. As seen in top panels: there is a recovery after the collapse. The recovery cannot be guaranteed as seen in bottom panel.

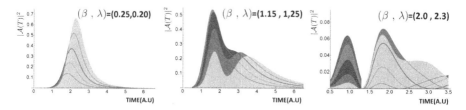

Fig. 3. The square of the amplitude for the first 5 orders of the Bessel function. The plots demonstrate the weakness of the full probability to instabilities along the time of the bitcoin transaction.

the full probability would have a range along the time where the completion of the transaction is done.

7   Conclusion

In this paper we have employed the formalism of Quantum Mechanics to derive various relations that gives account of the flux of bitcoins for a transaction. Essentially, we have derived amplitudes of probability as well as the full probability of transaction. In according to the plots, these probabilities might be subject to instabilities of system during the time by which the transaction is performed. This is reflected on the apparition of collapse of the transaction because the sensitivity of system to be eavesdropped as well as to the weakness of Internet network. In a future work we shall establish the conditions for getting a full unstoppable transaction in a network as might be regulated in a prospective Banking Internet that becomes crucial for a solid bitcoin-based transaction. In this manner, both buyers as sellers are full confident on the transaction so that the market is highly secure and the level of satisfaction for employing a currency entirely based on bitcoins appears to be high [18,19].

Acknowledgments. The author thanks to Engineer Juan Alfaro-Cabanillas because discussions on the bitcoin applicability in real markets and the potential realization in near future.

References

1. Low, K.F.K., Teo, E.G.S.: Bitcoins and other cryptocurrencies as property? Law Innov. Technol. **9**(2), 235–268 (2017)
2. Lo, Y.C., Medda, F.: Bitcoin mining: converting computing power into cash flow. Appl. Econ. Lett. **26**(14), 1171–1176 (2019)
3. Li, Y., Zhang, W., Xiong, X., Wang, P.: Does size matter in the cryptocurrency market?. Appl. Econ. Lett
4. Sakurai, J.: Advanced Quantum Mechanics, Revised edn. Addison Wesley, Boston (1993)
5. Cohen-Tannoudji, C.: Quantum Mechanics, vol. 1, 1st edn. Wiley, New York (1991)
6. Evans-Pughe, C., Novikov, A., Vitaliev, V.: To bit or not to bit? Eng. Technol. **9**(4), 82–88 (2014)
7. Tschorsch, F., Scheuermann, B.: Bitcoin and beyond: a technical survey on decentralized digital currencies. IEEE Commun. Surv. Tutor. **18**(3), 2084–2123 (2016)
8. Schack, R., Caves, C.M.: Explicit product ensembles for separable quantum states. J. Mod. Opt. **47**(2–3), 387–399 (2000)
9. Tromp, J.W., Dumont, R.S.: The thermal flux-flux correlation function and classical-quantum correspondence. Mol. Phys. **110**(9–10), 817–824 (2012)
10. Gan, F.F., Koehler, K.J., Thompson, J.C.: Probability plots and distribution curves for assessing the fit of probability models. Am. Stat. **45**(1), 14–21 (1991)
11. Lee, J.-H., Pilkington, M.: How the blockchain revolution will reshape the consumer electronics industry (Future directions). IEEE Consum. Electron. Mag. **6**(3), 19–23 (2017)
12. Peck, M.E.: The bitcoin arms race is on! IEEE Spectr. **50**(6), 11–13 (2013)
13. Nieto-Chaupis, H.: Encrypted communications through quantum key distributions algorithms and Bessel functions. IEEE XXV International Conference on Electronics, Electrical Engineering and Computing (INTERCON), pp. 1–4 (2018)
14. Li, H.-F., Zhu, L.-X., Wang, K., Wang, K.-B.: The Improvement of QKD scheme based on BB84 protocol. In: International Conference on Information System and Artificial Intelligence (ISAI), pp. 314–317 (2016)
15. Lukes, T.: A general expression for the average propagator in a disordered system
16. Glasser, M.L., Montaldi, E.: Some integrals involving Bessel functions (1993). arXiv:math/9307213
17. Humbert, P.: Proc. Edinb. Math. Soc. **3**(4), 276–285 (1933)
18. Grossman, J.H.: Passing cash from bank notes to bitcoin: standardizing money. J. Cult. Econ. **12**(4), 299–316 (2019)
19. Vo, A., Yost-Bremm, C.: A high-frequency algorithmic trading strategy for cryptocurrency. J. Comput. Inf. Syst

Author Index

Aguilera-Silva, L.   29
Araguillin, Ricardo   16
Arias, Roberto   273
Atiaja Atiaja, Lourdes   202

Barbosa-Santillán, Liliana I.   105
Bosmediano, Marcelo   337

Callejas-Cuervo, Mauro   120, 288
Camargo, Jorge E.   132, 176, 243
Campáz-Usuga, Pablo   297
Cárdenas Rengifo, David Leonardo   288
Castro-Ospina, Andrés E.   259
Chasi, Carolin   16
Chica, Fernando   154
Contreras Barrera, Juan Pablo   288
Cordoba, Ricardo   165

D'Haro, Luis   165
De La Bastida, Ronny   16
Díaz, Gloria M.   215, 259, 297
Dominguez, Marlon Steibeck   132
Ďuračík, Michal   120

Eiriz, Osana   229
Espí, Roberto   229

F. da Rocha, Adson   325
Flauzac, Olivier   40
Fonnegra, Ruben D.   297
Franco, Hugo   273
Freire, José Julio   63

García Martínez, Andrés   202
Gastelum-Rodríguez, G.   29
Góez Sánchez, David   3
Gonzalez, Carlos J.   40
Guanuche, Adriana   229
Gutierrez, Flabio   351

Hernández, Liliana   259
Hrkút, Patrik   120
Huertas-Herrera, Benjamin   3

Inga, Esteban   75
Isaza-Roldán, C. A.   89

Jimenez-Carrion, Miguel   351
Juma, Jonnathan   142

León-Paredes, Gabriel A.   105
Llano, Jhony   188
Lobaina Delgado, Alfredo   325
López Delis, Alberto   325
López-Leyva, J. A.   29
Lujan, Edwar   351

Marín-Castrillón, Diana M.   259
Meza-Arballo, O.   29
Mikušová, Miroslava   120
Moreno, Fredy A.   176
Morillo, Paulina   188

Narvaez, Erick   154
Narváez, Fabián   273, 312, 337
Naula, Luis   52
Nieto-Chaupis, Huber   364, 375
Nieto-Londoño, César   89
Nolot, Florent   40

Osorno-Castillo, Kevin   297

Palacios Játiva, Pablo   63
Pareja-Lora, Antonio   105
Parra-A., N.   132
Proaño, Julio   142

Quinayás, César   325
Quitiaquez, Patricio   89
Quitiaquez, William   89

Ramirez, Vanessa   188
Reinoso, Andres   142
ReyesVera, Erick   3
Ricardo Enciso, Nicolás   243
Rincón, Jaider Stiven   259
Rodríguez-Melquiades, Jose   351

Román-Cañizares, Milton   63
Romero, David   154, 165
Ruiz, Andrés   325
Ruiz, Milton   75

Saavedra, Carlos   63
Salamea, Christian   154, 165
Sanabia-Vincent, E.   29
Segovia, Andrés   52
Simani, Silvio   75
Simbaña, Isaac   89

Solsol, Irving L.   215
Sotomayor, Nelson   16

Talamantes-Álvarez, A.   29
Toapanta-Ramos, Luis   89

Vargas, Héctor F.   215
Vargas-Calderón, Vladimir   132
Velasco, Fernando   312
Vinck-Posada, Herbert   132

Zukowska, Joanna   120

Printed in the United States
By Bookmasters